# THE REVOLUTIONS OF 1848-9.

*Guiseppe Mazzini.*

# THE
# REVOLUTIONARY MOVEMENT
## OF 1848-9
## IN ITALY, AUSTRIA-HUNGARY, AND
## GERMANY.

### WITH SOME EXAMINATION OF THE PREVIOUS
### THIRTY-THREE YEARS.

BY

C. EDMUND MAURICE, *1843-*

AUTHOR OF " THE LIVES OF ENGLISH POPULAR LEADERS IN
THE MIDDLE AGES."

HASKELL HOUSE PUBLISHERS Ltd.
*Publishers of Scarce Scholarly Books*
NEW YORK, N. Y. 10012
1969

First Published 1887

HASKELL HOUSE PUBLISHERS LTD.
*Publishers of Scarce Scholarly Books*
280 LAFAYETTE STREET
NEW YORK. N. Y. 10012

Library of Congress Catalog Card Number: 68-25250

Standard Book Number 8383-0215-7

Printed in the United States of America

# PREFACE.

THE following book is the result of many years' work. It aims at showing the links which connected together the various movements in Germany, Italy, and the Austrian Empire in 1848-9. Many as are the books which have been written on the various parts of that struggle, I do not know of any attempt to link them together. How adventurous this effort is I am most painfully aware, and none the less so because I happen to know that the task was undertaken and abandoned by at least one writer who has many qualifications for it to which I can lay no claim. I allude to my friend Dr. Eugene Oswald, who has most generously assisted me in carrying out the work for which he was unable to spare the time. But I may say without arrogance that however deficient my history may be in the learning and ability which Dr. Oswald's would have shown, as well as in that lifelikeness which his personal share in the important rising in Baden would have enabled him to give to the descriptions; yet I shall at least have no temptation to any one-sided estimate of the merits of the various races concerned in the struggle, a temptation from which the most candid German could hardly escape. My only danger in that matter would be that I might be tempted to speak too favourably of *all* the movements of those various races; seeing

that during my investigations in the cities affected
by these movements, I received the most extreme
courtesy and kindness from German and Bohemian,
Magyar and Szekler, Saxon and Roumanian, Serb,
Croat, and Italian; and I feel nothing but pain at
any word of criticism I have uttered in these pages
that may jar on the susceptibilities of any of those
races.

It will be noticed, of course, that I have omitted
from this history any account of the French Revolution. My reasons for this have been given at the
beginning of the seventh chapter. But I may add to
what I have said there that I had long felt the disproportionate importance which many people attached
to the French Revolution of 1848, in regard to its
immediate influence on Europe. From Palermo, not
from Paris, came the first revolutionary outburst.
From Presburg, not from Paris, came the word that
shook Metternich from power, and secured a European
character to the Revolution. Under these circumstances, I conceived the idea of telling the story of
the European Revolution, without touching on the
French part of it, except in the most incidental
manner; so that the students of this period may be
able fairly to estimate the other influences which produced these great results, unblinded by the splendour which anything done in Paris seems always to
have for the student of revolution.

One other peculiarity in my book also needs some
explanation. I have, as far as possible, avoided references to authorities in notes. Such references only
worry the general reader, while the student will, I
think, be more helped by the list of authorities which
I append to this preface.

It now only remains for me to thank those friends who have helped me in my work.—For the German part of the Revolution, I have received much help from the kind loan of the " Neue Rheinische Zeitung " by the late Dr. Karl Marx. For the special Baden part of it I received help not only from Dr. Oswald but also from Dr. Karl Blind, who lent me pamphlets not otherwise accessible. For the Bohemian part of the narrative I owe much to the kind help of Dr. Gabler, Mr. Naprstek, Count Leo Thun the younger, and Dr. Rieger. For hints about the Viennese struggle I owe thanks to Dr. von Frankl, the well-known poet of the revolution, and also to Dr. Friedjung. For some general hints on the Slavonic question I am much indebted to Baron Helfert; and my obligation to Dr. Herbst I have acknowledged in a note. For general Hungarian information I owe thanks to Mr. Pulszky, to Miss Toulmin Smith, to General Klapka, to my kind friend Professor Felmeri of Klausenburg, to Dr. Lindner, Mr. Kovacs, Mr. Kovary, Mr. Boros, of the same town, and to Mr. Szabò, now Librarian of Klausenburg University, formerly a distinguished officer in General Bem's army; also to Mr. Fekete, Mr. Sandor, and Professor Koncz of Maros Vasarhely; and last but not least to Mr. Paget, the author of " Hungary and Transylvania." For special hints about the Saxon question I am indebted, amongst others, to Dr. Teutsch, to Professor Senz, and to the late " Obergespan " of Hermannstadt, Herr von Brennerberg, whose loss to the district I can well understand, since the acquaintance of a week enabled me to appreciate the singular justice of his mind, as well as his uniform kindness; while for information from the Roumanian point of

view I owe thanks to Mr. Barritzu. For information
on Serb questions I am indebted principally to Mr.
Polit, and Mr. Hadjiç of Neusatz, and Mr. Boscoviç
of Belgrade, for whose acquaintance I have to thank
the late Servian Minister in England, Mr. Mijatoviç.
The same introducer I have to thank for the kindness
shown me by Mr. Matkovicu of Agram. In the last
mentioned town I also received useful information
and help from Mr. Subek, and from the Librarian of
the South Slavonic Academy.

For help in Italian work I have to thank my old
friend Madame Venturi, Signor Ernesto Nathan,
Signor Cardinali, Signor Berti, Professor Villari,
Signor Guastalla, Professor Aurelio Saffi (the Ex-
Triumvir of Rome), Signor Galli, Dr. Sacchi, the
Syndic of Goito, the Librarian of the Biblioteca di Brera
at Milan, and my friend Signor Pizzi.—For help of
various kinds I have to thank Miss Wedgwood, Miss
Irby, Dr. Brandl and Mr. Garnett of the British
Museum.

I have also to acknowledge the kindness of Mr.
Diösy in allowing a copy to be taken of his picture
of Kossuth, for insertion in my book. This favour,
with other help, I owe to my friend Mr. B. Gunszt.

# CONTENTS.

# LIST OF ILLUSTRATIONS.

# AUTHORITIES CONSULTED.

## GENERAL HISTORY.

Metternich's Memoirs.
Menzel's Geschichte der letzten vierzig Jahre.

## GERMANY.

### GENERAL GERMAN HISTORY.

Arndt, Life of.
Blum, Life of.
Görres, Life of.
Marx, Neue Rheinische Zeitung.
Perthes, Life of.
Stein, Life of, by Professor Seeley.
Stenographischer Bericht des deutschen Vor Parlaments zu
    Frankfort.
——— des Fünfziger Ausschüsses.
——— der deutschen Constituirenden Versammlung.
Zimmermann Deutsche Revolution.

## PRUSSIA.

Humboldt Brief-Wechsel mit einem Jungen Freunde.
——— Letters to Varnhagen von Ense.
Schmalz Berichtigung einer Stelle in der Bredow-Venturinischen
    Chronik für das Jahr 1808.

## BADEN.

Goegg (Amand) Rückblick auf die Badische Revolution (from
    La Ligue des Peuples).
La Liberté de Penser (a journal containing pamphlets, &c., on
    the Baden Revolution).
Morel Der März-Aufstand und Die Badische Revolution.
Struve (Gustav) Geschichte der Volks Erhebungen in Baden.
    „   (Amalie) Erinnerungen, &c.

xii        AUTHORITIES CONSULTED.

## SCHLESWIG-HOLSTEIN.

Adressen an eine hohe deutsche Versammlung, &c., von Kiel.
Bunsen.  Memoir on Constitutional Rights of the Duchies.
Droysen.  The Policy of Denmark towards the Duchies.

## SWITZERLAND.

Der Untergang des Sonderbundes.

## AUSTRIA.

### GENERAL HISTORY.

Helfert.  Geschichte Oesterreichs.
Springer.  Geschichte Oesterreichs seit der Wiener Frieden, 1809.
Pillersdorf.  Rückblick auf die politische Bewegung in
Oesterreich.

## VIENNA.

Dunder.  Denkschrift über die Wiener October Revolution.
Grüner.  Geschichte der October Revolution.
Reschauer.  Das Jahr 1848.
Reichstag's Gallerie, &c.
Verhandlungen des Oesterreichischen Landtages 1848.
Violand.  Die Sociale Geschichte der Revolution in Oesterreich.
Wiener Boten.

## BOHEMIA.

Müller.  Die merkwürdigsten Tage Prags in der Pfingst—
Woche des Jahres 1848.
Pameti (Pamphlets and proclamations, &c., in the Archives of
Prague).
Schöpf.  Volks Bewegung in Prag.
Ständische Verhältnisse des Konigreichs Böhmen.
Stiles.  Austria in 1848-9.
Tomain.  Das Böhmische Staatsrecht.

## GALICIA.

Ausschlüsse über die jungsten Ereignisse in Polen.
Krasinski.  Panslavismus und Germanismus.
Krolikowski.  Mémoire sur l'Etat de Cracovie, 1840.
Zaleski.  Die Pölnische Frage.

## HUNGARY.

### GENERAL HISTORY.

Beschwerden und Klagen der Slaven in Ungarn, 1843.
Böhmisch-Slavische Helden in der Panslavismus.
Deak, Life of.
Görgei. My Life and Acts in Hungary.
Irby (Miss). Across the Carpathians.
Klapka. Memoirs of the War of Independence in Hungary.
Kossuth, Memoir of in a History of Hungary by E. O. S.
Kovari (Lasló) Okmanytar az 1848-9. (This book, though written in Hungarian, contains some important documents in German, of which alone I have been able to make use.)
Mailath (Count Johann) Geschichte von Oesterreich.
„ Der Ungarische Reichstag in 1830.
Paget. Hungary and Transylvania.
Pulszky. Meine Zeit mein Leben.
„ (Madame). Memoirs of a Hungarian Lady.
Smith (Toulmin). Parallels between Constitution and Constitutional History of England and Hungary.
Szechenyi (Vortrag über) Ludwig Fezstory.
Zur Geschichte des Ungarischen Freiheits-Kampfes Autentische Berichte.

## CROATIA AND SLAVONIA.

Aktenstücke zur Geschichte des Croatisch Slavonischen Landtages, by Pejakoviç.
Agramer Zeitung, 1843-8.
Deutsche Viertels-Jahr-Schrift (article called Mittheilungen aus Serbien).
Le Duc. La Croatie et la Confédération Italienne.
Serbes de Hongrie, &c.
Verhandlungen des Agramer Landtags in October, 1845.
Other pamphlets on the Croatian question.

## TRANSYLVANIA.

Bem. Feldzug in Siebenbürgen, by Czetz.
Bonar. Transylvania, its Products and People.
Deutsche Worte, a magazine.
Friedenfels, Joseph Bedeus von Scharberg.
Klausenburg, Collection of documents in Library of.

Lauriani.  Die Romänen der Oesterreichischer Monarchie.

Maros Vasarhely, Collection of Baron Apor at.

Roth.  Der Sprach-Kampf in Siebenbürgen.

Scharberg.  Die Verfassung Siebenbürgens.

Unterhaltungen aus der Gegenwart.

Vereinigung Siebënbürgens mit Ungarn vom Standpunkte der Sachsischen Nation beleuchtet.

Zieglauer.  Die Reform-Bewegung in Siebenbürgen.


## ITALY.

### GENERAL HISTORY.

Alfieri.  Opere.  Autobiography.

Bianchi (Nicomede), Storia della politica Austriaca rispetto ai Sovrani ed ai Governi Italiani dell' anno 1791, al Maggio del 1857.

Coppi.  Annali d'Italia.

D'Amato.  Panteon dei Martiri della libertà Italiana.

Farini.  Lo Stato Romano (really including much of other parts).

Foscolo (Ugo) Scritte politici inediti.  Jacopo Ortis.

—— Lettera a Conte Verri.

—— Lettera a Conte di Ficquelmont.

—— (Vita di).  Pecchio.

Gallenga.  Italy in 1848.

Gioberti Vincenzo (biography by V. G. in I Contemporanei Italiani).  Del Primato Morale e Civile degli Italiani.

Gualterio.  Gli Ultimi Rivolgimenti Italiani.

—— Delle Negative date dal Conte Solaro della Margherita.

La Concordia (paper published at Genoa).

La Farina.  Storia dell Italia dopo il Settembre del 1847.

Manzoni (Alessandro).  Cenni Sulla vita Sua.

Miscellanee politiche Genovesi (pamphlets, songs, &c., published at Genoa, and bearing on the revolution).

Mazzini, Life and Writings of (translated by E. A. V.).

Panizzi, Lettere ad, di uomini illustri, &c.

Ranalli.  Istorie Italiane dal 1846 al 1853.


## LOMBARDY AND VENETIA.

Andryane.  Mémoires d'un prisonnier d'Etat.

AUTHORITIES CONSULTED. xv

Anfossi (Francesco). Memorie sulla campagna di Lombardia del
 1848.
Biblioteca di Brera (Milan), Collections of Caricatures, Pam-
 phlets, and Proclamations in.
Cantù (Cesare). Editions and Lives of Monti and Parini.
Casati. Nuove rivelazioni su i fatti di Milano nel 1847-8.
Cattaneo. Dell' Insurrezione di Milano.
 „ Archivio Triennale.
Dandolo. Italian Volunteers and Lombard Rifle Brigade.
Gazzetta di Milano, 1848.
Manin, Documents et pièces autentiques laissées par.
Quadro politico di Milano (collection of pamphlets, &c.).
Vedovi (Timoleone). I martiri di san Georgio e di Belfiore.

## NAPLES AND SICILY.

Colletta. History of Naples (translated).
Ruggiero Settimo. Per Gabriele Colonna.

## PIEDMONT.

Balbo (Cesare) autobiography.
 „ Speranze d'Italia.
Brofferio. Storia di Piemonte.
 „ I miei Tempi.
Solaro della Margherita, Vita di per Biginelli.
 „ Memorandum Storico-Politico.
 „ Avvedimenti Politici.

## ROMAN STATES.

Artaud. Vie de Pie 7.
 „ Vie de Pie 8.
Balleydier. Storia della Revoluzione di Roma.
Beghelli. La Republica Romana del 1849.
Brasini. L' 8 Agosto 1848, Bologna.
 „ La Resistenza di Bologna nelle otto Giornate di
 Maggio, 1849.
D'Azeglio (Massimo) Degli ultimi casi di Romagna.
 „ Correspondance Politique.
Monitorio Romano, 1848 and 1849.
Orsini. Memoirs.
Pasolini (Memoir of), by his son, translated.
Protocollo della Republica Romana.

Republica Italiana del 1849 (anonymous clerical).

Rossi (Pellegrino). Vita di per Raggi (including other notices of him).

Torre (Federico). Memorie Storiche sull' intervento Francese (unfinished).

## TUSCANY.

Guerrazzi (Domenico) Apologia della Vita Politica. (His novels should also be read to estimate his influence.)

# CHIEF RACES OF AUSTRIAN EMPIRE.

## Hungary.

*Magyars*, ruling race; found in most parts of the Kingdom, but most largely in the Northern parts. Semi-Turkish race (non-Aryan). Various creeds; Calvinism the most distinctive (*i.e.*, the one that has most connected itself with the race-struggles). Chief town, Buda-Pesth.

*Croats*, chiefly found in Croatia, but sometimes in Slavonia and Dalmatia. Creed, Roman Catholic; Slavonic race; chief town, Agram.

*Saxons*, found in S.E. of Transylvania. Creed, mainly Lutheran; race, German; chief town, Hermannstadt.

*Serbs*, found chiefly in Slavonia, but also in Banat, Bacska, and in smaller numbers in other parts of Hungary. Creed, Greek Church; race, Slavonic; chief towns, Neusatz and Carlowitz.

*Slovaks*, found in North Hungary. Creed, Lutheran; race, Slavonic.

*Szekler*, found in N.E. of Transylvania. Creeds, various; race, same as Magyars; chief town, Maros Vasarhely.

*Roumanian*, or *Wallack*, in all parts of Transylvania, and a few in the Banat. Creed, Greek Church; race, mixed Dacian and Italian; chief town, Blasendorf.

*Italians*, found in Dalmatia and Istria.

## Western Austria.

*Germans*, found everywhere, but chiefly in Archduchy. Creed, mainly Roman Catholic; chief town, Vienna.

*Slovenes*, found in Krain, Carinthia, and Styria. Race, Slavonic.

*Czechs*, in Bohemia, Moravia, and Silesia. Creed, chiefly Roman Catholic; race, Slavonic; chief town, Prague.

## Galicia.

*Poles*, found in all parts. Creed, Roman Catholic; race, Slavonic; chief town, Lemberg.

*Ruthenians*. Creed, Greek Church; race, Slavonic.

*b*

# TABLE OF DATES.

TABLE OF DATES. xxiii

1849. Mar. 7. Dissolution of the Kremsier Parliament.
" 11. Capture of Hermannstadt by Bem.
" 12. Charles Albert declares war on Austria.
" 20. Formal announcement of new Austrian Constitution.
" 23. Battle of Novara. Abdication of Charles Albert.
" 28. Frankfort Parliament decides to offer Crown of Germany to King of Prussia.
" 29. Mazzini, Saffi, and Armellini made Triumvirs.
April 1. Capture of Brescia by Haynau.
" 3. King of Prussia refuses the Crown of Germany.
" 14. Declaration of Hungarian Independence.
" 17. Final meeting of Sicilian Parliament.
" 24. French arrive before Civita Vecchia.
" 25. Re-occupation of Pesth by the Hungarians.
" 27. Dissolution of Prussian Parliament.
May 14. Beginning of third Baden insurrection. King of Prussia recalls Prussian members from Frankfort Parliament.
" 15. Neapolitans capture Palermo.
" 20. Bologna captured by Austrians.
" 26. Proposals of Lesseps accepted by Triumvirs.
" 30. Frankfort Parliament resolves to adjourn to Stuttgart.
" 31. Oudinot rejects Lesseps' Convention.
June 4. Russian proclamation of intended invasion of Hungary.
" 13. Ledru Rollin's insurrection in Paris.
" 17. First Russian victory in Transylvania.
" 18. Final dissolution of German Parliament.
" 19. Austrians capture Ancona.
" 30. Roman Assembly decides to yield. Prussians surround Rastatt, which is centre of Baden movement.
July 3. French enter Rome.
" 15. Papal Government restored.
" 28. Death of Charles Albert. Hungarian Diet dissolves itself.
Aug. 5. Capture of Hermannstadt by Russians.

# CHAPTER I.

## THE TRIUMPH OF DESPOTISM. 1815—1819.

Condition of Europe in 1815. — Metternich's position. — Character of Alexander of Russia.—Metternich's attitude towards religion.—Madame de Krudener.—The Holy Alliance.—Aspirations of the Germans.—Stein v. Metternich.—Schmalz's pamphlet. —The Rhine Province.—Arndt and Görres.—The Small States of Germany.—Würtemberg.—Weimar.—The Jena demonstration. —The Burschenschaft.—The Wartburg demonstration.—The Murder of Kotzebue.—The Carlsbad decrees.—The Final-Act of Vienna.—Metternich's triumph.

IN the year 1814 Napoleon Buonaparte ceased to reign over Europe, and, after a very short interregnum, Clement Metternich reigned in his stead. Ever since the fall of Stadion, and the collapse of Austria in 1809, this statesman had exercised the chief influence in Austrian affairs; and, by his skilful diplomacy, the Emperor had been enabled to play a part in Europe which, though neither honourable nor dignified, was eminently calculated to enable that Prince to take a leading position in politics, when the other Powers were exhausted by war, and uncertain of what was to follow. But Francis of Austria, though in agreement with Metternich, was really his hand rather than his head; and thus the crafty Minister easily assumed the real headship of Europe, while professing to be the humble servant of the Emperor of Austria.

B

The system of the new ruler resembled that of Napoleon in its contempt for the rights of men and of nations ; but it was to be varnished over with an appearance of legality, a seeming respect for the rights of kings, and a determination to preserve peace and avoid dramatic sensations, which made it welcome to Europe, after eighteen years of almost incessant wars or rumours of wars.  As he looked round upon the countries that had fallen under his rule, the contemplation of the existing state of Europe seemed to promise the new monarch a fairly successful reign.  France had been satisfied by the preservation of Alsace and Lorraine, and by the sense that, from having been the focus of revolution, she had now become the corner-stone of legitimacy. England had at first seemed to give pledges to the cause of liberty by her promise of independence to Genoa, and her guarantee of the Sicilian Constitution ; but with the help of Castlereagh, whom Metternich described as " that upright and enlightened states- man," the Austrian Government had succeeded in persuading the English to consent to look on quietly while Genoa was absorbed in the Kingdom of Sardinia, and while the Anglo-Sicilian Constitution was destroyed by Ferdinand of Naples ; and the English zeal for independence had been happily diverted from the support of constitutions and civic liberties to the championship of the most contemptible of Napoleon's puppets, the King of Saxony.

The King of Prussia, who in 1813 had seemed in danger of becoming the champion of popular rights and German freedom, was now, with his usual feeble- ness, swaying towards the side of despotism ; and any irritation which he may have felt at the opposition to his claim upon Saxony, had been removed by the concession of the Rhine Province.

Among the smaller sovereigns of Europe, the King of Sardinia and the Pope alone showed any signs of rebellion against the new ruler of Europe. The former had objected to the continued occupation of Alessandria by Austrian forces ; while the representatives of the Pope had even entered a protest against that vague and dangerous clause in the Treaty of Vienna which gave Austria a right to occupy Ferrara.

But, on the other hand, the King of Sardinia had shown more zeal than any other ruler of Italy in restoring the old feudal and absolutist régime which the French had overthrown. And though Cardinal Consalvi, the chief adviser of the Pope, was following for the present a semi-Liberal policy, he might as yet be considered as only having established a workable Government in Rome. And a Pope who had been kidnapped by Napoleon was hardly likely to offer much opposition to the man who, in his own opinion, was the overthrower of Napoleon.

Yet there were two difficulties which seemed likely to hinder the prosperity of Metternich's reign. These were the character of Alexander I. of Russia, and the aspirations of the German nation.

Alexander, indeed, if occasionally irritating Metternich, evidently afforded him considerable amusement, and the sort of pleasure which every man finds in a suitable subject for the exercise of his peculiar talents. For Alexander was eminently a man to be managed. Enthusiastic, dreamy, and vain ; now bent on schemes of conquest, now on the development of some ideal of liberty, now filled with some confused

religious mysticism ; at one time eager to divide the
world with Napoleon, then anxious to restore Poland
to its independence ; now listening to the appeals of
Metternich to his fears, at another time to the nobler
and more liberal suggestions of Stein and Pozzo di
Borgo ;[1] only consistent in the one desire to play an
impressive and melodramatic part in European affairs.

But, amusing as Alexander was to Metternich,
there were circumstances connected with the condition of Europe which might make his weak love of
display as dangerous to Metternich's policy as a more
determined opponent could be. There were still
scattered over Europe traces of the old aspirations
after liberty which had been first kindled by the
French Revolution, and again awakened by the
rising against Napoleon. Setting aside, for the
moment, the leaders of German thought, there were
men who had hoped that even Napoleon might give
liberty to Poland ; there were Spanish popular leaders
who had risen for the independence of their country ;
Lombards who had sat in the Assembly of the Cis-
Alpine Republic ; Carbonari in Naples, who had
fought under Murat, and who had at one time
received some little encouragement, even from their
present King. If the Czar of Russia should put
himself at the head of such a combination as this,
the consequences to Europe might indeed be serious.

But the stars in their courses fought for Metternich ;
and a force, which he had considered almost as
dangerous as the character of Alexander, proved the
means of securing the Czar to the side of despotism.

[1] A Corsican of noble birth who left his country after it fell
under the rule of France, and whose influence was used with
Alexander to encourage him in a Liberal policy.

Nothing is more characteristic of Metternich and his system than his attitude towards any kind of religious feeling. It might have been supposed that the anti-religious spirit which had shown itself in the fiercest period of the French Revolution, and, to a large extent, also in the career of Napoleon, would have induced the restorers of the old system to appeal both to clerical feeling and religious sentiment, as the most hopeful bulwark of legitimate despotism. Metternich was far wiser. He knew, in spite of the accidental circumstances which had connected Atheism with the fiercer forms of Jacobinism, that, from the time of Moses to the time of George Washington, religious feeling had constantly been a tremendous force on the side of liberty ; and although he might try to believe that to himself alone was due the fall of Napoleon, yet he could not but be aware that there were many who still fancied that the popular risings in Spain and Germany had contributed to that end, and that in both these cases the element of religious feeling had helped to strengthen the popular enthusiasm. He felt, too, that however much the clergy might at times have been made the tools of despotism, they did represent a spiritual force which might become dangerous to those who relied on the power of armies, the traditions of earthly kings, or the tricks of diplomatists. Much, therefore, as he may have disliked the levelling and liberating part of the policy of Joseph II., Metternich shared the hostility of that Prince to the power of the clergy.

Nor was it purely from calculations of policy that Metternich was disposed to check religious enthusiasm. Like so many of the nobles of his time, he had come under the influence of the French philosophers of the eighteenth century ; his hard and cynical spirit had easily caught the impress of their teaching; and he found it no difficult matter to flavour Voltairianism with a slighttincture of respectable orthodox Toryism.

The method by which he achieved this end should be given in his own words : " I read every day one or two chapters of the Bible. I discover new beauties daily, and prostrate myself before this admirable book; while at the age of twenty I found it difficult not to think the family of Lot unworthy to be saved, Noah unworthy to have lived, Saul a great criminal, and David a terrible man. At twenty I tried to understand the Apocalypse ; now I am sure that I never shall understand it. At the age of twenty a deep and long-continued search in the Holy Books made me an Atheist after the fashion of Alembert and Lalande ; or a Christian after that of Chateaubriand. Now I believe and do not criticize. Accustomed to occupy myself with great moral questions, what have I not accomplished or allowed to be wrought out, before arriving at the point where the Pope and my Curé begged me to accept from them the most portable edition of the Bible ? Is it bold in me to take for certain that among a thousand individuals chosen from the men of which the people are composed, there will be found, owing to their intellectual faculties, their education, or their age, very few who have arrived at the point where I find myself?"

This statement of his attitude of mind is taken from a letter written to remonstrate with the Russian Ambassador on the patronage afforded by the Emperor Alexander to the Bible Societies. But how

much more would such an attitude of mind lead him
to look with repugnance on the religious excitement
which was displaying itself even in the Arch Duchy
of Austria !

And, to say the truth, men of far deeper religious
feeling than Metternich might well be dissatisfied
with the influence of the person who was the chief
mover in this excitement.

The Baroness de Krudener, formerly one of the
gayest of Parisian ladies of fashion, and at least
suspected of not having been too scrupulous in her
conduct, had gone through the process which Carlyle
so forcibly describes in his sketch of Ignatius Loyola.
She had changed the excitements of the world for
the excitements of religion, and was now preaching
and prophesying a millennium of good things to come
in another world, to those who would abandon some
of the more commonplace amusements of the present.
The disturbance which she was producing in men's
minds specially alarmed Metternich ; and, under what
influence it may be difficult to prove, she was induced
to retire to Russia, and there came in contact with
the excitable Czar.

Under her influence Alexander drew up a manifesto,
from which it appeared that, while all men were
brothers, kings were the fathers of their peoples ;
Russia, Austria, and Prussia were different branches
of one Christian people, who recognized no ruler save
the Highest ; and they were to combine to enforce
Christian principles on the peoples of Europe.  When
the draft of this proclamation was first placed before
Metternich it was so alien from his modes of thought
that he could only treat it with scorn ; and Frederick
William of Prussia was the only ruler who regarded

it with even modified approval. But with all his scorn Metternich had the wit to see that the pietism of Alexander of Russia had now been turned into a direction which might be made use of for the enforcement of Metternich's own system of government; and thus, after having induced Alexander, much against his will, to modify and alter the original draft, Metternich laid the foundation of the Holy Alliance.

But there still remained the troublesome question of the aspirations of the German nation; and these seemed likely at first to centre in a man of far higher type and far more steady resolution than Alexander. This was Baron von Stein, who, driven from office by Napoleon, had been in exile the point of attraction to all those who laboured for the liberty of Germany. He had declared, at an early period, in favour of a German Parliament. But Metternich had ingeniously succeeded in pitting against him the local feeling of the smaller German States; and instead of the real Parliament which Stein desired, there arose that curious device for hindering national development called the German Bund.

This was composed of thirty-nine members, the representatives of all the different German Governments. Its object was said to be to preserve the outward and inward safety of Germany, and the independence and inviolability of her separate States. If any change were to be made in fundamental laws, it could only be done by a unanimous vote. Some form of Constitution was to be introduced in each State of the Bund; arrangements were to be made with regard to the freedom of the press, and the Bund was also to take into consideration the question of trade and intercourse between the different States.

All the members of the Bundestag were to protect Germany, and each individual State, against every attack. The vagueness and looseness of these provisions enabled Metternich so to manage the Bundestag as to defeat the objects of Stein and his friends, and gradually to use this weakly-constituted Assembly as an effective engine of despotism.

But in fact Stein was ill fitted to represent the popular feeling in any efficient manner. His position is one that is not altogether easy to explain. He believed, to some extent, in the People, especially the *German* People. That is to say, he believed in the power of that people to *feel* justly and honourably ; and, as long as that feeling was expressed in the form of a cry to their rulers to guide and lead justly, he was as anxious as anyone that that cry should be heard. He liked, too, the sense of the compact embodiment of this feeling in some institution representing the unity of the nation. But, with the ideas connected with popular representation in the English sense, he had little sympathy. That the People or their representatives should *reason* or act, independently of their sovereigns, was a political conception which was utterly abhorrent to him.

In short, Stein's antagonism to Metternich was as intense as that of the most advanced democrat ; but it was not so much the opposition of a champion of freedom to a champion of despotism, as the opposition of an honest man to a rogue. Metternich wrote in his Memoirs, when he was taking office for the first time in 1809, "From the day when peace is signed we must confine our system to tacking and turning and flattering. Thus alone may we possibly preserve our existence till the day of general deliverance." This policy had

been consistently followed. The abandonment of
Andrew Hofer after the Tyrolese rising of 1809,
the adulterous marriage of Maria Louisa, the alliance
with Napoleon, the discouragement of all popular
effort to throw off the French yoke, the timely
desertion of Napoleon's cause, just soon enough to
give importance to the alliance of Austria with
Prussia and Russia and England, just late enough
to prevent any danger of defeat and misfortune ;
these acts marked the character of Metternich's
policy and excited the loathing of Stein.

As he had been repelled from Metternich by arts
like these, so Stein had been drawn to Arndt,
Schleiermacher, and Steffens by a common love of
honesty and by a common power of self-sacrifice ;
but he looked upon them none the less as, to a large
extent, dreamers and theorists ; and this want of
sympathy with them grew, as the popular movement
took a more independent form, until at last the
champion of Parliamentary Government, the liberator
of the Prussian peasant, the leader of the German
people in the struggle against Napoleon, drifted
entirely out of political life from want of sympathy
with all parties.

But it was not to Stein alone that the Germans of
1813 had looked for help and encouragement in their
struggle against Napoleon. The People had found
other noble leaders at that period, and it remembered
them. The King of Prussia remembered them too,
to his shame. He was perfectly aware that he had
played a very sorry part in the beginning of the
struggle, and that, instead of leading his people, he
had been forced by them most unwillingly into the
position of a champion of liberty. It was not, there-

fore, merely from a fear of the political effects of the
Constitutional movement, but from a more personal
feeling, that Frederick William III. was eager to
forget the events of 1813.

But if the King wished to put aside uncomfortable
facts, his flatterers were disposed to go much further,
and to deny them. A man named Schmalz, who
had been accused, rightly or wrongly, of having acted
in 1808 with Scharnhorst in promoting the Tugendbund,[1] and of writing in a democratic sense about
popular assemblies, now wrote a pamphlet to vindicate himself against these charges.

Starting from this personal standpoint, he went on
to maintain that all which was useful in the movement of 1813 came directly from the King; that
enterprises like that by which Schill endeavoured
to rouse the Prussians to a really popular struggle
against the French were an entire mistake ; that the
political unions did nothing to stir up the people;
that the alliance between Prussia and France in
1812 had saved Europe; and that it was not till the
King gave the word in February, 1813, that the
German people had shown any wish to throw off
the yoke of Napoleon.

This pamphlet at once called forth a storm of
indignation. Niebuhr and Schleiermacher both wrote
answers to it, and the remaining popularity of the
King received a heavy blow when it was found that
he was checking the opposition, and had even singled
out Schmalz for special honour. The great centre of
discontent was in the newly-acquired Rhine province. The King of Prussia, indeed, had hoped that

---

[1] A popular and patriotic society, for training the Germans in
resistance to the French yoke.

by founding a University at Bonn, by appointing
Arndt Professor of History, and Görres, the former
editor of the " Rhenish Mercury," Director of Public
Instruction, he might have secured the popular feeling in the province to his side.

But Arndt and Görres were not men to be silenced
by favour, any more than by fear. Görres remonstrated with the King for giving a decoration to
Schmalz, and organized petitions for enforcing the
clause in the Treaty of Vienna which enabled the
Bund to summon the Stände of the different provinces. Arndt renewed his demand for the abolition
of serfdom in his own province of Rügen, advocated
peasant proprietorship, and, above all, Parliamentary
Government for Germany.

The feeling of discontent, which these pamphlets
helped to keep alive, was further strengthened in the
Rhine Province by a growing feeling that Frederick
William was trying to crush out local traditions and
local independence by the help of Prussian officials.

So bitter was the anti-Prussian feeling produced
by this conduct, that a temporary liking was excited
for the Emperor of Austria, as an opponent of the
Prussianizing of Germany; and Metternich, travel-
ling in 1817 through this province, remarked that it
is "no doubt the part of Europe where the Emperor
is most loved, *more even than in our own country.*"

But it was but a passing satisfaction that the ruler
of Europe could derive from this accidental result of
German discontent. He had already begun to perceive that his opposition to the unity of Germany,
and his consequent attempt to pose as the champion
of the separate States, had not tended to secure the
despotic system which his soul loved.

Stein had opposed the admission of the smaller German States to the Vienna Congress, no doubt holding that the unity of Germany would be better accomplished in this manner, and very likely distrusting Bavaria and Würtemberg, as former allies of Napoleon. Metternich, by the help of Talleyrand, had defeated this attempt at exclusion, and had secured the admission of Bavaria and Würtemberg to the Congress. But he now found that these very States were thorns in his side.

They resented the attempts of Metternich to dictate to them in their internal affairs; and, though the King of Bavaria might confine himself to vague phrases about liberty, the King of Würtemberg actually went the length of granting a Constitution. Had this King lived much longer, Metternich might have been able to revive against him the remembrance of his former alliance with Napoleon. But when, after his death in 1816, the new King of Würtemberg, a genuine German patriot, continued, in defiance of his nobles, to uphold his father's Constitution, this hope was taken away, and the South German States remained to the last, with more or less consistency, a hindrance to the completeness of Metternich's system.

But the summary of Metternich's difficulties in Germany is not yet complete. The ruler of another small principality, the Duke of Weimar, had taken advantage, like the King of Würtemberg, of the permission to grant a Constitution to his people; and had been more prominent than even the King of Würtemberg in encouraging freedom of discussion in his dominions. This love of freedom, in Weimar as in most countries of Europe, connected itself with

University life, and thus found its centre in the celebrated University of Jena; and on June 18th, 1816, the students of the University met to celebrate the anniversary of the Battle of Leipzig. There, to the great alarm of the authorities, they publicly burnt the pamphlet of Schmalz, and another written by the play-writer Kotzebue, who was believed to have turned away Alexander of Russia from the cause of liberty, and now to be acting as his tool and spy.

The head of the Rhine police, conscious, no doubt, of the ferment in his own province, remonstrated with the Duke of Weimar on permitting such disturbances.

This opposition increased the movement which it was designed to check. Jahn, who had founded the gymnastic schools which had speedily become places of military exercise for patriotic Germans during the war, now came forward to organize a Burschenschaft, a society which was to include all the patriotic students of Germany. Metternich and his friends had become thoroughly alarmed at the progress of the opposition, but again events seemed to work for him; and the enthusiasm of the students, ill-regulated, and ill-guided, was soon to give an excuse for the blow which would secure the victory for a time to the champions of absolutism.

The desire for liberty seems always to connect itself with love of symbolism; and the movement for reform, naturally led to the revival of sympathy with earlier reformers. Actuated by these feelings, the students of Leipzig and other German Universities gathered at the Wartburg, in 1817, to revive the memory of Luther's testimony for liberty of thought; and they seized the opportunity for protesting against the tyranny of their own time.

Apparently the enthusiasm for the Emperor of Austria had not extended to Saxony; for an Austrian corporal's staff was one of the first objects cast into the bonfire, which was lighted by the students; while the dislike to Prussia was symbolized by the burning of a pair of Prussian military stays, and the hatred of the tyranny which prevailed in the smaller States, found vent in the burning of a Hessian pig-tail. The demonstration excited much disapproval among the stricter followers of Metternich; but Stein and others protested against any attempt to hinder the students in their meeting.

In the following year the Burschenschaft, which Jahn desired to form, began to take shape, and to increase the alarm of the lovers of peace at all costs. Metternich rose to the occasion; and boasted that he had become a moral power in Europe, which would leave a void when it disappeared. In March, 1819, the event took place which at last gave this "moral power" a success that seemed for the moment likely to be lasting.

Ludwig Sand, a young man who had studied first at Erlangen and afterwards at Jena, went, on March 23rd, 1819, to the house of Kotzebue at Mannheim, and stabbed him to the heart.

It was said, truly or falsely, that a paper was found with Sand, declaring that he acted with the authority of the University of ——. It was said also that Sand had played a prominent part in the Wartburg celebration. With the logic usual with panic-mongers, Metternich was easily able to deduce from these facts the conclusion that the Universities

must, if left to themselves, become schools of sedition
and murder.

The Duke of Weimar, with more courage, perhaps,
than tact, had anticipated the designs of Metternich
by a proclamation in favour of freedom of thought
and teaching at the Universities, as the best security
for attaining truth.

This proclamation strengthened still further the
hands of Metternich. Abandoning the position
which he had assumed at the Congress of Vienna,
of champion of the smaller States of Germany, he
appealed to the King of Prussia for help to coerce
the Duke of Weimar, and the German Universities.

Frederick William, in spite of his support of
Schmalz, was still troubled by some scruples of
conscience. In May, 1815, he had made a public
promise of a Constitution to Prussia ; Stein and
Humboldt were eager that he should fulfil this
promise, and even the less scrupulous Hardenberg
held that it ought to be fulfilled sooner or later.

But Metternich urged upon the King that he
had allowed dangerous principles to grow in Prussia;
that his kingdom was the centre of conspiracy
against the peace and order of Germany, and that,
if he once conceded representative government,
the other Powers would be obliged to leave him to
his fate.

The King, already alarmed by the course which
events were taking, was easily persuaded by Metternich to abandon a proposal which seemed to have
nothing in its favour except the duty of keeping his
word. Arndt was deprived of his professorship, and
tried by commission on the charge of taking part in
a Republican conspiracy ; Jahn was arrested, and

Görres fled from the country, to reappear at a later time in Bavaria as a champion of Ultramontanism against the hateful influence of Prussia.

Then Metternich proceeded to his master stroke. He called a conference at Carlsbad to crush the revolutionary spirit of the Universities. A commission of five members was appointed, under whose superintendence an official was to be placed over every University, to direct the minds and studies of students to sound political conclusions. Each Government of Germany was to pledge itself to remove any teacher pronounced dangerous by this commission ; and if any Government resisted, the commission would compel it. No Government was ever to accept a teacher so expelled from any other University. No newspaper of less than twenty pages was to appear without leave of a Board, appointed for the purpose, and every state of Germany was to be answerable to the Bund for the contents of its newspapers. The editor of a suppressed paper was to be, *ipso facto*, prohibited from starting another paper for five years in any state of the Bund ; and a central Board was to be founded for inquiry into demagogic plots.

These decrees seem a sufficiently crushing engine of despotism ; but there still remained a slight obstacle to be removed from Metternich's path. The 13th Article of the Treaty of Vienna had suggested the granting of Constitutions by different rulers of Germany; and, vaguely as it had been drawn, both Metternich and Francis felt this clause an obstacle in their path.

As soon, therefore, as the Carlsbad Decrees had been passed, Metternich summoned anew the different States of Germany, to discuss the improvement of this clause. The representatives of Bavaria and Würtemberg protested against this interference with the independence of the separate States ; and, although the representative of Prussia steadily supported Metternich, it was necessary to make some concession in form to the opponents of his policy.

It was, therefore, decided that the Princes of Germany should not be hindered in the exercise of their power, nor in their duty as members of the Bund, by any Constitutions. By this easy device Metternich was able to assume, without resistance, the Imperial tone, which suited his position. The entry in his memoirs naturally marks this supreme moment of triumph. " I told my five-and-twenty friends," he says, " what we want, and what we do not want; on this avowal there was a general declaration of approval, and each one asserted he had never wanted more or less, nor indeed anything different."

Thus was Metternich recognized as the undisputed ruler of Germany, and, for the moment, of Europe.

# CHAPTER II.

## FIRST EFFORTS OF CONSTITUTIONALISM,
### 1820—1832.

Effect of Napoleonic Wars on Italian Feeling.—Austrian promises and performances in Lombardy.—Vincenzo Monti.— Ugo Foscolo.—Alessandro Manzoni.—Federigo Confalonieri.— Position of Sardinia.—Relations of Sardinia with Austria.— Reaction under Victor Emmanuel.—Ferdinand I. of Naples.—The Carbonari.—The Spanish rising.—The Spanish Constitution.— The Neapolitan rising.—Guglielmo Pepe.—The Conference at Troppau.—Palermo and the Constitution of 1812.—Divisions in the Liberal Camp.—Ferdinand's attitude.—The movement in Piedmont.— Santa Rosa.—Charles Albert. —" Voleva e non voleva."—The Students' rising.—The rising in Piedmont, and causes of its failure.—Reaction in Italy.—The first martyr.— The Greek rising.—Alexander of Russia.—George Canning.— Breaking of the Holy Alliance.—The Movements of 1830-31.— The Frankfort Decrees.—Metternich's second triumph.

OF all the countries of Europe, none had been more affected than Italy, both for good and evil, by the Napoleonic wars; and in no part of Italy were the traces of these wars so evident as in Lombardy. Though settled liberty had been unknown there since the cities of the Lombard League had fallen under their petty tyrants ; though any sense, even of national independence, must have ceased since the sixteenth century; yet the real misery of the position of a conquered country, the sense of an absolutely alien rule, seems hardly to have been fully realised by the Lombards, until the Peace of Utrecht, in 1713, had substituted the Austrian rule for that of the Spaniards.   The Spanish tyranny, however cruel, had been softened to the Italians by the sense of community of race and similarity of language; and the readiness of the conquerors to inter-marry with the conquered had given hopes of an ultimate amalgamation between the races.   But under the German rule there were no such modifications of the evils of conquest.   The new rulers held aloof from the Italians; and the latter were reminded at every moment that they were not merely slaves, but slaves to an alien and unsympathetic master.

When, then, an Italian, at the head of a French army, offered the Lombards deliverance from German rule; when he organized them into a separate legion, and showed special trust in them throughout his wars; when he established the Government of the Cis-Alpine Republic, and held out before their astonished eyes the vision of an united Italy, it was natural that such appeals should awaken hopes of a newer life, and a prouder position in the councils of Europe.

It was true that their confidence had received terrible shocks.   The horrible treachery of the Treaty of Campo Formio, the manipulation of the Constitution of the Cis-Alpine Republic, the gradual changes which tended to absorb it into the French Empire; these had been tolerably clear signs to the Lombards of what they might ultimately expect from their so-called liberator.

Yet amid all these acts of violence and treachery, Napoleon had still kept before them the idea of a separate kingdom of Italy, if not in the present, then

in the not distant future.   If Napoleon failed them,
Eugène Beauharnais might realise the ideal with
which his step-father had mocked them; if Eugène
Beauharnais proved false, King Joachim of Naples
might lead them to freedom.

And then, most wonderful of all! came the announcement that the Austrian might become, in
his turn, the liberator.   In 1809, Archduke John
had promised to the Italians, in the name of the
Emperor Francis, "a Constitution founded on the
nature of things, and a frontier inaccessible to any
foreign rule.   Europe well knows," continued the
Archduke, "that the word of this Prince is sacred,
and that it is as unchangeable as it is pure.   It is
Heaven that speaks by his mouth."

General Nugent, the leader of the Austrian forces,
followed up this proclamation, at a later time, by
equally strong promises of Italian independence, and
as late as April 26, 1814, Lord William Bentinck,
the founder of the Sicilian Constitution of 1812, had
added his guarantee for the liberty, prosperity, and
independence of Italy.

The Italians, therefore, had some hopes of justice
from the Powers of Europe.   These were shaken by
the Congress of Vienna ; and the Lombards received
a new shock when they found how unreal were even
the seeming concessions made by that Congress.   A
central Congregation of Lombardy, which had no
power of initiating reforms, and hardly leave to utter
complaints, was the sole embodiment of the principle
of Italian independence; and the "frontier guaranteed
against the foreigner" was unable to exclude, not
only Austrian soldiers from the garrisons of Lombardy,
but even Austrian judges from her tribunals, and

Austrian professors from her universities; secret tribunals tried Lombards, who were arrested for they knew not what cause; taxes out of all proportion to the size of Lombardy drained the country for the benefit of other parts of the empire; and police dogged the footsteps of the most distinguished citizens.

Nor could Lombardy be even certain of her own sons. The wisest Lombards might well have been confused by the rapid changes of government which had taken place in the short space of eighteen years. They had seen Austrian tyranny give place to a Cis-Alpine Republic; they had passed from republican rule by somewhat confused stages under the despotism of Napoleon, a despotism which had in its turn to give way to the freer rule of Eugène Beauharnais; and lastly they had seen Beauharnais overthrown, and Austrian rule restored in a more crushing form than before.

Not merely their political judgment, but their sense of right and wrong had been unsettled by such changes. When men of high genius, like the poet Vincenzo Monti, could begin his literary career by a fierce poem against France, continue it by songs in praise of the French conquerors as promoters of liberty, then write eulogies on Napoleon's empire, and finally join in the inauguration of a library, which was to be the means of reconciling the Italians to their Austrian conquerors, it can scarcely be wondered at if men of lower intellect found themselves equally ready to worship each new ruler as he rose into power, and to trample on the memory of fallen heroes.

A man of nobler type than Monti expressed, perhaps still more clearly, the sense of despair which seemed likely to become the keynote of Italian feeling. Ugo Foscolo was, from his very birth, an embodiment of the confused state of Italy at that period. He was born in 1778, in the Isle of Zante, then a colony of the Venetian Republic, and in a condition of the utmost lawlessness. He was sent from thence to study at Padua, and thus grew up to manhood during the period of those continual changes in Lombardy which marked the period of the struggle against France. At one time he thought of becoming a priest, but soon devoted himself to literature.

The sole models for the Italian dramatists, at that period, were the writings of Vittorio Alfieri, whose feelings and literary taste had led him to adhere, as closely as he could, to the old classical traditions. At the age of nineteen Foscolo chose, as his first subject for a drama, the horrible story of Thyestes ; but though this work was received with great applause, his literary career was, for a time, cut short by the Treaty of Campo Formio.

His political convictions seem already to have been strongly developed, for he was forced to leave Venice to escape the persecution of the new Government. Yet the creation of the Cis-Alpine Republic revived his hopes, and he hastened to Milan to take a share in the new life. There he became acquainted with the two leading poets of the day, Vincenzo Monti and Giuseppe Parini. From the former he gained several hints in style ; from the latter he learnt the nobler lesson of hatred of corruption and servility. But the growing tyranny of Napoleon, the sense of the fickleness of his own countrymen, and the loathing of the rule of the Austrians, produced in Foscolo a bitter tone of cynicism and despair.

It was while in this state of mind that he fell in with Goethe's romance of Werther ; and on this he modelled the strange rhapsodical story of Jacopo Ortis, in which the hero, disappointed in love and politics, takes refuge, like Werther, in suicide. But while the German romance was merely the expression of a passing feeling, which the author took pleasure in throwing into an artistic form, the Italian story was the deliberate expression of Foscolo's most permanent state of mind, and was accepted as the embodiment of the feelings of many other Lombard youths.

Foscolo, after fighting for the independence of Italy against the Austrian invasion of 1815, withdrew in disgust to England; but some of those who would gladly have welcomed him as a fellow-worker still remained in Lombardy, and tried to form a nucleus of free Italian thought.

Of these, the most remarkable was Alessandro Manzoni, best known to foreigners as the author of "I Promessi Sposi." Manzoni's influence was more widely felt in Italy at a later period ; but the presence of such a man among the Lombard patriots of 1816-20 is too remarkable a fact to pass without notice. He, like so many other young nobles, had gone through a phase of eighteenth-century scepticism. But in 1808 he had been attracted by a beautiful Protestant lady, who, after her marriage to Manzoni, drifted into Roman Catholicism, and eventually led her husband to accept the same faith. Many of his old comrades denounced his conversion, and some even attributed it to evil motives. But they soon discovered that his new faith, far from weakening his Italian feeling, had strengthened, while in some sense, it softened it. The hard classicism of which Alfieri had set the fashion, and which Foscolo could not shake off, was repugnant to Manzoni, who desired to become the sacred poet of Italy, and who was recognized by Goethe as being " Christian without fanaticism, Roman Catholic without hypocrisy."

Manzoni disliked Eugène Beauharnais for wishing to derive his title to the kingdom of Italy from Alexander of Russia ; but he sympathized with the attempt of Murat, and was ready to act with those Lombards who wished to rouse Italian feeling in literature and politics.

But though men like Foscolo and Manzoni had a wider and deeper influence in all parts of Italy, the person who most attracted the hopes of the Lombards and the fear and hatred of Metternich, at this period, was a man whose name is now little remembered outside his own country. This was Count Federigo Confalonieri. He, like so many of the better men of his country, had become equally disgusted with French and Austrian rulers ; and, when a proposal was made by the Italian Senate in 1814 to secure from the allies an independent kingdom of Italy, to be governed by Eugène Beauharnais, Confalonieri headed a protest against the proposal. The Austrian spies seized the opportunity to stir up a riot against the Senate ; and in this disturbance Prina, one of the ministers, was seized by the mob and murdered, in spite of Confalonieri's indignant protest.

The Senate fled ; and the new Provisional Government of Lombardy sent Confalonieri to Paris, to plead for an independent kingdom of Lombardy. His appeal, however, was in vain ; and, when the Austrians recovered their rule, Confalonieri was banished from Milan. He soon, however, returned, and devoted himself to developing in all ways the resources of his country. He had studied in London and Paris the principle of mutual instruction ; and he founded schools for that purpose in Lombardy. He succeeded in getting the first steamboat built in Milan, introduced gas light, and encouraged all kinds of improvements, both artistic and industrial.

But his great work was the gathering round him, for literary and political purposes, of the great writers of Lombardy ; and he founded a journal called " Il Conciliatore," to which contributions were sent by the poet Silvio Pellico, by the historians Sismondi and Botta, by Manzoni and Foscolo, and, amongst others, by a certain Lombard exile, who was afterwards to earn a short and sad celebrity in Italian history, Pellegrino Rossi. Thus, as a great noble encouraging the material growth of his country, as the centre of a literary movement, and above all as a known champion of freedom, Confalonieri riveted the attention of all who knew him.

But, however zealous this small knot of Lombards might be for the progress and freedom of their country, none of them supposed that Lombardy could throw off the yoke of Austria without assistance from other Powers. The question therefore was, to whom they should look for help.

Their nearest neighbour, the King of Sardinia, had some special grounds for grievance against the Emperor of Austria, besides the tradition of dislike which he had inherited from Victor Amadeus. That unfortunate king had had reason to regret the prominent part which he had taken in defying the French Republic in 1796. For he found that Francis of Austria was eager on every occasion to take advantage of the weakness of his ally. When Savoy was hard pressed by the French, the Austrians had demanded that, in return for any help that they might give to the King of Sardinia, he should surrender to them part of the territory in Lombardy which had been secured to him by recent treaties. Victor Amadeus endeavoured to resist this proposal as long as he could ; but he was induced by the pressure of English diplomatists to consent that, if in the war any lands were taken from Austria, he would compensate the Austrians by part of the territory which they demanded.

Victor Emmanuel found in 1815 that alliance with Austria cost him as dear as it had cost his predecessor in 1796. For, even in the last desperate struggle against Napoleon, the Austrians demanded that the treaty of alliance between Austria and Sardinia should contain a clause for the destruction of the fortifications of Alessandria ; and in the Congress of Vienna they tried to take from Victor Emmanuel the district of Novara. By the help of Alexander of Russia these intrigues were defeated ; but the Austrians, in revenge, made all the delay that they could devise in evacuating Piedmont ; and, when they finally left it in 1816, they destroyed the fortress outside Alessandria. Under these circumstances it was natural enough that the King of Sardinia should bear a bitter grudge against the House of Austria.

But, on the other hand, there was great reason to doubt whether Victor Emmanuel could be persuaded to take the lead in any war that savoured of revolution. For, hostile as he was to the claims of Austria, the newly-restored king resented yet more strongly the changes which had been introduced during the

French occupation. On his restoration in 1814, he abolished by one sweeping Act all laws passed since 1800 in Piedmont; primogeniture, aristocratic privileges, ecclesiastical tribunals, tortures, secret inquisitions, were all restored. Even at the universities learned men were deposed, as likely to be friendly to the French, and were replaced by men who had no claim but their social rank. A system of espionage was introduced, at least as inquisitorial and degrading as that of Metternich, and it was soon found that to maintain that system it was necessary to sacrifice national dignity, and to have recourse to the great master in the art of tyranny. Thus it came about that Austrian officers were chosen to control the police in Turin.

In two important respects the government of Victor Emmanuel was even worse than that of Austria. Clerical injustice and oppression were as distasteful to Francis and Metternich as they had been to Joseph and Leopold; while in Piedmont, on the contrary, friars and monks were allowed a licence which speedily became a new source of evil. The other point of difference was that, tyrannical and unjust as the Austrian tribunals were in cases where political questions were involved, they were perfectly pure in cases between man and man unconnected with politics; whereas in Piedmont judicial decisions were sold to the highest bidder.

Under these circumstances, the eyes of the champions of Italian liberty naturally turned to that kingdom from which the last effort had been made for the unity of Italy.

Naples had contributed a very large proportion of those who had died for the cause of liberty in the earlier struggles, and even before that time had produced at least one man who had left his mark on sciences which tended to promote good government. Gaetano Filangieri had been one of the most distinguished writers on law and political economy, and had gained great influence at one period over Ferdinand I. of Naples. Ferdinand himself, though intensely weak, and capable of cruelty under certain circumstances, was not a man of habitually cruel character, nor even of so despotic a temperament as Victor Emmanuel of Sardinia.

But, like most of the sovereigns of Italy, he found himself compelled to rely more and more on Austria for the re-establishment of his power. He appointed Nugent, the Austrian general, as the head of his army, and a central council interfered with the liberties which had grown up in Naples. His refusal to carry out the promises of liberty which he had made in his time of difficulty naturally irritated his people against him, while the recollections of Murat stirred in them the desire for new efforts for freedom.

But the great ally which Naples supplied at this time to the cause of liberty was the Society of the Carbonari. Connected by vague traditions with some societies of the past, Carbonarism had received its first distinct political shape in the year 1811, when Murat was reigning in Naples. In 1814, when Murat had shown signs of a despotic spirit, it transferred its allegiance to King Ferdinand, then reigning only in Sicily. When Ferdinand had been restored to the throne of Naples, he found Carbonarism a dangerous element in his kingdom, and he began to prosecute the members of the Society. This had not, however, deprived the Carbonari of their monarchical sympathies; they merely transferred them from Ferdinand to his son Francis, who, having assisted at the establishment of the Constitution of 1812 in Sicily, was supposed to be committed to the cause of liberty.

A vague talk about equality, and a more definite demand for the independence of Italy, constituted the programme of the Carbonari. But the Society was surrounded by various symbols of an impressive character, and its rules were enforced by a secret and vigorous discipline. It was evident that, in some way, it was suited to the wants of the time; for it spread rapidly from Naples to other parts of Italy, and took root both in Lombardy and Piedmont. In Lombardy it speedily attracted the attention of the Austrian police, and in 1818 several arrests were made; but such attempts merely strengthened the growth of the movement, and Carbonarism soon appeared in Spain.

In the latter country the betrayal of the Constitutional cause had been, perhaps, baser than in any other part of Europe.

With the exception of Frederick William of Prussia, no sovereign had owed more to the zeal of his people in the struggle against Napoleon than Ferdinand of Spain. In 1812, before he had been restored to his throne, he had been forced to grant a Constitution to his people, which, on recovering full power, he had abolished; and anyone who ventured to speak of liberty had been exiled or imprisoned. Among those who had been forced to fly from the country was Rafael del Riego, who had been one of the earliest to rise on behalf of Ferdinand against Napoleon. He had succeeded, by the help of the Carbonari, in establishing relations with many of the discontented soldiers in the Spanish army; and in January, 1820, he suddenly appeared at Cadiz and proclaimed the Constitution of 1812.

His success was rapid, and Ferdinand was compelled once more to swear to maintain the Constitution.

This, the first Constitution proclaimed since the downfall of Napoleon, was remarkable for its democratic character.  Parliament was to have the power of making laws in conjunction with the king, and if they passed a law three times, the king was to lose the right of vetoing it.  Ministers were to be responsible to Parliament.  Freedom of the press was to be secured, and a Council of State was to advise the king on questions of peace or war and the making of treaties.  At the same time, the nation was to prohibit the practice of any but the Roman Catholic religion.

The news rapidly spread to Naples; for not only was there continual communication between the Carbonari of Spain and those of Naples, but even official duty would make speedy communication necessary, since Ferdinand of Naples was the next heir to the Spanish throne, and it was therefore held that this Constitution would be binding on him.  The Carbonari were ready for the emergency; and while some of them, in the city of Naples, were demanding concessions, the more revolutionary districts of Calabria and Salerno had already risen in open insurrection.  Ferdinand was able to arrest some of the leaders in the city; but he soon found that the insurrectionary spirit had spread even among the generals of his army.  Officer after officer declared for the Constitution; and even those who were not ready to take that step were suspected by, and suspicious of, their fellows.  Guglielmo Pepe, known as a supporter of the previous movement of Murat,

and at one time sentenced to death for his opposition
to the Bourbon rule, was marked out by the Carbonari
as their leader.   He at first hesitated to join them,
and was even chosen by Nugent to lead the king's
forces against the insurgents; but Ferdinand distrusted him, and opposed his appointment, and Pepe
was finally driven to accept the leadership of the
revolution.  On July 5th he gathered round him a
great body of the officers and soldiers, and led them
to Naples; and Ferdinand, finding that he had no
one to rely upon, yielded to the insurgents and consented to the appointment of a provisional Junta
(composed to a great extent of the previous supporters of Murat), and swore to accept the Spanish
Constitution.

Metternich was greatly startled at the completeness
of this popular victory.   He had been convinced
that, with a people like the Neapolitans, blood would
flow in streams; and he was alarmed to find that the
leading Carbonari were men of high character.   He
at once assumed that Alexander of Russia was at
the bottom of the conspiracy; and he set himself to
convert him once more to the side of order.   But
that fickle Prince seems never to have seriously
resumed the championship of liberalism in Europe,
after the death of Kotzebue; and though he may
have wished occasionally to play with the Carbonari,
and may have been flattered by their appealing to
him, he was much more anxious to put in force those
principles which M$^{me}$ de Krudener had taught him,
which forbade kings to keep faith with those subjects
to whom they had granted liberties.   He therefore
readily consented to come to Troppau, to consider
the best means of checking the Neapolitan insurrection.

In the meantime, suspicions had arisen between the Carbonari and the old followers of Murat, and the want of organization in their forces seemed to doom the insurrection to failure.

But a still more fatal cause of division was the attitude of Sicily. The news of the proclamation of the Spanish Constitution had, at first, been welcomed there; but the nobles of Palermo cherished the recollection of that short time of independence when Ferdinand, driven out of Naples, had ruled Sicily as a separate kingdom; the Sicilian Constitution of 1812, which was welcome to the nobles of Palermo, as more aristocratic in its character than the Spanish Constitution, was acceptable to all the Palermitans as the symbol of Sicilian independence. The cry, therefore, of " the Constitution of 1812 " was raised in Palermo, in opposition to the cry of " the Spanish Constitution."

A Neapolitan intriguer, named Naselli, did his best to fan the flame of this division; riots arose; and the news spread to Naples that the Sicilians were enemies of Naples, and were opposing the Spanish Constitution. The Palermitans, on their part, appealed to the King by the memory of the old fidelity which the Sicilians had shown him when he was in exile. The King, and some others, might have responded to this appeal; and General Florestano Pepe, who was sent to suppress the rising, ended by conceding to the Sicilians the right of deciding by popular vote between the two Constitutions. But the Neapolitan pride was excited; a cry arose that the King was surrendering an important part of the kingdom, and thereby violating the Constitution.

In the meantime, however, it had become clear

D

that the preference of the Palermitans for the Constitution of 1812 was not shared by the whole body of the Sicilian people. Messina, followed by other towns, rose on behalf of the Spanish Constitution; and, while the Neapolitans were preparing new forces to suppress the rising in Palermo, the Palermitans were sending their troops against Messina.

During this state of confusion the news arrived that the representatives of the Powers at the Congress of Laybach had urged pacific means of intervention, but at the same time had advised the Neapolitans to modify their Constitution.

Under these circumstances, considerable alarm was caused by the news that the King intended to go to Laybach. Ferdinand, to check this alarm, declared to the Parliament that, whatever happened, he would defend the fundamental principles of the Constitution, freedom of the press, equality before the law, sole right of representatives to vote taxes, independence of judicial power, and responsible ministry. This speech, instead of calming the fears of the people, raised new alarms; for it seemed as though the King were meditating already *some* changes in the Government; and the people declared that they could only allow him to depart if he went to defend the Spanish Constitution. But Ferdinand earnestly assured them that he had meant nothing against the Constitution, and that, if he could not defend the rights of the people and the crown by his words at Laybach, he would return to defend them by his sword.

The Duke of Ascoli, an old friend and confidant of the King, asked him privately for more specific directions; and Ferdinand urged him to try to maintain peace; but, if it should be necessary, to prepare for war.  With such promises, Ferdinand left Naples for Laybach in January, 1821.

In the meantime, the work of the Carbonari had been spreading in Piedmont; and other sects of a similar character, and with more definite objects, had sprung up by their side.  Unlike the Neapolitans, the Piedmontese Liberals had no French political traditions, either to encourage or to hamper them. Although the House of Savoy was French in its origin, both rulers and people had been forward in their resistance to the aggressions of the French Republic.  Their ideas of liberty were derived, not from France, but from their own poet, Vittorio Alfieri; and these ideas had been strengthened by the love of independence which they had developed in the struggle against France, and which was now wholly directed against Austria.

The risings in Spain and Naples had attracted the sympathies of the Piedmontese; and it was even rumoured that Victor Emmanuel I. himself had said that if his people demanded a Constitution he would grant it.  His minister, Prospero Balbo, who had previously served under Napoleon, was supposed to have Liberal leanings.

But while all these circumstances tended to connect the desire for liberty in the minds of the Piedmontese with the support of monarchical principles, and while the absence of any interest in political affairs on the part of the peasantry, or the artizans, prevented any strong democratic organization, it was yet necessary, if the movement was to be successful, that there should be some leader who was

not afraid of revolutionary measures.   Such a man
was Santorre di Santa Rosa, an officer who had
fought in the royal guard against the French, and
who was now a major of infantry in Turin.   His
sympathies were not only monarchical, but in some
respects even aristocratic; and when the Spanish
Constitution was first proclaimed, he was inclined to
prefer some other Constitution like that of Sicily, or
even the charter which had been granted in France.
But, with keen insight, he quickly perceived that
the Spanish Constitution had become a watchword
which was thoroughly understood by the people, and
that any new cry would only cause division.

Nor were the designs of Santa Rosa limited to his
own State.   He knew that no struggle for Piedmontese liberty could be successful which did not
aim at throwing off the yoke of Austria; and that
that could only be done by combining with the
other States, which were groaning under the same
oppression.   The patriots of Lombardy were willing
enough to act with the Piedmontese, for Confalonieri
was already in communication with the Neapolitans
and other Italian Liberals, and was ready to provide
arms for the rising.

But there was still needed a figure-head who
must be placed in front of the movement, if it was
to retain any appearance of monarchical Constitutionalism.

Whatever casual remarks Victor Emmanuel may
have let fall, it soon became evident that *he* was
disposed to resist the Constitutional movement, and
he even began to increase the guards about his
palace.   Charles Felix, his brother, the next heir to
the throne, was known to be a yet sterner champion

of despotism than the King himself; and it was
under these circumstances that the eyes of the
Liberals of Piedmont were for the first time turned
to the head of the younger branch of the House of
Savoy, Charles Albert, Prince of Carignano.

He had been brought up as a simple citizen in a
public school, and had specially attracted attention
by the favour which he had shown to Alberto Nota,
whom he had made his secretary. Nota was a
writer who had set himself to restore the national
comic theatre in Piedmont, who had excited the
suspicion of the courtiers of Victor Emmanuel by his
Liberal principles, and who had at last been banished
from Turin.

But, though the favour shown by Charles Albert
to Nota was the fact in the Prince's life which
had most impressed the Piedmontese, other influences had already been brought to bear on him;
for he had also studied at Paris under an Abbé, who
had impressed on him a loathing for the French
Revolution. He was only twenty-three, and was
still hesitating between the lessons of these rival
teachers.

But before Santa Rosa and his friends could carry
out their schemes, the first sign of protest against
tyranny in Turin was given from a different quarter.
Although the desire for liberty had not yet pene-
trated to the poorer classes of Italy, and though
the leadership of these movements naturally fell into
the hands of men of noble birth, like Confalonieri
and Santa Rosa, yet there was another class in the
State which was already full of the new ideas, and
which was eventually to play an important part as
a link between the more intelligent members of the

aristocracy and the still silent classes of the community. The University students of Germany, Austria, and Italy, from the time of the gathering at Jena in 1816 down to the fall of Venice in August, 1849, were to hold a position in the great movements of the time which affected considerably the character of those movements, both for good and evil.

The share of the Turin students in the Piedmontese rising of 1821 was touched with a certain character of boyish frolic. On January 11th, some of the University students appeared at the theatre at Turin in red caps. The police at once arrested them. But their companions rose on their behalf and demanded that they should be tried by the tribunals of the University. In this demand they hoped that the professors would support them; but the rector of the college was opposed to the movement, and the professors were unwilling to interfere. Thereupon the students took matters into their own hands, took away the keys of the University from the door-keeper, placed guards at all the entrances, defended the two principal gates with forms and tables, tore up the pavements, and barred the windows. Then they despatched two delegates to Count Balbo, to entreat him to set free their comrades, or to hand them over to the authorities of the University.

The representatives of the provincial colleges flocked to the assistance of the Turin students; and the sight of the soldiers, who were called out to suppress their rising, only roused them to more determined resistance.

The delegates returned speedily, followed by Count

Balbo himself, who promised to defend the cause of
the students before Victor Emmanuel, if they
would in the meantime remain quiet.  The students,
therefore, consented to wait for further news; but
the soldiers remained encamped outside the University.  Suddenly the attention of the soldiers
was attracted by some boys coming out of school;
and, irritated presumably at some boyish mischief,
they attacked the children with bayonets.  The
students, indignant at the sight, threw stones at
the soldiers, who thereupon charged the barricades
of the University, and a general massacre followed.

The news of this massacre caused the most furious
indignation in Turin, and tended to swell the
growing revolutionary feeling.  Charles Albert paid
a special visit to the hospitals to console those who
had been wounded by the soldiers.

But in the meantime the proceedings at the Congress
of Laybach were alarming the lovers of liberty.
The King of Naples, by all sorts of pretences, had
tried to lull to sleep the vigilance of the Junta at
home; but it soon became known that the Powers
had resolved to suppress the Neapolitan Constitution,
and in February, 1822, their forces were on the
march to Naples.  The Piedmontese Liberals were
eager to protest against this violation of national
independence; and their fears were further roused
by a rumour that Austria was renewing her demands
for the surrender of the Piedmontese fortresses.  These
rumours were specially rife in Alessandria, which
had known the degradation of an Austrian occupation; and Victor Emmanuel in vain tried to convince
the Alessandrians of the unreasonableness of this
panic.

On March 6th, Santa Rosa and his friends went to
Charles Albert and asked him to put himself at the
head of the movement; and it was now that Santa
Rosa discovered the character of the man with whom
he had to deal, and left on record that saying which
summed up the whole life of that unhappy Prince—
"Voleva e non voleva" (He would and would not).
On March 6th, says one writer, "I do not know if
Charles Albert *con*sented, but he certainly *as*sented "
to the proposals of Santa Rosa.

The rising was fixed for the 8th, but on the 7th
Charles Albert had changed his mind and wished
to delay the movement. Again Santa Rosa and
his friends urged him to act with them, but without
telling him on which day the insurrection was to
break out.

There was, indeed, no time to be lost; for suspicions had already arisen of the designs of the
Liberals, and arrests were being made. On March
10th, therefore, Count Palma seized on the citadel
of Alessandria and proclaimed the Spanish Constitution. Almost at the same time Captain Ferrero
occupied the little town of San Salvario and unfurled
the Italian flag in the church. Students and soldiers
readily joined the insurgents, and both King and
Ministers in Turin were seized with panic. Orders
came from the Powers at Laybach that Victor Emmanuel should march to Alessandria, and Balbo
called on all loyal soldiers to return to Asti.

But Santa Rosa was as firm in his purposes as the
Royalists were undecided. The Spanish Constitution was proclaimed in the fortress of Turin, and the
soldiers, who were sent to attack the people, fled
after a few shots; Charles Albert represented to the

King the wishes of the people; and on the night of March 14th, Victor Emmanuel abdicated in favour of his brother Charles Felix, appointing Charles Albert Regent in Turin. On the following day Charles Albert, in his capacity of Regent, swore to accept the Spanish Constitution.

But it was soon apparent that one vigorous man could not make a revolution successful, when he had to depend on a nobility many of whom were servile admirers of Austria, and on a Regent who "would and would not." Men were appointed to posts in the new administration who had no claim to their office except their rank. The leaders in Alessandria suspected the leaders in Turin; while the hopes of persuading Charles Albert to declare war on Austria grew fainter and fainter.

In the meantime, the new King, Charles Felix, was residing in Modena, under the protection of the Grand Duke. Francis IV. of Modena had shown himself the most distinctly tyrannical of all the princes of Italy; while his extravagance and indifference to the welfare of his people had startled even Metternich. His relationship to the House of Savoy had led him to sympathise at first with Victor Emmanuel in his irritation at the arrogance of Austria; but that very same relationship now led him to hope that he might succeed to the throne instead of Charles Albert, if the latter offended the ruling Powers. He therefore readily supported Charles Felix in his protest against the proceedings of the new Regent.

Charles Felix, on his side, was a man of more rugged and narrow spirit than Victor Emmanuel, and had none of the sense of national dignity which

occasionally interfered with the despotic inclinations
of his brother. When, therefore, he issued from
Modena a denunciation of the new Government, he
did not scruple to add that, if order were not
soon restored, his august allies would come to his
rescue. In the same letter he ordered Charles Albert
to go to Novara and place himself under the orders
of Della Torre. " I shall see by this," said Charles
Felix, "if you are still a Prince of the House of
Savoy, or if you have ceased to be so." Charles
Albert concealed this letter from his Ministers;
and, after a few days of hesitation, fled secretly to
Novara.

The feeble officials of Turin would have at once
deserted the cause; but, in defiance of their opinion,
Santa Rosa published a proclamation declaring that
the King was a prisoner in the hands of the enemy,
and that *he*, as Minister of Charles Albert, called on
them to stand by the Constitution and declare war
on Austria. One or two of the generals fled to Della
Torre, at Novara; but at the same time the Genoese
rose on behalf of the Spanish Constitution. Della
Torre sent orders to Santa Rosa, in the name of the
King, to resign his authority. Santa Rosa refused
to recognize the King while he remained in a
foreign country, and despatched a force against
Novara.

But, in the meantime, the news came that General
Pepe had in vain tried to rally his forces in defence
of the Neapolitan Constitution; that his bands had
been dispersed at the first attack of the Austrians ;
and that the Austrians, having crushed out the freedom of Naples, were marching northwards. The
Russian Ambassador thereupon entreated the Junta

to modify the Spanish Constitution.  Some of the
Ministers were inclined to consent; but Santa Rosa
knew that to lose the Spanish Constitution was to
lose the watchword of the Revolution; and no doubt
he felt the indignity of yielding to a foreign ambassador.  He therefore refused this proposal, and once
more despatched forces against Della Torre, who
was now preparing to march on Turin.

Colonel Regis, the leader of the Constitutional
forces, succeeded in reaching Novara before Della
Torre had begun his advance.  The armies met outside the town; but in the middle of the battle the
news arrived that the Austrians had crossed the
Ticino and were marching into the country.  Regis
and Ferrero fought gallantly; but the double forces
against them were too strong; and though they once
or twice repelled the Austrian attack, the want of
discipline of the Piedmontese soldiers, combined with
the superior force of the enemy, led to a crushing
defeat.  Santa Rosa, finding it impossible to defend
Turin, retreated first to Alessandria and then to
Genoa; but the men on whom he relied had lost
courage and hope; and he and such of his friends
as were fortunate enough to reach Genoa were soon
obliged to leave it again and to fly from Italy, most
of them to fight in foreign countries for the liberty
which they had lost at home.

The reaction set in with the greatest fury.  In
Piedmont the system of espionage was resumed with
double force.  The University was closed.  Under
the influence of favouritism, and in the absence of
any free expression of public opinion, corruption of
tribunals revived, and the Jesuits, who had lost
power during the Liberal interregnum, speedily re-

covered it. In Naples, the Austrians, after recommending mildness to Ferdinand, yielded to his demands for the right to punish; and the sense of his dishonourable position seems to have called out in him a savagery which he had not previously shown; while the presence of the Austrian troops irritated the country into a state of intermittent insurrection.

Lord William Bentinck attempted a protest in the English House of Commons against a second destruction of Sicilian independence; but Castlereagh defeated the motion, and Sicily fell back under Neapolitan rule.

Metternich specially devoted himself to restoring order in Lombardy. He established an Aulic Council at Vienna to superintend the affairs in that province, so as to crush out still further any local independence. At the same time a special committee was formed at Milan to enquire into the conspiracy. Several leading conspirators were arrested. One tried to save his friends by confessing his own fault; but the confession was used as a new clue by the police. Confalonieri was urged to save himself by flight; but he answered, " I will not retire in face of the storm which I wish to confront. Let what God will become of me !" He was soon after arrested; and, after being kept in doubt of his fate for nearly two years, he was condemned to death. His case excited sympathy even in Vienna, where the Empress interceded for his life; and at last, after long entreaty, his sentence was commuted to imprisonment for life in the fortress of Spielberg. There Metternich in vain tried to extort from him the betrayal of his fellow-conspirators. But the crafty statesman little knew the result of this treatment. One of those who suffered imprisonment about the same time describes the effect of Confalonieri's influence by contrasting him with the head of the Austrian police in Lombardy. "Confalonieri and Salvotti seemed to represent, in the eyes of the Milanese, the angel of Liberty and the demon of Slavery, striving not more for the success of their respective causes than for the triumph of their individual personalities. About Confalonieri gathered the prayers of honest people, of men of feeling hearts, who saw in him an unfortunate persecuted being whom adversity clothed with all the lustre of devotion and courage."

This passage strikingly exhibits that noble, but illogical, popular instinct which so often confuses the hero and martyr with the mere victim of unjust oppression. Confalonieri had undoubtedly organized an insurrection, and his arrest and imprisonment might fairly be justified by the ordinary rights of self-defence which exist in every Government. Yet the instinct of horror and pity for this imprisonment had a truth deeper than logic. Under the system of government then prevailing, the prison or the scaffold was the natural place for such men ; but the pity of it was that a system of government should prevail which logically necessitated the imprisonment of Confalonieri and the triumph of Metternich. And it was a sign of the deep folly of the latter that he called the attention of the public to this fact, and provided the cause of Italian unity with its first prominent martyr. The stories of Confalonieri's imprisonment spread from mouth to mouth, and were preserved as tender memorials. It was told, for instance, how, when his wife had visited him, he had tried to preserve the cushion on which her tears had

fallen, and how the guards had insisted on taking it
from him ; how his friends had devised a plan for
his escape, and he had refused to avail himself of it
because his fellow-prisoners would not be able to
escape with him ; and lastly, of the continual pressure
which had been brought to bear upon him to reveal
the secrets of his fellow-conspirators, and his steady
refusal to purchase health and liberty by their betrayal.

The defeat which despotism had sustained by the
imprisonment, and still more by the persecutions,
of Confalonieri would hereafter be plain.  At present
Metternich might think that he had conquered in
Lombardy ; but elsewhere he could not feel sure of
victory, for there came to him at this time two unmistakeable warnings that he was no longer to be
allowed to reign undisturbed in Europe.

Even at that very Congress of Laybach which
succeeded in crushing out the independence of Naples,
the question of Greece, which could not be so easily
disposed of, came before the Powers, and puzzled
considerably the mind of Metternich.  The pietistic
maunderings of Alexander might be made use of in
defence of the rights of Roman Catholic kings, but
he could not be persuaded that the principles of the
Christian religion justified him in supporting the
tyranny of the Turks over Christian populations.
He had indeed abandoned the Wallachian leader,
Alexander Ypsilanti, when he discovered that the
rising in Wallachia was simultaneous with the risings
in Naples and Piedmont ; but the Greeks could not
so easily be persuaded that their patron, the Czar of
Russia, had deserted their cause.

The Hetairiai of Wallachia and Greece had done
the same work which the Carbonari had accomplished

in Spain and Italy; and on April 4, 1821, the Greeks
suddenly rose at Patras and massacred the whole
Turkish population.  In three months the southern
part of Greece was free; and by January, 1822, a
Provisional Government had been formed, with Alexander Mavrocordatos at its head.

Religious feeling, classical sentiment, and the loathing of the barbarous rule of the Turks combined to
rouse in Europe an amount of sympathy which
Metternich could not afford to disregard.  He admitted the right of Alexander of Russia to sympathise
with the Greeks, both on the ground of Christian
sentiment and on the pretext of rights granted by
previous treaties with Turkey; and he even intervened diplomatically to secure concessions from the
Porte to its Christian subjects.

But, though he felt the danger of the precedent
which even this amount of concession to the revolutionary spirit would cause, Metternich yet believed
that, by timely compromise and judicious diplomacy,
he could bring back Alexander to sounder principles.
The influence of Capo d'Istria was indeed an antagonistic power in the Court of St. Petersburg; but, on
the other hand, Tatischeff, the rival minister at the
Russian Court, seems to have been a mere tool of
Metternich, and could be used effectively for the
interests of Austria.

So successfully did this diplomacy work, in Metternich's opinion, that on May 31, 1822, he writes ex-
ultingly in his memoirs, that he has "broken the
work of Peter the Great, strengthened the Porte
against Russia, and substituted Austrian and English
influence for Russian in Eastern Europe."  So he
wrote in May; in August of the same year "that

upright and enlightened statesman," Lord London-
derry, committed suicide. Then George Canning
became Minister for Foreign Affairs, and hastened
to cut the knot which linked the interests of Austria
with those of England.

The change in England's policy soon became
evident. No doubt the feeling of dislike to Metternich had been gradually growing in that country.
Its representatives had held aloof even from the
Congress of Laybach; and when, in 1822, the Powers
met again at Verona to encourage the French Cabinet
in their attempt to restore Ferdinand of Spain, England entered a decided protest against the proceedings
of the Congress. Nor did the protest remain a barren
one. The invasion of Spain by the French was followed by the recognition of the independence of the
Spanish colonies by England ; and when the absolutist
movement threatened to spread to Portugal, Canning
despatched troops to protect the freedom and independence of that country.

It is amusing to note the growth of Metternich's
consciousness of the importance of the opponent who
had now arisen. "A fine century," he writes at
first, "for these kinds of men ; for fools who pass
for intellectual, but are empty ; for moral weaklings,
who are always ready to threaten with their fists
from a distance when the opportunity is good."

But in the following year he writes : "Canning's
nature is a very remarkable one. In spite of all his
lack of discernment, the genius which he undoubtedly
has, and which I have never questioned, is never
clouded. He is certainly a very awkward opponent ;
but I have had opponents more dangerous, and it is
not he who chiefly compels me to think of him."

And in 1824 he sums up this difficulty, satisfactorily
to himself, in these words : " What vexes me with
the English is that they are all slightly mad.   This
is an evil which must be patiently endured, without
noticing too much the ludicrous side of it."

This outburst of insanity on the part of England
naturally drove Metternich back into the arms of
Russia; and this change became more congenial to
him when, in 1825, the fickle Alexander died and
was succeeded by the stern despot Nicholas.

It seemed, too, as if the Greek rising might end
about that time in the success of the Turks.   Ibrahim,
the Pasha of Egypt, had come to the rescue of the
Sultan, and was carrying all before him.   Marco
Botzaris, the chief general of the Greeks, had been
killed in battle; and in 1826 the garrison of Messo-
longhi blew up their fortress and themselves to avoid
surrendering to the Egyptian forces.

But Metternich soon found that, whatever objection
Nicholas might have to revolution elsewhere, he felt
as much bound to protect the Greeks as had Alexander before him ; and in August, 1827, Nicholas
consented to Canning's proposal that England, France,
and Russia should send a fleet to the Bay of Navarino to enforce an armistice between the Greeks and
the Turks.   Then followed the celebrated battle
which Wellington afterwards described as " that
untoward event."   This convinced even Metternich
that the results of the Greek insurrection would have
to be recognized by the Powers, and perhaps even
secured by force.   The Russian war of 1828 followed,
and Metternich had to admit that the European
alliance of 1814-15 was practically broken.

But though the effect of the Greek insurrection in

E

weakening the chances of Metternich's system was
certainly important, it soon began to be doubtful
whether the change would be permanent.  England,
indeed, in spite of the death of Canning and the
short rule of Wellington, was evidently hopelessly
lost to the cause of despotism.  But the revolutionary
movements of 1830-31 seemed to leave far less trace
of freedom in Europe than the previous risings of
1820-22.  The July monarchy of Louis Philippe
was soon forced to become Conservative; and the
Belgian revolution seemed to have little connection
with the other movements of Europe.  The Polish
rising and its sudden collapse only secured Nicholas
to the side of despotism.  The treachery of Francis
of Modena to Ciro Menotti destroyed for a time the
tendency to believe in revolutionary princes.  The
rising in Bologna, by compelling the intervention of
the Austrians, strengthened their hold over the
Papacy, and even enabled Metternich cheaply to pose
as the adviser of reforms which, out of respect for
the independence of the Papacy, he would not enforce.

But his greatest triumph of all was in Germany.
There Constitutions had been proclaimed in Bavaria,
Würtemberg, and Saxony ; and Metternich resolved
to follow up the Carlsbad Decrees by a still more
crushing enactment.  So it was decided at the Federal
Diet of 1832 that a German prince was *bound*, "as a
member of the Confederation, to reject petitions tending to the increase of the power of the Estates at the
expense of the power of the Sovereign," and further,
"that the internal legislation of the States belonging
to the German Confederation should in no case be
such as to do prejudice to the objects of the Confederation."

Thus Metternich had again triumphed; but it was for the last time.  Two forces of very different kinds were already in motion, to undo the work of his life. Two men were about to cross his path, very different from each other in moral calibre, in width of sympathy, and in the means at their disposal, but alike in that power of reaching the heart of a People, for want of which the leaders of the previous Liberal movements had failed in their objects.  These men were Giuseppe Mazzini and Louis Kossuth.

# CHAPTER III.

## FAITH AND LAW AGAINST DESPOTISM. 1825—1840.

Tuscany under Fossombroni.—"Il Mondo va da se."—The Antologia.—Romanticism v. Classicism.—Domenico Guerrazzi. —Giuseppe Mazzini.—His early career.—His experiences as a Carbonaro.—His plans in the fortress of Savona.—His first banishment.—Louis Philippe and the Italian Revolutionists.— Collapse of the rising of 1831.—Accession of Charles Albert.— Italian belief in him.—Mazzini's letter.—Charles Albert's position. —Mazzini's second banishment—His influence.—La Giovine Italia. —Its enemies and friends.—Charles Albert's cruelties.—The expedition to Savoy.—Menz and Metternich v. Mazzini.—The special position of Hungary.—The County Government.—The Germanization of the nobles.—The Diet of 1825.—Szechenyi. —The Magyar language.—Material reforms.—Metternich and Szechenyi. — Wesselenyi. — The Transylvanian Diet. — Poland and Hungary.—Serfdom in Hungary.—The Urbarium.—Francis Déak.—Wesselenyi at Pressburg.— Louis Kossuth. — His character.—His first work.—Arrest of Kossuth and Wesselenyi.— The protest.—Metternich's defeat.

WHILE Piedmont and Naples had been vibrating between revolution and despotism; while the government of the popes had been steadily growing more tyrannical and unjust; and while the rulers of Parma, Lucca, and Modena had remained (with whatever occasional appearance to the contrary) the mere tools of Austria, the government of Tuscany had retained a peculiar character of its own.

The vigorous programme of reform, introduced by

Leopold I. when the government first passed into the hands of the House of Austria, had not been further developed by his successors. But a tradition of easy-going liberality had been kept alive both under Ferdinand III. and Leopold II. Fossombroni, the chief minister of Tuscany, took for his motto "Il mondo va da se" (the world goes of itself); and thus a certain liberty of thought and expression continued to prevail in Tuscany that was hardly to be found in other parts of Italy.

This might have excited the alarm of the Austrian Government, and of the other princes of Italy; for conspirators condemned by them took refuge in Tuscany. But two circumstances protected this freedom. The fact that the ruler of Tuscany was a member of the House of Austria seemed to exclude him from the chance of ever becoming the leader of a purely Italian movement; and Metternich was, perhaps, not sorry to be able to show the opponents of Austria that an Austrian prince could be the most popular ruler in Italy. Secondly, Fossombroni, while so easy-going in internal matters, maintained a dignified independence in foreign affairs; and Ferdinand and Leopold had enough of the spirit of the founder of the dynasty to second the efforts of their Minister.

Thus, when the Austrian officials sent to Ferdinand a list of the Carbonari in Tuscany, with the request that he would punish them, he simply burnt the list; and when, on the death of Ferdinand in 1824, the Austrian Minister demanded that Leopold's accession should not be publicly notified until the terms of the notice had been approved by Austria, Fossombroni at once announced Leopold's accession as the only answer to this insolent demand. Lastly, in 1831, when the Austrians were trampling out the liberties of Bologna, Fossombroni prevented them from extending their aggressions in Italy by an invasion of Tuscany.

Here, then, it was natural that the thought of Italy, whether taking a literary or political form, should find its freest expression. The Conciliatore of Manzoni and Confalonieri had been suppressed in Lombardy, but its work was revived by the Florentine journal called the "Antologia." Manzoni's influence gained much ground here among the literary men, who connected the struggle between the old classicism of Alfieri, and the freer and more original writing to which the name of Romanticism was given, with the struggle for a freer life in Italy against the traditions of the past.

The writer who attracted the most attention, and whose name became most widely known among the Romantic School, was Domenico Guerrazzi. It is, perhaps, a little difficult for an Englishman to understand the attraction of this author's novels; but an Italian writer thus explains it: "The singularity of his forms and the burning character of his style, the very contradiction of principles that are perceived in his writings, gave to Guerrazzi the appearance of something extraordinary, which struck upon imaginations already excited by misfortunes and grief." Moreover, perhaps, Guerrazzi, more definitely than most of these writers, connected the literary movement with the political; and even in Tuscany he became an object of some alarm from his desire for Italian freedom.

He naturally gathered round him a knot of young men of more decided type than the ordinary contributors to the "Antologia;" and it was to him, therefore, that the proposal was addressed to revive in Leghorn a Genoese journal which had been just suppressed by the Sardinian Government. The proposal was probably made to Guerrazzi in the first instance by a young and enthusiastic Livornese named Carlo Bini; but the chief promoter of the enterprise was a young Genoese of between twenty and thirty years of age.

This youth was chiefly known as having recently sent to the "Antologia" at Florence an article on Dante which had been rejected by them, but which was subsequently inserted in another paper. Among his contemporaries at the University the new comer had already excited an enthusiasm which was not yet understood by the outer world. Such was the first appearance in public life of Giuseppe Mazzini.

Under the influence of a very earnest and remarkable mother, he had early been interested in the cause of Italian liberty, and he dated his first impression of the importance of this cause from an interview with one of the exiles who was about to leave Italy on account of his share in the struggle of 1821.

Mazzini had been intended by his father for the profession of the law; but he had already shown a decided preference for literature and politics; and while still at the University he had been influenced by the gloomy romance of Jacopo Ortis. But, though that strange book had deepened his feeling for the miseries of his country, the scepticism and despair which were its keynote could not long hold him in slavery. On him, as on all the greatest minds of Italy, Dante soon gained a powerful hold; and while he profoundly admired the "Divina Commedia," he

learned from the " De Monarchiâ " that mystic enthusiasm for Rome and that belief in the theological basis
for political principles which was to colour so deeply
his later career.

The journal which, with Guerrazzi's help, Mazzini
started at Leghorn was called the " Indicatore Livornese." It soon became so alarming even to the mild
Tuscan Government that after some warnings it was
suppressed.

Shut out for the moment from the literary expression
of his faith, Mazzini turned to more directly political
action. He felt that it was his duty to make use
of whatever existing machinery he could find for
carrying on the struggle for Italian freedom ; and
he therefore joined the Carbonari. The very for-
mula of the oath which was administered to him,
on entering this Society, seemed to suggest the in-
adequacy of this body for stirring up the faith of a
people. For, instead of speaking of work to be done
for the freedom or unity of Italy, the words of the
oath merely exacted implicit obedience to the Order.
Mazzini's spirit revolted alike against this slavery,
and against the solemn buffooneries with which the
rulers of the Order tried to impress those who joined
it with the sense of its importance.[1]  His irritation

---

[1] "He congratulated me on the fact that circumstances had
spared me the tremendous ordeals usually undergone; and
seeing me smile at this, he asked me severely what I should
have done if I had been required, as others had been, to fire off
a pistol in my own ear, which had been previously loaded before
my eyes. I replied that I should have refused, telling the
initiators that either there was some valve in the interior of
the pistol into which the bullet fell—in which case the affair
was a farce unworthy of both of us—or the bullet had really
remained in the stock : and in that case it struck me as some-

at the uselessness and tyranny of the Carbonari brought on him the stern rebuke of some of their leaders.

The July Insurrection of 1830, in France, woke new hopes in Mazzini, as in other Italians ; but before he could join in any active movement, he was arrested at Genoa, and, without trial, was soon after imprisoned in the fortress of Savona. The explanation given to Mazzini's father, by the Governor of Genoa, of the reasons for this arrest affords a striking picture of the despotism of the time. The Governor said that Giuseppe was a young man of talent, very fond of solitary walks by night, and habitually silent as to the subject of his meditations ; and that the government was not fond of young men of talent the subject of whose musings was unknown to it. The real cause of the arrest was Mazzini's connection with the Carbonari, which had been betrayed by a pretended member of the Society, who, however, declined to support his charge in public.

It was during this imprisonment that Mazzini came to the conclusion that the Society of the Carbonari had failed to accomplish the purpose for which it was founded, and that some new organization was required in its place. While he was considering the objects which such an organization should set before itself, there arose before his mind the idea of Italian unity. The failure of the local efforts of 1821 and 1831 had been due to the want of common action between the different Italian States ; and the mystic enthusiasm for Rome supplied a poetical argument in favour of

what absurd to call upon a man to fight for his country, and make it his first duty to blow out the few brains God had vouchsafed to him."—*Life and Writings of Mazzini, Vol. I.*

the practical conclusion which he drew from these failures. While too the treachery of Charles Albert and of Francis of Modena had left on Mazzini a deep-rooted distrust of kings, and inclined him to believe that a republic was necessary to solve the difficulties of his country, he was willing, as will presently appear, to accept any leader or form of government which should bring about the unity of Italy. Anarchy he loathed with all his heart. He thoroughly disliked the French doctrine of the Rights of Man; and he desired to assert authority when legitimately established.

But the great distinction between Mazzini and the other political leaders of his time was, that his aim was not merely to establish a form of government, but to imbue the people with a faith. The unity of Italy was not with him a mere political arrangement, but the working out of God's government over the world, a development of a nobler and better life.

This affected his attitude to the question both of the relation of classes to each other, and of the relation of Italy to the rest of Europe. Though he appealed to the working men of Italy with an effect that no previous politician had produced, he never appealed to them on the ground of purely selfish interests; for he felt that the special motives for improving their condition should always be subordinated to the general welfare of the nation. And it is a striking proof of the extent to which this side of his teaching has taken hold of his followers, that, in the demonstration to his memory at Genoa in the year 1882, among the banners borne in the procession, and inscribed with quotations from his works, was one on which were written the words " Fight not against the bourgeoisie, but against egotism, wherever it grows, under the blouse of the workman, as under the coat of the capitalist."

Italy too was to help in the regeneration of Europe, but not after the manner of the French Republic, by merely establishing a foreign tyranny, calling itself Republican, in the place of native kings.    Patriotism, with Mazzini, was not the hard, narrow thing which it became in the minds of too many of the leaders of the revolution.    The Peoples were to help each other in developing their own national life after their own fashion, and to respect each other's national claims as they claimed respect for their own.[1]

After long delay Mazzini was acquitted of the charge laid to him, no evidence being brought forward against him.    Thereupon the Governor of Genoa appealed to Charles Felix to set aside the decision of the judges, and to condemn Mazzini.    The King consented; and Mazzini was ordered to choose between banishment from Italy and confining himself to a place of residence in one of the small towns in the centre of Piedmont.    He believed that the former alternative would offer him freer scope for action; and he sailed for France.

The hopes of the Italian exiles had been roused,

[1] As an instance of his way of carrying out this idea may be mentioned his feeling to Savoy.    He felt that in race, language, and possibly in sympathy, Savoy might naturally gravitate towards France, while its geographical position and the modes of life of its inhabitants might naturally connect it with Switzerland. He therefore desired that by the deliberate vote of an elected Assembly, not by a fictitious Napoleonic plebiscite, Savoy should decide the question of its connection with Italy, France, or Switzerland.    Mazzini expressed a hope that it would decide in favour of Switzerland.

first by the July Revolution in France, and secondly by the risings at Modena and Bologna. General Regis, who had played such an important part in the Piedmontese insurrection of 1821, was organizing with other exiles an expedition, composed of Italians and French, to go to help the insurgents who were still holding out in Bologna.

But the hopes of the insurgents were doomed to disappointment. Louis Philippe, after playing with them for some time, came to the same sagacious conclusion about Revolution that he afterwards announced with regard to war, viz., that to talk about assisting a Revolution, and to assist a Revolution, were two different things.[1] Just as the expedition was on its march, orders were issued to abandon it, and a body of cavalry were sent to enforce the command. Some abandoned the attempt; but Mazzini and a few friends escaped to Corsica, which was still Italian in feeling, though French in government; and there they hoped to organize an expedition to help the Bolognese.

The Bolognese, however, though gallant enough in their own struggles, were unwilling to commit themselves to a wider programme than the defence of their own State. So they refused to send to Corsica the money which was necessary for the expeditionary force. The Austrians soon after entered the Papal territory; and when they had crushed out the insurrection they were in many cases welcomed by the inhabitants as a protection against the cruelties of the Papal troops.

[1] "Mais M. Bulwer parler de faire la guerre, et faire la guerre sont choses bien différentes."

Two other points in the insurrection alone need notice. One was, that at the surrender of Ancona Terenzio Mamiani, already known as a philosophic writer, refused to sign the conditions of capitulation, and was consequently forced to go into exile. The other was that, while the representatives of the Pope showed themselves, as a rule, utterly reckless in violating the conditions under which the surrender of the towns was made, one honourably distinguished himself by keeping his word. This was the Governor of Imola, Giovanni Mastai Ferretti, afterwards Pius IX.

The movement, however, in spite of its scattered and disconnected character, had excited attention in Piedmont, and several leading Piedmontese Liberals had determined to press Charles Felix to grant a Constitution. Of these Liberals, the most remarkable were Angelo Brofferio, the future historian of Piedmont; Augusto Anfossi, hereafter to play so brilliant a part in the rescue of Milan from Austria; and Giacomo Durando, whose book on Italian nationality was afterwards to hold an honourable place among the writings which stirred up Italian feeling. The conspiracy was, however, discovered; the leaders of the movement were arrested; and, while the prisoners were still awaiting their trial, Charles Felix died, and Charles Albert succeeded to the throne.

During the time between the failure of the insurrection of 1821 and his accession to the throne, Charles Albert's only important public act had been his service in the French Army, which was suppressing the liberties of Spain. Yet, in spite of this act of hostility to the Liberal cause, and in spite of the recollections of his previous desertion in 1821, the Liberals still had hopes that he would become their champion.

This is a fact which requires more explanation than can be found in the mere desire on the part of the reformers of Italy to choose some King to lead them against Austria. After the treachery of Francis of Modena, no Liberal expected *him* to return to the cause which he had deserted; and, when Francis of Naples had succeeded Ferdinand I., none of the passing hopes, which had pointed him out in earlier life as a possible constitutional champion, could save him from the hatred which his tyranny deserved.

Nor must we be misled by the subsequent history of Italy into the theory that there was anything special in the traditions of the kingdom of Sardinia which should lead Liberals to fix their hopes on a ruler of that country. Victor Amadeus of Sardinia had been the foremost of the allies of Austria in the war against the French Republic; and though there were continual causes of irritation between the aggressive House of Austria and the rulers of the little monarchy, these were not of a kind to have attracted the sympathy of any large body of Liberals outside Piedmont. The only movement for the unity of Italy, previous to the movement of 1821, had come from Naples; unless, indeed, Eugène Beauharnais had intended Lombardy to be the centre of a similar attempt.

When we take all these points into consideration we must come to the conclusion that there was something in the personal character of Charles Albert which riveted the attention of Italian Liberals almost in spite of themselves; nor could any appearances to the contrary induce them to doubt that he had at heart a desire for the liberty and unity of Italy such as no previous Italian Prince had entertained.

It was, perhaps, the greatest proof of this strange fascination that Mazzini, Republican as he was, yet thought it well to yield to the strong feeling of the Liberals of Italy, and to give Charles Albert one more chance of playing the part of a leader.

Mazzini, therefore, addressed to the new King a letter in which he called his attention to the enthusiasm with which his accession was greeted. " There is not a heart in Italy whose pulse did not quicken at the news of your accession. There is not an eye in Europe that is not turned to watch your first steps in the career now open to you." He told him that the Italians were ready to believe that his desertion of their cause was the mere result of circumstances; and that, being at last free to act according to his own tendencies, the new King would carry out the promises that he had first made as a Prince. He warned him that a system of terror would only provoke reprisals ; and that a system of partial concessions would not only fail to satisfy the wishes of the people, but would have an arbitrary and capricious character which would increase the existing irritation. " The people are no longer to be quieted by a few concessions. They seek the recognition of those rights of humanity which have been withheld from them for ages. They demand laws and liberty, independence and union. Divided, dismembered, and oppressed, they have neither name nor country. They have heard themselves stigmatised by the foreigner as the Helot Nation. They have seen free men visit their country, and declare it the

land of the dead. They have drained the cup of
slavery to the dregs; but they have sworn never to
fill it again." Mazzini then calls on Charles Albert
to put himself more definitely at the head of a
movement for Italian Independence, and to become
the King of a united Italy. The letter concludes
with these words : " Sire, I have spoken to you
the truth. The men of freedom await your answer
in your deeds. Whatever that answer be, rest
assured that posterity will either hail your name as
the greatest of men, or the last of Italian tyrants.
Take your choice."

Before we consider Charles Albert's answer, we
must call to mind, once more, his position. He came
to the throne in the very crisis of a conspiracy against
his predecessor, and had hardly been able to realize
what had been the intention of the conspirators towards himself. The Duke of Modena, who had
plotted to remove him from the succession (a proposal discussed at some length in the Congress of
Laybach), had just recovered his own Dukedom
by Austrian help, and was no doubt watching with
eager eyes any false step which his rival might make.
Charles Albert, with all his liberal sympathies, was
proud of being a prince of the House of Savoy ; and
he was surrounded by the courtiers of Charles Felix,
who must have persuaded him that the dignity and
independence of that House could only be maintained
by opposition to the movement for reform.

There was, too, another influence which must
never be forgotten in estimating the difficulties of
Charles Albert. He was a strong Roman Catholic,
at a time when the connection between reverence for
the Pope and reverence for the Church was, perhaps,

closer than it had been at most previous periods of the history of the Papacy. The commonplace tyrannies of Leo XII. and Pius VIII. had not wholly dispelled the halo which the heroic attitude of Pius VII.'s early days had shed round the Papacy; and it seems highly probable that the most puzzling act of Charles Albert's life, his share in the French invasion of Spain, had been due, to a large extent, to that strong religious sentiment which gathered in so peculiar a manner round the kings of Spain. A man influenced by such sentiments could not fail to remark that the most vigorous and determined of the insurgents of 1831 had directed their attacks against the Papacy; and it might well seem to him that a letter which called on him to oppose the Austrian restorers of the papal power was the utterance of an enemy to the religion of the country.

But the fact was, as Mazzini afterwards confessed, that any king who was to undertake the work which he had suggested to Charles Albert must possess at once " genius, Napoleonic energy, and the highest virtue. Genius, in order to conceive the idea of the enterprize and the conditions of victory ; energy, not to front its dangers—for to a man of genius they would be few and brief—but to dare to break at once with every tie of family or alliance, and the habits and necessities of any existence distinct and removed from that of the people, and to extricate himself both from the web of diplomacy and the counsels of wicked or cowardly advisers ; virtue enough voluntarily to renounce a portion at least of his actual power ; for it is only by redeeming them from slavery that a people may be roused to battle and to sacrifice."

If such were the qualities required by any prince

F

who undertook this office, what must have been needed from one who had to contend with a Power which had ten years before helped to crush out the aspirations of his people, and which was just then triumphantly ruling in the centre of Italy? A man of genius might have undertaken the task; Charles Albert was only a man who " would and would not." But, if Charles Albert refused to listen to Mazzini's appeal, he had no alternative but to protest against it; and he did so by banishing Mazzini, under pain of imprisonment if he should return to Italy.

Nevertheless, the letter had produced its effect on the nation. The demand for the unity of Italy had been openly and definitely made, and put forward as a boon to be struggled for by Italians, and not to be conferred by a foreign conqueror. The attention of the youth of Italy was at once attracted to the writer of the letter, and none the less that he was an exile. The personal fascination which he exercised even over casual observers may be gathered from the following letter, which seems to refer to this period. It was written by one of his fellow-exiles, describing his first sight of Mazzini in the rifle ground at Marseilles.

" I went into the ground, and, looking round, saw a young man leaning on his rifle, watching the shooters, and waiting for his turn. He was about 5ft. 8in. high, and slightly made; he was dressed in black Genoa velvet, with a large Republican hat; his long curling black hair, which fell upon his shoulders, the extreme freshness of his clear olive complexion, the chiselled delicacy of his regular and beautiful features, aided by his very youthful look, and sweetness and openness of expression, would have made his appearance almost too feminine, if it had not been for his noble forehead, the power of firmness and decision that was mingled with their gaiety and sweetness in the bright flashes of his dark eyes, and in the varying expression of his mouth, together with his small and beautiful moustache and beard. Altogether, he was at that time the most beautiful *being*, male or female, that I had ever seen, and I have not since seen his equal. I had read what he had published; I had heard of what he had done and suffered, and the moment I saw him I *knew* it could be no other than Joseph Mazzini."

It was under such auspices that the Society of Young Italy was founded. The general drift of the principles of that Society has already been sufficiently indicated in the account of Mazzini's meditations in the fortress of Savona. It was to make Italy free, united, Republican, recognizing duty to God and man as the basis of national life, rather than the mere assertion of rights. But the great point which distinguished it from all the other societies which had preceded it was that, instead of trusting to the mysterious effect of symbols, and the power of a few leaders to induce the main body of Italians blindly to accept their orders, it openly proclaimed its creed before the world, and even in the articles of association set forth the full arguments on which it grounded the defence of the special objects which it advocated. And the principles were further to be preached in a journal which was to be called, like the Society, " Giovine Italia."

But while he put forward a definitely Republican programme, Mazzini never fell into the French mistake of thinking that a knot of men, monopolizing power to themselves, can, by merely calling them-

selves Republicans, make the government of a nation
a Republic. While he fully hoped, by education, to
induce the Italians to accept a Republican Government, he was quite prepared to admit the possibility
of failure in that attempt, and to accept the consequence as a consistent democrat. This is distinctly
stated in the first plan of Young Italy.

" By inculcating before the hour of action by what
steps the Italians must achieve their aim, by raising
its flag in the sight of Italy, and calling upon all
those who believe it to be the flag of national regeneration to organize themselves beneath its folds—
the association does not seek to substitute that flag
for the banner of the future nation."

" When once the nation herself shall be free, and
able to exercise that right of sovereignty which is
hers alone, she will raise her own banner, and make
known her revered and unchallenged will as to the
principle and the fundamental law of her existence."

Plentiful as was the scorn and misrepresentation
showered upon Mazzini and his doctrines, the two
years from 1831 to 1833 brought a vast number of
supporters to the Society of Young Italy ; and the
revolutionary movement in other countries gained
organization and definiteness of purpose from this
model. In the meantime, the Government of Louis
Philippe was becoming more and more definitely
committed to the cause of reaction ; and every kind
of slander was being circulated by Frenchmen against
the Society of Young Italy. The theory that this
Society undertook to exterminate all who disobeyed
its orders was supported, by attributing to its action
any casual violence which might take place in the
streets of Paris ; and though Mazzini prosecuted one

of these slanderers for defamation a few years later, and compelled him to make a complete retractation in the law courts, the slander was too convenient to be allowed easily to drop.

On the other hand, men of the older type of revolutionist, who had drawn their ideas from the first French Republic, and had afterwards hoped to find their realization in the methods of the Carbonari, objected to Mazzini as "too soft and German" in his ideas.

But nevertheless some who were afterwards known in other ways came forward to contribute to the Journal of Young Italy. Amongst them may be mentioned the historian Sismondi and a future opponent of Mazzini, the Abate Vincenzo Gioberti. By 1833 the Society had established centres in Lombardy, Genoa, Tuscany, and the Papal States, and it was resolved to attempt an invasion of Savoy.

For, in spite of the promises which Charles Albert had held out of reforms in the government, the prosecutions for the conspiracy of 1831 were being carried on with renewed rigour, and the prisons of some of the chief towns of Piedmont were filled with men in many cases arrested on the barest suspicion, and who were threatened with death if they would not reveal the secrets of their fellow-conspirators. Such cruelties were used to extort confessions that Jacopo Ruffini, a young friend of Mazzini's, committed suicide in prison for fear he should be compelled to betray his friends.

The news of these acts quickened the eagerness of the Italians for the invasion of Savoy, and they desired to co-operate with men of other countries. Among these, there were few from whom they expected so much sympathy as the Poles. Unable to organize

successful insurrections in their own country, the
Poles were scattered over Europe, a revolutionary
element in every land in which they were to be
found.   They, like the Italians, had at first expected
sympathy from the July monarchy in France.  They,
too, had been bitterly disappointed.  But this had
not prevented them from maintaining a centre at
Paris; and many of those who had fought in vain in
1830 for the liberty of Poland came back to Paris
to learn there what further was to be done.

Amongst these came a man named Ramorino, a
Savoyard by birth, who had acted as a general in the
Polish struggle of 1830.  The part which he had
played in that insurrection was only known very in-
distinctly to most of the Italians who were organizing
the new expedition; but the mere fact that he had
been a leader in a war for liberty was enough to
make them desire his help.  Mazzini had gathered
from the Polish exiles the opinion generally held of
Ramorino by those who knew the facts of the insurrection of 1830.  He found that the reputation which
Ramorino had held at that period was very low,
both for trustworthiness and military ability; and he
opposed his election as leader of the expedition to
Savoy.  The only result of the opposition was a
charge against Mazzini of personal ambition.

The expedition had already been weakened by the
opposition of one of those fanatical revolutionists who
had before denounced Mazzini as too soft and German
in his ideas.  This man, who bore the honoured name
of Buonarotti, had complained of the members of the
expedition for admitting men of noble rank and some
wealth to the position of leadership in it, and he had
succeeded in detaching from the movement an im-

portant section of its supporters.   Mazzini, therefore, saw that, under these circumstances, to lose the friends of Ramorino would ruin the chances of the expedition; and, feeling that any further opposition would only excite division, he consented to act with Ramorino.

The new leader soon showed his true character by hindering the expedition as long as possible; but in February, 1834, he yielded to the pressure of Mazzini and began the march.   Unfortunately, Mazzini was seized with a fever on the route, and Ramorino, finding this obstacle to his treachery removed, ordered the columns to be dissolved and rode away.

Plenty of scorn was heaped upon the failure of this first expedition of Young Italy.   But Metternich, at any rate, judged more truly.   In April, 1833, he had written to the chief of his spies in Lombardy to warn him against the growth of a new revolutionary party, and particularly against the advocate Mazzini, one of the most dangerous men of the faction; and he told him to procure copies of the journal called "La Giovine Italia," and two copies also of Mazzini's pamphlet about guerilla warfare.   Menz, the spy in question, while believing that the journal of Young Italy was losing ground, yet considered that it was the most dangerous of the newspapers which circulated in Lombardy.

This request of Metternich's was, indeed, made a few months before the actual invasion of Savoy, and Menz, no doubt, began to think that after that failure the power of Mazzini would decline; but it is tolerably clear that Metternich did not share that delusion, and kept his eye steadily on the new leader.   Nor did even Menz believe that mere repression would now suffice to win the sympathies of the Lombards to Austria, and he proposed to divert the intellectual zeal of disaffected Lombards into a direction favourable to the State by offering prizes for the solution of questions in different branches of human knowledge.   From the winners of these prizes, he thought, might be chosen professors, inspectors, and directors of studies, and encouragement might be given to compositions of poems and paintings, of which "the subject, and even the colour," was to be dictated by Government.[1]

He further proposed that, with this object, an Academy of Poetry should be founded in Lombardy, under the absolute direction of the Austrian Government, who are to see that the nation should take part in an intellectual movement "with a correct view, and that these productions of the imagination, bearing the impress of a tendency profitable to the well-being of society, would, in their turn, act in a very favourable manner on the public spirit."

Further, as "the Circus was in the time of the Romans the secret means of the State for rendering the people submissive to the Government," . . . . so "the Austrian Government should give a very generous subsidy to the theatre of La Scala (at Milan); but it would be also desirable that it should make some sacrifice for the provincial theatres."   A few modifications of the Austrian code, some reduction on customs duties, and lessening of the restrictions on passports, are also suggested in the Report.   Such were the means by which the trusted

[1] Document 158 to Gualterio Gli Ultimi Rivolgimenti Italiani.

servant of Metternich hoped to counteract the influence of Mazzini and Young Italy.

But in the meantime another form of opposition to the power of Metternich was growing up in a country very different from Italy, both in its circumstances and the character of its people.

While, in all other countries of Europe, Metternich looked upon every approach to self-government with suspicion, and tried to crush it out either by force or diplomacy, both he and Francis recognized that in Hungary there were reasons for maintaining and even encouraging Constitutional feeling.

For here the Constitutional rights did not rest upon any revolutionary basis; at any rate, not upon any revolution of modern times. They were not connected with the sort of national aspirations which made the movements in Italy and Germany so alarming to Metternich. There was, as yet, no desire here to redistribute the country according to popular aspirations; all rights rested on clearly defined laws handed down from a distant past, and in many cases these rights had been the subject of a peaceable contract between the previous rulers of the country and the House of Austria. So much was this felt by Francis that he even appealed on one occasion to the Hungarian Diet for sympathy against the revolutionary methods of Liberal leaders of other countries.

But, indeed, had the liberty of the Hungarians depended, like that of other nations, on the assertion of the power of a central parliament, they might have been crushed as the other peoples had been; for from 1813 to 1825 no Diet met in Hungary. But the full force of Hungarian liberty dwelt in the

organization of those county assemblies which the
Magyars had probably derived from the conquered
Slavs. The Government could not enforce its laws
except through the county officers, all of whom, with
one exception, were elected by the landholders of the
district. That one Government official was bound to
call together once a year a meeting of the nobles and
clergy of the county. *There* the wants and grievances
of the district were discussed, and orders were sent
to the representatives of the county in the Diet at
Presburg to introduce bills to remedy those grievances.

These county assemblies could raise taxes and
levy soldiers ; and they not only possessed, but
exercised the right to refuse to obey the orders of
the King himself if, after discussion, such orders
proved illegal.

In the county elections all freeholders of Hungary
had votes; and in the smaller village elections the
suffrage was still wider. The electors in the villages
chose, not only legislators, but judges of their village
concerns. The non-freeholding peasantry were,
indeed, often oppressed ; the towns were in a
backward state as regards self-government; but yet
this system of county organization secured a wider
diffusion of general interest in political affairs than
prevailed in any other country of Europe.

At the same time, there were elements in Hungary
which might give Metternich some hopes that he
could drain out the forces of Hungarian liberty.
The Magyar nobles were drawn more and more to
Vienna; and a process of Germanization was going
on of so effective a kind that many of the nobles had
almost forgotten their own language. Thus, though

the Magyar aristocracy had more often acted as
champions of independence than the nobles of any
other country in Europe, they were gradually being
drifted away from the main body of the people, and
were becoming absorbed in the ranks of Austrian
officialism. But when the Spanish Revolution of
1820 began to stir men's minds, the discussions in
the Hungarian county assemblies took a wider range,
and representations were made to Francis which he
could not long resist. He did not at first, indeed,
realize the full force of the opposition, and in 1822
he tried to levy new taxes on the Hungarians without
summoning the Diet. But this attempt failed, and
in 1825 the Diet at Presburg was once more called
together.

It seemed, indeed, to some of those who afterwards
played a prominent part in the struggles of 1848 as
if little was gained by this Diet ; and as if it was
even less satisfactory than its predecessor of 1791.
But a movement was inaugurated on this occasion
which, though it may have contained in it the seeds
of future misunderstanding, and even of civil war,
was yet in its beginning as noble in its intention as
it was necessary to the welfare of Hungary ; and,
had it been pursued in the spirit of its first leader,
might have produced in time all the blessings
which have since been secured to Hungary, without
any of those terrible divisions and bitternesses that
hinder those blessings from producing their full
effect.

The leader of this new movement was Count
Stephen Szechenyi, a member of one of the great
families of Hungary. His father had held office at
the Court of Vienna, but had grieved over the

process of denationalization which was going on
among the nobles of Hungary.

Count Stephen was early trained to sympathize
with the desire for the restoration of Hungarian life.
He saw that the withdrawal of the great nobles from
Hungary to Vienna led to the mismanagement of
their estates, the growth of an evil class of money-
lenders, and the separation between the aristocracy
and the rest of nation.

The abandonment of the Magyar language was,
in his eyes, the great source of all evil; and the Diet
of 1825 afforded him the first opportunity of protesting against it. While the Hungarian nobles talked
German in private, they used Latin in the management of public affairs; and Szechenyi, as a protest
against this practice, spoke in the Magyar language
in bringing forward a question in the House of
Magnates.

But, before the Diet had risen, he gave a much
more solid proof of his zeal for his native tongue.
On November 3rd, 1825, he offered, in the House
of Magnates, to give a whole year's income, 60,000
gulden, to found a Society for promoting the Study
of the Magyar Language. His example was followed,
with more or less zeal, by other nobles; and in 1827
a Hungarian Academy was established by Royal
Decree.

The movement which Szechenyi had stirred up
was in danger of being brought to ridicule by some
of its supporters, for Count Dessewfy actually proposed that a law should be passed forbidding the
marriage of any Hungarian maiden who did not
know her native tongue; but this was resisted as too
strong a measure.

But though Szechenyi opposed these wilder schemes of his supporters, he was none the less ready to use all possible attractions for carrying out his chief object, the drawing Hungarian nobles back to their country. As one of these means, he established a horse-race at Pesth, and founded a union for training horses. He promoted, too, the material advantages of Hungary by introducing steamships on the Danube.

The work to which he devoted most attention was the erection of a suspension bridge, to connect Pesth with Buda. Szechenyi's enthusiasm in this matter seemed to many ludicrously disproportionate to the result to be obtained; but the fact was that he intended this work to give the opportunity for the first blow at that great injustice, the exemption of the Hungarian nobles from taxation. If he could induce the Magnates to consent that the burden of so important a national undertaking should fall in part upon them, they might be willing hereafter to accept a more just distribution of the whole burdens of the State.

While, however, Szechenyi was labouring to promote Hungarian national life, and was willing to sacrifice personal comfort, and any unjust privileges of his order, for the sake of that object, he remained essentially the Conservative Magyar Magnate. He not only shrank from any movement for Constitutional reform, but even hoped to accomplish his ends with the sympathy of the Austrian Government.

It was not indeed that he was deficient in courage, or in the tendency to speak his mind plainly in private conversation. He said boldly that " the promises of the King are not kept, that the law is always explained in favour of the King to the disadvantage of the people ; and, to speak plainly, affairs just now have the appearance as if the Constitution were being overturned." And in the same conversation he further nettled Metternich by suggesting to that statesman that his high position might prevent him from seeing some things.

Yet it was not merely offended vanity that irritated the ruler of Europe against Szechenyi. Metternich seems always to have had a preference for the thoroughgoing men among his opponents. He might hate and desire to crush them; but what pleased him was that he understood the logic of their position and, as he supposed, their motives. The moderate and Constitutional Liberals were always a puzzle to him. But when a man like Szechenyi actually thought that he could work with him, while undermining the centralization which was the essence of his schemes, and appealing to that positive form of patriotism which it was the object of Metternich to crush out, so inconsistent a position drove the Prince beyond the bounds of ordinary courtesy.

Taking advantage of his own high position and Szechenyi's youth, he told him that he was a man lost through vanity and ambition, asked him if he could really confess to his friends the kindly feeling to the Austrian Government which he had expressed to Metternich ; and, on Szechenyi making some admission of the difficulties of such a course, " Then," said Metternich, " you must be a traitor either to me or to your friends, that is to yourself."

But if Szechenyi's position was unintelligible to Metternich, he found it far easier to understand another nobleman who came forward a little later and played a different, but hardly less important, part.  This was Nicolaus Wesselenyi, the descendant of a family of nobles who had constantly held their own against both king and People.  The father of Nicolaus had been a fiery, overbearing man, who had indulged in private feuds, and who had fought scornfully for the special privileges of the nobles.  His son had all the fire of his family, and the same love of opposition, but directed by the circumstances of the time into healthier channels.

It was not, however, at Presburg that the Wesselenyis had hitherto played their principal part, but at the Diet which met at Klausenburg, in Transylvania.  The circumstances and organization of that peculiar province will be more naturally considered in connection with the movements which arose a few years later.  For the present, the important point to remember in connection with Wesselenyi's position is, that the Austrian Government tolerated an unusual amount of freedom in the Transylvanian Diet, in the hopes thereby of weakening that larger Hungarian feeling which gathered round the central Diet at Presburg.  When both the Hungarian and the Transylvanian Diets were called together in 1830, and a demand was made by the Emperor for new recruits for the army, the House of Magnates in Transylvania showed, under Wesselenyi's leading, a bolder and firmer opposition than the House of Magnates at Presburg.  In the central Diet, indeed, the chief opposition to the Emperor came from the Lower House, and the nobles were disposed to yield to the demands of Francis.  But Wesselenyi, with his splendid bearing and magnificent voice, stirred up a far more dangerous opposition in Transylvania; and the Government at

Vienna began to mark him out as their most dangerous opponent.

But in the meantime new questions were coming to the front in Hungary, and new leaders were being called forth by them. The Polish insurrection of 1830 had roused more sympathy in Hungary than probably in any other country of Europe; and a connection between the two nations was then established which had a not unimportant influence on the subsequent history of Hungary.

The wiser men among the Hungarian leaders saw the great defect which marred all struggles for liberty in Poland. Whatever aspirations may have been entertained by the Polish patriots of 1791, certain it is that, when Poland fell before the intrigues of Russia and Prussia, the new Constitution had not had time to bring about any better feeling between noble and peasant; and the Polish peasantry looked with distrust and suspicion on movements for freedom inaugurated by their oppressors.

The Hungarian reformers saw that, if they were to make the liberties of Hungary a reality, they must extend them to the serf as well as to the noble. In spite of the air of freedom of discussion which the County Assemblies of Hungary spread around them, there were, at this time, out of the thirteen millions of Hungarians, about eleven million serfs. These were not allowed to purchase an acre of the soil which they cultivated; they paid all the tithes to the clergy and most of the taxes to the State, besides various payments in kind to their landlords; their labour might be enforced by the stick; while for redress of their grievances they were obliged, in the first instance, to apply to the Court over which their landlord presided.

The reigns of Maria Theresa and Joseph II., while modifying the evils of the position of the serf, had taught him to look to the Court of Vienna, rather than to the Diet of Presburg, for help in his troubles.

The Edict of Maria Theresa, called the Urbarium, had granted the peasant the right of leaving the land when he pleased, or of remaining if he liked, while he complied with certain conditions ; and by this act he was allowed to bequeath the use of his land to his descendants. Further, a right of appeal had been granted from his landlord's decision to the official court at Buda, known as the Statthalterei. By the same law the labour to be performed by the peasantry had been fixed, instead of being left to the will of the lord, as heretofore.

The reforms of Joseph II. had, like most of his attempts, been too vigorous to be lasting ; but he had done enough to strengthen in the minds of the oppressed peasantry of Hungary the desire to look to the Emperor as their liberator. Thus the satisfaction of the claims of humanity had tended to weaken Constitutional freedom.

The bitter feeling between noble and peasant was illustrated most painfully in the year 1831, when an outbreak of cholera in Hungary was attributed by the peasantry to the poisoning of the wells by the nobles. Agrarian risings had followed, and more than fifty peasants had been hung without trial.

Such was the state of feeling when the Diet of 1832 met at Presburg. Had the leader of the movement for agrarian reform been a mere champion of Constitutionalism, the work of drawing together the peasant and noble might have been more difficult. But fortunately the work fell into the hands of a

G

man who, though not deficient in powers of oratory, was far less a popular leader than a thoughtful and humane student of affairs. This was Francis Deak, then thirty years of age, trained, like so many leaders of the time, for the bar, and already known as a speaker in the County Assembly of Zala. He was not a man of the delicate, cultured type of Szechenyi; nor did he possess the commanding figure and lion voice of Wesselenyi. He was broad and sturdy in figure, his face was round and humorous, and his eye twinkled with fun. Yet he was not without a deep shade of melancholy. He was a man who inspired in all who came near him a sense of entire trust in his honesty and steadiness of purpose; and this feeling, though unlike the enthusiasm which is roused alike by the highest genius and by merely popular gifts, was yet exactly the form of confidence needed to enable Deak to do the special work which lay before him.

The question of the reform of the Urbarium he at once made his own. Besides the miseries of the peasantry above mentioned, they were continually exposed to all kinds of petty tyrannies. Their horses were liable to be seized by tourists through the country, and soldiers were billeted upon them. Deak demanded the extension to the peasant of the right of buying land, and better security for person and property.

But it soon became evident that, whatever exceptions there might be to the rule, the Magnates of Hungary were not prepared to surrender their privileges. The point which the reformers specially insisted on in the new Urbarium was a clause enabling the peasant to free himself from his feudal dues by a legal arrangement with the landlord. Thirteen times the Lower House of the Diet passed the clause; thirteen times the House of Magnates rejected it; and when at last that House consented to pass it, the Emperor vetoed it.

The reformers were now clearly justified in calling on the people to recognize them as their champions against both nobles and sovereign. But in order to prevent this recognition the Government had forbidden any publication of the debates.

Wesselenyi had met this difficulty in the Transylvanian Diet by introducing a private press of his own, with the help of which he circulated a report of the proceedings. This so alarmed the Government that they dissolved the Transylvanian Diet and established an absolute ruler in that province. Wesselenyi then transferred his eloquence to the House of Magnates in Presburg, where he thundered against the Government for opposing the liberties of the peasantry, denouncing them in the following words: "The Government sucks out the marrow of nine million of men (i.e., the peasantry); it will not allow us nobles to better their condition by legislative means; but, retaining them in their present state, it only waits its own time to exasperate them against us. Then it will come forward to rescue us. But woe to us! From freemen we shall be degraded to the state of slaves."

But the work which Wesselenyi had half done for Transylvania was to be carried out for Hungary more thoroughly by a man who had been gradually rising into note. This was Louis Kossuth, of whom it may be said that, more than any other man in Europe, he was the author of the Revolution of 1848.

He was a few years older than Francis Deak, and, like him, was trained as a lawyer. He had been appointed, in the exercise of his profession, arbitrator between several wealthy proprietors and their dependants. In this position he gained the confidence of many of the peasantry, and he was also able to give them help in the time of the cholera.

He possessed a quick and keen sensibility, which was the source of many of his faults and of his virtues. A curious illustration of this quality is shown in his renunciation of field sports, in consequence of reading a passage in a Persian poet on the duty of humanity to all living things. No doubt it was to this sensibility that he owed a large part of that matchless eloquence which was to be so powerful an engine in the revolutionary war. It was connected, too, with the keen statesmanlike instinct which enabled him to see so often the right moment for particular lines of action ; and which, had it been united with a wider sympathy, stronger nerves, and a more scrupulous conscience, might have made his career as useful as it was brilliant.

This instinct it was which enabled him to see at this crisis that nothing could be effected for Hungary until the work done in the Diet was better known to the main body of the people. The private press which he now started may have been suggested to him by Wesselenyi's attempt in Transylvania ; but its work was carried out with an ingenuity and resourcefulness which were altogether Kossuth's own. The Government became so alarmed at this press that they wished to purchase it from him, but, wherever print was hindered, he circulated written correspondence. Nor did he confine his

KOSSUTH LAJOS.

reporting to the debates in the Diet of Presburg, for he circulated also reports of the county meetings.

The Count Palatine, the chief ruler of Hungary, tried to hinder this work; but the county officials refused to sanction this prohibition, and thus deprived it of legal force.

The Government was now thoroughly roused; and in May, 1837, Kossuth was indicted for treason, arrested, and kept for two years in prison without any trial.

But great as was the indignation excited by this arrest, it was as nothing compared to the storm which was aroused by the prosecution and imprisonment of Wesselenyi.  The Government had marked him out during the Transylvanian debates as an enemy who was to be struck on the first opportunity.  The printing of the Transylvanian reports would have been followed very speedily by a prosecution, had he not escaped into North Hungary; but his speech against the Government in the Presburg Diet gave a new opportunity for attack.

The enthusiasm which his prominent position, impressive manner, and high rank had caused had been strengthened in Transylvania by the extreme personal kindness which he had shown towards his peasantry; and one of them walked all the way from Wesselenyi's Transylvanian estate to Vienna to petition, on his own behalf and that of one hundred fellow-peasants, that their landlord might be restored to them.

Had Francis been still on the throne, it is possible that Metternich would have offered further resistance to the popular demands.  But Francis had died in 1835, the year before the closing of the Diet.  His successor, Ferdinand, though, chiefly from physical causes, too weak to hold his own against Metternich, was a kindly, easy-tempered man, not without a sense that even kings ought to obey the law.

But whether Metternich or Ferdinand were to blame in the matter, the concessions of the King were made in a hesitating and grudging manner which took away their grace, and made the defeat more vividly apparent both to victors and spectators.

A more popular Chancellor of Hungary, Anton Mailath, was appointed ; another member of the same family was made chief justice; and about the same time the Transylvanian Diet was restored. Hoping that he had now conciliated popular feeling, Metternich, in 1839, called together the Diet of Presburg and demanded four million florins and thirty-eight thousand recruits.

But the members of the Assembly had been instructed by their constituents to oppose any demands of the Government until Wesselenyi, Kossuth, and the members of a club who had been arrested at the same time, were liberated.  And while Deak still led the opposition in the Lower House, Count Louis Batthyanyi came forward as the champion of freedom in the House of Magnates.  Finally, the Emperor consented, not only to grant an amnesty to Wesselenyi, Kossuth, and others, but to pass that clause about the peasants' dues which he had vetoed in 1836. The Diet then voted the money, and was dissolved.

Thus, while in Italy a new faith was springing up which was to supply a force to the struggles for liberty that they had previously lacked, in Hungary the different, but hardly less effective, power of old traditions of Constitutional freedom was checking Metternich in his full career of tyranny, and forcing

him to confess a defeat inflicted, not by foreign diplomatists, but by that very people who had rallied
round Maria Theresa in her hour of danger, and who
had sternly rejected the advances of Napoleon when
he had invited them to separate their cause from that
of the House of Austria.

# CHAPTER IV.

## LANGUAGE AND LEARNING AGAINST DESPOTISM.
### 1840—1846.

Contrast between position of German language in North Germany and in Austrian Empire.—Condition of Germany between 1819 and 1840.—Literary movements.—Protest of the Professors of Göttingen against abolition of Hanoverian Constitution.—Effect of the protest on other parts of Germany.— Position and character of Frederick William III.—His struggle with the Archbishop of Cologne.—Accession of Frederick William IV.—His character and policy.—Ronge's movement of Church Reform.—Robert Blum's share in it.—Language movement in Hungary.—Position and history of Croatia.— Louis Gaj and the "Illyrian" movement.—"The Slavonic ocean and the Magyar island."—Kossuth's treatment of the Slavonic movement.—Count Zay's circular.—The "taxation of the nobles."—Szechenyi's position.—Deak's resignation.—The Croats at Presburg.—Kossuth's inconsistency.—Ferdinand's intervention in the struggle.—The struggle of races absorbs all other questions.—History of Transylvania.—The "three nations."—The position of the Roumanians.—Effect of Joseph II.'s policy in Transylvania.— The "Libellus Wallachorum."— Andreas Schaguna.—Stephan Ludwig Roth.—General summary of the effect of the revival of national feelings.

> 'Twas from no Augustan age,
> No Lorenzo's patronage,
> That the German singers rose;
> By no outward glories crowned,
> By no prince's praise renowned,
> German art's first blossom blows.

From her country's greatest son,
From the mighty Frederick's throne,
Scorned, the Muse must turn away.
" *We* have given thy worth to thee ; "
" Let our heart-beats prouder be ;"
Can each German boldly say.

So to loftier heights arose,
So in waves more swelling flows
German poet's minstrelsy.
He in ripeness all his own,
From his heart's deep centre grown,
Scorns the rule of pedantry.

So sang Schiller; and, while in Germany the Muse
was ascending to the heights in which Schiller gloried
to see her, the opposite process had been producing
opposite results under the rule of another German
sovereign.   Frederick II. of Prussia preferred bad
French to the best utterances of his own country;
and so the German Muse was free to develope in
her own way.   Joseph II. of Austria felt his heart
warmed with the greatness of German traditions; he
looked round on dominions inhabited by men of
different races and languages, and, perceiving that
these differences led to continual misunderstandings,
and hindered any great work of common reform,
resolved to extend the blessings of German language
and literature to all the races of his dominions.   To
them, he thought, a change would prove a bond of
union ; while neither Bohemian, Hungarian, nor
Croat could claim for their native tongues, however
dear to them, such glorious associations and traditions
as were already connected with the language which
was to take their place.

The consequence of this nobly intended effort has
been that German is, to this day, a badge of tyranny

to the majority of the people of the western half of the Austrian Empire; and if it has almost ceased to be so in the eastern half, that is simply because its supremacy has been replaced by the no less crushing tyranny of another language which was offered to the various populations of the Hungarian kingdom by its rulers, as a symbol of national freedom and unity.

The spirit of literary independence in North Germany, and the rivalry of languages in the Austrian Empire, were both forcing themselves on the attention of the public during the period of Metternich's rule. To outward appearance there was no time at which the condition of Germany must have seemed more helpless and hopeless than between 1819 and 1840. The German insurrections of 1831 could not be compared for their historical importance with either the English reform movement of the same period, or with the Italian uprisings; nor for dramatic brilliancy with the Polish insurrection of 1830. Even the Hanoverian Constitution of 1833, which seemed to be firmly established, went down four years later without a sword being drawn in its defence; while the heavy burdens of the Carlsbad decrees of 1819 and the Frankfort decrees of 1832 were made still heavier in 1834 by a new Edict, passed at Vienna, establishing courts of arbitration, elected by members of the Bund, to decide questions at issue between sovereigns and parliaments. If the Assemblies, in defending their rights of taxation, should refuse to appeal to this Court, the sovereign might then proceed to levy, without further delay, the supplies which had been granted by the previous Assembly.

Yet Germany was not dead. Apart from the continual assertions of independence by the South German States, the growth of German literature was keeping alive the sense of union between the different parts of the nation. Stein, after his retirement from political affairs, had devoted himself to the encouragement of German literature, and particularly of German history. For this purpose he brought together historians from different parts of Germany; and Perthes, the bookseller, who had helped to defend Hamburg against the French, exerted himself to promote a book trade which was to unite the North and South of Germany. Occasionally, some prince, like the Duke of Saxe-Coburg Gotha, would show an inclination to play the part of the Duke of Weimar as a patron of literature, but could only call attention thereby to such life as still remained, not evoke any new life. The German Muse was still to thrive by her own labours, and the great proof of the existence of a still independent literary class was given in 1837, when the King of Hanover suppressed the Constitution which his predecessor had established.

On November 17th, 1837, seven professors of Göttingen University drew up against this act of tyranny a protest which so ably connected the feeling of the true literary man and the true teacher with that of the independent citizen that it deserves to be given at length. They said that the whole chance of the success of their work depended not more certainly on the scientific worth of their teaching than on their personal blamelessness. Should they appear before the young students as men who would play carelessly with their oaths, then at once the blessing of their work would be gone ; and what importance could the oath of homage possibly have, if the King had received it from men who just before had audaciously violated another oath?   This protest was signed by Dahlmann, Albrecht, Gervinus, the brothers Grimm, Weber, and Ewald.   They were summarily dismissed from their offices by the King, who declared that he could buy professors anywhere for money, as easily as dancers. At once the greatest enthusiasm broke out in different parts of Germany.   In Leipzig and Königsberg subscriptions were opened for the professors, and in twelve hours the Leipzigers had subscribed nearly 1,000 thalers.   The subscription of Leipzig was followed by a public reception given to Albrecht and Dahlmann ; an address was delivered in which the professors were told that the whole heart of the German people beat with them.   The man who delivered this address, and who thus first made his appearance before the public, was the Leipzig bookseller, Robert Blum.   In Saxony the Constitution which had been won in 1831 was still nominally in existence, and the Prime Minister was even called a Liberal.   The Members of the Parliament hoped to seize this opportunity of putting Saxony forward as the champion of German rights ; but the Government shrank from that position, and seemed disposed even to check the independent movement among the people.

Now in spite of the steady courage that had shown itself among the literary men of Germany, the bulk of the nation was still essentially monarchical, and they needed some king at the head of the movement for freedom and unity.   However much of Liberalism might occasionally have been shown by some of the smaller princes of Germany, none of them were in a position to take the leading part in any common German movement.  The Emperor of Austria, even had his policy tended in that direction, was hindered by his connection with non-German territories from assuming such a leadership.  And the memories of 1813 gathered, if not round the King of Prussia, at least round his kingdom.  The institution of the Zollverein formed one point of attraction between Prussia and the Liberals of Germany ; the position of Prussia as the great Protestant Power strengthened her influence in Northern Germany ; and just at the time when the King of Hanover was dismissing the professors of Göttingen, the King of Prussia was supporting at the University of Bonn professors whom the Archbishop of Cologne was trying to suppress.  The prohibition of mixed marriages by the same Archbishop further excited Frederick William's opposition ; and, unable to secure obedience by other methods, the King seized and imprisoned the Archbishop.  An act of tyranny in the interests of liberty seems to commend itself more readily to Continental revolutionists than to those who have been bred up under the principle of mutual forbearance produced by Constitutional life ; and there can be little doubt that much of the strongest part of North German feeling was enlisted on the side of the King of Prussia.  But Frederick William III. was not a man to take the lead in anything.  By the mere accident of his position he had become the figure-head of the rising of 1813 ; and by the same accident he continued to attract the wishes, one can hardly say the hopes, of those who

desired to counteract in Germany the policy of
Metternich.  He could at no time have done much
to help forward the unity of Germany ; and he had
long since abandoned any wish to work in that
direction.

But while the excitement arising from the tyranny
of the King of Hanover, and the struggle of the King
of Prussia with the Archbishop of Cologne, were still
distracting Germany, Frederick William III. died,
and was succeeded by Frederick William IV.  The
new King was a man of somewhat poetical and enthusiastic temperament, with a strong religious bias,
desirous in a way of the welfare of his people, and
not ill disposed to play a Liberal part within due
limits.  He restored Arndt to his position at Bonn ;
he set free not only Jahn, but also the Archbishop
of Cologne ; he found a post for Dahlmann in the
University of Bonn; and he began also to talk Constitutionalism in a way which roused new hopes in
Germany.  He inspired no confidence in those who
looked more closely into matters ; but his career began
at a time when the Germans were in a state of eager
expectation, which had been quickened by a movement already preparing in other parts of Germany.
The first utterance of the new reformers was a protest
against religious superstition.  A Roman Catholic
priest, named Ronge, denounced the famous worship
of the Holy Coat at Treves.  This protest attracted
attention, and was followed by an attack on a number
of other corruptions of the Roman Catholic Church.
The movement spread ; a reformed Catholic Church
was founded in Posen and Silesia, and Ronge was
appointed minister of the first congregation of the
new faith.

It was in 1845 that the movement reached Saxony. Two years before, the Liberal Ministry had retired ; a complete reaction had set in, and Robert Blum had been subjected to a fine and four weeks' imprisonment for an article in which he had advocated publicity of trial. Nothing daunted by this, Blum threw himself heartily into the new movement, and, although a Roman Catholic himself, denounced the practice of the confessional and the celibacy of the clergy. The Ultramontanes raised a riot in which Blum was personally attacked, and the Saxon Ministry declared their determination to put down "the sects." Such a threat naturally gave new force to the reformers, and they raised the cry, so often to be heard in the coming Liberal movements, of " Down with the Jesuits!" That unfortunate Society, so often the object of hatred both to kings and Peoples, was in this case specially obnoxious to the Liberals from the patronage which was extended to it by the heir to the throne. When the Prince appeared to review the troops at Leipzig he was received in silence, and when he had retired to his hotel the crowd gathered round it with cries of " Long live Ronge!" and " Down with the Jesuits!" accompanied by the singing of "Ein fester Burg ist unser Gott," and followed by songs of a different description. Stones soon began to fly. Then the soldiers were called out, they fired on the crowd, and many were killed.

On the following day the students of Leipzig gathered to hear an address from Robert Blum. He urged them to abstain from violence, but to put into form their demand for legal remedies ; and for this purpose a committee was chosen. The following demands were laid before the Town Council—viz.,

that the preservation of order should be entrusted
to the civic guard ; that the soldiers should be removed from the town ; that inquiries should be made
into the circumstances of the riot, and a solemn burial
given to those who had been shot.  The Town Council
yielded, and though the soldiers were soon sent back
into Leipzig, a beginning had been made which might
lead to a larger reform.  Blum then founded a debating society ; and, at the end of 1845, he was chosen
representative of Leipzig in the Lower House of
Saxony.

But while the national feeling of Germany was
gathering round the intellectual leaders of that
country, the feeling for national peculiarities and
national language was producing widely different
results in those countries where the unfortunate
policy of Joseph II. had made the German language
a symbol of division rather than of unity.  The
movement for substituting the Magyar language for
the Latin (which had previously been customary in
the Diet at Presburg) was the revival of a struggle
which had begun in the very time of Joseph II.;
and, had Hungary been a homogeneous country, the
movement might have passed as naturally into a
struggle for freedom as the enthusiasm for German
poetry and German learning had chimed in with the
desire for German political unity.  But Hungary had
never been a country of one race or of common
aspirations.  Several waves of conquest and coloniza-
tion had passed over different parts of it, without
ending, in any case, in that amalgamation between
the different races which alone could secure national
unity.

Yet it is just possible that, had the leadership of

the Magyars fallen into the hands of a man of wider sympathies and more delicate feeling than Kossuth, an understanding might have been effected between the different peoples of Hungary. During the struggle against Joseph II., the other races seem to have submitted to the leadership of the Magyars, and to a great extent to have adopted the Magyar language, because it was not then thrust on them by force. But when, after the Diet of 1830, Hungary began to reawaken to the desire for liberty, signs of national feeling soon showed themselves among other races than the Magyars.

The first race who felt the new impulse were the Croats. They, more than any of the other peoples who had been annexed to the Kingdom of Hungary, had preserved their separate government and traditions of independence. In 1527 they offered the throne of Croatia to the Hapsburgs, without waiting for any decision by the Magyars ; and when Charles VI. was submitting to the Powers of Europe and to the inhabitants of his different dominions the question of the Pragmatic Sanction, Croatia gave her decision quite independently of the Diet at Presburg.

But apart from her actual legal rights to independence, there remained a tradition of the old period when the Kingdom of Croatia had been an important Power in Europe, and had extended over Slavonia and Dalmatia. But these claims were not undisputed. The hold which Venice had gained over Dalmatia and Istria had introduced into those provinces an Italian element; and when, in the sixteenth century, the Serbs were called into Hungary in large numbers, Slavonia had developed a variety of the Slavonic tongue which must have weakened

H

the absolute supremacy of the Croats. The sense, however, of a connection between the dialects of the different Slavonic States was a bond of union between those States which might at any time be drawn closer.

When, then, Szechenyi began to stir up the Magyars to develop their language and literature, it occurred to a Croatian poet to link together the different dialects of the Southern Slavs into one language. The Croatians had been so far in advance of their neighbours the Serbs that they had abandoned the Cyrillic alphabet, which had been introduced at the time of their first conversion to Christianity, and had adopted the ordinary Latin alphabet. But the Croatian dialect, by itself, would not have been accepted by the other Slavs; and the softer language and higher culture of the old Republic of Ragusa supplied a better basis for the development of the new language. Louis Gaj, the Croatian poet, had studied at the University of Leipzig, which seems to have been the centre of a good deal of Slavonic feeling; and he hoped to link together, not merely the three provinces of Croatia, Slavonia, and Dalmatia, but several, also, of the south-west provinces of Austria; and, on the other hand, he wished to draw into this bond of sympathy those Slavonic countries which still groaned under the Turkish yoke. It was necessary, however, to find a new name for a language which was a new combination of dialects. To call it the Croatian language would have implied a claim to superiority for Croatia which it was most desirable to avoid; and as none other of the Slavonic provinces could well be treated as the godmother of the new language, Gaj went back to the seventeenth century for a name.

At that period Leopold I. of Austria had granted special privileges to the *Illyrian* nation, and it was only in the eighteenth century that the *Illyrian* Chancellery at Vienna had been abolished. Here, then, was a name, recognized by Imperial authority in legal documents, and giving no superiority to any one of the Slavonic provinces over the others. To carry out his purposes, Gaj started a journal in 1835 to which at first he gave the name of the "Gazette of Croatia," but which he soon renamed the "National Gazette of Illyria." This newspaper was written in the new language, and the Hungarian authorities refused to sanction it. Nor were they the only opponents of the new movement. The Turkish Pasha in Bosnia was alarmed at the attempt to draw the subjects of the Sultan into closer alliance with the Slavs in Hungary; and he tried to persuade Francis that Gaj was attempting to shake the Imperial authority and found a separate kingdom. At the same time the Bishop of Agram warned the Pope of the evident tendency of this movement to give the upper hand to the members of the Greek Church, who formed the majority of the Southern Slavs, over the Roman Catholics of Croatia. But these efforts failed. Metternich saw in Gaj's movement an opportunity of weakening the Magyars; Francis sent a ring to Gaj, as a sign of his approval; and Gregory XVI. was so far from being influenced by the Bishop of Agram's appeal that he removed him from his see for having made it.

The fact that Francis had encouraged, and Metternich at all events not disapproved, this movement was enough to alarm the sensibilities of the Magyars; and when Gaj appeared in the Hungarian Diet of

1840, Deak rebuked him for his work. Gaj answered
in words which became afterwards only too memorable. " The Magyars," he said, "are an island in the
Slavonic ocean. I did not make the ocean, nor did
I stir up its waves; but take care that they do not
go over your heads and drown you." The words
were certainly not conciliatory; but they had been
provoked by the evident signs of hostility on the part
of the Magyars. If the latter had been content to
ignore the movement, it might have remained, for
their time at least, a purely literary effort; or, if it
had taken a political form, it might have drifted into
union with the Bohemian struggle against German
supremacy, or even into a crusade against the Turks.
It is, however, more than probable that the attempt
to found this new language would have been earlier
abandoned had it not been for the opposition which
it called forth. For Gaj, however zealous as a patriot,
and however ingenious as a philologer, seems to have
been deficient in the power of producing such a great
work of imagination as that which enabled Dante to
unite the not less diverse elements of the Italian
language.

But the Magyar cry of alarm at the demands of
the Slavs was now echoed by a fiercer voice than
that of Deak. In 1841, the year after the dissolution
of that Presburg Diet by which Metternich had been
so signally defeated, Kossuth started a paper called
the " Pesti Hirlap " (the Gazette of Pesth), which
soon became at once the most determined champion
of those liberties which Kossuth desired for his
countrymen, and the bitterest opponent of those
liberties which he grudged to the other races of
Hungary. For it was not merely in provinces

marked off from the Magyar world like Croatia, Slavonia, and Dalmatia, that a movement like Gaj's would produce effect. The Slavs were scattered about in nearly all the districts of Hungary, and though they might not all desire separate political organizations like those which the Croats demanded, the question of the preservation of their language concerned even those who had no separate political existence; and they too resented any attempt on the part of the Magyars to substitute for it the language of the ruling race. Kossuth was as indignant at this hindrance to his schemes of national unity as Joseph II. had been at the hindrances which had been thrown in the way of the Germanizing of the Empire. The same year, 1841, which saw the starting of the journal in which Kossuth was to vindicate the liberties of Hungary against Metternich, was also the year in which he dealt his first decided blow against the liberties of the Slavonic races of Hungary. At a general convention of the Hungarian Protestants, he proposed that certain of the schools in which the Slavonic clergy studied physical science, and other branches of knowledge, should be deprived of these teachings, and that mere practice in writing sermons should be substituted. This proposal was defended on the ground that Slavonic gatherings, unless carefully limited, must be a source of danger to the country. Any one who ventured to defend the Slavonic cause at this meeting was howled down, and Kossuth's motion was carried.

Fierce attacks on the Slavs and their language now appeared in the " Pesti Hirlap," and Kossuth refused to insert the answers to these attacks. Count Zay, who had just been appointed chief inspector of

the Protestant Congregations and Schools, openly
announced in a public circular his determination to
Magyarize the Slavs. The Slavonic speech, he said,
would prevent the Slavs from being firm in the
Protestant faith; and while they used that speech
they would not be capable of freedom, and could
not even be considered to have a proper share in
humanity. The Magyarizing of the Slavs was the
holiest duty of every genuine patriot of Hungary,
every defender of freedom and intelligence, and
every true subject of the Austrian House. Others
accused the Slavs of offering sacrifices to their old
deity Svatopluk; while that great bugbear, the fear
of Russian influence, was pushed forward on every
occasion. Slavonic hymns, previously sung in the
churches, were prohibited; and Magyar preachers
were thrust upon congregations who did not understand a word of the Magyar language.

It was while this bitter feeling was at its height
that the elections began for the Diet of 1843 at
Presburg, and for the Croatian Assembly at Agram.
The Hungarian elections turned, to some extent, on
the quarrel with the Slavs; but partly also on the
question, which was now coming to the front, of the
exemption of the so-called nobles of Hungary from
taxation. These "nobles" were not confined to
the great families who sat in the House of Magnates,
but included all the freeholders of the country; and
great injustice had arisen from the fact that the men
who laid on the taxes were, in the main, not those
who paid them. Szechenyi, as before mentioned,
had tried to diminish this injustice ; but the fiery
methods of Kossuth, and the growing tendency to
opposition to the Austrian rule, had alarmed Sze-

chenyi; and he shrank more and more from the leaders of the popular movement. It was not, however, merely the extreme character of their aims, nor their rough-and-ready methods, which alienated him; it was also their growing injustice to the Slavs. Szechenyi, who had been so much the first in reviving an interest in Magyar language and literature, now came forward, as President of the Hungarian Academy, to denounce any step for spreading the Magyar language which could offend the Croats. On the other hand, the peasant nobles of Hungary protested fiercely against the attempt to deprive them of their exemption from taxation, and they gathered at the county meetings in a riotous manner, breaking, in one case, into the Hall of Election, with knives in their hands, and shouting, "Freedom for ever! We will not pay taxes."

This fierce intimidation on the part of the opponents of reform provoked reprisals from the reformers. And, where they were unable to hold their own by intimidation, they resorted to bribery. One protest was made against this defection from the true principles of liberty which was of vital importance to the future history of Hungary. The election of Zala county had ended once more in the return of Francis Deak ; and the electors were gathered to hear the announcement of the election, when, to their dismay, Deak came forward and stated that, in consequence of the way in which the election had been conducted, he should refuse to sit as their representative. His friends pressed round him, some entreating him not to desert their cause; some even venturing to reproach him with cowardice in shrinking from the struggle. But he replied that,

if he went to the Diet after this election, he should
always " see bloodstains on his mandate." Thus,
at a crisis when they most needed a man who would
combine genuine popular feeling with moderation
and justice, the reformers were deprived of *the* leader
in the Lower House who possessed those qualities
in the largest degree.  As for Deak himself, it must
be remembered that he was sacrificing the undoubted
position of leader of the reforming party, at the time
when its objects were becoming more and more
definite, and its leadership was in consequence
growing more attractive to a man of courage and
patriotism.  Though he was still to play a useful
part in the coming struggles, it was of necessity a
secondary one ; and it was not till twenty-three
years later that he was to resume the first place in
the Hungarian national movement.

In the meantime the Croatian question had become
more complicated by an element of internal division.
In a district not far from Agram, there was established a complete settlement of Croatian "nobles,"
of a similar type to those who had been raising the
cry against equal taxation in the Hungarian counties.
These men claimed the right, much disputed by the
other Croats, to attend the county meetings at
Agram *en masse*, instead of returning representatives
like other citizens.  In this Diet of 1843, Count
Jozipoviç, leader of this band of " nobles," asserted
their right in a very imperious manner; and a fierce
fight followed in the streets of Agram.  Thus began
a contest which extended, with various degrees of
violence, over several years.  The Croatian Assembly, however, at first attempted to place their
claims in a moderate manner before the Magyars;

and instructed Haulik, Bishop of Agram, to assure
the Magyars of their desire to live on good terms
with them, if they were secured in those rights
which had been granted by law, and guaranteed by
the oath of the King. They pointed out that many
of them were ignorant of the Magyar language, and
that the Magyars were in many cases ignorant of
theirs. On the former ground they desired to
maintain the right of their representatives to speak
Latin in the Hungarian Diet. On the latter ground
they objected to censors being appointed over the
Croatian press, who were ignorant of the Croatian
language. The former right was the first to be
tested; for no sooner did the Croatian deputies begin,
according to old custom, to speak Latin in the Diet
of Presburg than they were interrupted by a
clattering of sabres from the Magyar members, and
a demand that they should speak in the Magyar
language. Thereupon Jozipoviç saw an opportunity
of making new friends for his cause; and, while he
disputed the legality of the election of his opponents,
he declared that he and his supporters were "body
and soul Hungarian." Kossuth at once assumed the
justice of the cause of Jozipoviç; and, while he was
eagerly opposing the privileges of the nobles in
Hungary, he thus supported in Croatia an aristocratic privilege of doubtful legality, and undoubtedly
disorderly and unjust in its effects. The Magyars
responded to Kossuth's appeal ; and the Lower
House of the Hungarian Diet passed a resolution
forbidding the use of any language but Magyar
in the Diet. The House of Magnates, doubtless
under the influence of Szechenyi, were disposed
to make concessions to the Croats ; but even

they were not able to do much to check the
storm.

In the meantime the Emperor had been trying to
exercise a moderating influence on these conflicts.
Finding the bitterness caused in Hungary by Gaj's
movement, Ferdinand prohibited the use of the name
" Illyrian " in newspapers and in public discussions;
but at the same time he promised to encourage the
development of the Croatian language, and urged the
Magyars to suspend for six years their prohibition of
Latin in the Hungarian Diet.    While, too, the Magyar
language was to be used in Church boards and legal
tribunals of Hungary, Hungarian officials were to
accept Latin letters from Croatia and the other outlying districts that were united with Hungary.    But
these proposals, unfortunately, did not satisfy the
feeling of the Magyars; and some of them actually ventured on the extraordinary statement that, if the Croat
boards could understand letters written in the Magyar
language, they must necessarily be able to compose
Magyar letters in answer; and they maintained that
the Croats ought not to be allowed to elect any
members to the Diet who could not then speak the
Magyar language.

Thus, although in all parts of the Kingdom of
Hungary there was a growing demand for freedom
and equality, each question in turn became complicated by this quarrel between the members of the
different races.    On the one hand, a proposal for
admitting men not hitherto recognized as "nobles"
to the possession of land was met by an amendment
to limit this concession to those who knew Magyar;
and this exclusion was rejected by only twenty-eight
votes against seventeen; while a proposal to limit

offices to those who could speak Magyar was rejected by a majority of only two. On the other hand, the Croats successfully resisted a proposal to allow Protestants to settle in Croatia as a part of the scheme for Magyarizing their country. But though these divisions hindered the co-operation of the members of the different nations who might have worked together for freedom and progress, it should always be noted that the desire of each nation was, in the first instance, for the development of a free national life, connected with true culture and learning, and independent of mere officialism. If the Magyars were tyrannical and overbearing towards the Croats, it was partly because they believed that these divisions (the fault of which they attributed to the Croats) were tending to strengthen the hands of their common oppressors. If, on the other hand, the Croats appealed to the Emperor for protection against the Magyars, it was not from any courtier-like or slavish desire to strengthen the hands of despotism; but partly because they felt that the position of the Emperor enabled him to judge more fairly between the contending parties, partly because they found from experience that Ferdinand of Austria was a juster-minded man than Louis Kossuth.

While the growth of national feeling in Hungary and Croatia was tending at once to a healthier life and to dangerous divisions, a much more remarkable awakening of new and separate life was showing itself in the province of Transylvania. The geographical isolation of that province from the rest of Hungary is very striking, even now that railways have connected the different parts of the kingdom; but in 1848 this isolation was far greater, and had a considerable effect on the political history of the time. The Carpathians almost surround the country, and form a natural bulwark. Between this high wall of mountains on the north-east and Buda Pesth stretches a vast plain. No province of the Empire contained a greater variety of separately organized nations. The Transylvanian Diet was not, like the other local assemblies, the result of an attempt to express the feelings of a more or less united people, but arose merely from the endeavour to give reasonable solidity to an alliance between three distinct peoples. Of the three ruling races, the first to enter Transylvania were the Szekler, a people of the same stock as the Magyar, but slower to take the impress of any permanent civilization. They conquered the original inhabitants of the country, a race probably of mixed Dacian and Roman blood, called Wallachs or Roumanians. Towards the end of the ninth century came in the Magyars, before whom the Szekler retreated to the north-east, where the town of Maros-Vasarhely became their capital. This town is on the River Maros, which, rising in the Carpathians, flows all across Transylvania.

The Magyars in the meantime extended their rule over all parts of Hungary, but the position which they gained in Transylvania was one of much less undisputed supremacy than that which they established in Northern Hungary; for in the former province they remained a second nation, existing by the side of the Szekler, neither conquering nor absorbing them.

Much of the country, however, was still uncolonized, and was liable to inroads from dangerous neighbours; so in the twelfth century a number of German citizens who lived along the Rhine, and some of the German knights who were seeking adventures, came into Transylvania to offer their services to the King of Hungary. The German knights were unable to come to a satisfactory agreement with the King, and went north to try to civilize the Prussians; but the citizens remained, acquired land, developed trade, and developed, also, a power of self-government of which neither Szekler nor Magyar were at that time capable. That portion of the country which has been colonized by the Saxons has a look of greater neatness and comfort than the rest. The little homesteads are almost English in their appearance, with, occasionally, gardens and orchards. Hermann-stadt, the capital of this district, bears traces of its former greatness in several fine old churches, a law academy, and picture gallery. Its fortifications must have been almost impregnable in old times, with strong watch-towers and walls of great height. The portions of the walls that remain show marks of the sieges of 1849. The Carpathians, on the south-east, are many miles distant, but the Rothenthurm Pass, through which the terrible Russian force made its way into the country, is visible in some lights.

These three ruling nations—the Magyar, the Szekler, and the Saxon—though separate in their organization, had more than one common interest. They were united by a common love of freedom and a common temptation to tyranny. In 1438 they formed a union against the Turks, which in 1459 was changed into a union in support of their freedoms and privileges, " for protection against inward and outward enemies, against oppression from above or insurrection from below." And when, in the

seventeenth century, they separated for a time from
Hungary, the three nations accepted the Prince of
Transylvania as their head.  When Transylvania
and Hungary had both passed under the rule of
Austria, Leopold I., in 1695, established a separate
Government for Transylvania, and Maria Theresa
increased the importance and the independence of
this position.  It will be noted that among the
objects for which the three nations combined is
mentioned "insurrection from below;" and this was
a bond of great importance; for, while the Magyar,
Szekler, and Saxon were enjoying an amount of
freedom and independence in Transylvania not
generally allowed by the House of Austria to its
subjects, the original population of the country, the
Wallachs, or Roumanians, as they prefer to be called,
were hated and attacked by the Szekler, made serfs
of by the Magyar, excluded from their territory by
the Saxons, and despised by all.  Even the full
benefit of the village organization, which was the
great protection of the Hungarian peasant, was not
extended to the Roumanians in Transylvania, for
they were never allowed to choose one of their own
men as president of the village community; and
while the landowners oppressed them in the country,
the Saxon guilds excluded them from the trade of
the towns.  So they remained a race of shepherds,
without culture and wealth, among the warriors of
the Magyar and Szekler, and the prosperous traders
of the Saxons.

When, then, the reforming zeal of Joseph II. was
extended to Transylvania, the Roumanians alone
hailed it with delight; for, while, in his eagerness for
a united Empire, the Emperor tried to sweep away

all the special organizations of separate self-government so dear to the ruling races, he introduced
sweeping reforms in favour of the serfs. He put
forth an Edict, securing to the peasant an amount
of liberty not hitherto enjoyed by him. No peasant
was to be hindered from marriage, or from studying
in other places, or from following different kinds of
work; none was to be turned out of his village or
land at bidding of the landlord; the power of the
landlord to impose new burdens (already restricted
by the Urbarium of Maria Theresa) was to be still
further limited ; and the county officials were to
protect the dependant from any oppression of his
landlord. The hopes of the Roumanians were
naturally raised by this Edict; and many of them
believed, when a general conscription followed, that
by entering the army they could escape serfdom.
The lords, backed by many of the officials, hindered
this attempt, and interfered to prevent the carrying
out of the Edict. Thereupon the Roumanians rose
in insurrection, under two leaders, Hora and Kloska;
and all those horrors followed which are naturally
connected with an agrarian rising of uncivilized serfs,
and the violent suppression of it by hardly more
civilized tyrants.

But among the bishops of the Roumanians, to
whom they always granted great authority, were
some who saw a better way than insurrection for the
cure of the sufferings of their countrymen. Having
observed that when the three dominant races were
protesting against the reforms of Joseph II. they
had appealed continually to historic rights, these
Roumanian leaders drew up a petition, which was
called the "Libellus Wallachorum," and was pre-

sented to the Diet of 1791.   It was in this document
that the Roumanians first put forward that claim to
descent from the ancient Romans which has ever
since exercised such influence on the imagination
of this singular race.   The petition further declared
that, in the first inroad of the barbarians, the Roumanians had continued to maintain that Christianity
which they had learned under the Roman Empire,
and that when the Magyars came into the country,
the Roumanians had voluntarily accepted the Magyar
chief as their leader; that though their name was
then changed by the invaders from Roumanians into
Wallachs, their independent rights were still secured.
They went on to say that even the union of the
three ruling races in 1438 had not been intended
originally to deprive the Roumanians of their rights;
it was not till the seventeenth century that they had
been crushed down into their present position.   They
therefore entreated that they might be restored to
all the civil and political rights which they had
possessed in the fifteenth century; that the clergy of
the Greek Church, to which they belonged, might be
placed on an equality with those of other religions;
and that, wherever the Roumanians had a majority
in any villages, those villages might be called by
Roumanian names.   The reading of this petition
was received by the representatives of the three
ruling races, after a brief silence, with fierce protests; only the Saxons thought it necessary to make
even vague promises of concession; and those promises were not fulfilled.

    But, when this demand had once been put into
form, the memory of it lingered on among the
Roumanians ; and in 1842, during the general

wakening of national feeling, they attempted again to make an appeal to the Transylvanian Diet for special recognition. Again they failed ; but their leaders did not, therefore, lose heart. Some of them, indeed, were disposed to resort to their old method of insurrection ; and a few years later they rose, under the leadership of a woman named Catherine Varga, and for a long time held their own against the Magyar officials. But it is to the suppressor of this movement, rather than to its leader, that the Roumanians look back as their national hero. This was Andreas Schaguna, who, at the time of Catherine Varga's insurrection, was holding the position of Archimandrite. He came down to the village, where the Magyar officials had not dared to penetrate, rebuked the Roumanians for their turbulence, and carried off Catherine Varga from their midst, no one daring to resist. But this, though a striking, was not a characteristic exercise of his authority. He was far from thinking that force was a remedy for the grievances of the Roumanians; and he devoted time and thought to the foundation of schools and the education of the people. This education he carried out, not by mere teaching, but by seeking out and advising those whom he saw fitted for more intellectual occupations, and helping them to become lawyers and doctors. Last, but by no means least, he tried to reduce into a more literary form the Roumanian language.

But it was not only in their own ranks that the Roumanians were now finding champions for their national cause. In 1842 appeared a pamphlet by a Saxon clergyman, named Stephen Roth, in which the writer protested against the attempt of the

I

Magyars to crush out the rival languages in Transylvania; for this, as he pointed out, was a new form
of tyranny.  In North Hungary, indeed, the movement had been accompanied by an attempt to improve
the condition of the peasant ; and the Magyar
language was held out to him as a new boon to
be added to the abolition of feudal dues.  But in
Transylvania little or nothing had been done by the
Magyars to improve the condition of the peasant ;
and therefore there could be no talk of *benefits*
there.  If there were to be one official language in
Transylvania, it ought, urged Roth, to be the
language of the majority of the population,' that is,
Roumanian ; and though it was undesirable to make
this or any other language universal, it was certain
that the ruling race would never be able to Magyarize
the Roumanians; who might, however, be pacified
by greater respect for their dignity as men, completer
recognition of their form of Christianity, better
means of education, provision for material need,
and a freer position.  This pamphlet of Roth's was
notable, as a sign of sympathy felt by a member of
the most cultivated race in Transylvania for the
complaints of the most uncivilized one.  But it is
no reproach to Roth to say that he was thinking,
at the time, as much of maintaining the rights of his
own race as of redressing the wrongs of the Roumanians.  For though the Magyars did not, as yet,
venture to lord it over a German People as they did
over Slav and Roumanian, they were yet trying, by
various underhand methods, to weaken the devotion
of the Saxons to their race and language.  Roth and
his friends tried to counteract this, partly by founding
unions for the encouragement of German culture;

and also by the more effective way of introducing
German immigrants from the old country. A movement of a similar kind had been inaugurated by
Maria Theresa about 1731; and for more than forty
years it had been carried on with success; the German
Protestants, who had been driven out of other
countries, finding a natural refuge in the wholly
Protestant Saxon settlement of Transylvania. Strange
to say, Joseph II. does not seem to have carried on
his mother's work; perhaps he had made himself too
unpopular in Transylvania to do it with success.
But Roth had special friends in the University of
Würtemberg; and in spite of the Liberal tendencies
of the King of that State, the taxation in that country
was specially heavy. When, then, in 1845, Roth
went to Würtemberg, so many citizens of that State
consented to emigrate to Transylvania in the following
year that the Government at Vienna and the
Magyars at Pesth became alike alarmed. Ferdinand
was persuaded that this was a Protestant invasion,
and probably, also, a Communistic attempt. The
Magyars, on the other hand, cried out that this was
part of an attempt to Germanize Transylvania. Roth
defended his cause, and refuted the charge of Protestant propagandism by showing that Roman
Catholic families were among the emigrants; while,
as to the idea of a Communistic proletariat, many
of those who had emigrated were well provided
with money, and some had been encouraged by the
former impulse given to the movement by the
Viennese Government. But a vague prejudice, once
excited, is rarely got rid of by mere statements of
fact ; and the Governments, both at Vienna and
Pesth, threw such difficulties in the way of the

emigrants, that they had to suffer great misery on their journey ; and these sufferings tended (with other grounds of prejudice) to excite much indignation against Roth. Nor would the Magyars, at any rate, feel more friendly to him when they found that an organ of the Croatian patriots at Agram claimed him as an ally against the overbearing demands of the Magyars.

Thus, then, it is clear that, during the period from 1840 to 1846, there was a general awakening both in Germany and Hungary of strong national feelings. In Germany those feelings, gathering round a common language and literature, prepared the way directly for a movement towards freedom; while in Hungary the divisions of races and languages hindered the full benefits of the revival, and gave a handle to the champions of despotism. Yet whether among Magyars, Croats, Roumanians, or Saxons, the movement was in itself a healthy one, tending to newer and more natural life, and weakening the traditions of Viennese officialism.

# CHAPTER V.

## DESPOTISM RETIRING BEFORE CONSTITUTION-ALISM, 1844—DECEMBER, 1847.

The Bandiera insurrection. Its results.—Career of Cesare Balbo, "Le Speranze d' Italia."—Vincenzo Gioberti. "Il Primato degli Italiani."—The insurrection of Rimini. "Ultimi casi di Romagna."—The risings in Galicia.—History of Cracow since 1815.—Causes of the failure of the Galician movement.—The seizure of Cracow. Palmerston's utterances thereon.—Change in Charles Albert's position.—The Ticino treaties.—Mistake of Solaro della Margherita.—"Long live the King of Italy!"—D'Azeglio's policy.—Aurelio Saffi.—Death of Gregory XVI.—State of Roman Government.—Parties in the Conclave.—Election of Pius IX.—His character and career.—The amnesty. Its effect.—Ciceruacchio. His work.—The Congress at Genoa.—Charles Lucien Bonaparte.—Death of Confalonieri.—State of Milan.—Pio Nono's reforms.—The clerical conspiracy.—The occupation of Ferrara. Its effect on Italian feeling.—State of Tuscany.—The Duke of Lucca.—Absorption of Lucca in Tuscany.—The struggle with Modena.—The massacre of Fivizzano.—Occupation of Parma and Modena by Austria.—State of Switzerland.—Position of Bern and Zürich.—The Concordat of Seven.—The refugee question in 1838.—The Aargau monasteries.—The Sonderbund.—The Jesuit question.—Metternich's feelings, real and pretended.—Palmerston's attitude.—Relations between Metternich and Guizot.—The decision of the Swiss Diet.—The Sonderbund war.—Effect of the Federal victory.—The Schleswig-Holstein question.—The official view and the popular view.—Metternich's way out of the difficulty.—Effect of the movement on Germany and Prussia.—State of Europe at outbreak of Sicilian insurrection.

THE divisions of opinion, which had been hindering progress in Hungary, had, in the meantime, been growing less prominent in Italy; so that the more active political leaders in the latter country were, for a time at least, aiming at a common programme. Yet this point had only been reached after much suffering and failure. Conspiracies with various objects had been rife in Italy, especially in the Papal States; but, though some passing attention was attracted by the cruelties exercised in their suppression, these risings had left apparently little mark on the country. But an insurrection took place in 1844 which proved a turning-point in Italian politics. The character and circumstances of the leaders excited a sympathy which impressed their memories on the hearts of their countrymen; while the failure of the rising led to a change in the general tactics of the Italian Liberals.

The rising in question was that organized by the brothers Emilio and Attilio Bandiera. These youths were the sons of a Venetian nobleman who was an admiral in the Austrian service, and who had attracted attention in 1831 by violating the terms of the capitulation of Ancona, and attempting to seize the exiles who, under protection of that treaty, were on their way to France. Emilio and Attilio had been compelled, while still boys, to enter the service of Austria; but they soon began to feel a loathing for the foreign rulers of their country; and, while in this state of mind, they came into contact with some of those who were already acting with the Giovine Italia. At last, in 1842, Attilio Bandiera wrote to Mazzini expressing the esteem and love he had learned to feel for him, his desire to co-operate with him, and his belief that the Italian cause was but a part of the cause of humanity.

This correspondence with Mazzini was maintained by means of another naval officer in the Austrian service, Domenico Moro; in the following year a passing struggle in Southern and Central Italy gave new hopes to the brothers. They fled from their ships and met Domenico Moro at Corfu. But a stronger influence than the fear of Austrian tyranny was put forward to hinder the brothers Bandiera from their attempts. Their mother wrote from Venice calling on them to return, and denouncing them as unnatural for their refusal. Even this pressure, however, they resisted, and they prepared to make their first rising in March, 1844.

The desire to free the Neapolitans, already distracted by so many insurrections, gave rise to this attempt, of which Cosenza was the head-quarters. Unfortunately, the plan of the rising had not been understood by some of the insurgents, and a preliminary effort was easily suppressed by the Neapolitan troops. Nothing daunted by this, the Bandiere planned a new march on Calabria. It was, unfortunately, on this occasion that the correspondence of the Bandiere with Mazzini was opened by the British Postmaster-General, and communicated by him to the Austrians. When, then, the brothers, accompanied by many recruits from various parts of Italy, marched upon Cosenza to deliver the prisoners who had been taken in the former unsuccessful attempt, they found guides prepared to deceive them; and in a wood near Cosenza they were met by a large body of gensdarmes, who had been warned of their coming. They repelled the attack, however, and retreated to Corfu to gather new forces; but the authorities had filled the minds of the inhabitants with the belief that the Bandiere

and their followers were Turks.  The people rose
against them; and when they again marched on
Cosenza they were easily overpowered and imprisoned,
and soon after condemned to death.  The brothers
received the news of their condemnation with cries of
" Long live Italy !  Long live Liberty !  Long live
our country!"   And, to the priests who tried to
exhort them to repentance, they answered that they
had acted in the spirit of Christ in trying to free
their brethren.

The effect of their death, and of all the circumstances of their rising, was deep and wide; and their
memory seems to have lived longer than that of any
previous martyrs for Italian freedom.  The bullets
with which they were shot were collected as sacred
relics ; and it was felt that a new impulse had been
given to the struggle against Austrian tyranny.  But
with the indignation at the treachery by which the
Bandiera brothers had suffered, and with the reverence for their memories, there arose in Italy a passing
wave of suspicion against Mazzini and the leaders of
the Giovine Italia, as people who wasted the lives
of the heroic youth of Italy in useless and ill-organized attempts.

It was at this period that two books, written in
1843, began to attract attention.  These were the
" Speranze d' Italia " of Cesare Balbo and the " Primato " of Vincenzo Gioberti.

Cesare Balbo was the son of that Count Prospero
Balbo who was supposed, in the reign of Victor
Emmanuel I., to have supplied a Liberal element to
the Government.   There had been, however, little in
Count Prospero's career to inspire any reasonable
confidence in him.  He served under Victor Amadeus

till the fall of Piedmont before the French ; but after the establishment of Napoleon's power he had returned to Piedmont and become head of the University of Turin. After the restoration of the House of Savoy he had taken office again under Victor Emmanuel, and had played the somewhat doubtful part, described above, in the movement of 1821. Cesare had been presented by his father, when a boy, to Napoleon ; and though Count Prospero had considered it a dangerous step, the young man had accepted office in Napoleon's Council of State in Turin, and subsequently had served under the same ruler in Tuscany. Although shocked at the kidnapping of Pius VII., he did not abandon the service of Napoleon until the fall of the French Empire in 1814. Yet, after the restoration of the House of Savoy, he entered the army of the King of Sardinia, and fought, first against Napoleon, and then against Murat. In 1821 he managed to remain on friendly terms with Santa Rosa, while he was at the same time advising Charles Albert to break with the Revolutionists, and was also trying to hinder the proclamation of the Spanish Constitution at Alessandria. Such was the man who now tried to tell Italy of her hopes.

While appealing to Gioberti as his master, and declaring his preference for a moderate party, Balbo dwelt on the want of national independence as the chief source of the evils of Italy, and particularly on the control exercised by the Austrians over the Pope. He urged his countrymen to put aside the old ideas of Dante, and not to go back further than 1814 for their conception of Italian Unity. He then proceeded to examine the different schemes for attaining this unity, and, rejecting alike the schemes of Monarchists and Federalists, as well as the plan for a closer unity put forward by the Republicans of the Giovine Italia, he pointed out as the only real hope for Italy the possibility of the fall of the Ottoman Empire and the consequent chance that Italy might be freed in the scramble which would follow.

It is well to dismiss this book of Balbo's first, because its only worth is that it shows what scraps of comfort were caught at eagerly by Italians at this period ; but, as a matter of fact, its publication was slightly later than that of the " Primato " of Vincenzo Gioberti, to which Balbo alludes in the preface to his book.

Gioberti has already been mentioned as having been a contributor to the journal of the Giovine Italia. Previously to that time, he had chiefly been known as a writer on ecclesiastical or theological subjects. Before the age of twenty, he had written a philosophical treatise on Man, God, and Natural Religion; and early in life he had also written on the " Wickedness of the Popes," and had tried to prove that that wickedness was due to their temporal power. At the University of Turin, the Professor to whom he looked up with the greatest reverence was driven from his post by the Jesuits, and this event awakened in Gioberti his bitter hostility to that Order. Gioberti's connection with the Giovine Italia brought him under the suspicion of the Piedmontese Government; and he was banished from the country shortly before Mazzini's expedition to Savoy.

In that expedition, however, Gioberti had refused to join; and he remained at Paris, where many of the Italian exiles were gathered. Among these, two of the most prominent were Pellegrino Rossi and

Terenzio Mamiani.   Both of these writers may have
confirmed him in his dislike of the Jesuits; though
they may also have exercised some influence in
alienating him from the Republicans.   He returned,
indeed, at this period to those philosophical writings
for which he was much better fitted than for the
active life of politics;  and, in 1842, he was offered a
Chair of Philosophy at Pisa.   But Solaro della
Margherita, the Minister of Charles Albert, succeeded
in persuading the Grand Duke of Tuscany to withdraw this appointment.   Such had been Gioberti's
career up to the time when he brought out the book
which, by a curious combination of circumstances,
was to make his name famous.

   This book, " Il Primato Morale e Civile degli
Italiani," professes to show why, and how, the
Italians should take the lead in the affairs of Europe.
The writer begins with a glorification of Italy,
though, at the same time, he complains that she has
too often neglected her mission; and he maintains, in
this connection, the necessity of combining philosophy
with political discussion.  Very early in the argument he goes back to Romulus; but, not content
with the comparative antiquity of that allusion, he
thinks it necessary to deduce the origin of civilization
from Noah.   He then considers the relation between
the Papacy and the Empire after the time of Charles
the Great, and the attitude of various Italian writers
and patriots towards the Papacy.   He incidentally
notices the fascination of Abelard for Arnold of
Brescia as one of the causes of that reformer's hostility to the Papacy, and as a warning to Italians not
to yield to the influence of French ideas.   It is to the
Guelphs that Gioberti looks for the embodiment of

the political wisdom of the Italians of the Middle Ages. Without the Papacy, there could be no real political unity for Italy, since through its influence alone could there be produced a union of morality, religion, and civilization. He deprecates all revolution, all encouragement of invasion, all imitations of foreign ideas. Unity, in the complete sense in which it was known in England and France, was, says Gioberti, an impossibility, because of differences in Government and dialect between the different States of Italy. He expresses a belief that Alfieri would have repented of his attacks on Popes and Kings if he had lived to see the dignified resistance of Pius VII. to Napoleon. The Pope would be obliged to act by peaceful means; and while forming an Italian Navy, and developing Italian colonies, he should carry on his work through a Federal Union, of which he would be the President. But, as the Pope must act by pacific means, there would be need of a military leader also for Italy; and he must be found in Piedmont. Literature had been slower in growth in Piedmont than in other parts of Italy; but in proportion to its backwardness in this respect was its superiority in military matters. Further, the House of Savoy had been softened by religion, and had never produced a tyrant. But moderate reforms were necessary in order to make the leadership palatable; especially a modification of the censorship of the Press, and greater encouragement to science and literature. In urging that Italy must take the lead of Europe, not merely in matters of civilization, but in thought, he dwells emphatically on the connection between philosophy and politics. But, above all, Italy should hold this position because she has

never fallen into the errors of Protestantism.
Passing from the independent States of Italy, he
dwells on the necessity of a union between Lombardy
and Piedmont; and then, after discussing what
qualities the different parts of Italy will contribute to
the general character of the whole, and dwelling on
the possible union among the literary men of Italy,
he concludes by insisting that religion can be the
only uniting force; and therefore that the Head of
the Christian World must be the Head of the Italian
League.

This curious book attracted considerable attention;
but although many expressed admiration for the
author, few committed themselves definitely to its
doctrines. The idea of a Pope as a liberator and
uniter of Italy clashed with all the experiences which
Italy had had of the Government of Gregory XVI.,
and Gioberti was forced to modify his words, and to
deny that he looked to the Pope then on the throne
to carry out his programme. This explanation led
him into a controversy with the Jesuits, which must
considerably have increased his popularity.

A third writer, who attracted some attention,
though far less than Balbo and Gioberti, was Giacomo
Durando, already mentioned as one of the conspirators
of 1831. He demanded a league between Peoples
and Princes, but utterly denied that any initiative of
Italian independence could come from the Pope.
His idea was a Kingdom of Italy divided into three
parts—Northern, and presumably Central, Italy to
be under the House of Savoy; the city of Rome and
some islands to be left to the Pope; and Southern
Italy to the King of Naples. He did not, however,
desire that the League should make war upon

Austria, but that it should wait, and be ready to resist attacks from that Power.

But while these writers were trying to formulate, in a literary manner, the programme of the Constitutional Liberals, the more fiery members of that party were anxious to show that they too could do something in the way of a political movement of a more determined kind; and it was in the Papal States, again, as the centre of the worst government of Italy, that this new programme of insurrection was put forward. A man named Pietro Renzi undertook to formulate the demands of this section of the party. The petition drawn up by Renzi went back to the time of Pius VII., to show that hopes of reform had once been held out, even in the Papal States. It dwelt on the fact that, from the time of the insurrections of 1821 to the death of Pius VIII. in 1831, there had been a steady growth of tyranny; that in 1831 the Papal Government would have fallen but for the intervention of Austria; that, when Gregory XVI. had been restored to his power, demands had been made for reform in the Papal Government which had been steadily opposed; that the Pope and Cardinal Albani were now encouraging robbers and murderers on the ground of the support which such men gave to the faith. " For eight or ten years past," Renzi declared, "it had not been the Pope or Rome or the Cardinals who had been governing the people of the Legations; but a sanguinary faction of the brutalized populace has been wearing the dress, and performing the functions of government." Many young men had been driven from the universities, or shut out from liberal professions, by the influence of the Jesuits ; and the clergy had usurped the con-

trol of all education. The leaders of the new
party, therefore, demanded twelve concessions.—1.
A general amnesty for all political offences from
1821 to that time.   2. Publicity of Debate ; trial
by jury, and abolition of confiscations and capital
punishment for political offences.   3. That laymen
should not be subjected either to the Inquisition nor
any other ecclesiastical tribunal.   4. That political
offences should be tried by the ordinary tribunals.
5. That municipal councils should be freely elected
subject to the approval of the Sovereign; that these
municipal councils should elect the provincial councils, and the provincial councils the Supreme Council
of State.   6. That the Supreme Council should
reside in Rome, superintending the public funds, and
should have a deliberative power in some matters, a
consultative in others.   7. That all offices, civil,
military, and judicial, should be held by laymen.
8. That public instruction, other than religious,
should be taken away from the clergy.   9. That the
censorship of the Press should be only employed in
the case of offences against God, the Catholic Religion,
and the Sovereign, and the private life of citizens.
10. That foreign troops should be dismissed.   11.
That the Civic Guard should be instituted, and entrusted with the maintenance of the laws and of
public order.   12. That the Government should enter
on all those social reforms which are required by the
spirit of the age, and of which all the *civil* governments of Europe have given an example.

Renzi resolved to enforce this programme by a
sudden attack on Rimini, in which he was completely successful; but an ally of his, who had raised
a revolt simultaneously in the lower Romagna, was

compelled to retire before the Swiss troops of the
Pope; and Renzi, apparently panic struck, retreated
into Tuscany.  Unfortunately, a reaction was then
taking place there.  Fossombroni had died in 1844,
Corsini, the Minister who was most in sympathy
with Fossombroni's policy, resigned in 1845; and the
chief of the Jesuit party took his place.  The Grand
Duke Leopold himself was at first disposed to be
friendly to Renzi; but, as the best protection to him,
he advised his escape to France.  Renzi soon returned,
and Metternich, alarmed at the intensity of Italian
feeling, denounced the Duke for protecting rebels,
and, under the influence of Austrians, Jesuits, and of
the Pope, Leopold consented to surrender Renzi to
Gregory XVI.

The attention of the country was still further
directed to this attempt by a pamphlet which came
out immediately after, and which was written by a
young Piedmontese nobleman, Count Massimo
Tapparelli D'Azeglio.  In this pamphlet D'Azeglio
complained that the Rimini movement had been
much misrepresented; but that the action of the
insurgents had no doubt been a blunder, because the
movement had been purely local, and they had not
considered how to use the forces of the whole of
Italy.  He then proceeded to denounce the corruptions of the Papal Government, and the cruelties
which had followed the suppression of this rising;
particularly the gross injustice of imprisoning a
lawyer because he had defended some of the prisoners.
After a denunciation in detail of the evils of the
Papal Government, he goes on to repudiate the use
of secret societies, as having failed in their purpose ;
calls on the Italians to unite in peaceable protest

against abuses, rather than in insurrection; and points to the Tugendbund of Germany as a model for Italian combinations. The pamphlet had little that was new in it, but attention was fixed upon the author, by the fact that he was immediately banished from Tuscany by the Grand Duke, and was, shortly after, welcomed in Piedmont.

Metternich's protest against this welcome might have been more decided had he not been hampered by the events which were occurring in Galicia. Ever since the insurrection of 1830, there had been a steady feeling of sympathy towards the Poles, not merely as an oppressed nation, but as *the* nation whose restoration was the chief duty and necessity of the champions of liberty. Kossuth declared, at a somewhat later time, that there was a close connection between the liberties of Hungary and those of Poland. Mazzini had been eager to co-operate, where it was possible, with the exiled Poles. Robert Blum had shown a special enthusiasm for their cause, and was ready to help in a rising in Posen. Every Slavonic race looked on the wrongs of the Poles as the typical instance of the oppression of the Slavs by the Great Powers of Europe; while, at the same time, they honoured them as the most famous fighters in the cause of Slavonic freedom. But it was in France that the greatest enthusiasm was felt for the Poles, and the most complete organization of the exiles existed. There a special military school was founded for them in 1843; and in 1846, after a preparation of three years, the democratic section among the Poles resolved to strike a decisive blow against Austria.

The city of Cracow, on the borders of Galicia, was

K

the one part of Poland which still maintained a nominal freedom. The political independence of Cracow had been secured by the Treaty of Vienna. The Austrian Government even then wished to absorb it into their own dominions; but, under pressure from Russia, Francis consented that Cracow should be a free town, governed by its own elected Chamber of Representatives, and surrounded by a district which was not to be occupied by Austrian troops; and it was also to exercise complete control over its army and police. The usual Austrian interpretation of liberty, however, was soon to be applied to the Republic of Cracow. Although free trade between Cracow and Warsaw had been secured by a regular treaty, the protecting Powers, as they were called (Austria, Russia, and Prussia), began soon to insist on prohibitive duties being introduced on the frontiers of Cracow. Its University, dating from the fourteenth century, had been secured in its properties and liberties by the Treaty of Vienna; but, unfortunately, a large portion of the lands from which the University drew its income lay within the dominions of the three protecting Powers, each of whom refused, under various pretexts, to give up its share of the land. As to the liberties of the University, the Austrian Government, in 1817, had declared that it would inflict a fine of 100 ducats on any parent who sent his sons to the University of Cracow; in 1822, the Russian Government followed this example by a decree forbidding Polish youths to study in any foreign country, under which title they specially included Cracow. In the meantime, the organizing Commission, which had been appointed by the Powers, was gradually destroying the Constitu-

tion which had been established by the Treaty of
Vienna.   The right to modify laws sent from the
Senate was first taken from the Chamber of Representatives; while, as to the control of the finances,
which had been specially mentioned in the Treaty,
the House of Representatives was informed that the
accounts were only to be shown to the Chamber in
order to convince them that the Senate had spent the
money, and that the Treasury was empty; though
the Commission graciously allowed the Chamber to
examine and make observations on the accounts, and
assured them that these observations should be sent
to the Senate.  The self-government of the University
was, in a similar manner, gradually taken from it;
and, under the excuse of a riot in 1820, the
great Powers, six years later, sent a Russian colonel
to act as supreme ruler of the University.    The insurrection of 1830 in Warsaw had, of course, given
excuse for further interference with the liberties of
Cracow; and, in 1831, Russian soldiers, for a time,
occupied the city.   It is hardly necessary to add that
the liberty of the Press, which had been specially
guaranteed by the Treaty of Vienna, had been
gradually crushed out; and a new Commission,
appointed by the three Powers in 1833, revised the
Constitution of Cracow, thereby setting aside the
claims of England and France to have their opinions
considered in any revision of the Treaty.   Torture
was revived for the purpose of extorting revelations
of crimes which had never been committed.   The
judges had, indeed, retained, for a time, the independence secured them by the Treaty; but in March,
1837, the Conference, as it was called, of the three
Powers abolished the offices of Mayors of the Com-

mune and Judges of First Instance, and transferred
their duties to officers of police.   In December of the
same year, the protecting Powers decided that the
question of the amount to be expended on the police
and militia should not be submitted to the Chamber.
Then the Chamber, at last, attempted an appeal to
the two Powers whose opinions had been wholly
ignored by the other signatories to the Treaty of
Vienna; but the appeal was, apparently, in vain, and
there seemed no remedy left but insurrection.

The centralizing principles of the Austrian Government, on this as on later occasions, paralyzing their
power of action in emergencies, Cracow was seized
and occupied by the democratic leader Tyssowski.
The Government Boards in Galicia were little able to
make head against the movement; and, if Tyssowski
had known how to appeal to the popular sympathies,
he might have been completely successful.  Unfortunately, however, the leaders of the insurrection
had not yet been able to establish that sympathy with
the peasantry of Galicia which alone would have
enabled them to carry out a really popular insurrection; and, instead of trying to enlist the sympathies
and interest of the peasants on behalf of the movement, Tyssowski's only idea was to terrorize them
into obedience.   He issued a proclamation, announcing that the whole Empire, during the time of revolution, is one and common property in the hands of the
revolutionary Government.  Every priest who opposed
the rising was to be deprived of his office; anyone who
refused to subscribe to the national cause was to be
seized and brought before a Governor chosen by the
insurgents; every inhabitant, on pain of death, was to
go to the place appointed him, as soon as he knew of

the outbreak of the insurrection. The peasantry, alarmed at hearing that many of them had been condemned to death for their unreadiness to assist the revolution, appealed to the officials to defend them; nor could they be conciliated by hearing that the insurgents were about to abolish all feudal dues and titles of rank, and to secure a certain amount of land to every peasant. These offers from unknown people could not induce the peasants to make friends with those who were threatening them with death. From more than seventy districts representatives came from the peasants to the official authorities at Tarnow to ask for military help against the revolutionary leaders; and they were advised to defend themselves and to arrest the agitators. On February 18th, 1846, the insurrection broke out, and one of the first actions of the conspirators was to fire on the peasants who had refused to join them. Then the peasants, stirred to desperation, rose; and a general massacre of the nobles began. The dark and underground methods of the Austrian Government, and the centralizing principle which had drained out the strength of the different local governments, had brought a double Nemesis on its founders. For while on the one hand the powerlessness of the local boards caused the early successes of the insurgents, on the other hand the world at large thought that the massacre of the nobles of Galicia must have been organized from Vienna, as a part of the regular Austrian policy.* This belief was likely to be

---

* I feel that some explanation is needed for the rejection of what was once one of the most deeply-rooted traditions among all Liberals who interested themselves in the politics of this period. I must, therefore, state that my chief authority for my

further strengthened by the events which followed. While Mieroslawski and some of the leaders of the insurrection surrendered to the Prussian troops, which had been despatched to prevent a rising in Silesia and Posen, Metternich struck the final blow at the independence of Cracow.   The account given above shows that there was little independence left to be destroyed in that unfortunate city; but somehow the actual destruction of liberties never excites so general a horror, especially in the diplomatic world, as the final removal of the *forms* of liberty. And Lord Palmerston, who does not seem to have responded to the previous appeal from the Assembly of Cracow, now addressed indignant remonstrances to Metternich, and uttered the remarkable words, " If the treaties of 1815 are null on the Vistula, they may be null on the Rhine and the Po."

 Thus the occupation of Cracow seemed to many to be an abandonment by Metternich of the semi-legal position which till then he had, in the eyes of diplomatists, maintained; while his supposed complicity in the massacre in Galicia roused against him the feelings of those humanitarians who do not understand the wickedness of choking out the moral and intellectual life of a nation, but who shrink with horror from any physical cruelty.   It is, therefore, no unnatural inference that the delay which Metternich showed in making any stern protest against Charles Albert's new position in Italy may have been due to the

account of the paralysis of the Austrian Government in the Galician insurrection, and their consequent innocence of any organized massacre, is Dr. Herbst, the well-known leader of the German Liberals in the Austrian Reichstag, who was in Galicia at the time of the insurrection.

paralysis caused by the storm of indignation roused
against Austria by the Galician massacres and the
annexation of Cracow. Charles Albert profited by
this weakness. He had been shifting as usual in his
policy, encouraged on the one side in moderate
reforms by the Liberal minister, Villamarina, and
dragged, on the other side, into extreme clericalism
by Solaro della Margherita. But, just about the time
when D'Azeglio arrived in Piedmont, events were
occurring which riveted on Charles Albert the hopes
of many who had not hitherto believed in the sincerity
of his desire for reform; and the same circumstances
gave him that position of champion of Italian independence which, in the eyes of perhaps a majority of
Italians, he continued to maintain till the fall of
Milan in 1848. The chief cause of this change of
feeling is to be found in the following circumstance.

In the year 1751 a treaty had been made between
Austria and Piedmont by which the former granted
to the latter the right of sending through Lombardy
the salt which they were selling to the Republic of
Venice. In consideration of this boon the King of
Sardinia renounced his trade with the Swiss cantons;
and the treaty was renewed in 1815, after Venice had
passed under the Austrian rule. In 1846 Ticino,
desiring to open a trade in salt with Marseilles,
asked the Piedmontese Government to allow them to
transmit their salt through Piedmont, and Charles
Albert consented.

The Austrian Government had for some time past
looked with suspicion on Charles Albert. Metternich
had never forgotten his passing outburst of Liberalism in 1821; and the continual search of the Italian
Liberals for some leader in the War of Independence

was naturally drawing people's eyes to Piedmont.
Few, and comparatively unimportant, as were the reforms that he introduced, they were enough to increase
the suspicions of Metternich; and, reformer or not, the
King of Sardinia was necessarily an enemy to the
House of Austria.   Moreover, Charles Albert had
recently given a tolerably clear hint of his own feelings; for he had struck a medal representing a lion
(the well-known badge of the House of Savoy) trampling on an eagle; and on the reverse side of the medal
appeared, " *J'attends mon astre.*"

The concession to the Canton Ticino lighted the
spark which had been smouldering in the breasts of
the Austrian rulers.   For of all the States of Europe,
this little canton had become specially obnoxious to
Austria in the last few years; and not long before
this Metternich and Charles Albert had worked
together to stamp out its freedom, and deprive it of
the right of sheltering those Italian exiles who were
dear to the Italian-Swiss from similarity in race and
language.   Metternich had failed in that effort, and
the Liberals had risen in the canton and overthrown
the Conservative Government and Austrian influence
together.   Any sign, therefore, of friendliness shown
by Charles Albert to the Ticinese was a special cause
of alarm to the Austrians.   They declared at once
that the treaty of 1751 had been violated; in April,
1846, they increased the custom duties on the wine
sent from Piedmont to Lombardy; and in order to
mark the hostility of the Act more plainly the same
decree declared that there would be no change with
regard to the wines coming from several of the other
Italian States.

Solaro della Margherita, though his Conservatism

naturally inclined him to sympathize with the Austrian Government, was a man who valued the independence and dignity of Piedmont; and he therefore consented to Charles Albert's proposal at once to lower the duties between Piedmont and France, in order to facilitate the commerce between those countries. The meaning of this act could not be misunderstood; and the Austrian ambassador, alarmed at the sudden defiance, made a proposal to recall the duty on Piedmontese wines, on condition that Charles Albert would consent to withdraw his concession to Ticino. Solaro della Margherita, in his anxiety for a friendly understanding with Austria, did not perceive that such a concession would give up the whole principle at stake, since it would admit the right of Austria to forbid Charles Albert to make what terms he pleased with the canton; so Solaro actually urged the King to agree to the proposal. But Charles Albert stood firm, and, greatly to Margherita's horror, D'Azeglio succeeded in persuading the people to get up a demonstration in Turin, at which cries were heard of " Long live the King of Italy!"

Charles Albert, however, though showing some signs of his usual irresolution, did not draw back from his policy of hostility to Austria; and he set himself to promote a railway which should connect Lombardy and Venetia more closely with Piedmont. The Austrians made some difficulty with regard to this railway, and it was on this occasion apparently that the point was carried against the rulers of Lombardy, to a great extent, by the energies of a Venetian lawyer, Daniele Manin, a name afterwards memorable in the records of Venice. In the meantime D'Azeglio had been working hard to convince the rest of Italy that

Charles Albert was preparing to put himself at the head of an Italian movement and to attack Lombardy. In Tuscany Professor Montanelli had already formed a Society for promoting the unity of Italy. Demonstrations were being made against the Jesuits, and petitions for changes in taxation and education were drawn up.

But it was in the Papal States that D'Azeglio most hoped to gain ground; and in Forli he came in contact with Aurelio Saffi, who, with D'Azeglio's encouragement, prepared an address from the people of Forli to one of the clerical rulers, calling attention to the growth of Italian feeling and the desire for action against the foreigner. The authorities became alarmed and Saffi's arrest and imprisonment were determined on, when the death of Gregory XVI. suddenly changed the whole position of affairs; and Charles Albert's newly-won fame was for a time dimmed by that of another hero of the popular imagination; while Gioberti's teaching, hitherto admired only in a small circle, and laughed at by many, was suddenly accepted as the utterance of an inspired prophet, and as embodying the conception of a profound statesman.

The state of Roman government at the death of Gregory XVI. was as follows:—The management of affairs was entirely in the hands of cardinals, or of laymen appointed by the Pope. The nobles and the rich were indeed conciliated to some extent by appointments which seemed a concession to lay feeling. The provincial councils, nominated by the Pope, laid taxes partly on property and partly on articles of consumption. The study of political economy was prohibited in the schools; and the study of law and medicine was but little provided for.

The press was under a triple censorship, that of the Inquisition, of the Bishop, and of the Governor of the province. The police, though vigorous in repressing political conspirators, were utterly unable to check highway robbery. In the tribunals which were administered by the clergy, the grossest corruptions prevailed. As a natural result of all this, the ablest and best men of the States were to be found, not in Rome, but some in France, some in Tuscany, and some in Piedmont. The government of Rome and its immediate neighbourhood was corrupt; and the government of the Legations in some cases became so cruel as to excite shame even in the Pope himself. And Monsignore Savelli, one of the worst of these tyrants, had been guilty of such a combination of corruption and cruelty that Gregory had been compelled to remove him from office.

Such was the state of affairs when Gregory XVI. died. Tremendous expectation was roused in the different provinces of the Papal States; an insurrection broke out in Ancona; and a colonel, who had distinguished himself for cruelty in that town, was killed. The cardinals at once despatched Savelli to suppress the rising. In the meantime the Conclave met, and the ambassadors of the different Powers began to intrigue for their respective candidates. Cardinal Lambruschini was one of the most powerful members of the sacred college; but he was hated for his injustice and partisan distribution of offices; and no sooner had the Conclave opened than attacks were made on him by Cardinal Micara, on this very ground. Lambruschini had been appointed by the influence of the Austrian Court, and might have been supposed to be their candidate. But whether it were that even the Austrians desired certain concessions to the policy of reform, which they had themselves supported after the rising of 1831, or whether it were that their influence was weakened by the events which had recently occurred in Galicia, they do not seem to have used very great pressure on behalf of Lambruschini.

On the other hand, there had recently arrived in Rome, as French ambassador, that same Pellegrino Rossi who had formerly been driven into exile by the success of the Austrians in 1815, who had contributed to the Conciliatore of Confalonieri, and who had played so important and influential a part among the Italian exiles in Paris. Rossi declared in favour of reform in the church, and demanded the election of someone who both wished and knew how to reform prudently and efficiently. The person naturally marked out as the candidate of the Liberals was Cardinal Gizzi, who had been known for milder government than that of any of the other Cardinals, and who had been singled out for exceptional praise by Massimo D'Azeglio. But where a bitter conflict of interests arises between the leading candidates, it is only natural that some unknown man should slip in; and, as the reformers were probably more in earnest and more united than the majority of the opponents of reform, other Liberal candidates were withdrawn; Giovanni Mastai Ferretti was elected Pope on June 16th, 1846, and, out of respect for Pius VII., took the name of Pius IX.

He was then fifty-four years old and had been originally intended for the Papal guard; but, being liable to epileptic fits, he had been refused admission. He had thereupon become a priest, and had, as

already mentioned, distinguished himself in 1831 by
the honesty with which he had carried out the terms
of the surrender of Imola.   He was so little known,
however, to the general public that a rumour arose,
after his election, that it was really Cardinal Gizzi
who had been chosen.   Nor were his future opponents startled at the choice.   Princess Metternich
wrote of him in her diary that he was a man of
exemplary piety, *" toute fois sans être exalté."*   Nor
was it till a month later that Pio Nono took the step
which was the foundation of his future popularity.
It was then that he issued a general amnesty in
favour of all those who had been condemned for
political offences.   The amnesty, indeed, was carefully guarded; for only those were admitted to it
who would sign a declaration confessing their previous offences, and promising future improvement.
Mamiani and others refused to sign this declaration,
and it would have been obvious to anyone who had
thought over the question that this was a demand
which could not be accepted by any men of spirit
and consistency.   But men's minds had been excited
by previous events; and the teaching of Gioberti led,
not only the Romans, but Italians in all parts of the
peninsula, to place a meaning upon this amnesty
which was certainly not intended by the Pope himself.   This belief in the reforming intentions of the
Pope was further increased by the bitter hostility
that he excited in that extreme party which had
thriven under Gregory XVI., and which was urged
on by Lambruschini, who, in his disappointed ambition, began to throw discredit on the election of his
rival and to plot against his authority.

The appointment of Cardinal Gizzi as Secretary of

State roused the hopes of the Liberals still further, and commissions were appointed to examine into the question of reforms. Yet Gizzi, who was the only cardinal with the most remote claims to the confidence of the Liberals, does not seem to have desired anything more than some slight administrative reforms. And it may be doubted whether the enthusiasm for Pius IX. would long have been sustained, had it not been fostered and directed by a man of a very different type from any of the philosophical writers on the politics of Italy.

This was Angelo Brunetti, better known by his nickname of Ciceruacchio. He was a man of poor birth, and simple habits, who by hard work had made a certain amount of money, while, by personal beauty, a peculiar kind of eloquence, and a thorough honesty of character, he had gained a special influence among the poorer classes in Rome. A kind of imaginative enthusiasm had evidently possessed his whole mind; and this was kindled to the highest degree by the idea of a reforming Pope. It was to Ciceruacchio, then, rather than to any utterance of the Pope himself, that the popular conception of Pius IX. was due. A kindly priest, wishing to do more justice than his predecessors, was reflected in Ciceruacchio's mirror as the liberator and reformer of Italy. The myth quickly grew. Demonstrations in honour of the Pope were organized by Ciceruacchio; and, as each new difficulty or hindrance arose in the path of progress, he was ready to assure his countrymen that these hindrances were all due to the wicked cardinals, and that Pius IX. was eager to remove them. And so, while the other princes of Italy were being asked to concede various limitations on their power, in Rome was heard continually the cry of "Viva Pio Nono Solo."

Thus it came about that this quiet and unpretending priest found himself magnified in the popular imagination into a leader of heroic proportions, half saint, half crusader. It was impossible for him to resist altogether the fervour of popular enthusiasm, and it soon spread far beyond the limits of the Roman State. In December, 1846, a Congress, nominally intended for scientific discussion, met at Genoa. These congresses had already begun to give opportunity for the expression of political opinion, and two circumstances tended to increase the importance of this particular meeting. One was, that 1846 was the centenary of the expulsion of the Austrians from Genoa, at the close of their temporary occupation during the Austrian War of Succession. The other was the presence in this Congress of Charles Lucien Buonaparte, Prince of Canino. He had already gained some reputation as a student of physical science, but his interest in politics was even greater than his zeal for learning; and he now came to the Congress to invite the men of science to carry on their discussions in the Papal States. From this he naturally passed to the praise of Pius IX. and of Charles Albert, and to the denunciation of Austria and Metternich.

Such an oration, especially when delivered on a non-political occasion, naturally excited the alarm of the Austrian Government; and that alarm was still further increased by the reappearance in Lombardy of the old feeling of irritation against Austrian rule. An attempt on the part of the Austrian Government to seize upon the funds of the Benevolent Societies of Lombardy, in order to appropriate them for their own purposes, had caused such a storm of indignation in the provincial Lombard Councils, that the Government had been compelled to withdraw the proposal. And as if this awakening of life had not been sufficiently significant, it was followed in December, 1846, by a still more alarming sign of popular feeling.

Count Confalonieri had been released from the prison at Spielberg by Ferdinand on his accession to the throne in 1835, but had been deprived of his civil rights, and sent to America. The news now reached Milan that, hearing of the new hopes aroused by the accession of Pius IX., Confalonieri had set sail for Italy, but had died on the way. Instantly a demonstration was organized in his honour, and Count Gabrio Casati, Podestà of Milan, took part in the funeral procession. Bolza, one of the group of Austrian officials who ruled Milan, took note of all who attended the ceremony ; and when it was followed by a proposal to form a committee for erecting a statue to Confalonieri, Bolza threatened to prohibit the committee altogether. He was not, however, able to hinder the growing popular feeling in Milan, and early in the following year, 1847, the bitterness was increased by a famine. Grain riots followed; and the Governor of Milan, as the only method for relieving the distress, prohibited the export of grain to foreign parts, except to the German provinces of Austria. Again that terrible canton of the Ticino protested against this infringement of a commercial treaty, made between herself and Austria ; and again the Austrian Government was compelled to yield, and to re-open the grain

trade with the Ticinese. Hymns to Pio Nono were
answered with cheers in the Milanese theatre; while
the Viceroy and his family were received, in the
same theatre, in dead silence.

In the meantime, Pio Nono's reforms, if not important, were numerous. On March 12th, 1847,
came out a modification of the censorship of the
press, of which the most important point was that
the censorship was to be administered in future by
four laymen and one ecclesiastic. On April 14th,
a Council of State was formed, to be chosen by the
Pope from delegates elected by the provinces; and
this Council was to be allowed to propound opinions
on certain questions of State. Finally, on July 5th,
the Pope granted a civic guard to Rome, and promised one to the provinces.

Metternich had now become thoroughly alarmed,
and, whether he sanctioned or not the attempt which
was now made in Rome, there seems to be little
doubt that the friends of Lambruschini did actually
organize a conspiracy against the Pope. The anniversary of the amnesty of 1846 was the occasion of
the discovery of this conspiracy. A popular demonstration had been prepared in honour of the day;
but when the organizers of this demonstration appeared, their first act was to call out the civic guard
to arrest the conspirators. Ciceruacchio paraded
the streets, attended by a great number of people.
Several of the conspirators were seized and imprisoned, others fled, and none attempted any resistance.

How far Metternich had sympathized with this
conspiracy can never be known ; but its failure
seemed to decide him to strike the blow which he

had been meditating.  It has already been mentioned that the Austrians had succeeded in introducing into the Treaty of Vienna a clause, permitting them to occupy some part of Ferrara.  Pius VII. had protested against this, as an injury to the Holy See. Cardinal Consalvi had expressed this protest in the following words:—" This clause," he said, " is an unprovoked aggression, deprived of all that could make a war legitimate under the rights of nations; an aggression against a weak and innocent State, which had solemnly proclaimed its neutrality in the war that agitates other States; an act outside every human right; and a treaty that is the consequence of an aggression of such a kind is essentially null and void."

Such a protest, and the fact that it was disregarded, emphasized the important truth that treaty rights, as understood in Europe, are simply the rights of the strong to divide the territories of the weak. Pius IX. had committed no act of aggression against Austria; and nothing new had arisen to justify the enforcement of a clause which had been allowed to remain in abeyance so long.  When the Powers of Europe had desired to compel Gregory XVI. to reform his dominions after the insurrection of 1831, Metternich had shrunk, with holy horror, from the idea of putting pressure on an independent Prince ; but now that Pius IX. had introduced reforms far short of those recommended by the Powers in 1833, Metternich seized the opportunity to despatch Austrian forces to Ferrara.

A cry of indignation arose from all parts of Italy. The Milanese seized the opportunity of the appointment of an Italian Archbishop of Milan to organize an Italian demonstration. A league was formed for commercial purposes between Rome, Sardinia, and Tuscany; and it was supposed that Pius IX. and Charles Albert would declare war upon Austria. Neither of those Princes, however, were ready for the emergency. Pius IX. hardly knew yet what attitude he should take up towards the Italian movement. Charles Albert was as usual hesitating between different policies. But fortunately, besides the moral objections to the occupation of Ferrara, it appeared that there were diplomatic doubts about the interpretation of the clause which excused it. And, while the mere cowardice and injustice of an insult to a weak State might have passed unavenged, the wrong interpretation of the word "*place*" in the clause of a treaty could not be permitted without a protest.

Lord Palmerston, however, had shown on more than one occasion his loathing of the policy of Metternich; and he was doubtless glad enough of this diplomatic excuse for forwarding the cause of Constitutional Liberty. Lord Minto was despatched to Italy to encourage the various princes to stand firm in the cause of reform; and in December, 1847, the Austrian troops consented to withdraw from Ferrara, after having succeeded, by their occupation of it, in consolidating against them an amount of Italian feeling such as they had hardly aroused till then.

The first and most startling expression of this feeling, and of the consequent determination of the Italians to break loose from Austrian influence, came from a prince whom Metternich had probably hardly recognized as an opponent. Leopold of Tuscany,

however much disposed to avoid collision with his
kinsman, the Emperor of Austria, could not altogether free himself from the rush of reforming zeal
which was spreading through Italy.  That triumph
of Austrian and Papal policy in Tuscany, which had
been signalized by the surrender of Renzi and the
expulsion of Massimo d'Azeglio, had lasted a comparatively short period, and even during that period
the reaction had not been complete.  The influence of
the Jesuits had increased in Tuscany after the fall of
Corsini, and that influence has always excited an
hostility which no other form of tyranny has produced;
and the University of Pisa, under the influence of
Cosimo Ridolfi, was specially zealous in protesting
against their influence.  As Ridolfi gained ground in
Leopold's Council, Metternich had become alarmed,
and tried to counteract his influence and to drive
him from office.  Leopold, however, refused to yield to
this pressure, and, as the reforming movement spread,
he advanced further and further in his sympathies
with Italian freedom.  Freedom of the press was
granted; many new journals were started; and when
the civic guard was conceded, great demonstrations
were held in Florence, and an attempt was made to
revive the memories of Francesco Ferruccio and
other heroes of the past.  Professor Montanelli,
already known as a writer, now took a prominent
part in the political movement, organized a deputation to Pius IX. to entreat him to grant liberty of
the press, to expel the Jesuits, and to declare war
upon Austria.  Domenico Guerrazzi, who had assisted
at the foundation of Young Italy, seconded the efforts
of Montanelli, and Leopold became, almost against
his will, marked out as a reforming sovereign.

The movement now spread beyond Tuscany and affected the dominions of the Duke of Lucca. This Duke was one of those eccentric princes who combined despotism and a reliance on Austria with a certain love of playing at Liberalism with foreign exiles. This game was not carried on with any of those ambitious objects which had led Francis of Modena to play with rebellion in 1831; but it rather arose from a love of clever literary lions, coupled with those tendencies to eccentricity which might be natural to a prince with no great responsibilities and a certain amount of cleverness. When, however, the Liberal movement spread to Lucca, he dropped his dilettantism and proposed to suppress Liberalism by force. Finding that the people rose against him, he consented to yield all which Leopold of Tuscany had granted; but his subjects were unwilling to trust a prince who was the ruler of so small a State under the influence of Austria, and who had only yielded to reform under sudden pressure; so they continued to make further demands. The Duke, weary of the struggle, and very likely desirous to avoid bloodshed, took advantage of a clause in the Treaty of Vienna which constituted the Grand Duke of Tuscany his heir, and resigned his dominions forthwith to Leopold. At the same time, he desired to exempt from this surrender the two towns of Pontremoli and Bagnone and to hand them over to the Duke of Modena. Leopold accepted the territory of Lucca; but, by the same clause which had constituted him the heir to the Duke of Lucca, he was bound, on acquiring the territory, to surrender to the Duke of Modena the district of Fivizzano. Now, of all the princes of Italy, none had been more utterly subservient to

Austria than the Duke of Modena, and the people of Fivizzano therefore resented the proposal to annex them to Modena. The Duke of Modena thereupon called on the Austrian Marshal Radetzky to help him to enforce his demands; and, while Leopold of Tuscany was preparing to fix a day for the surrender of Fivizzano, the Duke of Modena marched his troops into the town and massacred the unarmed inhabitants.

Both the Pope and the Grand Duke protested against this cruelty; and Leopold, wishing to keep Fivizzano in consequence of the people's preference for his rule, offered to make Charles Albert and the Pope arbiters between him and the Duke of Modena. In the meantime the citizens of Pontremoli and Bagnone sprang to arms in order to resist the entrance of the Duke of Modena. The Austrians had by this time sent forces to assist the Duke; but though they were able to secure the submission of Fivizzano, the Duke of Modena was forced to surrender Pontremoli and Bagnone. Less than a fortnight after this treaty the Duchess of Parma died, and the Duke of Lucca succeeded to her territory. Here he immediately found himself confronted by a new insurrection; but, unwilling to trouble himself further, he fled to Milan, leaving the Austrian troops to occupy Parma. This occupation and the despatch of forces to Modena tended to strengthen the bitterness which had already been roused by the occupation of Ferrara, so that, when the Austrians consented to the evacuation of that town, they merely incurred the shame of a diplomatic defeat without lessening the causes of Italian bitterness against them.

But the evacuation of Ferrara was not the only

diplomatic defeat which the year 1847 brought to Metternich. The blow which was to be recognized by all Europe as one of the most fatal which the cause of despotism had yet sustained was to come from a little State which seemed to stand outside the ordinary politics of Europe.

The territory of the Swiss Confederation had been increased by the Treaty of 1815; but this had by no means led to such a complete strengthening of Switzerland as the most patriotic Swiss would have desired. The aristocratic party had been restored in several of the cantons, and the customs duties on the frontiers of the separate cantons had been renewed. But what specially alarmed the Liberals of Switzerland was a clause, which the Papal Nuncio had introduced into the Treaty of Vienna, giving the monasteries of Switzerland an independent position. It must be remembered that the early struggles of the Swiss cantons against the House of Austria had been connected with the throwing off of the influence of the monks, who had been patronized by the Hapsburgs; and in the sixteenth, seventeenth and eighteenth centuries the combination of the Roman Catholic cantons had tended to strengthen the influence of foreign Powers in Switzerland, and in some cases had even endangered the unity of the Confederation. The extreme Roman Catholic party in Switzerland were, therefore, naturally inclined to oppose reform, and to weaken the Confederation. And after the July Monarchy of France had begun to show its Conservative tendencies, the Liberals of Switzerland began to fear that their reforms might be checked by outside influence. As early as the year 1831, Metternich, already alarmed at the Polish and Belgian

risings, as well as at the movements in Italy and
Germany, remarked that there was still another
question to which the Cabinets must devote their
attention, "the moral anarchy which reigns in Switzerland." And the expedition of Mazzini in 1833-4
increased the alarm of the Austrian Government. In
the steady-going canton of Bern there was always an
element of moderate Conservatism, which led the
Government to shrink from sympathy with the insurrectionary plans of other parts of Europe; and
they even called upon the other cantons to assist
them in suppressing the revolutionary movement.
But the sturdier Liberals of Zurich protested against
this circular, and led the way in internal democratic
changes, in which they were followed by several
other cantons. Utterances like those of Metternich
tended to draw the reformers together; and in March,
1832, while Metternich was no doubt meditating the
Frankfort Decrees, which he carried out a few months
later, the seven Liberal cantons formed a league in
which they bound themselves to stand by each other
in case of an attack on their freedom.

The cantons which entered into this concordat
were Bern, Zurich, Luzern, Solothurn, St. Gallen,
Aargau, and Thurgau. This league was considered
by its opponents to be a violation of the Swiss Confederation, though the champions of it would probably
have pleaded its purely defensive character. But the
Roman Catholic party felt themselves justified in re-
taliation; and they formed, in November, 1832, an
opposition league called the Sarnerbund. This Bund
steadily set itself to oppose reform; but the men of
Schwytz, who were at that time its leading spirits,
did not confine themselves to argument, but invaded

Luzern in 1833. Thereupon the Diet interfered, occupied Schwytz, and dissolved the Sarnerbund. The reforming party now began to spread their ideas, and the new University of Zurich, which was founded at this time, became a fresh centre of intellectual life. The fugitives from other countries gathered more and more to Switzerland, and the excitement roused in that country by Mazzini's expedition to Savoy led to the foundation of a society called Young Europe.

The great object to which the reforming party in Switzerland now devoted its attention was the breaking down of the authority of the clergy, and the placing education and marriage under the State instead of under the Church. Their scheme was embodied in fourteen articles which excited the indignation of the Roman Catholic cantons; on the appeal of the Roman Catholics to Gregory XVI., he declared these articles heretical; and a little later Louis Philippe intervened to prevent the canton of Bern from enforcing them in the Roman Catholic district of the Jura.

The struggle had now risen to great bitterness; and, at this period, the bitterness was much intensified by the domestic character of the quarrel. The Radical party and the Roman Catholic party struggled fiercely against each other in several of the cantons; and there were changes in the government, backwards and forwards, which temporarily affected the contest. The two changes, however, which were of a permanent character, and which had a vital effect on the destinies of Switzerland, were that which took place in 1838 in Bern and that in Luzern in 1841. Bern, though reckoned, on the whole, among

the Liberal cantons, in consequence of its undoubted
Protestantism, was yet under the control of a timid
and moderate party. This may have arisen from the
fact of its important position in the Confederation;
for though Bern divided at this time with Luzern and
Zurich the honour of being the meeting-place of the
Diet, yet it seems to have assumed, even at this
period, a certain superior and initiative tone.

Whether it was due to the sense of responsibility
inspired by this position, or to some other cause,
certain it is that the tone adopted by the Government
of Bern in matters of foreign policy by no means
satisfied the sterner Radicals of Switzerland. The
proposal of Bern for an anti-revolutionary proclamation in 1830 had been defeated by the protest of
Zurich; but when in 1838 Bern considered, not un-
favourably, the demand for the expulsion of a refugee,
the Radicals became furious.

This was one among many instances of that curious
irony of history by which great principles have to be
asserted in defence of persons who are in themselves
unworthy of protection; for the exile, whose surrender was now demanded by Louis Philippe, was
Louis Napoleon Buonaparte, who had recently made
his attempt on Strasburg. But the Radicals of Bern
rightly felt that the principle of asylum was more
important than the character of any particular refugee;
and when Louis Napoleon left Switzerland to avoid
being surrendered, the reforming party rose in indignation, and Bern became the centre of determined
Radicalism from that time. The change in Luzern
seems to have been due to an extension of the suffrage
which threw the power more distinctly into the hands
of the Roman Catholics, who were a majority in the

canton; and thus Luzern became the centre of the Roman Catholic movement.

But before that change had taken place, new elements of bitterness had been introduced into the discussion. Neuhaus, the new leader of the Bern Government, had been chosen president of the Confederation; and he had used the troops of the Confederation to help the Aargau Protestants in suppressing the monasteries in that canton. The majority of the Swiss Diet had, however, been unwilling to support Neuhaus in this action, and had even condemned the suppression of the Aargau monasteries. The Aargau Protestants, however, had refused to yield, except as to the restoration of two very small monasteries. The feeling on both sides had now risen to its highest point, and on September 13th, 1843, the six cantons of Luzern, Uri, Schwytz, Unterwalden, Zug, and Freyburg formed the alliance known as the Sonderbund. They appealed to the old treaties on which the Confederation was founded, and maintained that even the terms of the Confederation fixed by the Treaty of Vienna had not been observed in the matter of the protection of the rights of the Roman Catholics.

The compromise to which the Diet had assented in the Aargau question, and their non-interference on behalf of some monasteries at Thurgau, excited a special protest from the Sonderbund, and they demanded that the Diet should set these things to rights. So far the Sonderbund could scarcely be logically condemned by those who had joined the Protestant Concordat of Seven in 1832. But the Roman Catholic cantons went on to say that, if their demands were rejected, they would consider that the principles of the Confederation were so completely violated that they would secede from it.

The formation of the Sonderbund excited their opponents; and it was declared that France, Austria, and the Pope were intriguing against Switzerland. The Jesuits, as usual, were supposed to be the centre of the intrigues; and the cry was raised that they ought to be expelled from the Confederation. Hitherto they had chiefly settled in Schwytz and Freyburg; but it was believed that if a cry rose against them they would become less safe in those cantons; and Luzern, as one of the three chief towns of the Confederation, was supposed to be a safer resting-place; therefore, on September 12th, 1844, the Assembly of Luzern passed a resolution inviting the Jesuits to settle in Luzern.

Strange to say, Bern and Zurich had somewhat changed places during this period; for while the indignation against the former Government of Bern, caused by their abandonment of the right of asylum, had produced a strong and permanent Radical feeling in that canton, the bitter hostility to Christianity shown by some of the leading Radicals of Zurich had, on the other hand, scandalized the more moderate Liberals, and produced a Government less keenly Radical than that which now ruled in Bern. At this crisis, unfortunately, the Government of Bern took a step which could scarcely have tended to the order and unity of Switzerland. They appointed a committee to attack the Jesuits, and organized volunteer regiments, which they despatched against Luzern. And the want of confidence in the central power, which had been proclaimed by the Sonderbund, seemed to be almost justified by the action of the

Diet at their next meeting; for that body, while condemning the Bernese volunteers, refused to take any
steps to hinder their march. The attack of the
volunteers was, however, successfully repelled by
Luzern; and the Sonderbund soon after proceeded to
form a council of war for its own protection.

In the meantime, Metternich had become more and
more alarmed at the progress of affairs in Switzer-
land. The defeat of the efforts of Austria and
Sardinia to defend the Conservative cause in the
Ticino, and the subsequent alliance between the
Ticinese and Charles Albert, had strengthened the
fears which had been previously aroused in the
Austrian Government by the shelter given by the
Swiss to the European Revolutionists. Even in 1845
Metternich had despatched troops to the frontier of
Switzerland; he looked upon the struggle of the
Catholic cantons as a means for carrying out his
policy of weakening the union of Switzerland; and,
through the help of Solaro della Margherita, he succeeded in rousing Charles Albert's sympathies for the
cause of the Sonderbund. But to others he frankly
said that he was not fighting in the least for the
Jesuits—" They do not make us hot or cold;" and
instead of resting his appeal to the Diet on so doubtful
a ground, he earnestly entreated Louis Philippe to
prevent the violent substitution of a unitary and pro-
pagandist government " for the cantonal government
of Switzerland."

To say the truth, it was for the stability of Austrian
government in Italy that Metternich was now
alarmed; and Mentz had warned him that a strong
and united government in Switzerland would be
dangerous to Austria in Lombardy. When, then,

the election of a Radical government by the canton of
St. Gallen made the character of the coming Swiss Diet
tolerably certain, Metternich thought that the time
had come for decided action; and he desired that
before the meeting of the Diet, Austria, France,
Russia, and Prussia should declare that they would
not suffer cantonal authority to be violated. England,
however, Metternich well knew would be opposed to
him. Ever since the recognition of Greek independence in 1830 Metternich had become aware that a
statesman had arisen in England who, though inferior
to Canning in width of sympathy and capacity for
sudden and ready action, yet was Canning's equal in
strength of will, and in the thorough grasp of the two
convictions that Constitutionalism was better than
Despotism, and that Metternich was a dangerous
politician who should always be opposed.

Palmerston, indeed, had not accomplished any such
brilliant stroke of foreign policy as the breaking up
of the Holy Alliance, or the defeat of Absolutism in
Portugal, and had only played a late and subordinate
part in the Greek question. But he had helped to
save Belgium from the clutches both of France and
Holland. He had uttered as decided a protest as
was, perhaps, possible to him, against the Frankfort
Decrees. And he had recently intimated plainly his
opinion about the annexation of Cracow. The occupation of Ferrara had not at that time taken place;
but Palmerston's utterance about the Treaty of
Vienna on the Po had sufficiently indicated to Metternich the line which English feeling was taking
with regard to Italian policy. But, though certain
of the hostility of Palmerston, Metternich fully hoped
to counterbalance that danger by securing France to

his side. With Guizot he had long been on terms of cordial friendship; and each had sympathized with the other in various points of their political career. But, unfortunately for Metternich, in the Italian question Guizot had not seemed entirely sympathetic with Austria; for the Lombard exile, Pellegrino Rossi, who was now French ambassador at Rome, was the special friend and *protegé* of Guizot; and as it was primarily for the sake of Austrian rule in Italy that Metternich cared about the Swiss question, he might find that here, too, French opinion did not coincide with Austrian.

It soon appeared that Louis Philippe shrank from an alliance with Austria. He declared that any declaration by the four Powers, instead of hindering any outburst in Switzerland might hasten it; and Guizot was directed to propose that, instead of a common action by the four Powers, Austria should undertake alone the defence of the Sonderbund, France merely occupying some position in the territory of the Confederation. Metternich, however, remembered that during the intervention in the Papal States, in 1831-2, a French general had seized on Ancona, and had attempted a demonstration there, at first of a Republican character, and throughout entirely anti-Austrian. And he feared that, if he consented to Guizot's proposal, the French Radicals might turn the occupation of Swiss territory to their advantage.

While France and Austria were thus wasting their time in wrangling, the Swiss Diet met. Ochsenbein, an even more energetic man than Neuhaus, had been chosen President of the Confederation ; and on the 20th July, 1847, the Diet had declared that the

Sonderbund was incompatible with the Treaty of Confederation. This was speedily followed by the dismissal from the service of the Confederation of all those who held office in the cantons of the Sonder-bund ; and finally, in September, the Diet decreed that the Assemblies of Luzern, Schwytz, Freyburg, and Valais should be invited to expel the Jesuits from their territory. The Sonderbund probably felt that a direct military resistance to the whole forces of the Diet would be hopeless, and therefore they resolved to make a separate attack on some of the smaller cantons. With this view they prepared to march their troops from Luzern against Aargau, which they considered one of the centres of Protestant tyranny ; and about the same time the canton of Uri resolved to invade the Ticino. In both these cases the Sonderbund hoped to rouse a popular insur-rection on their side, but in this they were singularly mistaken.

Previously to 1815 Uri had exercised a special authority over Ticino, and had used it to thrust in German officials in place of Italian. The Treaty of Vienna had secured Ticino from these tyrannies ; but the Ticinese remembered them, and resented this new invasion. The troops of Uri were indeed able to gain one or two successes ; but the people of Ticino rose against them, and, after a short, sharp struggle, succeeded in driving them out of the canton. The expedition to Aargau proved equally unsuccessful, and, in the meantime, the Federal Diet was organizing its forces under the command of General Dufour, a Genevese. They resolved that Freyburg, as the nearest of the Sonderbund cantons to Bern, and as geographically separated off from its allies, should

be the first object of attack ; and on November 7,
Rilliet, the commander of the first division of the
Federal forces, issued the following order of the day
to his troops :—

"You are the first Federal troops who have entered
the Freyburg territory. Your bearing at this moment
will give the tone to the whole division. Consider
that you are entering on a Federal territory, that you
are marching against members of the Federation,
who for centuries have been your friends, and will
be so again. Consider that they are rather misled
than guilty. Consider that they are neighbours, and
that you ought to be fighting under the same flag.
Therefore be moderate ; refute the slanders of those
who are driving them on. Listen not to false
rumours, nor to foolish provocations to violence.
Listen only to your leaders, and leave to your opponents the responsibility of having fired the first shot
against the Federal flag. Soldiers ! I rely on you as
on myself; and do you trust in God, who marches
before the flag of good, right, and honour."

To the Freyburger Rilliet appealed to receive the
Federal troops as brothers and friends, and as obeying the God whom Protestants and Catholics alike
worship. "Lay down your arms," he said, "not
before us, but before our flag, which is yours also."

These appeals were not without result. At one of
the first towns at which the Federal troops arrived in
the canton of Freyburg, the townsfolk threw off the
authority of the Cantonal Boards, raised the Federal
flag, and admitted the Federal troops. Two slight
skirmishes took place after this between the Federal
forces and those of the canton ; but the former were
easily victorious. On November 12 the Federal

M

troops appeared before the town of Freyburg; and on
the 14th it was surrendered to them. Large numbers
of the citizens received them with cries of " Long live
the Confederates ! Down with the Sonderbund !
Down with the Jesuits !"

The leaders of the Sonderbund at Luzern were
startled at this sudden collapse, and resolved to
apply for foreign help; and it was on November 15,
1847, that the descendants of Reding and Winkelried
appealed to the descendants of Leopold of Hapsburg
for help against their fellow-confederates.

Metternich would gladly have intervened; and he
hastened to assure the Sonderbund that the Emperor
of Austria considered their cause a just one. Still,
however, he desired the co-operation of France; but
Guizot hesitated, and when Palmerston announced
that any demonstration in favour of the Sonderbund
would be met by a counter-demonstration by England
on the side of the Federal Diet, the French Government distinctly refused to have any share in intervention.

In the meantime the Sonderbund was rapidly
breaking down. The Protestant party had gained
the upper hand in the little canton of Zug, and persuaded the Government to surrender to the Diet even
before the Federal troops had appeared in the canton.
The occupation of Zug was speedily followed by a
march to Luzern. On November 23 the Federal
troops encountered the forces of Luzern and drove
them back after a sharp fight. On the following day
the War Council of the Sonderbund fled from Luzern
and the Federal troops entered it. After this defeat
there was no further serious resistance; by November 29 the last canton of the Sonderbund had sur-

rendered to the Diet, and on December 7 the Diet passed a formal resolution refusing to admit any mediation from the Great Powers. So ended the Sonderbund war; and whatever harshness the Diet and the Protestant cantons may have shown in the earlier part of the struggle towards their Catholic neighbours, they had at least consistently upheld the principle of national independence, and by their vigour and determination they had saved the unity of Switzerland and defeated Metternich.

Nor were these the only defeats which the ruler of Europe sustained in the year 1847. In Germany, too, there were signs that the old system was giving way. Metternich, indeed, had hoped that the King of Prussia had been about to abandon the policy which he had followed from 1840 to 1843; for in 1846 a meeting had taken place between Metternich and the King in which Frederick William had shown signs of alarm at the popular movement. But this change of feeling had been only temporary, for an event had occurred soon after which had given a new impulse to German national feeling, and re-awakened thereby the popular sympathies of the King of Prussia.

On July 8, 1846, the King of Denmark, Christian VIII., issued a proclamation in which he declared that he should consider the provinces of his Crown as forming one sole and same State. This was felt to be undoubtedly aimed at the independence of Schleswig-Holstein. That Duchy had, since the middle of the fifteenth century, been recognized as a separate province, of which the King of Denmark was duke (till that time Schleswig had been a fief of Denmark and Holstein of Germany).

In the seventeenth century a practically absolute
Government had been established in Denmark; but
in 1830 the liberties of that country had been restored, and soon after a cry had arisen from some of
the Radical party at Copenhagen in favour of the
conquest of Schleswig.

But the object of the popular party and that of
the King were entirely unlike; the Democratic party
desiring to assert what they considered a national
principle by the separation of Schleswig from Holstein and its absorption in Denmark; the King
wishing to absorb Schleswig-Holstein whole into
the Danish dominions, without consideration for
anything but selfish aggrandizement. As a compromise between his own aims and those of the
people of Copenhagen, Christian, in 1831, conceded
separate assemblies to Holstein and Schleswig; but
he had followed this up by steadily trying to Danize
the Duchies. Danish officers were introduced into
their army and navy, even into their private ships;
Danish teachers were appointed in the University of
Kiel; the liberty of the Press was continually interfered with, and arms were removed from the forts of
Schleswig-Holstein to Copenhagen. Thus it became
evident that the proclamation of July, 1846, was
merely another step towards the complete denationalization of the Duchies.

Metternich was in a difficult position. On the one
hand he was bound by the Treaty of Vienna to assert
the rights of Austria to protect Holstein as a member
of the German Confederation; on the other hand he
knew that by so doing he was strengthening that
German national feeling which he so much dreaded.
"In the University of Heidelberg," wrote Metternich,

"in the municipal councils of German towns, in the gatherings of professors and of choral societies, the cry is being raised for the Fatherland." The professors of Heidelberg had sent a special address to the Holsteiners, and it was clear on every side that German sentiment was rising to boiling point. Under these circumstances Metternich tried to steer between the dangers of encouraging popular feeling and that of neglecting to assert the legal influence of Austria. Finally, he persuaded the Federal Diet, on September 17, 1846, to pass two resolutions—First, that, apart from his letter of July 8, the King of Denmark should respect all the rights which he had promised to respect in a private letter of August 22; but, secondly, that, "while the Confederation pays just honour to the patriotic sentiments shown on this occasion by the Confederated German States, it regrets the passionate accusations and irritations which were produced by this circumstance."

So for the moment Metternich hoped to stave off the natural results of this outburst of popular feeling. But he could not prevent the effect which that outburst would produce on the more impressionable character of the King of Prussia. One of those who had had much opportunity of observing that king remarked that whoever was a favourite with him for the time and managed to indulge his fancies had the game in his own hands; and the Ministers who then enjoyed the confidence of Frederick William were eager to encourage him in complying with the popular feeling. So, in spite of Metternich's warnings, the King of Prussia, in January, 1847, had summoned to Berlin the representatives of all the Provincial Estates to discuss affairs. "The King," said Princess Metternich, " has promulgated this Constitution without force and without virtue, which is nothing to-day, but which to-morrow may change into thunder and destroy the Kingdom."

But the concessions which the King of Prussia was making only embodied a feeling which was stirring in various parts of Germany. A terrible famine in Silesia was quickening the desire of the poorer classes for some change in their condition; the booksellers and literary men were uttering various demands for freedom of the Press; and when a meeting of the Baden Liberals at Offenburg tried to formulate these demands, the organizers of the meeting were threatened with a prosecution which never took place.

Such, then, was Metternich's position towards the close of 1847; discredited as a champion of legality by the annexation of Cracow, looked on with suspicion by many orthodox Catholics in consequence of his attempt on Ferrara, his power as a ruler and his reputation as a diplomatist alike weakened by the result of the Sonderbund war. The result of these various failures was seen in the attitude both of kings and peoples. The King of Prussia was breaking loose from Metternich's control; France was suspicious and England hostile; Charles Albert was assuming more and more an attitude of defiance to Austria; the Pope was drifting gradually into the position of a champion of Italian Liberty; German national feeling, which Metternich had hoped to stamp out in 1834, was bubbling up into new life under the triple influence of the Schleswig-Holstein question, the King of Prussia's reforms, and the growing Liberalism of Saxony and Baden; while

Hungary, which had seemed hopelessly divided, was gradually solidifying into opposition to Austrian rule. Such were the chief points in the spectacle which presented itself to Metternich as he looked upon Europe. Yet he was far indeed from thinking of yielding in the struggle, or of abandoning in the slightest degree his faith in his great system. He was still prepared to crush Switzerland and Charles Albert, to lead back the Pope and the King of Prussia into wiser courses, to quench the spirit of German enthusiasm, to wear out Hungarian opposition, to recover the friendship of France, and to defy the enmity of England. Such results seemed still possible when, in an Italian island to which Metternich had not recently given much attention, there first broke out that revolutionary fire which, under judicious guidance, was to spread over Europe and overthrow the system of Metternich.

# CHAPTER VI.

## FIRST MUTTERINGS OF THE STORM.
### SEPTEMBER, 1847—MARCH, 1848.

State of Naples and Sicily under Ferdinand II.—The birds and the King.—The conspiracy.—The September rising and its results.—Christmas in Naples.—The 12th of January in Palermo. —The insurrection spreads to Naples.—The first Constitution of 1848.—The effect in Rome—in Tuscany—in Genoa.—The editors of Turin.—" Voleva e non voleva."—The government of Milan.— The Milanese view of their rulers.—Count Gabrio Casati.— Ficquelmont.—The " Panem et Circenses " policy.—Giambattista Nazari.—His speech in the Congregation.—Its effect.—Rainieri and Spaur on Nazari.—The grievances of different parts of Lombardy. — Condition of Venetia. — Charles Bonaparte in Venice.—Damele Manin.—Niccolo Tommaseo.—Manin's programme.—Moncenigo's treachery.—Manin's imprisonment.—The tobacco massacres at Milan.—Their effect.—Metternich's programme of Italian reform.—" Viva el sangue Palermitano !"— The "Administrators " in Hungary.—The programme of Kossuth and Deak.—The Constitutional victories in Hungary.—State of Vienna.—The division of classes.—The ruling trio.—Effect of Ferdinand's accession in Vienna.—The " Lese-Verein."—Hye-Andrian.—Kuranda and Schuselka.—The German movement in Vienna considered morally.—The Archduke John's toast.—The relations between rich and poor.—The anti-Jesuit feeling.—The illegal soup-kitchen. — The " Professional" opposition. — Die Sibyllinische Bücher.—" The Austrian has no fatherland."—The censorship.—Metternich's policy in Switzerland—in Lombardy.

THE failure of the struggles for liberty in Naples and Sicily in 1821 had not prevented continual abortive insurrections from breaking out after that period;

and, while these attempts produced no immediate results except the strengthening of tyranny, they were yet gradually teaching Sicilians and Neapolitans the two great lessons of confidence in each other and distrust of the Bourbons. Francis had succeeded to Ferdinand I., and Ferdinand II. again to Francis; and, unless there were some slight variety in the forms of cruelty and tyranny, the change of kings may be said to have brought no change to the peoples whom they governed. Corruption and espionage prevailed both in Naples and Sicily. The only perceptible distinction between those two countries was that the clergy exercised rather more tyranny in Naples, while in Sicily robbery and brigandage were more rife. The Bourbons, like the Hapsburgs, sought to keep alive the disunion between the different races of their subjects, thus hoping to increase their own power; and so Sicilian Ministers were brought to govern Naples, and Neapolitan commissioners sent to Sicily. The desire for reform awakened by the accession of Pius IX. was a bond between all the different countries of Italy, and the King of Naples recognized this by suppressing all newspapers in his dominions that praised Pius IX. But Ferdinand was not to be left altogether without warning before the blow against his power was actually struck. In June, 1847, he paid a visit to Sicily to inspect the military defences of the island. In visiting Messina he found several statues of himself, but the ears of all of them had been stopped up. The King was alarmed; for, whether he understood or not this significant practical joke, he saw at least that some insult was intended. Perhaps he was able to accept the explanation of his courtiers that "the birds had chosen the ears of the royal

statues to build their nests in." At Palermo he
received another hint as to the nature of the birds
who had paid this homage to royalty, for there he
was met by a petition for freedom of the Press. He
angrily rejected this request, and refused to make
any inquiry into the growing misery of the Sicilians.
More soldiers and stronger forts, he considered, were
the only needs of the country.

Yet at this very time an insurrection was preparing
of a far more dangerous character than the spasmodic
outbursts in Messina and Calabria which had disturbed the repose, but scarcely endangered the throne,
of Ferdinand's predecessors. The Sicilians and
Neapolitans had now learned to act together, and
planned a simultaneous rising in Calabria and Sicily.
The revolutionists were to march upon the nearest
fortified places, and eventually to seize Naples, where
they were to proclaim the Unity of Italy. According
as circumstances guided them, they were either to
compel the King to accept the Constitution, to depose
him in favour of his son, to choose a new dynasty, or,
if necessary, to proclaim a Republic; but in any case
they were to assert the unity and independence of
Italy.

Some hint of an approaching outbreak seems to
have reached the ears of the King or his Ministers;
for in August two artillery officers and some other
citizens were arrested in Palermo. "But," says La
Farina, the Sicilian historian, "nothing could be
discovered, since the Sicilians knew better than any
nation how to stand firm in preserving silence in all
tortures: an ancient virtue not yet destroyed by
modern corruption."

The miserable local jealousies which had hindered

the former struggles for liberty had for a time disappeared; but there was still in this conspiracy, as in every other, the natural division between the impetuous and the prudent, between the party of speedy action and the party of delay. And while the fiery spirits of Messina and Calabria were eager for an immediate rising, the citizens of the two capitals, Palermo and Naples, were in favour of slower action. At Messina, therefore, the first outbreak took place. On September 1 some officers met at an inn in that town to celebrate the promotion of one of their generals by a dinner. The conspirators seized this opportunity for an outbreak, and surrounded the inn as if from mere curiosity; but when sufficient numbers had gathered they suddenly unfurled the tricolour flag and raised the cries of " Viva Italia!" " Viva Pio Nono!" " Viva la Costituzione!" The officers at last became alarmed, and, rushing out, summoned the soldiers and ordered them to fire. They hesitated to obey, and listened to the appeal of the conspirators, who urged their common cause and the duty of Neapolitans and Sicilians to stand together against their common oppressor. Discipline, however, proved stronger than patriotism; the soldiers fired, and several Sicilians fell, amongst them Giovanni Grillo, the youth who had played the part of the birds in stopping the ears of the King's statues.

The insurgents retreated; but a shoemaker named Sciva, who was at work near the scene of action, left his shop and rushed forward to rally them; and a priest named Kriny also fought gallantly in their ranks. The movement, however, had been too hastily organized; the insurgents were either forced to fly or were arrested on the spot, and Sciva, the shoemaker, was condemned to death. The authorities, indeed, hoped to persuade him to save his life by betraying his friends; but he refused, even on the scaffold, to accept a pardon on such terms, and died bravely. Kriny, as a priest, had his sentence commuted from death to imprisonment. Grillo died of his wounds.

Desperate efforts were made by the Government to obtain information as to the details of this conspiracy. Three hundred ducats were offered to anyone who would kill the chief conspirators; a thousand to anyone who would arrest them. But, though the leaders of the insurrection were hidden in the houses of very poor men, no one could be found to betray them, even for the sake of so large a reward. Even where the Government had made sure of their prey, it sometimes slipped through their hands. One of the insurgents was brought wounded to a house, and his hiding-place was discovered and surrounded by soldiers; but, by a false alarm, the guards were frightened away and the wounded man conveyed elsewhere. The owner of the second place of refuge was arrested, but the fugitive was again enabled to escape. His wound brought on fever, and he remained hidden for fifteen days without food, sucking the end of a sheet for nourishment; he was then so exhausted that his friends thought him dead and carried him to a church; but he revived, and was at last shipped to Marseilles, where he recovered.

A people so vigorous and determined were obviously not far from freedom. The heroism of the Sicilians had strengthened the courage of the Neapolitans; and on Christmas Day the latter rose to the cry of "Evviva Palermo!" This demonstration, however, was only the forerunner of the Revolution; for it was still from Sicily that the first successful action was to come. So little did the Sicilians care to conceal their intentions that a pamphlet was circulated fixing January 12 as the day for the actual rising. The police, thinking that they would be able easily to suppress the movement, began to make arrests; but their efforts were in vain.

La Farina, who afterwards became a member of the Sicilian Assembly, gives the following account of the rising:—

"On the night that preceded the 12th January, 1848, the streets of Palermo were silent and deserted; but in the houses the citizens were wakeful, agitated by fears and hopes. At the dawning of the new day the soldiers were in arms in fortified places and in their own quarters; some battalions of infantry and gensdarmes occupied the public places of the prefecture of police and of the royal palace, where the General De Majo, the Lieutenant of the King, General Vial, Commandant of the Piazza, and other royal officers, were assembled in council. The cannons of Castellamare were drawn out for a festival, for it was the birthday of Ferdinand II., and the roads were extraordinarily full of people; all were waiting for the conspirators to appear, for the sign to be given, for the first cry to break out, when Buscerni, a bold and ready youth, weary of delay, raised on high a musket that he had held concealed, and cried resolutely, 'To arms! To arms!' Then Pasquale Miloro came out armed into the street of the Centorinari; the abbot Ragona and the priest Venuti exhorted the people to rise in

the name of God.   There ran up to them, in arms,
the advocate Tacona, Giuseppe Oddo, Prince Gram-
monte, Baron Bivona, Lo Cascio, Pasquale Bruno,
Francesco Ciaccio, Giancinto Carini, Amodei, Enea,
and a few others.   Giuseppe La Masa bound to a stick
a white pocket-handkerchief, a red one, and a green
ribbon, and waved the three Italian colours.   Santa
Astorina went about distributing tricolour ribbons
and cockades."

"At the sight of the arms, and of the small number
of those who bore them, the crowd grew thin and
dispersed; the shops were closed, and the few eager
men remained alone.   A few of the unarmed remained with them to divide the honour and perils of
the attack; and among these, distinguished by the
loftiness of their mind and remarkable probity, were
Vincenzo Errante and the Baron Casimiro Pisani.
They were not disheartened; they stood firm and
bold in their resolve; the bells of the Church of
Orsola sounded an alarm, those of the Convent of
the Gangia answered them; the Revolution had become irrevocable.   Small bands were forming themselves here and there.   They had neither rules,
orders, nor plans; they did not barricade the streets;
they did not make trenches, as is usual in other
cities; they did not make head in any one position;
troops of children preceded them, dancing and
singing; they drew near to the troops, watched
their motions and acts, and returned to warn the
insurgents even while the blood was dropping from
the blows that they had received.   One band of the
insurgents put to flight a military patrol in the
street of the Albergava; others had the same
fortune in the Raffadale street, at the church of San

Gaetano, near the gate of St. Antonino, in the street of Calderari, and in other places. Thus passed the whole day; two of the insurgents, among whom was L'Amodei, were dead, and ten soldiers; the wounded were more numerous. The insurgents withdrew within the Piazza of Fiera Vecchia, which since the morning had been the centre of the movements and the seat of a committee formed of the first insurgents. There were not more than fifty who had firearms; a company of infantry would have been sufficient to disperse them; but the soldiers remained immovable in the positions which they had taken up, because, remembering the year '20, they had determined not to advance into the populous quarters of the city. To this it is necessary to add that all the houses were lighted for the festival, and that the balconies of the windows were crowded with men, women, and children, who all clapped their hands and gave loud Vivas to Italy, the Sicilian Constitution, and Pio Nono; a spontaneous, unexpected, and universal agreement of the people which made the rulers lose their heads and the soldiers their hearts. In the night the insurgents were recruited from the country districts and the neighbouring communes. The first to arrive were sixty countrymen from Villabate; then others from Misilmeri and from other places. By the next day Fiera Vecchia contained about 300 men armed with guns, and as many more armed with scythes, billhooks, knives, spits, and those iron tools which the popular fury changes into arms. The fortress of Castellamare bombarded the city; the artillery of the royal palace was dragged along the Cassero; but the insurgents attacked, stormed, and destroyed the police commissariats and made themselves masters of the military hospital of San Francesco Saverio; the soldiers who remained prisoners were embraced as brothers, and provided with every accommodation which they needed."

Brilliant as these successes sound, the victory was not yet complete; and to diplomatists, at any rate, the result seemed still uncertain. The Consuls of Austria, France, and Sardinia tried to persuade the insurgents even now to yield, on condition of obtaining a pardon. An attack made by La Masa on the Royalist forces was repelled, and several of the revolutionary committees fled from Palermo. But many of the leaders stood firm, and Mariano Stabile declared that Sicily should recover her ancient liberties, and that Ferdinand and not the people was the rebel. At the same moment the bells sounded, and the Royalist artillery was brought to bear upon the city. For three hours the struggle lasted; but at the end of that time the Royalists were driven back. The Neapolitan soldiers, grown savage by their defeats, began to sack private houses and commit various acts of cruelty; and when the foreign Consuls went again to the Governor's palace to ask for mercy to the insurgents, they were fired upon.

In the meantime new insurgents were pouring in from the country districts, and the revolution was developing a government. Mariano Stabile was made secretary of the Governing Committee, and Ruggiero Settimo, an old man of seventy who had held office under the original Constitution of 1812, and who had helped to proclaim the Spanish Constitution in Sicily in 1820, was chosen President. Nor was the movement any longer confined to Sicily. The

Neapolitans had risen in Salerno.  The King, in a panic, had dismissed Del Caretto, the head of the police, from office; and General Ruberti, the Commandant of the fortress of St. Elmo, had told the King that he would not fire upon the people.  A demonstration in favour of the Constitution of 1820 had taken place; and when the rain threatened to disperse the people, the umbrellas which were opened displayed the Italian colours.

Alarmed at the risings in Naples and Sicily, and uncertain on whom he could depend, Ferdinand, on January 29th, conceded a Constitution to Naples. At the same time he entreated Lord Minto to intervene between him and the Sicilians.  Neither Neapolitans nor Sicilians, however, were entirely satisfied.  In the Kingdom of Naples the Constitutionalists met with much opposition from the supporters of the old system, and some skirmishes followed between these two parties.  In Sicily the Liberals demanded that the granting of a Constitution should be followed by an adhesion to an Italian Confederation.  They therefore answered Lord Minto's appeal by a renewed attack on the fortress of Castellamare, which they succeeded in capturing after four hours' fighting, and thus destroyed the last hold of Ferdinand over Palermo, and left in his hands no important Sicilian position except the citadel of Messina.  The hopes thus raised were soon increased by the appointment of two men who had recently suffered imprisonment for their liberal opinions.  These were a lawyer named Bozzelli, who became Prime Minister, and the new head of the police, Carlo Poerio, who belonged to a family which had given many champions and sufferers to the cause

N

of Liberty, and who had himself been imprisoned in the previous year. When, then, the Constitution was actually promulgated on February 12, the hopes of the Neapolitans had risen to their highest pitch. The Constitution itself was but a poor affair, far less encouraging to popular hopes than its Spanish predecessor of 1820. It was founded, indeed, on the French Constitution of 1830, and the Parliament was therefore composed of two Houses, the upper one nominated by the King. A nominal freedom of the Press was secured, but carefully limited, especially in matters treating of religion. And there seems to have been hardly any security for Ministerial responsibility. But the granting of a Constitution against his will by a Bourbon King was, whatever its deficiencies, a fact which naturally supplied a spark to the combustible material to be found in all parts of Italy.

The news of the movement in Sicily had already kindled new hopes in Rome. There matters had been proceeding more slowly than in the first months of Pius IX.'s rule. Even Ciceruacchio had begun to think that a more definite programme might be accepted by the Pope; and on December 27, 1847, he drew up a list of the reforms which he thought especially needed in Rome. In these, while professing continued zeal for Pio Nono, he put forward requests of a kind not likely to be conceded; such as the removal of the Jesuits, the abolition of monopolies, and the emancipation of the Jews; while other demands were so vague that the Pope might easily have seemed to concede them without much trouble. For instance, Ciceruacchio required that the Pope should show confidence in the people, that individual liberty should be guaranteed, and that restraint should be put on excessive exercise of power.

The Pope, though not disposed to accept the exact programme of Ciceruacchio, was influenced by this address, and on December 31, 1847, he issued a decree promising separate and independent responsibility to each of the Ministers. When, then, the news arrived of the Sicilian insurrection, the enthusiasm in Rome rose to the greatest height; and when the Pope next appeared in public, people scattered flowers in his way, and Ciceruacchio displayed a banner bearing the words, " Santo Padre fidatevi nel Popolo " (Holy Father, have confidence in the people). Still, it was rumoured that the wicked cardinals were holding back the good Pope, and that they were opposing the armaments voted by the Council of State.

During the excitement caused by this fear the news arrived that the Sicilians had been successful, and that Ferdinand had granted a Constitution to Naples. Again the Romans rose, and this time with the cry of, " Away with the men of bad faith! Long live the secular ministry! Give us arms! " A Minister appeared on the balcony, promising the people a secular ministry and increase of the army. This was actually conceded a few days later, and Ciceruacchio once more called upon the people to have confidence in the reforming Pope. The news of the Sicilian and Neapolitan movements steadily spread northwards, and in Tuscany they chimed in with the new belief that Leopold was a reforming sovereign.

But matters took here a rather different complexion from that which they had assumed in Rome. The zeal of the Tuscans had been kindled by their struggle

with the Duke of Modena, and the free life of
Tuscany had attracted many democratic Italians;
while, on the other hand, though Leopold might have
wiped out the memory of the surrender of Renzi, he
could not cease to be a Hapsburg, and could never
attract to himself the same imaginative enthusiasm
which was kindled by the dream of a reforming
Pope.    At any rate, the first spark of a revolutionary
movement had been kindled by Guerrazzi in Leghorn,
before the success of the Sicilians had been known;
and though Ridolfi had suppressed the movement
and imprisoned Guerrazzi, the bitterness caused by it
still remained.    And even when the news of the
Neapolitan Constitution reached Florence, the Tuscan
reformers hastened to congratulate, not the Neapolitan Ambassador, but a representative of the revolutionary Sicilians who happened to be in Florence.
But Leopold was ready to yield with a much better
grace than Ferdinand; and when, on February 17,
the Constitution appeared it was found, in the matter
of religious liberty, to be considerably in advance of
the Neapolitan Constitution.

In the Kingdom of Sardinia the city of Genoa
supplied the same kind of element which the Tuscans
found in Leghorn.  The questionable manner in which
that city had been annexed to Piedmont had left, no
doubt, a continual soreness and readiness for revolution among the Genoese; while, on the other hand,
its important geographical position and great commercial reputation had led Charles Albert to push
forward its development as much as possible.    It
soon came to the front during the movement for
reform, and its citizens tried to urge on Charles
Albert whenever he hesitated.  As he drifted gradu-

ally in the direction of bolder action, the Genoese were ready to encourage festivals in his honour, and on the occasion of a demonstration in November, at Genoa, a citizen had called out to him, "Charles Albert, cross the Ticino and we will follow thee." When, then, the news arrived of the Sicilian rising, the Genoese sent to Turin a petition for the expulsion of the Jesuits and the concession of a national guard. In the meantime the editors of leading newspapers in Turin were meeting to decide on the policy which they should support, and Count Cavour, who had hitherto been disinclined to Liberal movements, proposed that they should demand a Constitution. D'Azeglio, Durando, and others, supported the proposal, and Cavour was despatched to present it to the King.

While Charles Albert was still hesitating, the news of the Neapolitan Constitution arrived. The people of Turin at once made a demonstration in honour of the event, and Pietro di Santa Rosa[1] proposed in the Municipal Council that that body should support the petition for the Constitution. The Municipal Council, though previously a reactionary body, accepted the proposal by a large majority. But Charles Albert still hesitated. On February 7th, he held a meeting of his Council, in which he at first refused to discuss the question whilst the crowd was gathering outside. On their dispersal, he began to consider the proposals, and the discussion lasted for eight hours. When the sitting of the Council was concluded, the representatives of the Municipality arrived, but were received very coldly by Charles Albert. While

---

[1] I do not know what relation he was to the more celebrated Santa Rosa of 1821.

things were still in this state, a message arrived
from the Governor of Genoa that, unless the Constitution was proclaimed, it would be necessary for
the King to place Genoa in a state of siege. At last
he consented to grant what was called a Statuto, of
which the terms seemed at first very indefinite, while
the delays in carrying it into execution irritated the
more decided reformers. But the faith of Charles
Albert's admirers was as robust as that of the
admirers of Pius IX. Banquets were held in his
honour, and those who took part in these exulting
demonstrations had at least the excuse for their
joy that the promise of the Statuto had roused the
irritation of the Austrians ; and Radetzky even
threatened to occupy Alessandria. But Radetzky
and the Austrians had enough to think of nearer
home.

The Government of Milan was at this time in a
very peculiar condition, seeing that there were not
less than seven people who were, in different ways,
responsible for the maintenance of order in the town
or its neighbourhood. Of these, the nominal head
was probably Rainieri, the Viceroy ; but he seems
to have been a man of less vigour than some of those
who acted under him; and though willing enough
to do acts of violence, yet not able altogether to
control his subordinates. The second, probably, in
nominal importance was Spaur, the Governor of
Milan: a Tyrolese nobleman, credited, even by his
opponents, with some remains of honourable feeling,
but crushed in spirit by his habit of constant de-
ference to the Court, and to Metternich. Next came
Torresani, the head of the police, a man who must
have been in some respects pleasanter to deal with

than the other rulers; for, though not disinclined to cruelty and tyranny, he managed to cover them with a certain Italian wit and courtesy which must have been rather a relief, as a contrast to the tone of some of his colleagues.  Thus, for instance, on one occasion the Town Council remonstrated with him for the action of the police in a riot, and urged that he should take measures for preserving order among his subordinates; Torresani chose to interpret the idea of order in his own fashion, and the next day issued a stern public notice against disorderly meetings, while at the same time he sent a polite note to the Council, pointing out that, by this pro- clamation, he had met their wishes for the preser- vation of order.

But if Torresani could soften by witticisms the necessary savageries of his position, any deficiencies in roughness on his part were amply atoned for by his subordinate Bolza, who was looked upon as the completest embodiment of the spirit of cruelty in the Government.  On the other hand, the craft and treachery of the system were best represented by a Bohemian named Pachta.  He was one of those men whose complete loss of reputation in private affairs fits them to become useful engines of despotism. He had been known previously as having swindled a lady out of some jewels which she had entrusted to him; and he had plunged so heavily into debt, that nothing but his favoured position protected him from arrest.  He held some nominal office in the Council at Milan; but his real duty was to act as a spy upon his colleagues.  Indeed, it may be said that that description might, with more or less force, apply to all the rulers of Milan, and to many others of the Government officials. A spy was set by the Home Government upon Torresani, and another to watch that spy. Rainieri was entrusted with one set of police, Spaur with another, Pachta with another. But while all these men divided the civil administration of Milan, there stood at their back the one man who did enjoy more of the permanent confidence of the Government than anyone else in Lombardy. This was the celebrated Field-Marshal Radetzky.

It is somewhat strange that this man, who has been considered, by many of those interested in these movements, as one of the most complete embodiments of Austrian cruelty, was yet looked upon by the Milanese at this time mainly as a theatrical buffoon. In the caricatures which are preserved at Milan, Rainieri generally appears as a hypocrite, sometimes cunning, sometimes maudlin; Bolza as a ferocious ruffian; while in Pachta and Torresani the appearance of cruelty is modified by a slightly idiotic expression. But Radetzky is invariably the theatrical blusterer, who might have supplied Shakespeare with a model for Ancient Pistol. Such was the Government with which Lombardy was blessed under the Metternich system.

On the other hand, the only official embodiment of popular feeling during the longest period of this rule had been the Town Council of Milan. The Central Congregation which had embodied the Austrian idea of a Lombard Constitution had been deprived of all freedom of utterance; but the Town Council was no doubt considered a more harmless body, and therefore had been allowed a certain amount of freedom. Since 1838 this Council had been presided over by Count Gabrio Casati, who has probably received more praise and more blame than he deserved.  He seems to have been a man by no means deficient either in courage or patriotism; and had he continued to exercise his office during a period when passive resistance and formal protests were still useful weapons, he might have left a reputation somewhat like that of Speaker Lenthall or Lord Mayor Beckford in our own History.  As it is, he was called on by circumstances to play a part in the struggle against Austria for which he was unfitted; and, while he has received undue praise from those who have accepted him as the embodiment of Milanese heroism, he has, on the other hand, been somewhat too fiercely condemned by those who noted his actual shortcomings, and could not make allowance for the difficulty of his position.  During the first years of his office he did his best to bring before Metternich and his colleagues the evils which prevailed in the Government of Lombardy; and when the growth of the Italian movements led to the demonstrations in favour of the Italian Archbishop of Milan, and the solemn funeral to Confalonieri, Casati showed his sympathy with the popular feeling, and protested against the various acts of cruelty which were perpetrated in the suppression of these movements.  Indeed, so prominent a part did Casati play in these matters that Sedlnitzky, the head of the Viennese police, wrote to Spaur to tell him to keep his eye on Casati, and to see that on the next occasion a Podestà of better principles was elected.

In October, 1847, Metternich added a new element to the confusion of the Milanese Government by

sending a new agent to share the authority of the
other rulers of Lombardy. This new emissary was
Count Ficquelmont, whose work was of a much more
definite character than his official position. This
work was, in fact, the carrying out of that part of
Menz's programme which had been modelled on the
Circus shows of the Emperors of Rome. This was
to be effected by the introduction of Fanny Ellsler
and other people of a similar character to the
pleasure-loving population of Milan. But the mission
only succeeded in eliciting new signs of discontent.
Ficquelmont and his protegées appear in the collection
of Milanese caricatures ; and a popular agreement
to abstain from theatre-going was so rigorously
carried out that, on one evening, only nine tickets
were sold for the principal theatre in Milan.

But, before this remarkable abstention had come
into force, a new character had been given to the
Lombard resistance to Austrian rule. The Central
Congregation of Lombardy had suddenly awakened
to life ; and the grievances under which the country
suffered had been placed before their rulers at Vienna
with a clearness previously unknown. The author
of this sudden change affords one of those curious
instances of men who do a great and important work
for their country, and then pass suddenly into ob-
scurity before their reputation has spread beyond
narrow limits. Giambattista Nazari was a lawyer
of Treviglio. All that seems to be known of him
previously to his election to the Central Congregation was that he was a man of moderate fortune,
with a large family; but both those facts may be
taken as adding something to the courage of his
public action. Treviglio is a town in the district of

Bergamo; the people of that district, presumably
with Austrian sanction, had accepted Nazari as their
representative, and on December 8 or 9, 1847, he
came forward in the Central Congregation to give,
for the first time since 1815, free and peaceable
expression to the wants of the people of Lombardy.

"Illustrious Congregation," he said, "it does not
require much shrewdness to discern that for some
time past there have been in this province manifest
signs of discontent shown by all classes of citizens,
as the rulers themselves ought to have known every
time that they have tried to deaden its effects.    And
from whence does the agitation which has thus been
produced arise—an agitation which increases the
more they try to restrain it?    From whence comes
this universal disquiet?    From whence this suspicion
between governors and governed?    The latter have,
perhaps, just reasons to complain; and if they have,
who ought to present those reasons to the Prince?
For my part, I do not see that anyone can be better
interpreters of the desires of our country than we;
since, even in our private condition, we are sharers
of the good and evil which are the fruits of good and
evil institutions; and since, moreover, we have the
precious office of discovering the needs of the populations and of presenting them at the Imperial
Throne.    In order, then, that that agreement between ruler and people which alone can secure the
quiet of the State may be restored, I am resolved to
propose that you should choose as many men as
there are provinces in Lombardy, and give them a
commission to examine specially into the present
conditions of the country; and when they have
discovered the causes of discontent, to refer them to

the whole Congregation in order to give fitting opportunity for petitions. This I say and advise, from a desire for the public good, from affection for my Prince, and from a sentiment of duty. For as citizen I love my country, as subject I desire that the Emperor should be adored and blessed by all, and as deputy I should think that I had failed to keep my oaths if I did not say what was imposed on me by the duty of not being silent."

On December 11 this protest of Nazari's was presented in due form to the rulers of Milan, and produced from them the sternest rebukes. The awkward point of the protest was that, both in form and substance, it was undoubtedly legal, and could not therefore be wholly disregarded. Accordingly, Rainieri told Spaur that it was desirable that a commission should be appointed; but that, instead of being composed of representatives chosen from the Lombard provinces, it should be limited to those few people who were noted for their zeal and attachment to the Austrian Government. Further, such commissioners were not to assume that discontent existed, nor even to make mention of such discontent in their discussions. At the same time, Nazari was to be told that he had acted irregularly in bringing forward his motion, and Torresani was to be directed to keep a special watch on this dangerous agitator.

Spaur thereupon addressed the Congregation, telling them that the Viceroy had consented to Nazari's proposal, provided that the Congregation limited itself strictly to the powers entrusted to it by the Constitution; and, further, that the Government was occupying itself with the wishes of the Lombard provinces, and that the Viceroy had left to Spaur's decision the appointment of the members of the Commission. Spaur concluded with a rebuke to Nazari for the want of confidence that he had shown in him, as President of the Congregation, in not communicating to him his intended motion. Nazari answered that he had wished to take upon himself the sole responsibility of his act; and that, as to the proposed previous application to Spaur, he would rather be wanting in confidence than respect; for that if he had told Spaur of his intention, and Spaur had tried to persuade him to be silent, he would have been compelled to be rude enough to disobey him.

In the meantime the motion had created the greatest enthusiasm, and many Milanese hastened to pay their respects to Nazari; four thousand visiting cards were left on him, and petitions flocked in from various places in support of his movement. In the Provincial Congregation of Milan, indeed, the supporters of Nazari encountered the same kind of official obstruction which their leader had met with in the Central Congregation of Lombardy, for the President refused to join his colleagues in signing the petition. Thereupon the members of that body threatened to resign; and the Viceroy, who had just declared Nazari's protest irregular, urged the President to yield. But the movement had spread far into the provinces. Many of the provincial towns had their own causes of grievance against the centralizers of Vienna. Pavia had been deprived of its arsenal; Brescia had been compelled to close its armourers' shops, Bergamo its ironmongeries; Cremona had lost one trade, Salo another; Como and other towns had lost their linen trade. Everywhere there had been signs of the sucking out of the strength of the country by the Central Government at Vienna. Nazari's protest, therefore, naturally attracted sympathy far beyond Milanese circles; and amongst other petitions came one from the old Lombard capital of Pavia asking that it might be specially represented on the Commission proposed by Nazari, and suggesting special reforms needed in Lombardy and Venetia.

But by far the most remarkable of the Lombard petitions produced by Nazari's protest was one which was apparently signed by the Lombards irrespective of their provincial divisions. In this the petitioners call upon the Central Congregation to keep alive the courage which had been shown by Nazari's protest. They remind the deputies of the promises previously made by the Austrian Government, and the breach of them. They declare that "The Lombards were formerly distracted by discordant hopes, but are now almost miraculously unanimous in their desires;" and they call on the deputies "to speak out the whole truth, to proclaim that they have faith in God, and that they leave to others the infamy of lying." . . . . . They call upon them " To declare the abuses of the Tribunals which are concealed by secret bribery; the arrogance of the police, the puerile corrections of the censorship; but above all to proclaim the great truth of nationality, to demand a federal union, and to remind Austria of her proclamation of April 16, 1815, in which she promised to conform the institutions of Lombardy to the character of the Italians. Ten million Italians are now united by an agreement between princes and people, defended by a flourishing army, and sanctioned by the authority

of the Pope." The petitioners then proceed to call
attention to the success of Hungary in its Constitutional struggle ; and they point out that, while
Austria had held out hopes of a special representation for Lombardy and Venetia, she had, in fact,
drawn the power more and more to Vienna, while
the Press had been subjected to the most petty persecutions. " An invisible network of information, con-
jectures, suspicions, has surrounded all the citizens.
The Government is arbitrary both by ignorance and
violence. It is only the representatives of the people
who can explain *that;* and they must show that all
these evils spring from the first great falsehood of a
people that has not the life of a people, of a kingdom
that has not the life of a kingdom. Lombardy is
governed by foreign laws and foreign persons. It is
taxed for the benefit of Austrian industries, while a
barrier of customs duties separates it from Italy."

It is worth noting that now, for the first time, the
leaders of Italian political movements began to consider the special grievances of the poor. As Mazzini
had roused the working men to care for the liberty
and unity of their country, so a common suffering had
gradually taught the wealthier leaders to care for the
troubles of their poorer neighbours; and these petitions enumerate a number of taxes which specially
weighed on the poor. The tax on salt was the
material burden most generally felt; while the lottery,
with its deliberate encouragement of the spirit of
gambling, increased the moral loathing of the Lombards for the Austrian rule. But the crushing out
of national feeling and intellectual life were still the
two main complaints of these petitioners; and, besides
the more general proofs of these mentioned above,

the petitioners dwelt with great emphasis on the conscription which carried off the youth of the country
for eight years.  And they finally demand that the
representatives of the people should ask for " A complete and irrevocable separation in every branch of
the administration; that they should be governed by
a person, not by a foreign people; " and that " their
own nationality, history, language, and brotherhood
with other Italians should not be considered as crime
and rebellion."   They finally close with the words,
" To-day you can still speak of peace.   The future is
in the hands of the God of Justice."

The petition of Nazari had, as already mentioned,
produced effects in the Lombard provinces; but it
had also called out sympathy, though a little more
slowly, in the neighbouring province of Venetia.
There the hand of Austria seemed to have weighed
more heavily than even in Milan.  Perhaps the
absence of old traditions of internal freedom, and the
terrible corruption which had hastened the fall of its
independence, may have had something to do with the
silence of Venice.   Perhaps, too, the sense of the
singular baseness of the crime, by which they had
become possessed of the Venetian district, may have
goaded the Austrians into greater tyranny than even
that which they exercised in their other dominions.
But, whatever was the cause, there seems to be no
doubt, as one of the historians of the time puts it,
that Venice was then reckoned " the least sturdy city
in the kingdom, and the one least disposed to movement."   But even Venice could not be shut out from
the influence of the Italian spirit, and the first sign
of awakening life was called out, curiously enough,
by a Buonaparte.   The Prince of Canino, who had

already succeeded in turning Scientific Congresses at Genoa and Milan into opportunities for political demonstrations, had come, in September, 1847, to Venice to preside in the Geological Section of the Congress. There he had introduced a discourse on Pius IX., which was received with loud applause; and when the Austrian police compelled him to leave the State, people followed him on his road with cheers of sympathy. But the spark which Charles Buonaparte had lighted required other hands to keep it alive; and it appeared that there was no one in the Venetian Congregation bold enough to take up the part which had been played at Milan by Nazari.

Under these circumstances, Daniele Manin, the lawyer, who had already opposed the Austrian Government about the Lombardo-Venetian railway, came forward to take upon himself the office from which the official members of the Congregation had shrunk. He presented a petition calling on the members of the Venetian Congregation to imitate the example of Nazari, ending his appeal with the words, "It is unjust and injurious to suppose that the Government has granted to this kingdom a sham national representation."

This address of Manin's was sent to the Congregation on December 21st. On the same day Niccolo Tommaseo addressed a letter to Baron von Kübeck, one of the Viennese ministry, asking for permission to print a discourse which he had just delivered at Venice on the Austrian press law. In this discourse he had shown that the Austrian law was in theory more liberal than the Piedmontese law, but that it was not carried out, a fact which he illustrated by

o

the signatures to a petition which was then being circulated in favour of the proper enforcement of the Austrian law. "If this petition be granted," said Tommaseo, "the country will find peace, and Austria an honourable security." He ended with a remarkable warning—"If the movements of the brothers Bandiera alarmed the Austrian Government, how much more will there be danger now that the altar is no longer on the side of the throne?"

Tommaseo had already been marked out by the Government as a dangerous person. He had been the first to introduce Mazzini to the public by securing the publication of his article on Dante which had been refused by the "Antologia," and he had joined with Mazzini in the revolutionary struggle of 1833. It was therefore as a pardoned man that he had been allowed to return to Venice; and the authorities were doubly indignant that he should venture to come forward again. But Manin's attempt to stir up the Venetian Congregation attracted the hostility of the Government more than Tommaseo's petition. He had already protested against a new form of official cruelty—the shutting up of a political prisoner in a lunatic asylum; and Palffy had threatened to let the prisoner out and shut up Manin instead. But it seemed for a time as if his attempt to stir up the Venetian Congregation would fail, for he could get no member to present his petition for him. Nothing daunted, however, he printed it, and sent it himself to the Congregation. This act soon attracted attention, and several provincial governments sent in similar petitions.

Still the Venetian Congregation would not stir; so, on January 8, Manin sent in a second petition, in

which he no longer confined himself to vague appeals,
but set forth the necessary programme of reform.
He demanded that the laws should be published and
obeyed, that no obedience should be required to
unpublished laws, and that the territories of Lombardy and Venetia should form a separate kingdom,
not a province, "still less a mere outlying village of
Vienna. We ought to be governed," he said, "according to our character and customs; to have a
true national representation, and a moderately free
press which could control and enlighten the chiefs
of the Government and the representatives of the
nation." . . . . "The germs planted by the laws of
1815 had not developed, and only a madman or an
archæologist would refer to them as a guide." He
then proceeded to demand that the Viceroy of Lom-
bardo Venetia should be completely independent of
all but the Emperor; that the finances and the army
should also be separated from the government at
Vienna; that the communal governments should be
more independent than at present, and that trials
should be by jury, and should be oral and public; that
the power of the police should be limited, and that
a moderate law should be substituted for the existing
censorship of the Press; that a civic guard should be
granted; that citizens should be made equal before
the law; that Jewish disabilities and feudal tenures
should be abolished, and that there should be a
general revision of the laws.

Manin's petition alarmed the timid spirits of the
Congregation; and one of them named Moncenigo
sent it to Governor Palffy. Manin had already
protested against the appointment of this Moncenigo
on the sham Commission of Enquiry which the Vice-

roy had granted; and no doubt personal irritation
combined with political cowardice to prompt Moncenigo's breach of confidence.  But, whatever its
motives, this act of servility produced a protest from
another lawyer, who, while denouncing Moncenigo's
act as unworthy of the dignity of a commissioner,
alluded to the period of Napoleon's rule as one of
greater freedom than had ever been allowed by
Austria.  The police had in the meantime been preparing a report for the criminal tribunal; and on
January 19, 1848, Manin was suddenly seized and
carried off to prison on the charge of disturbing the
public peace.

In the meantime the Milanese movement had been
assuming a more serious character.  Demonstrations
at the theatre, or abstentions from it, songs and other
public expressions of opinion, were continually alarming the authorities.  That separation, too, between
the altar and the throne, to which Tommaseo had
called attention, was even more marked in Milan
than in Venice; and Radetzky a little later ordered
his soldiers not to attend the sermons or the confessional of the Milanese clergy, "since they are
our enemies."  But this ferocious commander was
resolved at all hazards to drive the Milanese to extremities; and he soon found an opportunity for
carrying out his plans.  One of the most universal
forms of protest against the Government in Lombardy
was the determined abstention from tobacco on the
ground that it was a Government monopoly.  This
protest began on January 1, 1848, and it seemed at
first as if it would be allowed to pass without remark.
But Radetzky, in spite of the advice of Torresani,
ordered his soldiers to appear in public, smoking.

This order was carried out on January 2, 1848.   In some parts of the town this demonstration provoked nothing but a few hisses from the crowd; but in one part, where the police and soldiers had collected in large numbers and many citizens had gathered to watch the smokers, the soldiers suddenly turned upon the crowd with their bayonets and charged them. Casati remonstrated with Torresani, but could get no redress, and was even himself assaulted by the police when he appealed to them.

This, however, was merely the preliminary of Radetzky's proceedings.   The following afternoon a much larger force of soldiers appeared in Milan, and every one of them was smoking.   The crowd gathered as before, and was, as usual, largely composed of boys.   Suddenly two of the sergeants gave a signal, and the soldiers, drawing their swords, rushed upon the crowd, wounding many boys seriously and killing an old man of seventy-four.   The crowd fled at the attack; but the soldiers followed them, breaking into the shops in which they took refuge, destroying what they found there, and killing or wounding those whom they came across.   In one place they broke into an inn, gave the hostess several severe wounds in the head, besides beating violently a little girl of four years old.

Throughout the city these scenes of barbarity continued during the greater part of the day, and naturally aroused the most tremendous indignation. Similar smoking demonstrations took place in Brescia, Cremona, and Mantua; but in these places they seem to have passed off without a riot.   In Pavia and Padua, on the other hand, the smokers came into collision with the students, who fought with their bare fists against the soldiers' swords. In Milan the indignation was not confined to the opponents of Austria. Monsignore Oppizzoni, who was on the whole a supporter of the Government, headed a deputation to the Viceroy in which he used these words:—"Your Highness, I am old, and have seen many things. I saw the profanation of the Jacobins and the cruelty of the Russians; but I never saw nor heard of before such atrocious acts as have happened in the days just past."

Companies of ladies met at the Casa Borromeo to collect funds for the wounded. In all the principal cities of Lombardy funeral rites were performed for those who had died in the riots; and the people refused to walk in the Corso Francesco, which had been the scene of the principal massacre, and went instead to another street, which they renamed the Corso Pio Nono. Even some of those who had served the Austrian Government raised a protest against these atrocities. Count Guicciardini, for such a protest, was deprived of his office; while the Councillor, Angelo Decio, declared that he would resign if the Government would not put a restraint on the undisciplined soldiers. The Viceroy, taken aback at this sudden outburst of indignation, promised reforms and dismissed some of the troops from Milan.

But the saner members of the Austrian Government had completely lost hold of affairs, and Radetzky had become the sole ruler of Milan. He harangued his troops in one of those bombastic addresses whose absurdity seemed to take even a deeper root in men's minds than the atrocity of his acts. " Let us not," he said, " be forced to open the wings of the Austrian eagle which have never yet been clipped." This calm

ignoring of Austerlitz and Marengo specially tickled
the fancy of the Milanese; more particularly as
Radetzky was credited, whether justly or unjustly,
with having played a somewhat ignominious part in
the latter battle. A few utterly inadequate and
trivial reforms were won from Metternich by the
spectacle of the Sicilian revolution, the growing
popularity of the Pope, and the Neapolitan Constitution. On January 18 it was proposed that the
Viceroy should transfer himself from Milan to Verona;
that he should be surrounded by persons better informed than his subordinates were; that the Government of Milan should be made more strong; and that
some of the members of the Central Congregation of
Milan should be summoned to Vienna. How absurdly
unlike these concessions were to the real wishes and
needs of the Lombard people it is scarcely necessary
to point out; but, had the concessions been far more
important, they would have been utterly worthless
while they were accompanied by the closing of the
clubs, the arrest of suspected persons, and, above all,
while Radetzky still ruled Milan.

It was to a population excited by this state of
things that there came the news of the Neapolitan
Constitution. The Milanese at once flocked to the
Cathedral to return thanks, and on the walls of
Milan were written up the words, "Viva il sangue
Palermitano! Seguiamo l'esempio di Sicilia! Il
pomo e maturo." And near these inscriptions was
drawn the picture of a house in ruins, and over it,
"Casa d'Austria." New riots followed, and the
Universities of Pavia and Padua were closed by
authority. But it was felt that the electric current
had now spread right through Italy from Palermo

to Milan; and, on the very day before the University
of Pavia was closed, a secret circular was issued by
the friends of Italy at Milan urging that further demonstrations should be abandoned for the present on
the ground that "the cause of Italy is now secure."

And though Metternich was still disposed to dispute that view, though he still held to the opinion
which he had uttered in August, 1847, that "Italy
was a mere geographical expression," he yet felt the
shock of the Sicilian insurrection, and was willing to
secure friends in other parts of the Austrian dominions
by more important concessions than those which he
had made to Lombardy and Venetia. *The* most
important, or at least the most obvious, of these
popular victories had been gained in Hungary.
There, indeed, Metternich had ingeniously contrived
to defeat his own purpose, to weaken that division
which had been gradually growing between the
different sections of his opponents in Hungary, and
to throw into the hands of Kossuth far more power
than he had previously possessed. At the close of
the Diet which had met in 1843 these elements of
division were more various and more prominent
than at any other period of the struggle. Besides
the quarrel between Magyar and Slav, there had
grown up a difference of opinion between the Magyar
champions of reform. For while Kossuth was advo-
cating the strengthening of the county governments
as the great hope for Hungarian liberty, Baron
Eötvös was urging the necessity for making the
central parliament stronger at the expense of the
local bodies. But Metternich, as if determined to
consolidate the various elements of opposition against
him, shortly after the dissolution of the Diet, took a

step which, while it seemed to justify Kossuth's
belief in the importance of county governments,
silenced at the same time all those who were opposed
to Kossuth, whether on grounds of race or party,
and roused the dislike to Metternich's system to a
height not previously known in Hungary. Mailath,
the popular Chancellor of Hungary, was removed,
and his successor, Apponyi, was directed to supersede the Hungarian County Assemblies by administrators appointed by himself.

No step could possibly have been taken more likely
to defeat Metternich's own objects; for if there was
one institution round which all the peoples of Hungary
rallied, it was their County Governments. Kossuth
felt the strength of his position, and tried to remove
the causes of division. For the moment he seemed
even disposed to abandon his extreme anti-Slavonic
policy, and opposed a proposal for compelling the
use of the Hungarian language in elementary schools.
The opposition to the Administrator system in the
counties seemed to Kossuth an opportunity for
bringing forward the whole body of reforms which
he had long desired. The movement for relieving
the peasants of their burdens had naturally widened
the circle of those who took interest in political affairs;
and a famine which was quickening the political
feeling of the Silesian peasants and of the artizans of
Berlin had also spread to Hungary, and was making
the ordinary grievances of the peasant doubly grievous
to him. Along with the demands for the relief of
the peasantry from their burdens, Kossuth and his
friends now put forward proposals for Constitutional
reforms. Deak, though no longer a member of the
Assembly, gave his assistance in putting their plans

into shape, and for the first time there was formed, in 1847, a complete programme of the Hungarian Liberals. Their demands were: Publicity of parliamentary debates; a parliamentary journal in which speeches were to be published in full; triennial elections and regular yearly meetings of the Diet; improvement of the government of the towns and enlargement of their right of election to the Diet; universal taxation of all classes; the abolition of forced labour of the peasant, and of other restrictions on his mode of life.

But while it was of importance that the reformers should thus be able to put into shape their programme of reform, it was round the "Administrator" question that the real fight gathered, and Metternich was urged to make at least some concessions on this point. When, then, the Diet met in 1847, Kossuth found himself supported by many who might have shrunk back from parts of his policy before. Count Batthyanyi had formerly acted with Szechenyi; but he now arrived at the conclusion that the opposition of that nobleman to Kossuth was unwise, and he drifted more and more into the position of the Leader of Opposition in the House of Magnates. Eötvös, too, however much he may have retained his belief in the importance of a centralizing line of policy, yet could not refuse to stand by his countrymen in defence of County Government against the Administrators of Metternich. Batthyanyi and Eötvös were thus willing to suspend their special grounds of opposition to Kossuth; but it was still impossible for them to carry with them the House of Magnates; and Kossuth's great influence in the country was increased by the fact that the centre of reform was

rather to be found in the class of professional men to
which he belonged than in the nobles who had been
previously looked to as the leaders of the country.
The Diet of 1847, therefore, saw a repetition of the
struggle of the two Houses which had formed so
prominent a part of the parliamentary history of
1839. In the Lower House Kossuth carried a
measure for enforcing municipal taxes on nobles,
and it was thrown out by the House of Magnates,
who called upon the Lower House to limit themselves to votes of thanks or to express their grievances
in general terms.

But neither the land question nor the question of
parliamentary liberty were felt by the Hungarian
leaders to be as important at this crisis as the rescue
of the counties from the tyranny of Metternich's
Administrators; and it was the struggle on this
point which was brought to a crisis by the news of
the Sicilian Revolution and of the growing discon-
tents in Milan. Again Metternich was disposed to
make concessions, and again his concessions were so
framed as to be utterly inadequate to the occasion.
He declared that the Administrators should only be
appointed under exceptional circumstances; and that
the present Administrators should be withdrawn
when the exceptional circumstances in the counties
were removed. This proposal was unwelcome to all
parties; and so much force did the discontent of the
country gain that on February 29 a motion in favour
of reform in the representation was carried in the
House of Magnates. When this resolution had passed
the House of Representatives Szechenyi entered in his
diary the words, " Tout est perdu."

In the meantime the Hungarian movement had

been keeping alive hopes which in late years had
begun to show themselves in Vienna.   In that centre
of the Metternich system it was not wonderful
that political death had been more complete and
unmistakeable than in any other part of Europe.
While in other parts of Europe the press was interfered with, here Count Sedlnitzky, the head of the
police, had it completely under his control.   In other
parts of the Empire national feeling was discouraged.
Here, for even reminding the Austrians of the popular
efforts against Napoleon, Hormayr was driven from
the Archduchy of Austria.   In other parts of the
Empire local affairs might sometimes be interfered
with, but were often passed over as unimportant; in
Vienna officials were thrust into the place of the
elected Town Council.   Nor was there any assembly
at all fitted to be the mouthpiece of Austrian discontent in communications between the people and
the Government.   The only assembly which met at
Vienna, except the Town Council, was that of the Estates of Lower Austria.   This assembly represented
mainly the aristocracy, even the richer burghers not
possessing more than a nominal voice in their councils.
Therefore, even if this body had possessed as much
freedom as was allowed to the Hungarian Diet, they
could not have rallied the people round them, because
they did not understand their wants and had no
sympathy with them.   Indeed, the barrier between
rich and poor, noble and serf, seems to have been
more marked, or at any rate more painfully felt, in
the province of Lower Austria than in any part of
the Empire, except, perhaps, Bohemia.   For in
Vienna there was rapidly growing up all the miseries
of a city proletariate.   The protectionist tariff made

dear the articles of food, while the absolute suppression of public discussion, and the obstacles thrown in the way of any voluntary organization, prevented even the benevolent men among the wealthier classes from understanding anything of the wants of the poor.

So far were the Government from interfering to correct this evil that, when, in 1816, the citizens of Salzburg petitioned for a reduction of taxes, on the ground that people were dying of hunger in the streets, Francis rebuked the citizens for the arrogance of this appeal, and marked Salzburg out for special disfavour in consequence. But the crushing out of genuine education was so complete that the poorer classes in Vienna were for a long time unable to see how their misery was increased by the arrangements of the Government. They saw that no leader in the well-to-do classes seemed to concern himself in their affairs. For while healthy political and intellectual life was repressed in Vienna, that town was not, after all, an unpleasant abode for those who gave themselves up to mere self-indulgence. Menz's precedent of the Roman circus was followed here also; and Vienna became known as the "Capua der Geister." Thus, deprived alike of sympathy and power of self-help, the poor could only show their bitterness in occasional bread-riots, the reports of which were carefully excluded from the papers of the Government. One result of this utter depression was that the Viennese eagerly caught at any signs of moderation, or the most superficial tendency to Liberalism, in any of their rulers; and, being at the centre of affairs, they were naturally able to get hints of differences among the official people which were

unknown to the citizens of other towns.   Thus they
knew that the Government, which to outsiders seemed
wholly concentrated in Metternich, was, at least
nominally, divided between three persons—Metternich, the Archduke Louis, and a Bohemian nobleman
named Kolowrat.   The third of this trio was credited
with the desire for a certain amount of liberty; and
it was supposed to be by his encouragement that the
National Bohemian Museum was founded in Prague
and became a centre of Slavonic culture.   Kolowrat's
Liberal sympathies would not have counted for much
in any other place or time.   But the fact that he was
an opponent of Metternich was enough to gain him
some sympathy from the Viennese; and when, after
the death of Francis, Metternich tried to get rid of
Kolowrat, he only increased the general sympathy for
one who was thus marked as his opponent.

The death of Francis, an event hardly felt in the
rest of Europe, was of considerable importance to
Vienna; not so much from any actual changes which
it produced as from the new hope which it aroused.
A dull flame of a sort of loyalty to the House of
Hapsburg still lingered in the breasts of the Viennese; and the sole consolation which reconciled them
to their abject condition was the belief that they
were at least carrying out the wishes of the Head of
that House.   Such a consideration, if, from one point
of view, it may be described as a consolation, yet
increased the sense of despair of any redress of
grievances.   But the accession of the Emperor Ferdinand changed this feeling.   He at least was credited with the desire for a milder policy; while the
fact that he had suffered for years from epileptic fits
made it easier to believe that he was not responsible

for the failure to carry out his own plans; and thus a heavier burden of hatred was thrown upon Metternich. It was not, indeed, confined to his political opponents. The Archduchess Sophia, the wife of the Heir Apparent, had reasons of her own for disliking him; and his own arrogance, backed by the arrogance of his wife, roused against him the opposition of that aristocratic part of the community which was inclined to favour his general policy. On the other hand, the admission of the Archduke Francis Charles, the heir to the throne, to the Council of the Emperor, tended to increase the belief in the Liberal tendencies of Ferdinand. But the concession in 1842 of the permission to establish a Reading and Debating Society was considered by the Viennese the greatest triumph of Liberal principles.

The formation of this Society was sanctioned by Ferdinand, while Metternich was temporarily absent on a journey for his health. Ferdinand was induced to consent to it, by his respect for his former tutor Sommaruga, who had taken a part in its formation. This Society speedily became a centre of all kinds of discussion; and Sedlnitzky, the head of the police, soon began to suspect and hamper it, and thereby to point out to the rising reformers their natural leaders. Professor Hye, a man, as it afterwards appeared, of no very great strength of purpose, praised this Society as a power in the State which had been gained by the spirit of Association. A police spy at once hastened to the Court; the Council was called together; and a proposal was made to deprive Hye of his professorship. Archduke Louis had the good sense to oppose this proposal; but the fact that it had been made speedily got wind, and attracted a certain amount of sympathy to Hye. Newspapers and pamphlets, too, somehow gained ground under the new *régime;* and three writers especially acquired an influence in stirring up public feeling not unlike that which had been exercised by Balbo, Gioberti, and others in Italy.

A writer named Andrian took up the question of reform from the aristocratic side, stirred up the Landtag in Bohemia to assert the Constitutional rights of which they had never been entirely deprived, and also influenced the Estates of Lower Austria to strengthen their body by admitting a more complete representation of the citizens. Schuselka, on the other hand, called upon the Emperor to turn from the nobles as untrustworthy, and rely for his help on the citizens. But the man who seems to have drawn most support and attention to his opinions was Ignatz Kuranda. He did not venture to propound his ideas in Austria, but started a paper in Leipzig called the *Grenz Boten.* To this all Austrians who desired reform, whether from the aristocratic or democratic point of view, hastened to contribute. And the Government soon became so much alarmed at these writings that they demanded that both Kuranda and Schuselka should be expelled from all the States of Germany. It was a sign, perhaps, that Metternich's power was beginning, even at that time, to wane, that he was unable to obtain this concession; and then the paid writers of the Government set themselves to answer the reformers. This attempt, of course, only produced new writers on the side of Kuranda; and so the movement gathered additional force.

But however excellent the awakening of intel-

lectual freedom might be, no steady movement of
reform could be inaugurated at this period which
did not sooner or later gather round the national
principle.　Neither Vienna nor the Archduchy had
any traditions of national life; while the Austrian
Empire, which, in its separate form, was not half a
century old, was the very negation of the national
principle.　While, therefore, the Viennese looked for
lessons in Constitutional freedom to the neighbouring
State of Hungary, their only hope of sharing in a
national life seemed to rest on their chance of absorption in Germany.　Hence arose a movement in many
ways hopeless and illogical, and the cause of much
injustice to other races; but which, nevertheless,
supplied a strength and vigour to the reformers of
Vienna which they would otherwise have lacked.
They have been denounced for wishing to sacrifice
the position of their city as the capital of a great
Empire by consenting to its absorption in another
nation, in which it would play, at best, only a
secondary part.　Yet the desire to take a share in
the common struggles, common traditions, and common hopes of men of the same language and race is
surely a nobler aspiration than the ambition to be
the centre of a large number of jarring races, held
together by military force or diplomatic intrigue.
Circumstances and History had made the desire of the
Viennese impossible of execution; but this desire
had none the less an element of nobility in it, which
should not be disregarded.　The first to give prominent utterance to the new aspiration was the
Archduke John, who, at a banquet in Cologne, proposed a toast which he afterwards to some extent
tried to explain away, but which was long remem-

bered by the Germans. " No Prussia! No Austria!
One great united Germany, firm as its hills!" At
that period, the most satisfactory bond between
Austria and Germany would have been found in the
Zollverein which had been established by Prussia.
A German named List came to Vienna in 1844 for
the purpose of encouraging this union; and a banquet was held in the Hoher Markt at Vienna at
which List gave the toast of "German Unity," which
was welcomed with loud cheers, while the health of
Metternich, proposed by the American Consul, was
received in dead silence.

In the meantime, the discussions on public affairs
were growing more and more keen; and, as the news
arrived of the various rebuffs to Metternich mentioned in the last chapter, the reformers gained
heart. Yet it still seemed doubtful whether they
could enlist the sympathy of the poorer classes on
the side of Constitutional liberty. The Estates of
Lower Austria, however willing to make certain
concessions to popular feeling, showed none of that
care for the improvement of the condition of the poor
which had been prominent in the Hungarian Diet,
and also in the Lombard petition. The horrible
contrast between wealth and poverty, during the
distress of 1846 and 1847, is illustrated by the following facts:—In the year 1846 a widow in Vienna
killed one of her children and set it before the
others for food. About the same time, a Viennese
banker gave a dinner at which strawberries were
produced costing in our money about a pound
a-piece!

This awful contrast would naturally prevent the

poor from feeling any keen sympathy for reform movements inaugurated by the wealthier classes; yet, in this very year 1846, some of the poorest citizens of Vienna began, for the first time, to show a strong desire for the removal of Metternich from office. The ground of this new outburst of feeling was the belief that Metternich's championship of the Sonderbund arose from his strong sympathy with the Jesuits. It is difficult to discern the exact ground of the bitter feeling of the poor of Vienna against this Order. The Emperor Francis had disliked and discouraged the Jesuits as much as their bitterest opponents could wish; nor had Ferdinand been able to secure them any prominent position in the State; while Metternich's real feeling towards them was, as before remarked, by no means so friendly as the Liberals supposed. The citizens of Vienna could therefore hardly believe that these men were the pampered favourites of fortune; and the only explanation of the universal hatred towards them must be that their air of mystery and power made them natural objects of suspicion to men who had been driven desperate by poverty, and who were not able to discover the causes of their misery. Whatever the reason may be, there is little doubt that Metternich's supposed sympathy with the Jesuits on this occasion roused bitterness against him in the hearts of many whose poverty had hitherto made them callous about questions of government.

But a more reasonable bond between the poorer classes and the reforming leaders was soon to be established. The discussions of the Viennese Reading and Debating Club had been concerned during

these terrible years with the condition of the poor;
and, on April 10, 1847, the leaders of the Club
held a meeting to prepare for the organization of a
soup-kitchen. They soon formed a Committee, under
the leadership of the future Minister Bach, and
issued an appeal for help. For issuing this appeal
without the previous sanction of the censorship the
Committee received a stern rebuke from Sedlnitzky;
and though, after some discussion, the police allowed
the appeal to appear, the officials complained continually of the independent action of this Committee,
and tried to hamper it in every way.

It was not merely, however, as the centre of efforts
for the relief of the poor that the Debating Club and
those who supported it attracted the sympathy of
the reformers. Both there and in the University
there were ever-growing signs of political life. Professor Hye had fiercely denounced the annexation of
Cracow, and had encouraged his pupils to debate the
subject of the freedom of the Press; and Professor
Kudler had promoted the study of political economy.
The books of both these professors were prohibited
by the Government, and, in consequence, were widely
read. More prominent still, as champions of University Reform, were the leaders of the medical
profession. The Court physicians had succeeded,
for a time, in bringing the Medical Faculty under
the complete supervision of the Government; but in
1844 the students undertook to draw up new rules
which should emancipate their course of study from
this subservient position; and, after three years'
struggle, in September, 1847, they won the day, and
established a government for their Faculty which
was independent of Metternich. This new institu-

tion attracted the sympathies of the freest spirits of
Vienna, and the growth of clubs was favoured by
the leading medical professors.

It was obvious that the great movements which
were stirring in Italy would affect the feeling of the
Viennese; but the result was perhaps less in Vienna
than in other parts of Europe, because of the dislike
felt for the Germans by the Italians. And, in spite
of the growing desire for a German national life, the
Viennese could not throw off the coarse Imperialism
which naturally connected itself with the position of
their city; nor could they get rid entirely of the old
theory of Joseph II., that enlightenment and culture
must necessarily come to all races from the Germans.
But the desire to reconcile the love of liberty with
the instinct of domination showed itself curiously
enough in a pamphlet which appeared in 1848 called
"Die Sibyllinische Bücher," by Karl Möring, an officer
in the army. Möring, like Schuselka, called on the
Emperor to become a citizen king, and to break down
all monopolies and oligarchical distinctions. But,
while this writer wished to let the Italians go as
being unnaturally connected with the Empire, he
desired to compensate the Emperor for this loss by
the annexation of the Balkan provinces; and he
uttered the warning that, unless freedom were
granted, the Austrian Empire would break up, and
Magyars and Czechs on the East and West would
found separate kingdoms. "The Empire," says
Möring, "can reckon thirty-eight million subjects,
but not one political citizen; not one man who, on
moral and political grounds, can be proved to be an
Austrian. . . . The Austrian has no Fatherland."

This pamphlet produced a great effect, for it ap-

pealed at once to the two great rival aspirations of
the Austrian Liberals; and perhaps it attracted all
the more attention from the fact that the writer was
a captain in the army. Metternich, however, steadily
refused to believe in the extent of the discontent,
and rebuked Sedlnitzky for the warnings that he
brought.  It was evident that Metternich was determined to fight to the last, and, if possible, to
ignore to the last the dangers that were surrounding
him.   Kolowrat, after a fierce struggle, succeeded in
securing a new College of Censorship, which he
thought would be more favourable to literature; but
no  sooner was it established than Sedlnitzky succeeded in turning it into a new engine of oppression,
and so heavy a one that the booksellers feared that
their trade would be entirely crushed out.

And, while Metternich and his followers were
prepared to deal in this manner with the people of
Vienna,  he at least was equally determined to
crush those other opponents whom he considered
the most troublesome at the moment.  On January
12, 1848, the Austrian Government had, in concert
with France and the German Confederation, threatened Switzerland with a commercial blockade, to be
followed by armed intervention, if the Swiss attempted to make any change in their Constitution
without the consent of the three Great Powers; and
Metternich was preparing for a conference to devise
means for carrying out this threat.  With his Lombard
subjects he was prepared to deal still more summarily; and, on February 22, the following Edict
was issued for that province.  In case of riot, sentence of death was to be given in fifteen days by a
Commission, without appeal to the Emperor.  Every-

one who wore certain distinctive badges, sung or recited certain songs, wore or exhibited certain colours, applauded or hissed certain passages in a drama or concert, joined in a crowd at a given place of meeting, whether for the purpose of raising subscriptions or of dissuading from acting with certain persons, might be imprisoned, banished, or fined to the extent of 10,000 lire. Such were the measures by which Metternich was hoping to crush out the growing freedom of Europe, when the shock of the French Revolution once more disturbed his calculations.

# CHAPTER VII.

## THE DOWNFALL OF DESPOTISM. MARCH, 1848.

Character of the French Revolution of 1848.—Its unlikeness to the revolutions in the rest of Europe.—Position of South German States.—Würtemberg.—Bavaria.—Baden.—Struve and Hecker. —The Offenburg Meeting.—Bassermann's Motion.—The procession to Carlsruhe.—The risings in Würtemberg—in Bavaria—in the small States—in Saxony.—Effect of French and German risings in Vienna.—Kossuth's speech of March 3.—Its importance.—Its effect on Vienna.—Dr. Löhner's Motion.—The " Eleven Points." —Effect of the reform movement on the rulers of Austria.— The Meeting at Heidelberg.—Heinrich von Gagern.—Division between Students and Professors in Vienna.—The deputation of March 12.—The meeting of March 13.—The " first free word."—The " Estates."—The insurrection.—The workmen's movement.—Pollet.—The fall of Metternich.—Intrigues of Windischgrätz and the Camarilla.—Kossuth in Vienna.—Austria " on the path of progress."—The insurrection in Berlin.—Its character and success.—Bohemia in the sixteenth and seventeenth centuries.—Policy of Ferdinand II. and III.—of Maria Theresa—of Joseph II.—The language question.—The March movement in Prague.—Gabler.—Peter Faster.—The language revives.—The first meeting at the Wenzel's-bad.—The two petitions.—The mission to Vienna.—Contrast of Metternich's treatment of Lombardy with that of other parts of the Empire.—The secret proclamations.—The final concessions.—Augusto Anfossi.— His programme.—The rising of the 18th of March.—The appeal to O'Donnell.—The " Five Days."—Flight of Radetzky.—Difference of Venetian movement from the other movements.— Manin's imprisonment and its effects.—His release.—The Civic

Guard.—Death of Marinovich.—Magyars and Croats.—Venice free. — Palffy's treachery. — General summary of the March risings.

THE reign of Louis Philippe had indirectly produced stirrings of thought in France which were at a later period to have their influence on Europe; and which, indeed, may be said to be affecting us at this moment. But the time for this influence had not yet arrived; and the immediate result of that reign had been in some measure to confirm France in the secondary position in European affairs to which the fall of Napoleon had naturally brought her. The foreign aggression, which had been favoured by the Ministers of Charles X., had given place to intrigues like those relating to the Spanish marriages; the despotic policy which had forced on the revolution of July, 1830, had made way for manipulation and corruption; and aristocratic pretensions for the arrogance of bourgeois wealth. Attempts at reform were defeated rather by fraud than by force; and, though the immediate cause of the revolution was an act of violence, it was to the cry " A bas les corrompus " that the revolutionists rushed into the parliament of Louis Philippe. The questions, therefore, with which France had to deal, vitally important as they were, were not those which were agitating Europe at that period. And, if the subjects in which France was interested were not yet ripe for handling by the other nations of Europe, still less could the watchwords of the European revolution be inscribed on the banner of France. The principle of nationality, the development, that is, of a freer life by the voluntary union of men of the same race and language, was not one which could interest the French. The first movement for distinctly national independence in Europe had been the rising of Spain against the French in 1808: the second, the rising of Germany in 1813; and, though there might be in France sentimental sympathies with Greeks and Poles, these were due rather to special classical feeling in the one case, and traditions of common wars in the other, than to any real sympathy with national independence. France, at the end of the previous century, had offered to secure to Europe the Rights of Man, and had presented them instead with the tyranny of Napoleon; the rights of nations had been asserted against her, and the national movement would be continued irrespective of her.

It may sound a paradox, but is none the less true, that this absence of French initiative in the European revolution of 1848 is most strikingly illustrated in those countries which seemed most directly to catch the revolutionary spark from France, viz., Würtemberg, Bavaria, and Baden. The States of South Germany had, ever since 1815, been a continual thorn in the side of Metternich. A desire for independence of Austria had combined with an antagonism to Prussia to keep alive in those States a spirit with which Metternich found it very hard to deal. Würtemberg had been the first to hamper his progress towards despotic rule; while the size of Bavaria and its importance in the German Confederation had enabled its rulers to maintain a tone of independence which Metternich could not rebuke with the same freedom which he used towards the princes of less important States. But it was in the smallest and apparently weakest of the three States of Southern Germany that the movement was being matured which was eventually to be so dangerous to the power both of Austria and France. The Grand Duchy of Baden had had, since 1815, a very peculiar history of its own. The Grand Duke had been one of those who had granted a Constitution to his people not long after the Congress of Vienna. A reaction had, however, soon set in; no doubt, to some extent, under the influence of Metternich. But it was not till 1825 that the opposition of the people of Baden seemed to be crushed and a servile Parliament secured. Again a Grand Duke of Liberal opinions came to the throne in 1830; but he, in his turn, was forced to bend to Metternich's power, and to submit to the Frankfort Decrees in 1832; and in 1839 Metternich succeeded in getting a Minister appointed who was entirely under his control. But these public submissions on the part of the official leaders made it easier for a few private citizens to keep alive the spirit of opposition in Baden.

In 1845 Gustav Struve had come forward, not merely to demand reform in Baden, but also to prophesy the fall of Metternich. For this offence he was imprisoned; but he continued to keep alive an element of opposition in Mannheim, where he founded gymnastic unions, and edited a journal in which he denounced the Baden Ministry. But, though Struve seems to have been one of the first to give expression to the aspirations of the Baden people, the man whom they specially delighted to honour was a leader in the Chamber of Deputies named Hecker, a lawyer of Mannheim, who had gained much popular sympathy by pleading gratuitously in the law courts. He was elected to the

Chamber of Deputies in 1847; and he soon began to distinguish himself by his championship of German movements, and, more particularly, by his sympathy with the reform movement in the German Catholic Church and with the German aspirations of the people of Schleswig-Holstein. By an accidental circumstance, he and another Baden representative named Izstein attracted a large amount of attention to themselves; for, happening to stop at Berlin in the course of a journey, they were suddenly, and without any apparent reason, ordered to leave the town. This was believed to be the first occasion on which a representative of the people had been treated in this contemptuous manner; and thus the names of Hecker and Izstein became more widely known in Germany than those of the other leaders of the Baden movement.

The struggle in Switzerland naturally had its effect in Baden; and the Grand Duke began once more to assert those Constitutional principles which he had held when first he came to the throne. He did not, however, keep pace with the desires of the reformers; and so, on September 12, 1847, the Baden Liberals had met at Offenburg, and demanded freedom of the Press, trial by jury, and other reforms, amongst which should be mentioned, as a sign of Struve's opinions, the settlement of the differences between labour and capital. It was for their action at this meeting that the reformers had been threatened with the prosecution which never took place.

But, in the meantime, the rush of German feeling was adding a new element to the reform movement in Baden. Amand Goegg had been trying to revive the demand for a German National Assembly. The religious reforms of Ronge, which had excited so much interest in Saxony, also attracted sympathy in Baden. Struve's gymnastic unions kept alive the traditions of Jahn; and song, as usual, came to the help of patriotism. These causes so hastened the movement for German unity that, on February 12, 1848, Bassermann moved, in the Baden Chamber, that the Grand Duke should be petitioned to take steps for promoting common legislation for Germany. This motion, coming from a man who was never reckoned an advanced Liberal, naturally hastened the awakening of German feeling; and on February 27 the Baden Liberals met at Mannheim, and decided to summon a meeting at Carlsruhe, at which they intended to put forward the demand for a really representative German Parliament. Thus it was on ground already prepared that there now fell the news of the French Revolution; and when, on March 1, the leaders of the procession from Mannheim entered Carlsruhe, wearing the black, red, and gold of United Germany, the Ministry were ready to make concessions; and, on March 2, the Second Chamber of Baden demanded the repeal of the Carlsbad Decrees of 1819, of the Frankfort Decrees of 1832, and of the Vienna Decrees of 1834; and they further required that the Government should take means to secure representation of the German people in the Bundestag.

While Baden was striking the keynote of German unity, the other small States of Germany were preparing to take it up. In Würtemberg the Ministers had grown, in latter days, somewhat tyrannical; and, when the citizens gathered in Stuttgart to demand freedom of the Press and a German Parliament, the

President of the Council advised the King to summon troops to his aid. But the King was more Liberal than his Ministers; he consented to call to office a Liberal Ministry; and the Chamber which was now formed speedily decreed the abolition of feudal dues. In Bavaria the power exercised by Lola Montez over the King had long been distasteful to the sterner reformers. She had attempted, indeed, to pay court to the Liberals; but she had given such offence to some of the students of Munich as to provoke a riot which led to the closing of the University. The nobles and Jesuits would now have gladly sacrificed the King's favourite to the people; but the Baden rising had fired the Bavarian Liberals with a desire for much greater reforms. Their hatred of the Jesuits quickened their zeal; for that body was supposed to divide with Lola Montez the conscience of the King. Animated by these various causes of indignation, the Bavarian Liberals were ready enough for action; and on the news of the Baden movement they broke into the arsenal at Munich, provided themselves with arms, and demanded a German Parliament. The King consented to summon, at any rate, a Bavarian Parliament for the present; but, unable to fall in readily with the popular movement, and resenting the opposition to his favourite, he abdicated a few weeks later in favour of his son. The spark, once lighted in the South, spread among the smaller States of Germany. In Hesse Cassel the Elector tried to offer some opposition; but the citizens of Hanau marched upon Cassel and compelled the Elector to yield. In Hesse Darmstadt the Grand Duke yielded more readily, under the influence of his Minister, Heinrich von Gagern. In Nassau the

movement received additional interest from the
seizure by the victorious people of the Johannisberg,
which belonged to Metternich.

But the most interesting of the struggles was that
in Saxony.  Robert Blum was present at a ball in
Leipzig when the news arrived of the French Revolution.  He at once hastened to consult his friends;
and they agreed to act through the Town Council of
Leipzig, and sketched out the demands which they
desired should be laid before the King.  These were:
"A reorganization of the Constitution of the German
Bund in the spirit and in accordance with the needs
of the times, for which the way is to be prepared by
the unfettering of the Press, and the summoning of
representatives of all German peoples to the Assembly
of the Bund."  The Town Council adopted this address on March 1, and sent a deputation with it to
Dresden; and, on the 3rd, the people gathered to
meet the deputation on their return.  The following
is the account given by the son of Robert Blum:—

"By anonymous placards on the wall, the population of Leipzig was summoned, on the evening of
March 3, to meet at the railway-station the deputation returning from Dresden.  Since the space
was too narrow in this place, the innumerable mass
marched to the market-place, which, as well as the
neighbouring streets, they completely filled.  In
perfect silence the thousands awaited here the arrival
of the deputation, which, at last, towards nine o'clock,
arrived, and was greeted with unceasing applause.
Town Councillor Seeburg spoke first of the deep
emotion of the King; after him spoke Biedermann.
But the crowd uproariously demanded Robert Blum.
At last Blum appeared on the balcony of the Town

Council House. His voice alone controlled the whole market-place, and was even heard in the neighbouring streets. He, too, sought, by trying to quiet them, to turn them away from the subject of the address and of the King's answer. But the people broke in uproariously even into his speech with the demand, ' The answer! The answer!' It could no longer be concealed that the petitions of the town had received harsh rejection. Then came a loud and passionate murmur. The masses had firmly hoped that the deputation would bring with them from Dresden the news of the dismissal of the hated Ministers. But Blum continued his speech, and they renewed their attention to him. ' In Constitutional countries,' said he, ' it is not the King, but the Ministers who are responsible. They, too, bear the responsibility of the rejection of the Leipzig proposals. The people must press for their removal.' He added that he would bring forward in the next meeting of the Town Representatives the proposal that the King should dismiss the Ministry, ' which does not possess the confidence of the people.' Amidst tremendous shouts of exultation and applause, the appeased assembly dispersed."

Blum was as successful with his colleagues as with the crowd; and the Town Council now demanded from the King the dismissal of his Ministers, the meeting of the Assembly, and freedom of the Press. The King tried to resist the last of these three proposals, pleading his duty to the Bund. But even the Bundestag had felt the spirit of the times; and, on March 1, had passed a resolution giving leave to every Government to abolish the censorship of the Press. The King seemed to yield, and promised to

ROBERT BLUM.

IL VASCELLO, ROME (*taken since the siege*).

fulfil all that was wished; but the reactionary party
in Dresden had become alarmed at the action of the
men of Leipzig; and so, on March 11, when the
men of Leipzig supposed that all was granted,
General von Carlowitz entered their city at the head
of a strong force, and demanded that the Town
Council should abstain from exciting speeches; that
the Elocution Union should give up all political
discussion; that the processions of people should
cease; and, above all, that the march from Leipzig
to Dresden, which was believed to be then intended,
should be given up. These demands were met by
Blum with an indignant protest. " Five men," said
he, " who manage the army cannot understand
that, though their bullets may kill men, they cannot make a single hole in the idea that rules the
world." The Town Councillors of Leipzig were
equally firm. Carlowitz abandoned his attempt as
hopeless; and on March 13 the King summoned a
Liberal Ministry, who abolished the censorship of
the Press, granted publicity of legal proceedings,
trial by jury, and a wider basis for the Saxon parliament, and promised to assist in the reform of the
Bund.

In the meantime the success of the French Revolution had awakened new hopes in Vienna. Soon
after the arrival of the news, a placard appeared on
one of the city gates bearing the words, " In a
month Prince Metternich will be overthrown! Long
live Constitutional Austria! " Metternich himself
was greatly alarmed, and began to listen to proposals for extending the power of the Lower Austrian Estates. Yet he still hoped by talking over
and discussing these matters to delay the executions

Q

of reforms till a more favourable turn in affairs
should render them either harmless or unnecessary.

But great as was the alarm caused by the South
German risings, and great as were the hopes which
they kindled in the Viennese, the word which was to
give definiteness and importance to the impulses
which were stirring in Vienna could not come from
Bavaria or Saxony.   Much as they might wish to
connect themselves with a German movement, the
Viennese could not get rid of the fact that they
were, for the present, bound up with a different
political system.   Nor was it wholly clear that the
German movement was as yet completely successful.
The King of Prussia seemed to be meditating a
reactionary policy, and had even threatened to
despatch troops to put down the Saxon Liberals;
and the King of Hanover also was disposed to resist
the movement for a German parliament.   It was
from a country more closely bound up with the
Viennese Government, and yet enjoying traditions
of more deeply rooted liberty, that the utterance
was to come which was eventually to rouse the
Viennese to action.

The readiness of the nobles to accept the purely
verbal concession offered by Metternich in the matter
of the " Administrators " had shown Kossuth that
there could be no further peace.   But he still knew
how and when to strike the blow ; and it was not by
armed insurrection so much as by the declaration of a
policy that he shook the rule of Metternich.   On
March 3 a Conservative member of the Presburg
Assembly brought forward a motion for inquiry into
the Austrian bank-notes.   Kossuth answered that the
confusion in the affairs of Austrian commerce pro-

duced an evil effect on Hungarian finances; and he
showed the need of an independent finance ministry
for Hungary. Then he went on to point out that
this same confusion extended to other parts of the
monarchy. "The actual cause of the breaking up
of peace in the monarchy, and of all the evils which
may possibly follow from it, lies in the system of
Government." He admitted that it was hard for
those who had been brought up under this system to
consent to its destruction. "But," he went on, "the
People lasts for ever, and we wish also that the
Country of the People should last for ever. For
ever too should last the splendour of that Dynasty
whom we reckon as our rulers. In a few days the
men of the past will descend into their graves; but
for that scion of the House of Hapsburg who excites
such great hopes, for the Archduke Francis Joseph,
who at his first coming forward earned the love of
the nation,—for him there waits the inheritance of a
splendid throne which derives its strength from freedom. Towards a Dynasty which bases itself on the
freedoms of its Peoples enthusiasm will always be
roused; for it is only the freeman who can be
faithful from his heart; for a bureaucracy there can
be no enthusiasm." He then urged that the future
of the Dynasty depended on the hearty union between the nations which lived under it. "This
union," he said, "can only be brought about by
respecting the nationalities, and by that bond of
Constitutionalism which can produce a kindred feeling. The bureau and the bayonet are miserable
bonds." He then went on to apologize for not
examining the difficulties between Hungary and
Croatia. The solution of the difficulties of the

Empire would, he held, solve the Croatian question too. If it did not, he promised to consider that question with sympathy, and examine it in all its details. He concluded by proposing an address to the Emperor which should point out that it was the want of Constitutional life in the whole Empire which hindered the progress of Hungary; and that, while an independent Government and a separate responsible Ministry were absolutely essential to Hungary, it was also necessary that the Emperor should surround his throne, in all matters of Government, with such Constitutional arrangements as were indispensably demanded by the needs of the time.

This utterance has been called the Baptismal speech of the Revolution. Coming as it did directly after the news of the French Revolution, it gave a definiteness to the growing demands for freedom; but it did more than this. Metternich had cherished a growing hope that the demand for Constitutional Government in Vienna might be gradually used to crush out the independent position of Hungary, by absorbing the Hungarians in a common Austrian parliament; and he had looked upon the Croatian question as a means for still further weakening the power of the Hungarian Diet. Kossuth's speech struck a blow at these hopes by declaring that freedom for any part of the Empire could only be obtained by working for the freedom of the whole; he swept aside for the moment those national and provincial jealousies which were the great strength of the Austrian despotism, and appealed to all the Liberals of the Empire to unite against the system which was oppressing them all. Had Kossuth remained true

to the faith which he proclaimed in this speech, it
is within the limits of probability that the whole
Revolution of 1848-9 might have had a different
result.

The Hungarian Chancellor, Mailath, was so alarmed
at Kossuth's speech that he hindered the setting out
of the deputation which was to have presented the
address to the Emperor.   But he could not prevent
the speech from producing its effect.   Although
Presburg was only six hours' journey from Vienna,
the route had been made so difficult that the news
of anything done in the Hungarian Diet had hitherto
reached Vienna in a very roundabout manner, and had
sometimes been a week on its way.   The news of
this speech, however, arrived on the very next day;
and Kossuth's friend Pulszky immediately translated
it into German, and circulated it among the Viennese.   A rumour of its contents had spread before
the actual speech.   It was said that Kossuth had
declared war against the system of Government, and
that he had said State bankruptcy was inevitable.
But, as the news became more definite, the minds of
the Viennese fixed upon two points: the denunciation of the men of the past, and the demand for a
Constitution for Austria.   So alarmed did the Government become at the effect of this speech, that
they undertook to answer it in an official paper.
The writer of this answer called attention to the
terrible scenes which he said were being enacted in
Paris, which proved, according to him, that the only
safety for the governed was in rallying round the
Government.   This utterance naturally excited only
contempt and disgust; and the ever-arriving news
of new Constitutions granted in Germany swelled the

enthusiasm which had been roused by Kossuth's speech.

The movement still centred in the professors of the University. On March 1 Dr. Löhner had proposed, at one of the meetings of the Reading and Debating Society, that negotiations should be opened with the Estates; and that they should be urged to declare their Assembly permanent, the country in danger, and Metternich a public enemy. This proposal marked a definite step in Constitutional progress. The Estates of Lower Austria, which met in Vienna, had, indeed, from time to time, expressed their opinions on certain public grievances; but these opinions had been generally disregarded by Francis and Metternich; and, though the latter had of late talked of enlarging the powers of the Estates, he had evidently intended such words partly as mere talk, in order to delay any efficient action, and partly as a bid against the concessions which had been made by the King of Prussia. That the leaders of a popular movement should suggest an appeal to the Estates of Lower Austria was, therefore, an unexpected sign of a desire to find any legal centre for action, however weak in power, and however aristocratic in composition, that centre might be.

Dr. Löhner's proposal, however, does not seem to have been generally adopted ; and, instead of the suggested appeal to the Estates, a programme of eleven points was circulated by the Debating Society. When we consider that the Revolution broke out in less than a fortnight after this petition, we cannot but be struck with the extreme moderation of the demands now made. Most of the eleven points were concerned with proposals for the removal either of forms

of corruption, or of restraints on personal liberty, and
they were chiefly directed against those interferences
with the life and teaching of the Universities which
were causing so much bitterness in Vienna.   Such
demands for Constitutional reforms as were contained
in this programme were certainly not of an alarming
character.   The petitioners asked that the right of
election to the Assembly of Estates should be extended to citizens and peasants; that the deliberative
powers of the Estates should be enlarged; and that
the whole Empire should be represented in an
Assembly, for which, however, the petitioners only
asked a consultative power.   Perhaps the three
demands in this petition which would have excited
the widest sympathy were those in favour of the
universal arming of the people, the universal right
of petition, and the abolition of the censorship.   The
expression of desire for reform now became much
more general, and even some members of the Estates
prepared an appeal to their colleagues against the
bureaucratic system.   But the character and tone of
the utterances of these new reformers somewhat
weakened the effect which had been produced by
the bolder complaints of the earlier leaders of the
movement; for, while the students of the University
and some of their professors still showed a desire for
bold and independent action, the merchants caught
eagerly at the sympathy of the Archduke Francis
Charles, while the booksellers addressed to the
Emperor a petition in which servility passes into
blasphemy.

These signs of weakness were no doubt observed
by the Government; and it was not wonderful that,
under these circumstances, Metternich and Kolowrat

should have been able to persuade themselves that they could still play with the Viennese, and put them off with promises which need never be performed. Archduke Louis alone seems to have foreseen the coming storm, but was unable to persuade his colleagues to make military preparations to meet it. In the meantime the movement among the students was assuming more decided proportions; and their demands related as usual to the great questions of freedom of speech, freedom of the Press, and freedom of teaching; and to these were now added the demand for popular representation, the justifications for which they drew from Kossuth's speech of March 3.

But, while Hungary supplied the model of Constitutional Government, the hope for a wider national life connected itself more and more with the idea of a united Germany. Two days after the delivery of Kossuth's speech an impulse had been given to this latter feeling by the meeting at Heidelberg of the leading supporters of German unity; and they had elected a committee of seven to prepare the way for a Constituent Assembly at Frankfort. Of these seven, two came from Baden, one from Würtemberg, one from Hesse Darmstadt, one from Prussia, one from Bavaria, and one from Frankfort. Thus it will be seen that South Germany still kept the lead in the movement for German unity; and the President of the Committee was that Izstein, of Baden, who had been chiefly known to Germany by his ill-timed expulsion from Berlin. But, though this distribution of power augured ill for the relations between the leaders of the German movement and the King of Prussia, yet the meeting at Heidelberg was not prepared to adopt the complete programme of the Baden leaders, nor to commit itself definitely to that Republican movement which would probably have repelled the North German Liberals.

The chief leader of the more moderate party in the meeting was Heinrich von Gagern, the representative of Hesse Darmstadt.  Gagern was the son of a former Minister of the Grand Duke of Nassau, who had left that State to take service in Austria, and who had acted with the Archduke John in planning a popular rising in the Tyrol in 1813.  Heinrich had been trained at a military school in Munich.  He had steadily opposed the policy of Metternich, had done his best to induce the Universities to co-operate in a common German movement, and had tried to secure internal liberties for Hesse Darmstadt, while he had urged his countrymen to look for the model of a free Constitution rather to England and Hungary than to France.  During the Constitutional movement of 1848 he had become Prime Minister of Hesse Darmstadt; and he seems to have had considerable power of winning popular confidence.  Although he was not able to commit the meeting to a definitely monarchical policy, he had influence enough to counteract the attempts of Struve and Hecker to carry a proposal for the proclamation of a Republic; and his influence steadily increased during the later phases of the movement.

It was obvious that, in the then state of Viennese feeling, a movement in favour of German unity, at once so determined and so moderate in its character, would give new impulse to the hopes for freedom already excited by Kossuth's speech; and the action of the reformers now became more vigorous because the students rather than the professors were guiding the movement. Some of the latter, and particularly Professor Hye, were beginning to be alarmed, and were attempting to hold their pupils in check. This roused the distrust and suspicion of the students; and it was with great difficulty that Professors Hye and Endlicher could prevail on the younger leaders of the movement to abstain from action until the professors had laid before the Emperor the desire of the University for the removal of Metternich. This deputation waited on the Emperor on March 12; but it proved of little avail; and when the professors returned with the answer that the Emperor would consider the matter, the students received them with loud laughter and resolved to take the matter into their own hands. The next day was to be the opening of the Assembly of the Estates of Lower Austria; and the students of Vienna resolved to march in procession from the University to the Landhaus.

In the great hall of the University, now hidden away in an obscure part of Vienna, but still retaining traces of the paintings which then decorated it, the students gathered in large numbers on the 13th of March. Various rumours of a discouraging kind had been circulated; this and that leading citizen was mentioned as having been arrested; nay, it was even said that members of the Estates had themselves been seized, and that the sitting of the Assembly would not be allowed to take place. To these rumours were added the warnings of the professors. Füster, who had recently preached on the duty of devotion to the cause of the country, now endeavoured, by praises of the Emperor, to check the desire of the students for immediate action; but he was scraped down. Hye then appealed to them to wait a few days, in hopes of

a further answer from the Emperor. They answered
with a shout that they would not wait an hour; and
then they raised the cry of "Landhaus!" Breaking
loose from all further restraint, they set out on their
march, and, as they went, numbers gathered round
them. The people of Vienna had already been appealed to, by a placard on St. Stephen's Church, to
free the good Emperor Ferdinand from his enemies;
and the placard further declared that he who wished
for the rise of Austria must wish for the fall of the
present Ministers of State. The appeal produced its
effect; and the crowd grew denser as the students
marched into the narrow Herren Gasse. They passed
under the archway which led into the courtyard of
the Landhaus; there, in front of the very building
where the Assembly was sitting, they came to a dead
halt; and, with the strange hesitation which sometimes comes over crowds, no man seemed to know
what was next to be done. Suddenly, in the pause
which followed, the words "Meine Herren" were
heard from a corner of the crowd. It was evident
that someone was trying to address them; and the
students nearest to the speaker hoisted him on to
their shoulders. Then the crowd saw a quiet-looking
man, with a round, strong head, short-cropped hair,
and a thick beard. Each man eagerly asked his
neighbour who this could be; and, as the speech proceeded, the news went round that this was Dr.
Fischhof, a man who had been very little known
beyond medical circles, and hitherto looked upon as
quite outside political movements. Such was the
speaker who now uttered what is still remembered as
the "first free word" in Vienna.

He began by dwelling on the importance of the day

and on the need of "encouraging the men who sit there," pointing to the Landhaus, "by our appeal to them, of strengthening them by our adherence, and leading them to the desired end by our co-operation in action. He," exclaimed Fischhof, "who has no courage on such a day as this is only fit for the nursery." He then proceeded to dwell at some length on the need for freedom of the Press and trial by jury. Then, catching, as it were, the note of Kossuth's speech of the 3rd of March, he went on to speak of the greatness which Austria might attain by combining together " the idealist Germans, the steady, industrious, and persevering Slavs, the knightly and enthusiastic Magyars, the clever and sharp-sighted Italians." Finally, he called upon them to demand freedom of the Press, freedom of religion, freedom of teaching and learning, a responsible Ministry, representation of the people, arming of the people, and connection with Germany.[1]

In the meantime the Estates were sitting within. They had gathered in unusually large numbers, being persuaded by their president that they were bound to resist the stream of opinion. Representatives as they were of the privileged classes, they had little sympathy with the movement which was going on in Vienna. Nor does it appear that there was anyone among them who was disposed to play the part of a Confalonieri or Szechenyi, much less of a Mirabeau or a Lafayette. Many of them had heard rumours of the coming deputation; but Montecuccoli, their president, refused to begin the proceedings before the regular hour. While they were still debating this point they heard

[1] The word " Anschluss " seems hardly to imply so complete a union as was afterwards aimed at by the German party in Vienna.

the rush of the crowd outside; then the sudden
silence, and then Fischhof's voice.  Several members
were seized with a panic and desired to adjourn.
Again Montecuccoli refused to yield, and one of their
few Liberal members urged them to take courage
from the fact of this deputation, and to make stronger
demands on the Government.

But before the Assembly could decide how to act
the crowd outside had taken sterner measures.  The
speakers who immediately followed Fischhof had
made little impression ;  then another doctor, named
Goldmark, sprang up and urged the people to break
into the Landhaus.  So, before the leaders of
the Estates had decided what action to take, the
doors were suddenly burst open, and Fischhof entered
at the head of the crowd.  He announced that he
had come to encourage the Estates in their deliberations, and to ask them to sanction the demands embodied in the petition of the people.  Montecuccoli
assured the deputation that the Emperor had already
promised to summon the provincial Assemblies to
Vienna, and that, for their part, the Estates of Lower
Austria were in favour of progress.  " But," he
added, " they must have room and opportunity to
deliberate."  Fischhof assented to this suggestion,
and persuaded his followers to withdraw to the courtyard.  But those who had remained behind had been
seized with a fear of treachery, and a cry arose that
Fischhof had been arrested.  Thereupon Fischhof
showed himself, with Montecuccoli, on the balcony ;
and the president promised that the Estates would
send a deputation of their own to the Emperor to
express to him the wishes of the people.  He therefore invited the crowd to choose twelve men, to be

present at the deliberations of the Estates during the drawing up of the petition. While the election of these twelve was still going on, a Hungarian student appeared with the German translation of Kossuth's speech. The Hungarian's voice being too weak to make itself heard, he handed the speech to a Tyrolese student, who read it to the crowd. The allusion to the need of a Constitution was received with loud applause, and so also was the expression of the hopes for good from the Archduke Francis Joseph.

But, however much the reading of the speech had encouraged the hopes of the crowd, it had also given time for the Estates to decide on a course, without waiting for the twelve representatives of the people; and, before the crowd had heard the end of Kossuth's speech, the reading was interrupted by a message from the Estates announcing the contents of their proposed petition. The petition had shrunk to the meagre demand that a report on the condition of the State bank should be laid before the Estates; and that a committee should be chosen from provincial Assemblies to consider timely reforms, and to take a share in legislation. The feeble character of the proposed compromise roused a storm of scorn and rage; and a Moravian student tore the message of the Estates into pieces. The conclusion of Kossuth's speech roused the people to still further excitement; and, with cries for a free Constitution, for union with Germany, and against alliance with Russia, the crowd once more broke into the Assembly. One of the leading students then demanded of Montecuccoli whether this was the whole of the petition they intended to send to the Emperor? Montecuccoli answered that the Estates had been so disturbed in their deliberations that they

had not been able to come to a final decision. But
he declared that they desired to lay before the
Emperor all the wishes of the people. Again the
leaders of the crowd repeated, in slightly altered
form, the demands originally formulated by Fischhof.
At last, after considerable discussion, Montecuccoli
was preparing to start for the Castle at the head of
the Estates when a regiment of soldiers arrived.
They were, however, unable to make their way
through the crowd, and were even pressed back out
of the Herren Gasse.

The desire now arose for better protection for the
people ; and a deputation tried to persuade the
Burgomaster of Vienna to call out the City Guard.
Czapka, the Burgomaster, was, however, a mere tool
of the Government ; and he declared that the Archduke Albert, as Commander-in-Chief of the army,
had alone the power of calling out the Guard. The
Archduke Albert was, perhaps next to Louis, the
most unpopular of the Royal House ; he indignantly
refused to listen to any demands of the people, and,
hastening to the spot, rallied the soldiers and led
them to the open space at the corner of the Herren
Gasse, which is known as the Freyung. The inner
circle of Vienna was at this time surrounded with
walls, outside of which were the large suburbs in
which the workmen chiefly lived. The students
seem already to have gained some sympathy with the
workmen ; and, for the previous two years, the discontent caused by the sufferings of the poorer classes
had been taking a more directly political turn.
Several of the workmen had pressed in with the
students, in the morning, into the inner town ; and
some big men, with rough darned coats and dirty

caps over their eyes, were seen clenching their fists for the fight. The news quickly spread to the suburbs that the soldiers were about to attack the people. Seizing long poles and any iron tools which came to hand, the workmen rushed forward to the gates of the inner town. In one district they found the town gates closed against them, and cannon placed on the bastion near; but in others the authorities were unprepared ; and the workmen burst into the inner town, tearing down stones and plaster to throw at the soldiers.

In the meantime the representatives of the Estates had reached the Castle, and were trying to persuade the authorities to yield to the demands of the people. Metternich persisted in believing that the whole affair was got up by foreign influence, and particularly by Italians and Swiss ; and he desired that the soldiers should gather in the Castle, and that Prince Windisch-grätz should be appointed commandant of the city. Alfred Windischgrätz was a Bohemian nobleman who had previously been chiefly known for his strong aristocratic feeling, which he was said to have embodied in the expression " Human beings begin at Barons." But he had been marked out by Metternich as a man of vigour and decision who might be trusted to act in an emergency. Latour, who had been the previous commandant of the Castle in Vienna, showed signs of hesitation at this crisis ; and this gave Metternich the excuse for dismissing Latour and appointing Windischgrätz in his place. To this arrangement all the ruling Council consented ; but, when Archduke Louis and Metternich proposed to make Windischgrätz military dictator of the city, and to allow him to bring out cannon for firing on the people, great opposition arose. The Archduke John was perhaps one of the few Councillors who really sympathized with Liberal ideas; but several of the Archdukes, and particularly Francis Charles, heartily desired the fall of Metternich; and Kolowrat shared their wish. This combined opposition of sincere reformers and jealous courtiers hindered Metternich's policy; and it was decided that the City Guard should first be called out, and that the dictatorship of Windischgrätz should be kept in the background as a last resource.

In the meantime the struggle in the streets was raging fiercely. Archduke Albert had found, to his cost, that the insurrection was not, as he had supposed, the work of a few discontented men. The students fought gallantly; but a still fiercer element was contributed to the insurrection by the workmen who had come in from the suburbs. One workman was wounded in his head, his arm, and his foot; but he continued to encourage his friends, and cried out that he cared nothing for life; either he would die that day, or else " the high gentlemen should be overthrown." Another, who had had no food since the morning, entreated for a little refreshment, that he might be able to fight the better; and he quickly returned to the struggle. In those suburbs from which the workmen had not been able to break into the inner town, the insurrection threatened to assume the form of an attack on the employers. Machines were destroyed, and the houses of those employers who had lowered wages were set on fire. It was this aspect of the insurrection which encouraged the nobles to believe that, by calling out the Guard, they would induce the richer citizens to take arms against the workmen; and this policy was carried still further when, on the application of the Rector of the University, the students also were allowed the privilege of bearing arms. But the ruse entirely failed; the people recognized the City Guard as their friends, and refused to attack them; and the rumour soon spread that the police had fired on the City Guard. It was now evident that the citizen soldiers were on the side of the people; and the richer citizens sent a deputation to entreat that Metternich should be dismissed.

But the Archduke Maximilian was resolved that, as the first expedient proposed by the Council had failed, he would now apply some of those more violent remedies which had been postponed at first. He therefore ordered that the cannon should be brought down from the castle to the Michaelerplatz. From this point the cannon would have commanded, on the one side the Herren Gasse, where the crowd had gathered in the morning, and in front the Kohlmarkt, which led to the wide street of Am Graben. Had the cannon been fired then and there, the course of the insurrection must, in one way or other, have been changed. That change might have been, as Maximilian hoped, the complete collapse of the insurrection; or, as Latour held, the cannon might have swept away the last vestige of loyalty to the Emperor, and the Republic might have been instantly proclaimed. But, in any case, the result must have been most disastrous to the cause both of order and liberty; for the passions which had already been roused, especially among the workmen, could hardly have failed to produce one of those savage struggles which may overthrow one tyranny, but which gener-

ally end in the establishment of another.   Fortunately,
however, the Archduke Maximilian seems to have
had no official authority in this matter; and, when he
gave the order to fire, the master gunner, a Bohemian
named Pollet, declared that he would not obey the
order, unless it was given by the commander of the
forces or the commander of the town.   The Archduke then appealed to the subordinates to fire, in
spite of this opposition; but Pollet placed himself in
front of the cannon, and exclaimed, " The cannon are
under my command; until there comes an order from
my commander, and until necessity obliges it, let
no one fire on friendly, unarmed citizens.   Only over
my body shall you fire."   The Archduke retired in
despair.

In the meantime the deputation of citizens had
reached the castle. At first the officials were disposed
to treat them angrily, and even tried to detain them
by force; but the news of the concession of arms to
the students, the urgent pressure of Archduke John,
and the continued accounts of the growing fury of
the people, finally decided Metternich to yield; and,
advancing into the room where the civic deputation
was assembled, he declared that, as they had said his
resignation would bring peace to Austria, he now resigned his office, and wished good luck to the new
Government.   Many of the royal family, and of the
other members of the Council, flattered themselves
that they had got rid of a formidable enemy, without
making any definite concession to the people.   Windischgrätz alone protested against the abandonment
of Metternich by the rulers of Austria.   Metternich
had hoped to retire quietly to his own villa; but it
had been already burned in the insurrection; and he

soon found that it was safer to fly from Vienna and
eventually to take refuge in England.   He had, however, one consolation in all his misfortunes.   In the
memoir written four years later he expressed his cer-
tainty that he at least had done no wrong, and that
"if he had to begin his career again, he would have
followed again the course which he took before, and
would not have deviated from it for an instant."

When, at half-past eight in the evening of March
13, men went through the streets of Vienna, crying
out "Metternich is fallen!" it seemed as if the march
of the students and the petition of Fischhof had produced in one day all the results desired.   But neither
the suspicions of the people, nor the violent intentions
of the Princes, were at an end.   The Archdukes still
talked of making Windischgrätz dictator of Vienna.
The workmen still raged in the suburbs; and the
students refused to leave the University, for fear an
attack should be made upon it.   But, in spite of the
violence of the workmen, the leaders of the richer citizens were more and more determined to make common
cause with the reformers.   Indeed, both they and the
students hoped to check the violence of the riots,
while they prevented any reactionary movement.   The
Emperor also was on the side of concession.   He
refused to let the people be fired on, and announced,
on the 14th, the liberties of the Press.   But unfortunately he was seized with one of his epileptic fits;
and the intriguers, who were already consolidating
themselves into the secret Council known as the
Camarilla, published the news of Windischgrätz's
dictatorship, and resolved to place Vienna under a
state of siege while the Emperor was incapable of
giving directions.   The news of Windischgrätz's ac-

cession to power so alarmed the people that they at
once decided to march upon the castle; but one of
the leading citizens, named Arthaber, persuaded
them to abandon their intention, and, instead, to send
him and another friend to ask for a Constitution from
the Emperor. A struggle was evidently going on
between Ferdinand and his courtiers. Whenever he
was strong and able to hold his own, he was ready
to make concessions. Whenever he was either ill, or
still suffering from the mental effects of his illness,
the Government fell into the hands of Windischgrätz and the Archdukes, and violent measures were
proposed.

Thus, though Arthaber and his friends were received courteously, and assured of the Constitutional
intentions of the Emperor, yet at eleven o'clock on
the same night there appeared a public notice declaring Vienna in a state of siege. But even Windischgrätz seems to have been somewhat frightened by the
undaunted attitude of the people; and when he found
that his notice was torn down from the walls, and
that a new insurrection was about to break out, he
sent for Professor Hye and entreated him to preserve
order. In the meantime the Emperor had, to some
extent, recovered his senses; and he speedily issued
a promise to summon the Estates of the German and
Slavonic provinces and the Congregations of Lombardo-Venetia. But the people had had enough of
sham Constitutions; and the Emperor's proclamation
was torn down. This act, however, did not imply
any personal hostility to Ferdinand; for the belief
that the Austrian Ministers were thwarting the good
intentions of their master was as deeply rooted, at this
time, in the minds of the Viennese as was a similar

belief with regard to Pius IX. and his Cardinals in the minds of the Romans; and when the Emperor drove out in public on the 15th of March, he was received with loud cheers.

But, as Ferdinand listened to these cheers, he must have noticed that, louder than the "Es lebe der Kaiser" of his German subjects and the "Slawa" of the Bohemians, rose the sound of the Hungarian "Eljen." For mingling in the crowd with the ordinary inhabitants of Vienna were the Hungarian deputation who had at last been permitted by the Count Palatine to leave Presburg, and who had arrived in Vienna to demand both the freedoms which had been granted to the Germans and also a separate responsible Ministry for Hungary. They arrived in the full glory of recent successes in the Presburg Diet; for, strengthened by the news of the Viennese rising, Kossuth had carried in one day many of the reforms for which his party had so long been contending. The last remnants of the dependent condition of the peasantry had been swept away; taxation had been made universal; and freedom of the Press and universal military service had been promised. Szechenyi alone had ventured to raise a note of warning, and it had fallen unheeded. In Vienna Kossuth was welcomed almost as cordially as in Presburg; for the German movement in Vienna had tended to produce in its supporters a willingness to lose the eastern half of the Empire in order to obtain the union of the western half with Germany. So the notes of Arndt's Deutsches Vaterland were mingled with the cry of " Batthyanyi Lajos, Minister Präsident!" Before such a combination as this, Ferdinand had no desire, Windischgrätz no power, to maintain an obstinate resistance; and, on March 16, Sedlnitzky, the hated head of the police, was dismissed from office. On the 18th a responsible Ministry was appointed; and on the 22nd Windischgrätz himself announced that national affairs would now be guided on the path of progress.

In the meantime that German movement from which the Viennese derived so much of their impulse had been gaining a new accession of force in the North of Germany. In Berlin the order of the Viennese movements had been to some extent reversed. There the artizans, instead of taking their tone from the students, had given the first impulse to reform. The King, indeed, had begun his concessions by granting freedom of the Press on the 7th of March; but it seemed very unlikely that this concession would be accompanied by any securities which would make it a reality. The King even refused to fulfil his promise of summoning the Assembly; and it was in consequence of this refusal that the artizans presented to the Town Council of Berlin a petition for the redress of their special grievances. The same kind of misery which prevailed in Vienna had shown itself, though in less degree, in Berlin; and committees had been formed for the relief of the poor. The Town Council refused to present the petition of the workmen; and, in order to take the movement out of their hands, presented a petition of their own in favour of freedom of the Press, trial by jury, representation of the German people in the Bundestag, and the summoning of all the provincial Assemblies of the Kingdom. This petition was rejected by the King; and thereupon, on March 13, the people gathered in large numbers in the streets. General Pfuel fired on them;

but, instead of yielding, they threw up barricades, and a fierce struggle ensued.

On the 14th the cry for complete freedom of the Press became louder and more prominent; and the insurgents were encouraged by the first news of the Vienna rising.  The other parts of the Kingdom now joined in the movement.  On the 14th came deputations from the Rhine Province, who demanded in a threatening manner the extension of popular liberties. On the 16th came the more important news that Posen and Silesia were in revolt.  Mieroslawsky, who had been one of the leaders of the Polish movement of 1846, had gained much popularity in Berlin; and he seemed fully disposed to combine the movement for the independence of Posen with that for the freedom of Prussia, much in the same way as Kossuth had combined the cause of Hungarian liberty with the demand for an Austrian Constitution.   In Silesia, no doubt, the terrible famine of the previous year, and the remains of feudal oppression, had sharpened the desire for liberty; and closely following on the news of these two revolts came clearer accounts of the Viennese rising and the happy tidings of the fall of Metternich.

The King of Prussia promised, on the arrival of this news, to summon the Assembly for April 2; and two days later he appeared on the balcony of his palace and declared his desire to change Germany from an Alliance of States into a Federal State.  But the suspicions of the people had now been thoroughly aroused; and on March 18, the very day on which the King made this declaration, fresh deputations came to demand liberties from him; and when he appealed to them to go home his request was not complied with.  The threatening attitude of the soldiers, and the recollection of their violence on the preceding days, had convinced the people that until part at least of the military force was removed they could have no security for liberty.  The events of the day justified their belief ; for, while someone was reading aloud to the people the account of the concessions recently made by the King, the soldiers suddenly fired upon them, and the crowd fled in every direction.  They fled, however, soon to rally again ; barricades were once more thrown up ; the Poles of Posen flocked in to help their friends, and the black, red, and gold flag of Germany was displayed.  Women joined the fight at the barricades ; and, on the 19th, some of the riflemen whom the King had brought from Neufchatel refused to fire upon the people.  Then the King suddenly yielded, dismissed his Ministers, and promised to withdraw the troops and allow the arming of the people.  The victory of the popular cause seemed now complete ; but the bitterness which still remained in the hearts of the citizens was shown by a public funeral procession through Berlin in honour of those who had fallen in the struggle.  The King stood bare-headed on the balcony as the procession passed the palace ; and on March 21 he came forward in public, waving the black, red, and gold flag of Germany.

But while the movements for German freedom and unity were strengthening the cause of the Viennese and destroying the hopes of Metternich, two other movements for freedom, which might have helped to produce a newer and freer life in Europe, were preparing the way, against the wishes of their leaders, for that collision of interests between the different

races of Europe which was to be the chief cause of
the failure of the Revolution of 1848. Of these movements the one least known and understood in England is that which took place in Bohemia. In order
to understand it we must recall some of the events of
earlier Bohemian history.

Bohemia, like Hungary, had, in the sixteenth
century, freely elected Ferdinand I. of Austria as
her King. Nor had the Bohemians, at that time, the
slightest desire for closer union with any of those
other Kingdoms which happened to be under the rule
of the same Prince; nay, they would have avoided
such union, even in matters where common action
seemed the natural result of common interests. Ferdinand I., indeed, and some of his successors, did undoubtedly desire a closer bond between the different
territories subject to the House of Austria; but,
during the sixteenth century, their efforts in this
direction were, in the main, defeated. The continual
wars against the Turks, indeed, did necessitate common military action; and, to that extent, they paved
the way for a closer union; but, in spite of this ground
for fellow feeling, no public recognition of any common bond between Bohemia, Austria, and Hungary
could be obtained at that period from the Estates of
Bohemia.

The seventeenth century, however, had produced
a great change in the relations between Bohemia and
the House of Austria. The ill-fated and ill-organized
struggle for liberty and Protestantism, which was
crushed out in 1620 at the Battle of the White Hill,
was followed by a change in the objects aimed at by
the House of Austria in their government of Bohemia.
Considering his military successes, it must be admitted

that Ferdinand II. was even generous in his action towards Bohemia, so far as the forms of Constitutional Government were concerned. For in 1623 he restored its old Constitution, re-established its independent law-courts, and declared that he had " no intention of destroying or diminishing the rights of our faithful subjects of this Kingdom."

But, alongside of the restoration of Constitutional forms, there went on an organized system of oppression by which Ferdinand II. was endeavouring to crush out the Protestant faith and the Bohemian language. While, on the one hand, the old Bohemian nobles were banished or executed, the German Dominicans and members of other Roman Catholic orders were at the same time destroying all the Bohemian literature on which they could lay their hands; and some Bohemians tried to save these relics of the past by carrying them to Stockholm, where, it is said, the remains of their early literature can still be found. Without any direct change in the law, German officials were gradually introduced into the chief offices of State in Bohemia; and German became the language of ordinary business relations. Thus, by a natural process, the Bohemian language underwent the same change of position which the English language experienced in the twelfth and thirteenth centuries; that is, it ceased to be a literary language, and became merely a popular dialect of peasants and workmen.

But Ferdinand II. soon found that he could not carry out completely his purpose of Romanizing and Germanizing Bohemia without departing from that Constitutional line which he had attempted to follow in 1623. He could not trust a Bohemian Assembly to carry out his plans; and in 1627 he issued an ordinance which remained in force till 1848. By this edict the King claimed the right to add to, alter, or improve the Government of the country at his own pleasure. Yet even this he claimed to do in virtue of a previously existing royal right ; the judges took advantage of this admission to interpret the new ordinance in the light of Ferdinand's previous promises to respect the Bohemian Constitution ; and this interpretation was justified by the fact that Ferdinand, in the very same year in which he issued the ordinance, reiterated the Constitutional promises which he had made in 1623. The explanation of this apparent contradiction is that Ferdinand II. cared more for the unity of the Roman Catholic Church than for centralizing the Government of the Austrian dominions; and the same might be said of his successor, Ferdinand III. Nevertheless, from motives of convenience, both these Princes resided very little in Prague and much in Vienna; and thus those court officials who give the tone in these matters to the Government gradually gathered together, rather in the Archduchy of Austria than in the Kingdom of Bohemia; while the process of centralization was still further encouraged by that denationalizing movement which dated from the Battle of the White Hill.

With the growth of an alien aristocracy there naturally grew up that union of class bitterness with race bitterness which intensifies both ; and the difference of faith between the conquerors and conquered added another element of division. An attempt of the peasants to shake off the yoke of their conquerors led to the destruction of privileges which they had hitherto possessed; and thus the Estates of Bohemia became even more aristocratic than those of the neighbouring countries. Under such circumstances the gradual absorption of the Government of Bohemia in that of the other lands of the House of Austria seemed the natural consequence of the Austrian policy in the seventeenth century ; and Maria Theresa propounded a plan for a Central Assembly in which Bohemia, Hungary, and Galicia were to share a common representation with the Archduchy of Austria. These schemes, like all measures for moderate unification in the Austrian dominions, received a fatal shock from the impetuous policy of Joseph II. The claim to Germanize Bohemia by force awoke in that country, as it had done in Hungary, a desire for new national life and a zeal for the old national literature. The opposition to Joseph did not, indeed, take so fierce a form in Bohemia as it assumed in Hungary and the Netherlands ; but it was strong enough to induce Joseph's successor, Leopold II., to restore the old Constitution of Bohemia.

In Bohemia, as in Hungary, the spirit of national independence had now embodied itself in the desire to preserve and revive the national language; and in 1809 a new impulse was given to this desire by the discovery of a parchment which had been wrapped round the pillars of a hall, and which was found to contain some old Bohemian poems. These poems were believed to belong to the thirteenth or fourteenth century; and the Bohemians held them to be superior to anything which had been produced by the Germans at that period. As a matter of course, German scholars at once came forward to try to disprove the authenticity of these poems ; and the fight raged hotly. The expulsion of the Bohemian language from its literary position seemed to many to have deprived this struggle of any living interest. But writers were arising who were determined to show that that language could still be made a vehicle of literary expression; and they even hoped to make it the centre of a Slavonic movement. For the Bohemian language had a kind of offshoot in the North of Hungary among the race of the Slovaks; and the interest which the poet Kollar and the philologer Szaffarik were stirring up in the Slovak dialect was adding new force to the Bohemian movement. The historian Palacky increased the effect which was produced by these writers; and, what is more remarkable, men whose names showed an evidently German origin became fascinated by this new movement. Count Leo Thun entered into a controversy with Pulszky about the worth of the Slavonic languages; and one may still see in Prague the statue of Joseph Jungmann, who was one of the first founders of unions for reviving the national language. A struggle of the Bohemian Estates in 1837 to maintain their control over taxation was sufficient, though unsuccessful, to increase considerably the interest felt by their nation in their political life. And thus it came to pass that, when, in March, 1848, the news of the French Revolution came to Prague, it found the Bohemians ready for the emergency.

A young man named Gabler, who had been in Paris in 1846, was requested by some friends who were gathered in a café to read the account of the French rising and explain its details. On the following day more people came to the café to hear the news ; discussion began, and suggestions were made as to the best way of adapting the French movement to the needs of Bohemia.   German was still the language of intercourse between educated people in Prague ; and the discussions were at first carried on in that language.   But among those who came to the meetings was a publican named Peter Faster ; and, while the discussion on various questions of reform was going on, Faster broke out suddenly into a speech in Bohemian.   Instantly, the whole assembly joined in the national cry of " Slawa."   Other speeches followed in the same language ; the fashion quickly spread ; and soon all adherents of the new movement began speaking the national language. A committee was now formed for the preparation of a petition; and a unanimous summons was circulated, calling on the Bohemians to meet at the Wenzel's-bad on March 11.

This bath-house stands in a garden at some little distance from the main streets of Prague, and it was overlooked by barracks.   One picquet of cavalry was seen in the streets, the rest remained in the barracks.   Slowly the streets near the bath-house filled ; at about half-past seven the doors opened ; and half an hour later appeared Peter Faster, a lawyer named Trojan, and others.   They announced that they had called the meeting for the purpose of proposing a petition to the Emperor.   The petition[1]

---

[1] This petition must be given at length in order that students of the Revolution may realize the peculiar character of the Bohemian movement, since this is the only one of the March risings in which the claim of an oppressed people to live in peaceable equality beside their former oppressors was, for the time, successfully established.

was adopted with little trouble, and a committee of twenty-five was appointed to present it. The petition was as follows : " A great event in the West of Europe is shedding its light, like a threatening meteor, over to us. It has scarcely begun ; but this great movement which we guessed afar off is carrying away Germany's allied States with it. There is much excitement near the frontiers of Austria ; but Your Majesty and the allied Princes have controlled the movement, while you have magnanimously placed yourselves at the head of it, to warn it from a dangerous abyss and from bad ways. The time has become new and different ; it has brought the people nearer the Princes, and lays on the people the duty of rallying round their Princes, offering confidence and entreating for confidence in the days of danger.

" Prague's faithful people, touched by the universal movement, ruled by the impulse to go before the monarchy in loyalty and truth, lays at the feet of Your Majesty its most heartfelt thanks for being allowed to speak from their full heart to their beloved King and Master. May their words find echo and just appreciation. Our confidence in God and our conscience leads us to hope that it will.

" New and unwonted is the benevolence of this high permission ; if we are less choice in our words and expressions, if we seem immodest in the extent of our petitions, our King's fatherly consideration will graciously put a right construction on our acts. Two different national elements inhabit this happy Kingdom, this pearl in your Majesty's illustrious imperial crown. One of them, the original one, which has the nearest right to its land and King, has hitherto been hindered in its progress towards culture and equal rights by institutions, which, without being hostile or denationalizing, yet naturally involve a partial wiping out of original national feeling as the condition of obtaining recognition as citizens.

" The free development of both nations, the German and Bohemian, which are united by fate, and both of which inhabit Bohemia, and a similar striving after the objects of a higher culture, will, by strengthening, reconciling, and uniting them in brotherhood, lay the foundation of the welfare of both nations.

" Bohemia has not yet reached that high position which it ought to have attained, in order to meet forcibly the serious events which are developing themselves ; and this failure arises from the superiority which has hitherto been granted to the German element in legal and administrative arrangements. It is not mere toleration, it is the equalizing of the two nationalities by legal guarantees which can and will bind both nations to the throne.

" But the guarantees for this excellent and sacred result, so much to be desired by every patriot, whether German or Bohemian, do not consist in the cultivation of language only. It consists in the essential alterations of the institutions which have hitherto existed, in the removal of the barriers which hinder intercourse between Prince and People, and at the same time in universal, benevolently guarded, popular instruction by school and writing."

After more to the same effect, and after dwelling at some length on the need of publicity in national affairs, the petitioners formulate their demands in eleven points. The first and second of these are concerned with the equalization of the races and with the Constitutional development hinted at in the

S

previous petition ; but they also include a proposal
for the restoration of the union between Bohemia,
Moravia, and Silesia, to be effected by an annual
meeting in common of the Estates of the three provinces.   The third is concerned with communal freedom and the condition of the peasantry.   The fourth,
fifth, sixth, and seventh relate to those ordinary
securities for civil and religious freedom which were
being demanded at this time by all the nations of
Europe.   The eighth clause of the petition demands
" the appointment to offices of men who know completely and equally both the languages of the country."
The ninth is concerned with the popularization of the
military service.   The tenth with the redistribution
of taxation, especially the abolition of taxes on articles
of consumption ; while the eleventh deals with the
equalization of education between German and
Bohemian, and the freedom of teaching at the
universities.

The gathering at this first meeting was rather
small; but the news of the movement rapidly spread.
On the 12th a meeting of the Town Councillors was
held in the Rath Haus; and, on the 15th, the students
met to draw up a petition of their own.   They had
soon caught the excitement of the time; and had
been stirred up by a German-Bohemian named Uffo
Horn to take separate action.   Guided and restrained
by Gabler, they consented to help in preserving order,
and embodied their petition in eight clauses.   In
these they not only demanded the ordinary liberties
of teaching for which other universities were contending, but also pleaded for the right to full instruction
both in Bohemian and German; for the power to
visit foreign universities; for the development of

physical education, and for the right to form unions among the students, after the fashion of those recently sanctioned by a statute of the Munich University. It is worth noting that they also demanded that the test of fitness for State service should be made severer.

The news of the rising in Vienna came to encourage and strengthen the Bohemian movement; and on March 18 the students of Prague sent a letter of exulting congratulation to the students of Vienna on their services to the cause of freedom. But the Bohemian movement was not yet to be turned out of that quiet course which distinguished it among the Revolutions of the period; and on Sunday, March 19, the deputation that was to bear the wishes of the Bohemians to the Emperor met in the streets of Prague to hear a silent mass before starting for Vienna. Prague, like Vienna, has been so much altered in recent years that it is difficult to realize the exact scene of this event. At the top of the long avenue which now ornaments the Wenzelsplatz there was, in 1848, a large gate called the Rossthor; and this was closed on March 19 so that no traffic should disturb the service. Within the gates stood a statue of St. Wenzel; and round this the deputation gathered, wearing scarves of the Bohemian colours, white and red, edged with the Austrian black and yellow, to show their zeal for the unity of the Empire. Outside the group formed by the members of the deputation stood the newly-formed students' legion and some others of the National Guard. The Archbishop took the leading part in the mass; but, after it was over, the Bishop of Prague gave out a Bohemian hymn, which was heartily joined in by the people. To

impress the citizens still further with the solemnity
of the occasion, Faster and Trojan had issued an
address, declaring that the deputation left their
families and property under the protection of the
citizens of Prague; and, on the other hand, a committee chosen by the citizens appealed to the deputation to impress upon the Emperor the danger of
delays and unfulfilled promises, and expressed a desire
for a closer union between the Peoples of the Austrian
Empire.

When the ceremonies were over, the deputation
started, led by Faster and Trojan. Faster took
charge of the petition from the citizens of Prague;
Trojan carried the petitions from the provincial towns
of Bohemia; while a chosen band of the students
were to present the University petition. The people
who were gathered at the station joined in Bohemian
songs; and the ladies showered flowers and ribbons
as the train moved off. After the departure of the
deputation, the citizens' committee set themselves to
check any violent movement among the workmen, by
making special arrangement for providing work for
the resident workmen in Prague. Soon came the
news that the deputation had been warmly welcomed
in Vienna. A great part of the National Guard had
turned out to greet them; the Emperor had addressed
them in Bohemian; and Count Kolowrat had said that,
though he was seventy-one years old, and had served the
State for fifty years, yet his last days were the happiest,
because he could now advise according to his heart.

In striking contrast to this, the most peaceable of
all the March risings, was the movement which was
going on at the same time in Lombardy. It seemed,
indeed, as if the Austrian Government were deter-

mined to drive the Lombards into violent action. In
Vienna Metternich was at least talking about extending the power of the Estates; in Hungary Kossuth
was able to speak freely in the Presburg Diet;
in Bohemia the Government seemed to drop into
the hands of the people almost without an effort;
but in Lombardy the savage proclamation of February had been followed on March 2 by an announcement from Spaur that the people must abandon all
hope of any reform in the organic institutions of
Lombardy which could imply a relaxation of the
union with other parts of the Monarchy; and so
rigorously were the repressive laws carried out that
on March 11 there were 700 political prisoners in
Milan.

Yet, in spite of this tremendous rigour, there were
still signs of the irrepressible aspirations of the Lombards. On March 10, a feast was held in Brescia
in honour of the proclamation of the French Republic;
and the Italian soldiers quartered in that town showed
sympathy with this demonstration. Even during
the actual rising at Vienna, Metternich still showed
his determination to hold down Lombardy by force;
he suddenly recalled Spaur and Ficquelmont from
Milan, and sent Count O'Donnell, a man of fiercer
type, to take the place of Spaur. Even Metternich's
idea of Lombard reform was not changed by the
rising in Vienna; for on March 16 there appeared
in Milan a proclamation which must either have been
prepared by Metternich just before his fall, or
adopted by the Camarilla directly after it; and in
this the Lombards were offered exactly the same
programme of reform which had been proposed to
them in January.

But in the meantime the people were not idle. The Italians in Vienna managed to keep up a secret correspondence with their countrymen in Lombardy, and to warn them that new troops might be sent against them; while the Milanese managed to circulate secret proclamations which stirred the hopes of their fellow Lombards. On the 16th or 17th of March one of these proclamations appeared, containing a final protest against all the tyrannies exercised by Austria in Lombardy since 1815, down to the massacres of 1848. The composers of the proclamation concluded by finally declaring their resolution " to feel as Italians, to think as Italians, to will once for all to be Italians; to resolve to break once and for all the infamous treaty that has sold our liberties without our consent; to exercise our rights as men, our revenge as Italians." Thus, by some mysterious freemasonry, the champions of liberty in Milan had gradually been drawn together and prepared for action; and when on the 17th of March the news arrived that the Viennese insurrection had succeeded, that liberty of the Press had been granted, and that the Congregations of Lombardy as well as the estates of the other parts of the Empire were to be called together, the news gave the signal for insurrection. The Congregations which, up to the time of Nazari's speech, had been so silent and helpless, and whose uselessness had been further proved by the failure of that very protest, could not be accepted as the representatives of national life; and the suggestion of freedom of the Press while Radetzky remained in Milan could only supply a subject for a caricature.

The leading spirit in the Milanese movement, so far as it is possible to single out any individual, was

Augusto Anfossi. He had been born in Nice and
educated by the Jesuits. That education, in this as
in so many other cases, had produced the most violent
reaction; and Anfossi's first claim to distinction was
a bitter attack on his former teachers. In consequence of this, he had been compelled to fly to
France; and he had served for a time in the French
Army; but his hopes had been raised by the accession of Charles Albert; and he had returned to Piedmont to experience the disappointment shared by the
other Liberals of that period. The punishments
which followed the risings of 1831 had driven him
again into exile; and he had then joined in the rising
of the Egyptians against the Turks. But the movements of 1848 once more called his attention to Piedmont; and he now hastened to Milan and drew up a
proclamation which was adopted and issued by the
leaders of the insurrection. How little these leaders
could have foreseen the actual result of the struggle
may be gathered from the contents of the proclamation; for, eloquent and enthusiastic as are its opening words, its demands fall far short of the claim for
that complete independence which the Lombards
were for a time to achieve; while so little did the
Milanese recognize the determined savagery of their
opponents that the seventh demand made in this proclamation was that " neutral relations should be established with the Austrian troops, while we guarantee
to them respect and the means of subsistence." But
the only really important point in the proclamation
was its final summons to the people to meet at
three p.m. the next day in the Corsia dei Servi; and
this appeal roused not merely the hopes, but the
impatience of the people.

Three hours before the time appointed, while
Casati and the Municipal Council were deliberating
in the Broletto, or town-hall, they heard loud shouts
in the streets of "Death to the Germans!" and
"Long live Italy!" Then a crowd bearing sticks
covered with the Italian colours entered the Broletto, and required that Casati and the leading
Councillors should come with them at once to
O'Donnell, to demand the establishment of a Civic
Guard, and the placing of the police under the
municipal authorities.    Cesare Correnti, one of the
Council, urged the leaders of the movement to trust
to the municipality; but Enrico Cernuschi, one of
the organizers of the movement, refused to yield to
this suggestion; and a man named Beretta seized
Casati by the arm to lead him to the Governor.
O'Donnell was startled at this sudden demonstration;
and Casati, on his part, was equally astonished at the
position into which he had been forced.  He shook
hands with O'Donnell and encouraged him to look
on him as a friend; and it was, perhaps, in reliance on
this help that O'Donnell ventured at first to refuse
the proposals to subject the police to the Municipal
Council and to surrender their arms to the Civic
Guard.  Cernuschi, however, insisted that O'Donnell
should not only yield these points, but that he should
sign his name to his concessions.  O'Donnell, in
terror, consented; and then Casati desired to send a
messenger to Torresani, the head of the police, to
secure his approval of the concessions.  But the
movement had gone far beyond Casati's control;
and, while his messenger was hastening to put the
matter before Torresani in proper diplomatic form,
Cernuschi and his friends had rushed to an armourer's
shop to avail themselves of their new privilege.

But, as they still wished to place the Municipal Council, as far as possible, at the head of their movement, they carried their arms to the Broletto, where they demanded to be enrolled in the new Civic Guard. In the meantime, Torresani had refused to act without Radetzky's authority, and Radetzky was furious at the news of O'Donnell's concessions. Hearing that one of his officers, who was ill in bed, had offered to give his sanction to these concessions, the savage General threatened to have him dragged from his bed and shot, if he did not at once recall the order; and troops were despatched to the Broletto to suppress the movement. Casati, indeed, had fled from the scene of action, and taken refuge in a private house; but the people, who had brought the arms to the Broletto, closed the gates against Radetzky's force; and, though they had only fifty guns with them, they prepared to defy the Austrian cannon, backed by more than 2,000 soldiers. The proposal to capitulate was rejected with scorn; and, from seven to nine p.m., this little band, many of them boys, defended the Municipal Council Hall. But it was impossible to conquer against such odds; and at last the Austrian soldiers broke in, attacked all whom they found there, whether armed or unarmed; hurled down into the streets some boys whom they found on the roofs, hung one little child, and marched off the rest of their prisoners to the castle, to be tortured by Radetzky.

But, as they were actually on their way to the castle, the victorious soldiers met some of their comrades who were flying before the citizens. Augusto Anfossi had been, in the meantime, reducing into order the gallant, but undisciplined defenders of their country; and, before the morning of the 19th, stones and wood had been put together and fastened with iron; and thus secure barricades had risen in many of the streets. Amongst other interesting materials for the barricades may be mentioned O'Donnell's carriage, which had been seized for this purpose. Radetzky, startled at the vigour of the opposition, wrote to Ficquelmont that "the nature of this people is changed as if by magic; fanaticism has infected every age, every class, and both sexes." In his alarm he offered to grant the demand which had been made in the morning, that the police should be placed under the command of the Municipal Council. Casati would, even then, have accepted this as a settlement of the struggle; but he was now quite powerless. For, while he was signing decrees, and appointing as head of the police a man who was still prisoner to the Austrians, the bells throughout Milan were ringing for a storm.

At no stage of the struggle were there greater efforts of heroism than on this 19th of March. At the bridge of San Damiano two men held at bay a whole corps of Austrians; not far from the Porta Romana another champion carried off some youthful scholars, one after another, on his shoulders, in the face of a body of Croats. Guns were often wanting, but the insurgents used swords and sticks instead. The Tyrolese fired from the tower of the cathedral upon the people, and the cannons from the Piazza Mercante played upon them; but three cannoneers were killed, and at last the cannon were captured by the Milanese. The 19th of March was a Sunday; and, as the congregation came out from mass in the church of San Simpliciano, they were attacked by the Austrians and driven back into the church.

Food was brought them from neighbouring houses; and they retained their position till four o'clock in the afternoon, when they succeeded in making their escape. Nor were there wanting touches of the Milanese humour to relieve the terrors of the fight; boys sometimes exhibiting a cat, sometimes a broom-stick with a cap on it, as a mark for the Austrians to fire at. But the fiercest fight raged at the Porta Nuova, on the south side of the town, where Augusto Anfossi commanded in person. There a band of Austrian grenadiers brought their cannon to bear on the defenders of the city; and Anfossi had a long and fierce struggle before he could drive them back. At last, however, he made his way to the gate; and, lifting on high the Italian flag, he kissed it, and planted it on the arch of the gateway.

On the 20th the Austrians began to show signs of giving way. The Tyrolese fled down the giddy stair-cases of the Cathedral tower and escaped through secret passages; and the family of Torresani fell into the hands of the insurgents. But the Milanese, though they had seen their children spitted on the bayonets of the soldiers, their women insulted, and the prisoners tortured by Radetzky, were ready to take charge of the family of one of their worst tyrants, and to protect them from violence. Even the brutal Bolza, when he became a prisoner in their hands, was carefully guarded from ill-treatment; and he is said to have been so much impressed by this unexpected magnanimity that he died penitent. Again offers of compromise were made by the Austrians, and a truce of fifteen days was proposed till the officers could hear from Vienna. Again Casati hesitated; but again his hesitation had no effect on the struggle.

On the 21st the Genio Militare, one of the chief barracks of the city, was attacked by the insurgents. The struggle was continued for some time with great fierceness on either side; but at last a cripple, named Pasquale Sottocorni, came halting up on his crutch and set fire to the gate; then the defenders, unable to hold out any longer, surrendered to the people. This day was also memorable for the capture of Radetzky's palace, and in it of the wonderful sword with which he had threatened to exterminate the Milanese.

In the meantime the other towns of Lombardy had been hastening to send help to their capital. At Como, immediately on the arrival of the news of the Viennese success, bands had collected with lighted torches, crying, " Long live Italy! Long live independence!" The guards were redoubled, but refused to act. The people surrounded the Town Council House, demanding a Civic Guard, which was quickly granted; in a short time Como was free, and the soldiers of Como were on their march to Milan. It was on March 18 that the news of the Milanese rising reached Bergamo; and the people at once rose, crying, " Long live Milan!" and " Death to the Germans!" The Archduke Sigismund, who was in the town, was compelled by the people to hold back his troops, while a Capuchin monk led the citizens to Milan. In Brescia the rising seems to have been almost simultaneous with that of Milan. The first attack was made on the Jesuits; but religious hostility was quickly merged in a desire for national independence, and the cry soon rose for a civic guard. Prince Schwarzenberg, who was in command of the terrible fortress which frowns upon Brescia, hoped easily to overawe the city. But the people gathered in

the Piazza Vecchia, and after a fierce struggle,
drove back the soldiers. Schwarzenberg was compelled to yield to the demands of the people; the
municipal authorities in vain endeavoured to hinder
the movement; and in a short time many of the
Brescians had united with the country folk of the
neighbouring district and were marching to Milan. At
Cremona about 4,000 soldiers had laid down their arms
before the citizens had attacked them.

In the meantime Augusto Anfossi had been dangerously wounded, and was obliged to abandon the
defence; but his place was taken by Luciano Manara, a
youth of twenty-four, who led the attack on the Porta
Tosa, on the east side of Milan. Arms had now been
freely distributed among the insurgents, and a professor of mathematics from Pavia superintended the fortifications and assisted Manara in the attack. For five
hours the assault continued, Manara rushing forward
at the head of his forces and effecting wonders with
his own hand. Recruits from the country districts
co-operated from outside the city with the Milanese
insurgents within. At last the gate was set on fire,
the position was captured, and the name of Porta Tosa
was soon afterwards changed to that of Porta Vittoria.
The Austrian soldiers had now become heartily tired
of the struggle. Radetzky had arranged his troops
in so careless a manner that he was unable to supply
them properly with food, and sixty Croats surrendered from hunger. Radetzky was now convinced
of the uselessness of continuing the struggle; and,
though he had just before been threatening to bombard
the city, he now decided to abandon it. So, on the
evening of the 22nd of March, the glorious Five Days
of Milan were brought to an end by the retreat of
the Austrians from the city.

This rising had for the time being freed the greater part of Lombardy; but there was yet another Italian city under the Austrian rule, which was achieving its own independence in a somewhat different way. The risings in Vienna, Berlin, Prague, and Milan, though they produced many acts of heroism, and some of wise forethought, did not call to the front any man of first-rate political capacity, nor could they be said to centre in any one commanding figure. In Venice, on the other hand, the movement centred from first to last in one man. The imprisonment of Daniel Manin had been the point of interest to Venetians, the typical instance of their grievances; and more than one circumstance tended to strengthen this feeling. Manin's sister had died from the shock of hearing of her brother's arrest; and his wife had organized a petition for his release which had been signed by the Podestà of Venice and ninety-nine other persons of well-known character. His own legal ability had enabled Manin to dwell more forcibly on the points of illegality in his arrest. But when he and his friends urged his claim to be either tried or set free, the authorities pleaded that they could not release him until they heard from Vienna. This answer must have tended still more to mark him out as a victim of that centralizing force which was endeavouring to crush out Italian feeling; while the fact of his descent from the last Doge of Venice added a touch of historic sentiment to the other points of interest in his case. Manin's arrest had been quickly followed by that of Tommaseo, and in any talk among the patriots of Venice the discussion of these arrests was sure to arise.

In Venice, too, the same kinds of demonstrations

of popular feeling took place during January and
February which had shown themselves in Milan.
Whenever German music was performed in public all
the Italians left the place.   Men went about in black
gloves; women refused to appear in gala costume at
public ceremonies; and even those who went to the
theatre attended there not so much for the sake of
the performance as to applaud passages about a
betrayed country, or to get up cheers for the Neapolitan Constitution.

Such was the state of feeling when, on March 16,
a boat arrived from Trieste, bringing news from
Vienna.   The chief informant brought with him the
fragments of a portrait of Metternich which had been
torn to pieces as a symbol of his fall.   Then the
Venetians rose and demanded the release of Manin
and Tommaseo.  The Governor referred the petitioners
to the criminal court; but the crowd resolved to take
matters into their own hands, and broke into the
prison to rescue the two leaders.   Manin, however,
refused to leave the prison until the president of the
tribunal had signed the order for his release.   The
president readily complied with this request; and
Manin and Tommaseo were carried home on the
shoulders of the people.  The Venetians then proceeded to attack the fortress; the Croat soldiers
rushed out to repel them, and succeeded in driving
them back.   But the next day there was a new
gathering in the streets. Palffy, the Military Governor
of Venice, appealed to Manin to preserve order; but
Manin replied that he could only do so if a civic
guard were granted, and if the soldiers were recalled
to their barracks.   The head of the police remonstrated against the proposal for the Civic Guard, and

asked that it should, at any rate, be placed under his
authority.   Thereupon Manin seized his gun and said
that if the police interfered with the Civic Guard he
would himself head a revolt.   Palffy was a Hungarian,
and so was Zichy, the Civil Governor of Venice; and
neither of them were disposed to push matters to extremities.   Although, therefore, Palffy was at first
inclined to make difficulties, and to appeal to the
Governor of Lombardy for orders, he yielded at last,
and the municipal authorities began to organize the
Civic Guard.

But the fears of the Venetians were not yet over.
Marinovich, the Governor of the Castle, was a hard
man, who had irritated the workmen of the arsenal
against him ; and the authorities had persuaded him
to resign his command and to leave Venice.   But,
on March 22, while Manin and his friends were deliberating on the next step to be taken, a messenger came to announce to them that Marinovich
had suddenly returned to the arsenal, and had there
been attacked and killed by the workmen.   Thereupon Manin at once decided that the Civic Guard
should be sent to seize the arsenal.   The Admiral
Martini tried to offer opposition ; but Manin succeeded in entering with some of the guard, and
then rang the workmen's bell and demanded arms
for the workmen of the arsenal.   It was well for
the Venetians at this time that there was so great
a hostility between Magyars and Croats.   On a
previous day, the Croats had desired to fire on the
unarmed crowd ; but a Hungarian officer, named
Winckler, had thrown himself in their way, and had
declared that they should fire first at him.   When
the news came of Marinovich's death, Zichy proposed

that the Croats should act with the Civic Guard; but the Croat soldiers refused, desiring instead to bombard the town. This latter proposition, however, was defeated, not only by the Hungarian officers, but by many of the soldiers; for the garrison contained many Italians, who seized this opportunity for joining the cause of their countrymen. During the confusion that arose from this division of opinion, the head of the Civic Guard went to Palffy to demand that the defence of the town should be placed in the hands of the citizens. Palffy hesitated; but, in the meantime, Manin was proclaiming the Venetian Republic in the Piazza of San Marco. Palffy consented to resign his authority to Zichy, and by 6.30 p.m. Zichy had signed the evacuation of Venice by the Austrian troops.

Palffy now desired to leave Venice as soon as possible. The chief of the Civic Guard tried to prevent his escape; but Manin trusted to Palffy's honour, and allowed him and some of his followers to depart in a steamer which was to stop at Pola with despatches, ordering the recall of the Venetian fleet which was stationed there. But no sooner was Palffy safely out of Venice than he compelled the captain to change his course, to sail to Trieste, and to surrender to the Austrian authorities. Of course, Manin had made a mistake in trusting so implicitly to the honour of an enemy. Perhaps we should thank God that there are people who are capable of those mistakes. Manin, at least, does not seem to have changed his line of conduct in consequence; for when, a few days later, a steamer full of Austrian private citizens came near Venice, and the Venetians wished to go out to attack

T

them, Manin prevented them from doing so, saying, " Let us leave such conduct to Metternich."

Thus, then, in this wonderful month of March, 1848, the whole system of Metternich had crumbled to the ground.  The German national feeling, which he had hoped to crush out, was steadily ripening and embodying itself in a definite shape.  The feeling for that "Geographical Expression" Italy had proved strong enough to drive Radetzky from Milan and Palffy from Venice.  The rivalry between the Bohemians and Germans of the Austrian Empire seemed, for the moment, to have been merged in a common desire for liberty ; and the Hungarian opposition, which Metternich had hoped to manipulate, had shaken him from power and from office, and had secured liberty to Vienna and practical independence to Hungary.  Of the terrible divisions and rivalries which were to undermine the new fabric of liberty, the story will have to be told in the succeeding chapters.  But the vigour, heroism, and self-sacrifice which had been brought to light in this early part of the movement will always make the March Risings of 1848 memorable in the history of Europe.

# CHAPTER VIII.

## THE STRUGGLE OF THE RACES—APRIL TO JUNE, 1848.

Apparent unanimity between races of Austrian Empire in the March risings.—Unreality of this appearance.—Local aspirations. —The Serbs of Buda-Pesth.—The Magyar politics in Pesth.— The first Hungarian Ministry.—Szemere's Press Law and its failure.—The answer of the Ministry to the Serb petition.— Position and History of the Serbs in Hungary.—Treatment by Magyars and Austrian Kings.—Growth of Serb literature.—The deputations from Neusatz and Carlowitz.—Velika-Kikinda.— Position and character of Rajaciç.—Of Stratimiroviç.—The summoning of the Serb Assembly.—Croatian movement revived.— The Croats and the "twelve points."—Joseph Jellaciç.—Pillersdorf and the Bohemian deputation.—The meeting at the Sophien-Insel.—The second petition.—The Germans of Bohemia and Moravia.—Opening of the Vor-Parlament at Frankfort.—Blum's influence.—Struve's proposals and their effect.—The Slavonic question at Frankfort.—The Polish phase of it.—The Bohemian question evaded by the Vor-Parlament.—The Committee of Fifty and Palacky.—The discussion between the National Committees in Prague.—Schilling's insults.—The appeal to the Austrian Government and its failure.—The summons of the Slavonic Congress.—The difficulties in Vienna.—The April Constitution. —The Galician movement.—The rising of May 15 and the flight of the Emperor.—Effect of the May movement on Bohemian feeling—on Hungarian feeling.—The Serb meeting of May 13. —The Roumanian meeting of May 15.—The Saxon opposition to the Union.—The alliance between the Magyars and the Szekler.—The fall of Transylvanian independence.—The first collision with the Roumanians.—Their position, and character of their rising.—Alliance between Croats and Serbs.—The attack

on Carlowitz of June 11.—The Slavonic Congress at Prague.—
The difficulties in Prague.—Windischgrätz and the Town Council.
—The quarrel between the students of Prague and the students
of Vienna.—The Slavonic petition.—The rising of June 12.—
The fall of Prague and its consequences

FEW points were more remarkable in the March
Risings of 1848 than the apparent reconciliation
between those champions of freedom who had been
separated from each other by antagonism of race.
Gaj and his friends had hastened to Vienna to join in
the general congratulations to that city on its newly
won freedom.  The Slavonic students of Prague had
been  equally  sympathetic ;  and  members  of  the
different races of Hungary had expressed their satisfaction in the successes of Kossuth.  But this sudden
union was necessarily short-lived ; for it sprang from
a hope which could not be realized ; the hope,
namely, that the Germans and Magyars would join
in extending to each of the Slavonic races of the
Empire those separate national freedoms which those
two great ruling races had secured for themselves.
Thus proposals soon began to be made for the formation of a district which was to be called Slovenia,
after the Slovenes who inhabited the province of
Krain, and other south-western provinces of the
Austrian Empire.  At the same time, the Slovaks of
North Hungary desired to be formed into a separate
province, in which they could freely use the Slovak
language and profess the Lutheran creed, undisturbed
by Magyar language or Magyar Calvinism.  Lastly,
on March 15, Ivan Kukuljeviç, who, next to Gaj, was
the most distinguished of the Croatian patriots,
carried, in the Agram Assembly, an address to the
Emperor, asking him to summon the old parliament

of the three kingdoms of Croatia, Slavonia, and Dalmatia.   But, though all these demands contained
within them the seeds of future quarrels, the first
actual outbreak was not to come either from Slovenes,
Slovaks, or Croats.   The first token of the "rift
within the lute," which, if it could not "make the
music" of Liberty "mute," would at least weaken
its sound and introduce discord into its harmony,
showed itself in connexion with a branch of the
Slavonic race to which little allusion has yet been
made.

Those who have visited Buda-Pesth will remember
how, when they had left the modern magnificence of
Pesth and crossed the suspension-bridge which joins
it with Buda, they have come to a pause at the foot
of the steep rock which confronts them.   Then, if,
instead of ascending to the fortress of Buda, they
turned southwards along the shores of the Danube,
in a short time they would have found themselves in
a district in complete contrast with the rest of the
capital, where an air of poverty, hardly found elsewhere in the town, is combined with an originality
and picturesqueness of decoration which is neither
German nor Magyar.   Little cottages, coloured yellow, blue, or white, are built up against the rock in
all kinds of irregular ways; in some places the rooms
are below the street, and the gay appearance is
increased by signs outside the shops, showing what
articles can be procured there.   The bright handkerchiefs on the heads of the women, and the gay
colours worn by both sexes, give a somewhat Eastern
aspect to the streets and market-place.   Such is the
Raizenstadt, the quarter of the Serbs, long looked
down upon by their Magyar countrymen.   There,

on March 17, the representatives of about a hundred districts of the neighbourhood gathered to prepare a petition for leave to use their national language in national affairs. This roused the fierce opposition of the Magyar youth of Pesth; and the Committee of Safety which had just been formed found itself unable to protect the Serbs from violence. If, indeed, the spirit of Kossuth's speech of March 3 had been still triumphant, compromises might have been found which would have hindered the claims of the Serbs from provoking actual war. But the sudden outburst of statesmanlike feeling which produced that speech was not of long duration; and, even if Kossuth had desired to conciliate the subject-races of Hungary, there were those at his back who would never have consented to such tolerance.

The fiery youth of Pesth supplied an element to the Magyar revolution very different from that which generally found expression in the Diet at Presburg; and this element had been so necessary to Kossuth's purposes that it was impossible to disregard its influence. Three days before the Serb meeting a great gathering had been held in a café at Pesth, which had been followed on the 15th by a march of the Hungarian students, headed by the poet Petöfy, to the Town Council, to demand the concession of twelve points. Some of these points were being secured on that very day by the deputation which had gone to Vienna; others were already conceded in principle by the Diet at Presburg ; one of them, the proposal for the union of Transylvania with Hungary, was to be the seed of future mischief, but was, at present, acceptable to all parties of the Magyars. It was not so much, then, by political theories that the youth of Pesth were distinguished from the quieter spirits of Presburg; it was rather the fiery manner in which they made their demands, and the dogmatic intolerance with which they insisted on particular formulas.

Moreover, the Presburg policy, if one may so call it, was weakened in its effect by that attempt to reconcile hopeless opposites which is the great difficulty of all moderate parties. Count Louis Batthyanyi, when he was appointed as the first responsible Minister of Hungary, thought himself bound to form his Ministry, so far as possible, by a combination of the different representatives of the rival parties; and he not only hoped to find a basis for common action between the growing Conservatism of Szechenyi and the growing Radicalism of Kossuth, but he even gave a place in his Ministry to Count Esterhazy, who sympathized to some extent with the Camarilla at Vienna. Baron Eötvös, who had been the champion of centralization when Kossuth was arguing for County Government, was also a member of this Ministry; while Meszaros, the War Minister, might be supposed to combine opposite principles in his own person; for, while he had contributed to Kossuth's paper, the "Pesti Hirlap," his last public action had been to serve under Radetzky in his attempt to suppress the liberties of Milan. Batthyanyi, indeed, hoped that, by introducing Deak into the Ministry, he should secure an influence which should reconcile these various incongruous elements; but such a task was beyond even Deak's powers. By his honourable abstention from the Diet of 1843, he had deprived himself of his former influence; and, though he accepted the place offered him by Batthyanyi, and honestly tried to work with his different colleagues, yet, as the movement became more and more revolutionary, he fell further into the background.

The weakness of this Coalition Ministry was first brought into prominence by Bartholomaus Szemere, a cold, hard man, who had had little previous influence on politics. He was appointed to draw up the new regulations with regard to freedom of the Press; and produced a law which was of so reactionary a character that the students of the Pesth University burnt it publicly in front of the Town Hall, and sent a deputation to the Diet to entreat them to repeal the law and to change the seat of government to Pesth. Batthyanyi consented to the repeal of the law; but rejected, for a time, the other proposal of the students; and the Ministry remained at Presburg, weakened by the sense that the strongest element of Magyar feeling was centred in Kossuth and the Pesth party, and that this feeling would eventually overpower the more moderate patriots. Under these circumstances it was natural that the weak Ministry at Presburg should sacrifice to their fiery opponents the claims of those races with which neither party had any deep sympathy; and when, on March 24, the Serb petition came before the Ministry, they answered that the Hungarians would not endure that any nationality except the Hungarian should exist in Hungary.

But the Serbs of the Raitzenstadt were but the feeble representatives of a much more powerful body, which was scattered over various parts of Hungary and found its chief centre in the province of Slavonia. It was during the sixteenth century that the great immi-

gration of the Serbs into Hungary had taken place. All
the important history of this race had been connected
with their struggle against the Turks; and it was as
fugitives from Turkish tyranny that they took refuge
in Hungary.    They arrived just about the time when
Hungary had accepted the rule of the House of Austria,
and, finding that Ferdinand I. was more zealous than
his Magyar subjects in resistance to the Turks, and
that some of the Magyars were even willing to call in
the Turks to their assistance, the Serbs naturally became
the champions of the House of Austria against the
Magyars.    As a reward for this loyalty, the Austrian
rulers granted various privileges to their new subjects; and, in 1690, Leopold I. gave special invitation
to the Serbs to come over from the Turkish provinces
and to settle in the district assigned to them.    To
those who lived in that district was granted the right
of choosing the Patriarch of their own Church, their
own Voyvode, or military leader, and their own
magistrates; while those living actually on the
frontier were placed under a special military government which was administered from Vienna, and were
rewarded for their military services by freedom from
taxation.    The Magyars, indeed, did not abandon the
hope of drawing the Serbs to their side; and when,
in the beginning of the eighteenth century, Rakoczi [1]
attempted to set up an independent principality in
Transylvania, he appealed to the Serbs to assist him
in his attempt.    But their gratitude to the House of

---

[1] Rakoczi is still to a great extent a national hero among the
Magyars, as is shown by the name of the Rakoczi March, which
is given to one of the national airs; for the Magyars, in the
seventeenth and beginning of the eighteenth centuries, were
willing to risk the separation of Transylvania from Hungary if

Austria, strengthened in this instance by a dislike to the Calvinism of Rakoczi, kept them firm in their championship of the Austrian cause.

The House of Austria, on the other hand, showed as little gratitude to the Serbs in the early part of the eighteenth century as they did to the Magyars in the nineteenth; and Joseph I. and Charles VI. steadily violated the promises which had been made by Leopold. The concession of religious liberty was found to be not inconsistent with a vigorous Jesuit propaganda for the crushing out of the Greek faith. A small émente in a Serb town gave excuse for further interferences with liberty; and, as the Magyars gained in strength, Charles VI. resorted to the mean device of submitting to the Diet of Presburg the list of privileges which he had granted to the Serbs, and asking if the Diet would be pleased to approve them; and, on receiving the refusal which he had expected, he declared that he could not uphold these privileges against the wish of the Hungarian Diet. The Serbs in Hungary were, in many cases, reduced to the position of serfs; the districts of the Banat and Batschka, which had formed part of the Serb settlement, were given up to Hungary in 1741 by Maria Theresa; the Voyvodeschaft was abolished, and so, at a later period, was the Patriarchate also. Maria Theresa, indeed, would have desired to redress some of the grievances of the Serbs; but the need which she felt for the help of the Magyars, first in the War of Suc-

thereby they could secure an independent background to their struggles for liberty against Austria, much as the Venetians in 1859 were thankful for the liberation of Lombardy from Austria, though it involved the loss to Venetia of fellow-sufferers under Austrian oppression.

cession, and afterwards in the Seven Years' War, compelled her to disregard the interests of the subject-
races when they clashed with those of her more
powerful allies.   In spite, therefore, of several insurrections and continual meetings of Congresses, the
Serbs failed to recover their former privileges; and a
few concessions which were made to them by Leopold II. were speedily withdrawn by Francis.

During the latter part of the eighteenth century a
new hope came to the Serbs in the growing development of their national literature.   A school was
founded at Carlowitz by the Patriarch of the Serbs;
printing-presses were set up, and writers were
gradually produced by this education, one of whom,
named Obradoviç, composed the first essay in the
Serb dialect; while Karadziç, another writer, gathered
up the old songs, proverbs, and stories of the country
and tried to reduce the dialect into grammatical
forms.   The movement of Szaffarik and Kollar in
North Hungary gave new hopes to the Serbs and
other Slavs in the development of their literature;
and it was whilst this feeling was growing that Gaj
put forward his plan for the Illyrian language.
Gaj's movement was, to some extent, an apple of
discord among the Serb national party; for, while
some of them were eager to join in any union of the
Slavs, many of the more powerful of the clergy
objected altogether to the abandonment of the old
Cyrillic alphabet which had been introduced by the
Bishops Cyril and Methodius, who converted the
Slavs to Christianity.   And while, as was mentioned
in a former chapter, Gaj was suspected by the Roman
Catholics of wishing to swamp them in a union with
the members of the Greek Church, the Greek clergy

among the Serbs, on the other hand, feared a movement which seemed likely to have its centre in the
Roman Catholic province of Croatia. Thus there
had grown up two centres of the Serb movement in
two towns situated within a few miles of each other.
Neusatz, or Novi Sad, the most important town of
Slavonia, was the centre of the literary and trading
part of the Serb community; and Carlowitz, or
Karlovci, was the head-quarters of the Metropolitan,
and the centre of the clerical section of the Serb
national party.

It was from Neusatz, then, that, on April 8, 1848,
a deputation arrived at Presburg and declared that,
while they were in sympathy with the March movement, and had no desire to separate from Hungary,
they yet wished for protection for their national
language and customs. They therefore demanded
the re-establishment of the Patriarchal dignity and
of the office of Voyvode; requesting, further, that
the power of the latter officer should be extended
over the territories which the Serbs had reconquered
from the Turks. Kossuth answered that the Magyars
would do their best to respect national feeling, and
to give the Serbs a share in the freedom which the
Magyars had won; but that only the Magyar language
could bind the different nationalities together.
Batthyanyi echoed the words of Kossuth in an even
stronger form. "Then," the Serbs answered, "we
must look for recognition elsewhere than at Presburg." "In that case," answered Kossuth, "the
sword must decide." "The Serbs," retorted one of
the deputation, "were never afraid of that." And
so the glove was thrown down. A few days later
came a deputation from Carlowitz with the same

object; for the clergy, however little sympathy they might feel with Gaj's movement, feared, as heartily as the citizens of Neusatz could do, the interference of the Magyars with Serb independence. The Magyars seem to have learned already the tyrannical arts of Metternich; for they met the petition of the clergy with the threat that they would extend to the Roumanians the liberties granted to the Serbs; and they were, no doubt, proportionately disappointed when the deputation answered that they were perfectly ready to share their rights with the Roumanians.

The quarrel thus begun soon led to an actual outbreak. In the town of Velika-Kikinda, in the Banat, there had arisen one of those disturbances which are the natural marks of a revolutionary period. The peasantry, excited by the changes in their position, had begun to expect still further advantages. A worthless adventurer had become a candidate for one of the village judgeships, and had promised that, if elected, he would recover for the peasantry, without compensation to the present possessors, all the lands that their lords had taken from them. He was elected, but was, of course, unable to carry out his promises; and the disappointed peasantry rose in indignation and made a riot. The soldiers were called out to suppress the movement, but were repelled and disarmed; the magistrates' houses were broken open, and two of them were killed. Thereupon the Magyars sent down a Commissioner to inquire into the riot; the people were ready to surrender the murderers to justice; but the Commissioners seized the opportunity to declare that all the Serb villages in the neighbourhood were concerned in a communistic rising; and, in consequence, they placed them under martial law.

The Serbs now despaired of getting any justice from the Magyars, and determined to appeal from them to the Emperor. They desired, however, still to act legally; and they therefore resolved that the petition to the Emperor should be drawn up by an Assembly which had been convoked in a legal manner. The only official leader to whom they could appeal was their Metropolitan, Rajaciç. He was an old man, and unwilling to bestir himself in politics. He hesitated, therefore, to comply with the request of his countrymen; but a man of more determined spirit was ready to take the lead among the Serbs. This was George Stratimiroviç, one of those erratic characters who add picturesqueness to a revolutionary movement. He came from a Serb family which had settled in Albania; but he had been brought up in Vienna in a military school, and had entered the Austrian Army, which he had been compelled to leave on account of an elopement. Since that time he had started a popular journal, and had joined in the Serb deputation to the Hungarian Diet. His fiery and determined character had attracted the more vigorous politicians among the Serbs; and, though only twenty-six years of age, he was chosen President of the National Serb Committee which was now being formed. The impulse given to the movement by Stratimiroviç was further quickened by the alarm which was roused among the Serbs by the appointment of a new Governor to the fortress of Peterwardein, which overlooked Neusatz. This decided the National Committee to act at once; and, gathering together the Serbs from those other provinces of Hungary which

had once been under their rule, they organized in
Neusatz a deputation which was to rouse Rajaciç to
a sense of his duty. Along the road to Carlowitz
they marched with banners and flags, singing the old
national airs, and telling of the exploits of Voyvodes
and Patriarchs who had saved their country in former
times. Rajaciç was greatly impressed by this deputation; and, after notifying his decision to the Count
Palatine, as the legal ruler of Hungary, he summoned
the Assembly to meet on the 13th of May.

In the meantime, the attitude of the Croatians was
alarming the Hungarian Diet. As mentioned above,
they had determined from the first to claim a separate
Assembly for Croatia, Slavonia, and Dalmatia, and
also a separate national guard. Kossuth and some
of his friends seemed more disposed, at this time, to
make concessions to the Croats than to the Serbs.
But the bitter struggles of 1843 to 1846 had destroyed
the hope of smoothing over the breach with soft words;
and, even while Kossuth was promising to sanction
the use of the Croatian language in Croatian affairs
and to protect their nationality, he was at the same
time denouncing their separatist tendencies as shown
in their desire for a separate Assembly. The Croatians,
on their part, resented fiercely the visit of certain
youths from Pesth, who came to demand their acceptance of the " twelve points." The growing sympathy
between the different subject-races of Hungary had
led the Croats to protest against the proposal to absorb
Transylvania in Hungary. The question of the abolition of the forced labour of the peasants, and of the
introduction of peasant proprietorship, was complicated in Croatia by the existence of village communities which managed the land on the old tribal system;

and therefore the Croats maintained that it was impossible to pass the same land laws for Hungary and
for Croatia.   The question of religious equality was
connected in the minds of the Croats with the fear of
an invasion by Magyar Protestants to denationalize
Croatia.   But the great cause of the Croatian dislike
to the "twelve points" lay not so much in their objection to any particular reform as in their resentment
at the arrogant attempt to thrust upon them whole-
sale formulas concocted at Buda-Pesth.   On the other
hand, the Magyars considered that they had a special
grievance, both against the Croats and against the
Emperor, in the sanction which Ferdinand had given
on March 23, without waiting for Magyar approval, to
the election of Joseph Jellaciç as Ban of Croatia.
Jellaciç was colonel in one of the regiments stationed
on that military frontier which was specially under
the control of Vienna; and he was chiefly known for
his share in a not very successful campaign in Bosnia;
while rumour connected his appointment with the
favour of the Archduchess Sophia.   This appointment, therefore, was doubly distasteful to the Hungarian Diet, as being at once an exercise of court
influence and an assertion of the independence of
Croatia against the power of the Magyars.

But while these various causes were working together to undo the harmony which had been established in the beginning of March, another race struggle
was coming to a head, in a different part of the Austrian Empire, which was to have as vital an effect on
the history of that Empire as any produced by the
struggle between the Magyars and the subject-races
of Hungary.   We left the Bohemian deputation enjoying their welcome from Ferdinand and Kolowrat in

Vienna, and sending happy messages to their fellow citizens in Prague; and on March 24 Pillersdorf, who was now the most important Minister at Vienna, announced the concession by the Emperor of most of the demands of the people of Prague. There were, however, three exceptions on very vital points. The Emperor declared that the equalization of nationalities was already secured by a previous ordinance, and therefore needed no new legislation; that the special law court for Bohemia, which the petitioners wished to see established in Prague, must be left to the consideration of the Minister of Justice; and that the proposal to reunite Moravia and Silesia to Bohemia must be decided by the local Assemblies of the respective provinces.

Some of the quieter citizens of Prague were willing to accept this answer; but the more determined patriots called upon their friends to attend a meeting on the Sophien-Insel, a green island which lies just below the Franzensbrücke in Prague, and which is used by the citizens as a great place for holiday gatherings. Here the more vigorous spirits of Prague uttered their complaints against the Emperor's answer. They pointed out that the local Estates, to which Ferdinand wished to refer some of the questions submitted to him, were mediæval bodies, having no real representative character; and that only an assembly freely elected by the whole people would be competent to decide on these questions ; that, as to the ordinance to which the Emperor referred for securing equality between Bohemians and Germans, that ordinance had ceased for two hundred years to have any effect; and that a law passed in a formal manner was therefore necessary as a guarantee for the desired equality;

while with regard to the question of the union between
Bohemia, Moravia, and Silesia, the claim for that union
rested on the historical, national, and geographical
connections between those lands.  The petitioners,
accompanied by the national guard, then marched to
the house of the Governor of Bohemia, and induced
him to sign their new petition.  On April 8 Ferdinand answered this petition in a letter, promising
complete equality between the German and Bohemian
languages in all questions of State Administration
and public instruction.  He further promised that a
Bohemian Assembly should be shortly elected on the
broadest basis of electoral qualifications, and should
have the power of deciding on all the internal affairs
of Bohemia.  Responsible central boards were to be
set up; and the new Assembly was to consider the
question of the establishment of independent district
law courts, and the abolition of the old privileged
tribunals; while the question of the union between
Bohemia, Moravia, and Silesia was to be decided by
a general Assembly, in which all three provinces
would be represented.  Public offices and legal boards
in Bohemia were to be filled exclusively by men who
knew both the German and Bohemian languages; and
the Minister of Public Instruction was to make provision for the thorough education of Bohemian and
German teachers.

There seemed to be nothing in these concessions
which was likely to irritate either the German or the
Bohemian party; but the work of Germanizing
Bohemia, so ruthlessly inaugurated by Ferdinand II.
after the Battle of the White Hill in 1620, could not
be entirely undone by the March insurrection of
1848.  Several towns in Bohemia had been com-

pletely Germanized, and they looked with the greatest
suspicion on the movement for restoring the Bohemian language to its natural place as an educational
and literary power; while they regarded, with hardly
less suspicion, any attempt to weaken the hold of
Vienna on Prague, or to restore in any degree a
Bohemian national life. The towns of Saatz and
Reichenberg, particularly, seem to have retained
the German impress most thoroughly, and were extremely jealous of the claim of Prague to take the
lead in a Bohemian movement. In Moravia the
German party were able to appeal to some feeling of
provincial independence against the absorption of
that province in Bohemia; while the Germans who
had been born in Bohemia, but who had subsequently settled in Vienna, naturally caught the
infection of that intense German feeling which connected itself with the March movement in Lower
Austria. It must not be supposed, however, that
this division of feeling ran strictly parallel with the
lines of hereditary descent. Men of undoubtedly
German name and German origin had accepted
heartily the language and traditions of the conquered
people; while names that were as certainly Slavonic
were found among the leaders of the German party.
Another element of confusion of the party lines arose
from the change which had come over the religious
feelings of the two races respectively. In Prague at
any rate, especially among the aristocracy, the championship of that cause of Bohemian independence
which had been dear to the followers of John Huss,
and to the subjects of the Winter King, was often
connected in 1848 with strong Roman Catholic sympathies. This irregularity in the division of parties

might have been expected to soften the bitterness of
the growing antagonisms; and, if the discussion of
the question at issue had been confined to the Germans and Bohemians of the Austrian Empire, there
seems some reason to hope that, under freer institutions, the bitterness of local and national divisions
might have been weakened, and a satisfactory solution of the claims of the different races might have
been arrived at.

But a new element of discord was now to be introduced into the struggle; and the great movement for
the unity and freedom of Germany became for a
time a source of tyranny, and a new and more fatal
cause of division between the races of the Western
half of the Austrian Empire.  This collision is the
more to be regretted because, until its occurrence,
the leaders of the German movement had exhibited
the same dignity and moderation of temper which
had been shown in the early phases of the Bohemian
movement.  On March 31, the very day of the
meeting in the Sophien-Insel, the representatives of
the German nation arrived in Frankfort, to open
that Preparatory Parliament which was to be the
first step towards German unity.  One who saw
this opening scene has thus described it :—
" Under a wavy sea of German flags, through a
crowd of green trees of freedom, covered with
flowers and crowns, walked the members of the
Preparatory Parliament.  They were surrounded and
accompanied by thousands of excited women, as they
went from the Imperial Hall of the Roman Emperors to their work in that Church of St. Paul,
which from thenceforth for nearly a year would

contain the best men of Germany, the holiest hopes
of the nation."

Nor were their early efforts unworthy of the
nation whom they represented; for it seemed likely
that the wisest men would be able to get their
due influence in the Assembly. And this was the
more remarkable, because the ease with which they
had accomplished the first steps of their work seems
to have led many of the Assembly to fear that there
was some deeper plot in the background; and both
in the city and among the members of the Assembly
a rumour spread that troops were on the march to
put down their meeting. A panic seized the Deputies, and bitter reproaches were interchanged.
Violence seemed likely to follow, when Robert Blum
came forward to reconcile the opposing factions.
"Gentlemen," said he, "from whence shall we get
freedom, if we do not maintain it in our dealings
with each other, in our most intimate circle?" He
went on then to point out, that the immediate causes
of quarrel were mere matters of form and not of
principle; and that it was the duty of the Assembly
to maintain the reputation of the German people for
calm decision. For any tumults that were made in
that Parliament would be settled out of doors not by
shouts, but by fists, and perhaps by other weapons.
"We will first," he continued, "reverence the law
which we ourselves have made, to which we voluntarily submit. If we do that, gentlemen, then not
only will the hearts of our people beat in response to
us, but other nations too will stretch out their arms
in brotherly love to the hitherto scorned and despised
Germans, and will greet in the first representative body,

which has come here, the full-grown true men, who are as capable of obtaining freedom as they have shown themselves worthy of it." The influence of his clear voice, powerful figure, and determined manner added to the natural effect of his eloquence in bringing the Assembly to a wiser state of mind.[1] Another sign of the power which these men showed, of responding to appeals which were addressed to their higher instincts, was given in answer to one of the Baden representatives, who called on them to accept as their fundamental maxim that " Where the Lord does not build with us, there we build in vain." At these words all the Assembly rose to their feet.

The same triumph of gentle and moderating influences was shown in their reception of a programme presented to them by Struve on behalf of the Committee of Seven. This programme contained fifteen propositions, in which the desire for liberty and national life which animated all sections of the Assembly was combined with Republican aspirations, so strong among the Baden leaders, and with those Socialistic proposals which were as yet entirely in the background of German politics. Thus, for instance, the list begins with a proposal for the amalgamation of the army with the Civic Guard, in order to give a really national character to the army; while another clause proposes equality of faiths, freedom of association, and the right of communities to choose their own clergy and their own burgomasters. On

---

[1] Englisn readers may be reminded by this scene of that fiery debate on the Grand Remonstrance, when the members of the House of Commons would " have sheathed their swords in each other's bowels, had not the sagacity and great calmness of Mr. Hampden, by a short speech, prevented it."

the other hand, the 12th clause aims at the settlement of the misunderstandings between labour and
capital by a special Ministry of Labour, which should
check usury, protect workmen, and secure them a share
in the profits of their work; while the 15th clause proposes the abolition of hereditary monarchies, and the
introduction into Germany of a Federal Republic on
the model of the United States of America.  This
medley of various ideas which Hecker and Struve
desired to force upon the Assembly was finally referred to a Committee, which in the end would sift out
what was practicable and embody it in a law.  Even
in the burning question of the relations between the
Frankfort Parliament and their antiquated rival the
Bundestag, Blum's influence was used in moderating
the violence of the disputes between those who wished
to drive the older institution to extremities and those
who wished to make for it a golden bridge by which
it could pass naturally into greater harmony with
modern ideas.

So far, then, the German national movement had,
on the whole, been guided wisely and moderately;
but when the discussions began about the basis of
the election of the future Assembly there quickly
appeared that German national arrogance which was
destined to inflame to so intolerable an extent the
antagonism of feeling between the rival races in
Bohemia.  It was, indeed, unavoidable that the
German movement in Austria should be met by
some expression of friendliness and some attempt at
common action on the part of the Frankfort Parliament; but the desire to welcome all Germans into the
bosom of the newly-united Germany became at once
complicated with the question of the best way of dealing

with those districts where Slavs and Germans were so closely mixed together. This question, indeed, would in all probability have been summarily answered by the German Parliament in favour of absolute German supremacy and of the absorption of Bohemia in Germany; but the Slavonic question in the South could not be considered apart from that other phase of it, which was concerned with the mutual relation between Poles and Germans in the Polish districts of the Kingdom of Prussia. Even the most extreme champions of German supremacy were influenced in their decision of this *North* Slavonic question by their desire to restore an independent Poland as a bulwark against Russian oppression; and they could not deny that the claims of the Poles to the possession of Posen, at any rate, were as justifiable morally and historically as their claims to that part of their country which had been absorbed by Russia. They were desirous, therefore, of making concessions to Slavonic feeling in Posen; and this desire was increased by the connection which Mieroslawsky had established between the struggle for Polish freedom in Posen and that for German freedom in other parts of Prussia. Under these circumstances they could not wholly disregard in Bohemia the feeling which they humoured in Posen; and thus it came to pass that the Preparatory Parliament, unwilling either to abandon German supremacy or to violate directly the principle of unity and autonomy of race, came to the conclusion so common to men under similar difficulties, to throw the burden of the decision on others. They therefore passed a vague resolution which might be differently interpreted by different readers, while they left the practical decision of the

question to the Committee of Fifty which was to
govern Germany from the dissolution of the Preparatory Parliament on April 4 till the meeting of
the Constituent Assembly on May 8.

It was this Committee, therefore, which undertook
the decision of the relations to be established between
Bohemia and the new free Germany. The new
body proved bolder than the Preparatory Parliament; for it took a step which, though it may have
been intended in a conciliatory spirit, yet involved
the distinct assertion of the claim to treat Bohemia
as part of Germany. They invited the Bohemian
historian Palacky to join with them in their deliberations, and thus to sanction the proposal that Bohemia
should send representatives to the German Parliament. Palacky answered by a courteous but firm
refusal of the proposal, based partly on the grounds
of previous history, partly on the needs of Bohemia,
and partly on the necessity of an independent Austrian
Empire to the safety and freedom of Europe. He
pointed out that the supposed union between Bohemia
and Germany had been merely an alliance of princes,
never of peoples, and that even the Bohemian Estates
had never recognized it. He urged that Bohemia
had the same right to independence which was
claimed by Germany; but that both would suffer if
extraneous elements were introduced into Germany.
He urged that an independent Austria was necessary
as a barrier against Russia, but that Germany could
be united only by a Republican Government; and,
therefore, Austria, which must necessarily remain an
Empire, could not consent to a close union with
Germany without breaking to pieces.

In spite, however, of this rebuff, the German

leaders at Frankfort were so eager to secure their
purpose in this matter that they sent down messengers to Prague to confer with the Bohemian National
Committee.  A long discussion ensued, turning partly
on the independence of the Austrian State, partly on
the nationality of Bohemia.  The Bohemians urged
that the Germans were endeavouring to force upon
them traditions which they had rejected for themselves; that the Frankfort Parliament had repudiated
the old Bund on account of its unrepresentative
character; and yet they demanded that Bohemia
should recognise a union which rested on the arrangements which had been destroyed, a union about which
the Bohemians had never been consulted as a nation.
The Germans, on their side, attempted to advance
certain arguments of expediency in favour of a closer
union between Bohemia and Germany.  But a certain
Dr. Schilling, who does not seem to have been one
of the original messengers from Frankfort, declared,
with brutal frankness, the real grounds of the German
proposal.  If Austria did not become German, he
said, the Germans of Austria would not remain
Austrian.  The five million Germans in Austria
would not stay to be oppressed by the twelve million
Slavs.  The freedom and culture of Bohemia was, he
declared, entirely German.  The idea of freedom could
not be found among the Slavs; and it was therefore
necessary, in the general interests of freedom, that
Bohemia should be absorbed in Germany.

Palacky bitterly thanked Schilling for the frankness of his speech; and expressed his regret at
hearing that the Germans would not stay where they
could not rule, and where they were obliged to be
on an equality with others; while another of the

Bohemians exclaimed that the Bohemians had shown their love of liberty by their resistance to the attempts to Germanize them. But Schilling seemed entirely unable to appreciate the feelings of his opponents; and, with a naïve contempt for logic, he declared that, *because* Nationality was just now the leading idea of the Peoples, *therefore* all the Slavs who belonged to the German Bund must be absorbed in Germany! Kuranda, the former champion of Viennese liberty, tried to soften the effect of Schilling's insults. He abandoned any claim based on the old German Bund, and declared that the Assembly at Frankfort was not so much a German Parliament as a Congress of Peoples, a beginning of the union of humanity. But this ingenious change of front could not destroy the effect of Schilling's words; and perhaps the Bohemians could not understand why a Congress of the Peoples should find its centre at Frankfort any more than at Prague.

But though the Bohemians had failed to convince the German Committee that Bohemia had as much right as Germany to a separate existence, they still hoped that the Austrian Government would protect them from an attack which seemed directed both against their national rights and against the integrity of the Austrian Empire. So they despatched to the Minister of the Interior a protest against the proposal to hold elections for the Frankfort Parliament in Bohemia. Such elections, they declared, would lead to a breach of the peace of the country, to Communistic and Republican agitations, and to attempts to break up the Austrian Empire. The Bohemian Assembly, they urged, would disavow the legal right of such representatives when they were elected; and

thus any really satisfactory alliance between Austria
and Germany would be hindered by this attempt.
The Ministers in Vienna were, no doubt, troubled in
their mind about this question of the relations between Germans and Bohemians.  On the one hand,
they desired to conciliate a people whose national
interests led them to seek protection in a union with
the rest of the Austrian Empire.  But, on the other
hand, they felt it difficult to disregard the intense
German feeling which was growing in Vienna, and
which was shared by important towns in Bohemia.
Therefore, after, no doubt, considerable deliberation,
the Ministry resolved to announce to the Bohemians
that they might either vote for the representatives in
the Frankfort Parliament or abstain from voting, as
seemed best to them.  This seems, of all conclusions,
the most unreasonable which could have been arrived
at.   The union with Germany might or might not be
defensible; but it was obviously a step which must
be taken by the whole nation or by none.  Of all
possible political arrangements, none could be more
intolerable than the permission to certain citizens of
a country to retain their civil rights and residence in
that country, and at the same time to be free to claim,
*according to their own fancy*, the special protection
secured by citizenship in another State.

The National Committee of Prague, finding that
the Government at Vienna were unable or unwilling
to protect them, resolved on stronger measures of
self protection; and on May 1 they issued an appeal to
all the Slavs of Austria to meet on the 31st of the same
month in Prague, to protest against the desire of the
Frankfort Parliament to absorb Austria in Germany.
This appeal was signed by Count Joseph Matthias

Thun, whose relative, Count Leo Thun, had taken
an active part in forming the National Committee; by
Count Deym, who had headed the first deputation to
Vienna; by Palacky and his son-in-law Dr. Rieger;
by the philologer Szaffarik, and by less well known
men.  But at the same time the Bohemian leaders
were most anxious to try to maintain the connection
with Austria and to observe a strictly deferential
attitude towards the Emperor.  They therefore appealed again to the Emperor and his Ministers to
withdraw the indirect sanction which they had given
to the proposed Bohemian elections to the Frankfort
Parliament.  They pointed out that Austria had
never belonged, in regard to most of her provinces,
to the German Bund; and that the question of
whether or no Bohemia should join herself to Germany was clearly one of those internal questions
with reference to which she had been promised the
right of decision.  They further urged that the
Emperor had acted on a different line with regard to
the union between Moravia and Bohemia; and although the claim for this latter union rested on old
treaties and laws, he had decided that it should only
be restored by a vote of the respective provincial
Assemblies, and the Bohemians had been perfectly
willing to accept a compromise on the subject.  How
much more reasonable then was it that the Bohemians should claim the right of deciding on the
question of an entirely new relation between their
country and Germany?  Again they warned him of
the violence which might be the consequence of such
elections; and they entreated him to consider also
that any attempt on the part of the Frankfort Parliament to make a Constitution for all the lands of

the Bund, would be a violation of the independence
of the Emperor of Austria and of all his subjects.
This last argument might, at an earlier stage, have
produced an effect on some at least of the Ministers
to whom it was addressed; for they had already
announced that Austria could not be bound by the
decisions of the Frankfort Parliament.  But affairs
in Vienna were at this time hastening towards a
change, which was materially to affect the relations
of that city with the other parts of the Empire.

The Ministry, which had been formed after the
fall of Metternich, was little likely to satisfy the
hopes of the reformers.   Kolowrat and Kübeck, who
had been supposed to be rather less illiberal than
Metternich, but who had worked with him in most
of his schemes, were prominent in this Ministry; and
another member of it was that Ficquelmont who
had hoped to pacify Milan by help of dancers and
actresses.   Only one member of the Ministry, the
Freiherr von Pillersdorf, had any real reputation for
Liberalism; and even he had been a colleague of
Metternich, and had done little in that position to
counteract Metternich's policy.   Finding it impossible, therefore, to put any confidence in the official
rulers of their country, the Viennese naturally
turned their attention to the formation of some
Government in which they could trust.   On March
20 a special legion had been formed composed of the
students of the University; and a Committee was
soon after chosen from those professors and students
who had played a leading part in the Revolution.
This Committee, which was at once the outcome and
the guide of the Students' Legion, became the centre
of popular confidence and admiration.   Thus then

there arose, in the very first days of the Revolution, a marked division of interest and feeling between the real and nominal rulers of Vienna. Some such antagonism is perhaps the scarcely avoidable result of a revolution achieved by violence, especially when the change of persons and forms produced by that revolution is so incomplete as it was in Vienna. Those who, by mere official position, are allowed to retain the leadership of followers with whom they have no sympathy, are constantly expecting that reforms which were begun in violence must be necessarily continued by the same method; while the actual revolutionary leaders can hardly believe in their own success, and are constantly suspecting that those who have apparently accepted the new state of things, are really plotting a reaction.

In Vienna these mutual suspicions had probably stronger justification than they have in most cases of this kind. The courtiers, who had plotted against Metternich, had as little desire for free government as the Jacobins who overthrew Robespierre; and Windischgrätz was gradually gathering round him a secret council, who were eventually to establish a system as despotic as that of Metternich. On the other hand, it cannot be denied that the gallant lads who had marched in procession to the Landhaus on March 13, and who had defied the guns of Archduke Albert, were unwisely disposed to prefer violent methods of enforcing their opinions. Thus, when, on March 31, a law regulating the freedom of the Press was issued, as distasteful to the Viennese as Szemere's had been to the Hungarians, the Viennese students at once proposed to follow the example of the students of Pesth, and burn the law publicly.

Hye persuaded them to abandon this attempt; and he, with Fischhof, Kuranda, Schuselka and other trusted leaders, went on a deputation to Pillersdorf, to entreat him to withdraw the law. Pillersdorf assured them that this law was only a provisional one, and that amendments would soon be introduced into it; but, a few days later, Count Taaffe, another member of the Ministry, publicly contradicted Pillersdorf's statement, and spoke of the Press law as being a permanent one, though he promised that it should be mildly administered. Perhaps the students may be excused if they felt no great respect for such a Ministry. Nor were their feelings conciliated by what they considered a growing tendency on the part of the Ministry to make concessions of local liberties to the provinces.

After the first enthusiasm for Kossuth had a little subsided, the Viennese began to reflect that the concession of a separate ministry to Hungary might be a dangerous source of weakness to the central Government; while the growing demands of the Bohemians seemed likely to injure both the position of Vienna, and the cause of German unity. But the Viennese were in many cases aiming at the two incompatible objects of maintaining the position of Vienna as the capital of the Austrian Empire, and gaining for it a new position as the second or third town of United Germany. But a more reasonable cause of discontent arose from the fact that, while parliaments were conceded to Hungary and Bohemia, the Constitution which had been promised in March to the Austrian Empire was as yet unrealized.

Dr. Schütte, a Westphalian by birth, organized a demonstration in favour of a mass petition. Schütte was arrested by the police, and banished from Vienna as a foreign agitator; and, while this irritated the students still further, the Ministry on their side were alarmed at finding that they had failed to secure the one advantage which they had hoped to reap from the power of the students.  The men who had succeeded in retaining office after the March Rising, had trusted that the intellectual youths, who had fought for freedom of the Press and freedom of teaching, would have discouraged the coarse socialistic agitations of the workmen, and have separated themselves altogether from their movements.  But, though the extremer forms of Socialism found little favour among the leaders of the University, the sympathy between the students and the workmen grew ever closer.  If the workmen complained of an employer, the students went to him and warned him to behave better; if any poor man needed money, the students organized the collection; if the cause of a workman was suffering by the undue length of a trial, the students called upon the judges to do their duty; if the workmen wished to state some special grievance in the form of a petition, the students composed the petition for them, or found a lawyer who would do it gratuitously.  Reductions of the hours of labour and higher wages frequently resulted from these efforts.

This combination naturally alarmed the authorities, and they showed their fears both by coercion and concession.  On the one hand they arrested Schütte and other agitators; on the other hand they consented on April 25 to issue the long promised Constitution.  The Constitution, however, at once disappointed the petitioners.  The proposed Parlia-

ment was to consist of two Chambers; the Upper
Chamber to be composed of Princes of the royal
House, of nominees of the Emperor, and of 150 landlords chosen by the landlords; and the assent of both
Chambers and of the Emperor was to be necessary
before the passing of a law.  This Constitution was
objected to both by the students and the workmen;
the former condemning it on the ground of its aristocratic character, the latter becoming discontented
when they found that the issue of this document did
not free them from the payment of rent.

The revolutionary enthusiasm of the students was
further whetted by the events which were taking
place in Galicia.  That unfortunate province had
been so hampered by the effects of the abortive movement of 1846, that it had not been able to join in the
March insurrection of the rest of Southern Europe.
But by the beginning of April even the Galicians
had taken heart; and they sent a deputation to the
Emperor asking for a State recognition of the Polish
language, a separate army for Galicia, and the concession of the different liberties which were then being
demanded throughout the Empire.  Even the Preparatory Parliament of Frankfort had passed a resolution in favour of the reconstitution of Poland; and
the students of Vienna were prepared to be far more
generous in their recognition of Galicia's claim to a
share in Polish independence, than the Frankfort
Parliament had been in its attitude towards Posen.
So alarming did the movement appear to the Austrian
Governor of Galicia, that he forbade any emigrants to
return to his province unless they could prove that
they had been born there.  The Galicians rose in
indignation, and imprisoned the Governor; but he

was set free, and, after a sharp struggle, the insurrection was suppressed.

But, if their Polish sympathies tended to rouse the revolutionary fervour of the Viennese students, their anger, on the other hand, was kindled by the growing tendency of the rich merchants to abandon the position which they had taken up in March, to accept the April Constitution, and to fall into more peaceable methods of action.   Even the Reading and Debating Club, which had been the first centre of the Liberal movement, was now the object of hostile demonstrations on the part of the students.   The Students' Committee had been strengthened by the adhesion of many of the National Guard, and had received the name of the Central Committee; Hoyos, the commander of the National Guard, was alarmed at this sign of revolutionary feeling, and forbade his subordinates to take part in any political movement. The Central Committee entreated him to withdraw this prohibition, to which Hoyos answered that he would withdraw his prohibition if the Central Committee would dissolve itself.   The Committee met to consider this proposal; but, while they were still sitting, a report arrived that the soldiers and the National Guard had been called out to put them down by force.   The truth appeared to be, that the soldiers had been called out to suppress a supposed attack by the workmen; but that, finding that no such attack was intended, the military leaders seemed disposed to turn their hostility against the University. Thereupon the students at once rose and marched to the Castle.   It seems that their exact object was at first uncertain; but on someone demanding of them their intentions, Dr. Giskra, one of their leaders,

answered with a shout, " Wir wollen einen Kam-
mer " (we want a single Chamber.)    The cry was
taken up by the students; Pillersdorf advised the
Emperor to yield, and on May 16 Ferdinand issued
a proclamation granting a one Chamber Constitution.
But whether the shock had been too much for his
feeble health, and had struck him with a panic, or
whether he yielded to the advice of his courtiers,
Ferdinand suddenly resolved to leave Vienna, and
on May 17 he fled secretly to Innspruck.

These events produced a somewhat peculiar effect
on opinion in various parts of the Empire.    In
Bohemia the extreme national feeling had been
hitherto represented by the Swornost, a body corre-
sponding almost exactly to the Students' Legion in
Vienna; and they had been held somewhat in check
by the noblemen and citizens, who had organized the
March movement.    But the Vienna rising of May
15, and the flight of the Emperor, roused the
indignation of men like Count Thun and Count
Deym; and they decided to take the important step
of breaking loose altogether from the Viennese
Ministry, summoning a special Bohemian assembly
in June, and inviting the Emperor to take refuge in
Prague.    The Swornost, on their part, felt some re-
luctance to take any steps which seemed to condemn
the abolition of the Upper Chamber by the Viennese;
but the bitter hostility, which the Germans of Vienna
had so repeatedly shown against the Bohemians
during the months of April and May, prevented
the possibility of any understanding between the
Democrats of Prague and those of Vienna; and
thus the students of Prague were ready to approve,
not only the assertion of Bohemian indepen-

dence, but even the proposed deputation to the Emperor.

Kossuth, on his part, saw in these events an opportunity for increasing the growing friendliness between the Magyars and the Emperor; and he induced the Hungarian Ministry to invite Ferdinand to Pesth. This attitude of the Magyar leaders was due to one or two causes. In the first place the Viennese, as mentioned above, had been growing alarmed at the separate position granted to Hungary, and had feared that they would lose their hold over that kingdom altogether. This naturally produced an attitude of hostility or their part, which provoked a counter-feeling of antagonism in the Magyars; and thus the latter became more friendly to Ferdinand as the representative of the anti-democratic principle, and therefore the opponent of the ruling spirits of Vienna. There was also a second reason of a stranger kind, which placed the leaders of the Magyar movement in hostility to the Democratic party in Vienna. In spite of the strong German feeling which prevailed among the leading Democrats of Vienna, it was the opinion of some of those Hungarians who were best acquainted with that city, that the change from indirect to direct elections, which was one of the results of the May rising, would tend to increase the power of the large Slavonic population of Vienna.

But the great cause of the growing sympathy between the Magyars and the Emperor was the attitude taken up by the latter in the questions at issue between Hungary and Croatia. Although the appointment of Jellaciç, as Ban of Croatia, had been considered as an undue exertion of the power of the Court to the disadvantage of the Magyars, yet the

independent tone which Jellaciç had adopted since his
appointment, seemed to alarm the Emperor as much
as it did Batthyanyi or Kossuth.   Immediately after
his appointment, Jellaciç announced that " the Revolution has changed our relations to our old ally,
Hungary " ; and that " we must take care that the
new relation shall be consistent with independence
and equality "; and he had then proceeded to summon the Assembly of Croatia, Slavonia and Dalmatia
to meet at Agram in June.   This independent attitude had brought rebukes upon Jellaciç from Ferdinand and the Hungarian Ministry alike ; and the
Croatian Council, while appealing to the Emperor to
strengthen the hands of the Ban, had threatened that,
if pressed too hard by the Magyars, they would take
measures to defend themselves.  It was not unnatural,
therefore, that at this moment the Croats should be
more disposed to sympathise with the Democrats of
Vienna; and that Kossuth should try to draw closer
the bond between the Emperor and the Magyars.

It might indeed seem that the appeal of the Bohemians to the Emperor under these circumstances
would have brought them out of sympathy with the
Slavs of Croatia and Slavonia; but not only did the
Emperor refuse to go to Prague, but the Tyrolese
followed up that refusal by a sharp rebuke to the
Bohemians for their proposal of a Slavonic Congress
in Prague.   Though, however, the Slavs of Hungary
looked forward to the Slavonic Congress, and were
willing to accept Prague as the centre of their political deliberations, it was in the Hungarian provinces
themselves that the most vigorous action in defence
of their rights was at present to be found.  For while
the Croatian Council were protesting against the

Emperor's rebuke to Jellaciç, the Serbs were gathering for their Conference of May 13 in Carlowitz,
and resolving to send deputies to the Croatian
Assembly, and to the Emperor himself, and also to
choose representatives for the Prague Congress.
Crnojeviç, who had been sent by the Magyars to
enforce martial law on the Serbs of the Banat and
Bacska, after the riot at Kikinda, denounced the
meeting, and called on Rajaciç to prevent it. Rajaciç
would have hesitated about further action, but
Stratimiroviç and his more fiery friends answered
the threat by burning Crnojeviç's letter publicly;
and the meeting took place in defiance of his warning.

From every district where the Serb language was
spoken, there came to Carlowitz representatives wearing the old national costume. Carlowitz is little more
than a village; and it would have required a large
city to provide for the crowds who arrived on this
occasion. Hundreds, therefore, lay out by night in
the streets, to wait for the meeting in the morning.
In the garden which lies between the Archbishop's
library and the small room where the archives of
Carlowitz are kept, there met on May 13 the
Assembly of the newly-roused Serb people. Rajaciç
appeared, accompanied by some of the clergy, and
presented to the Assembly the old charters which
had been granted by the Emperor in 1690 and 1691,
and on which the liberties of the Serbs were based.
Physicians, lawyers, and young students denounced
the abolition of their Voyvodschaft, claimed back the
provinces which Maria Theresa had abandoned to
Hungary, and demanded the removal of all hindrances
to the development of their life, language, and history.
They then proceeded to revive the old dignity of

Patriarch in the person of Rajaciç, and to choose as
their Voyvode a man named Suplikaç, who was then
serving in the army in Italy. Finally they appointed
a committee to prepare rules, and gave it the power
to call the Assembly together when circumstances
required it. Hrabowsky, the commander of the
fortress of Peterwardein, had been uncertain what
attitude he should assume towards this movement.
Sometimes he seemed to be personally friendly to the
Serbs; but, in his official position, he felt doubtful
whether to support the extreme Magyar authority,
or to wait for orders from Ferdinand; and this confusion of mind led him to give doubtful and contra-
dictory answers to the Serb deputations which waited
on him. Under these circumstances, the Serbs were
compelled to rely, even more markedly than before,
on the support of their own countrymen, and of those
races whom a common oppression had driven into
sympathy with them. It was not only to the Croatians and Bohemians that they now appealed; even
the Germans of the Bacska were expected to look
with friendly eyes on the Serb movement, and
Stratimiroviç believed that beyond the old Serb
provinces there were races to whom they might look
for alliance.

For while the Serbs were still discussing their
grievances and the remedies for them, the Roumanians were meeting in their village of Blasendorf to
make their protest against Magyar rule. They, like
the other Peoples of the Empire, had been disposed
to sympathise with the March movement; but when
it became known that the Magyars at Pesth had put
forward as one of their twelve points the union of
Transylvania with Hungary, the Roumanians became

alarmed. Had the Transylvanian Diet met under the extended suffrage now granted in Hungary, the Roumanians would have had a majority in the Diet; and the influence of this majority would have been far more important under the new parliamentary system than in the old days of centralised officialism. If, on the other hand, they were to be absorbed in Hungary, they naturally feared that the fanaticism of the Magyars in enforcing the use of the Magyar language, would be directed with even greater vigour against the despised Roumanians, than it had been against Serbs and Croats; and that the Greek Church to which the Roumanians belonged, and which had always been at a disadvantage in Transylvania, would be crushed, or, at any rate, discouraged. The tradition of their Roman descent recorded in the Libellus Wallachorum, had given some of them hopes for leadership in Transylvania, and had strengthened, even in the less ambitious, the desire for a dignified equality. Animated by these motives, they met on May 15 at Blasendorf.

This little capital of the Roumanian race lies in one of the large open plains of Transylvania. It is still little more than a straggling village of low huts; but it is apparently as important to the Roumanians as Carlowitz is to the Serbs and Hermannstadt to the Saxons. Crowds of the strange figures, whom one may still see in the villages of Transylvania, flocked in to this meeting, covered with their rough sheepskins and dark, flowing hair, and showing in their handsome faces at once the consciousness of the new life that was awakening, and their pride in those dim traditions of the past, which were supposed to unite them with the glories of ancient Rome. Even here,

too, there were found some of the ruling race, who
were prepared to make common cause with this, the
most despised and oppressed of the races of Hungary;
for a Magyar noble named Nopcsa was prominent in
the meeting. But now, as ever, the chief hope for
the Roumanians was in their clergy, and specially in
their bishops; and Lemenyi, the bishop of the United
Greeks,[1] appeared side by side with the more popular
and influential Schaguna. Speaker after speaker
dwelt on the great traditions of the Roumanian
nation, and their determination to obtain an equality
with the Magyar, Szekler, and Saxon. They avowed
their loyalty to Ferdinand, and declared that they
had no desire to oppress any other nation; but that
they would not suffer any other nation to oppress
them; that they would work for the emancipation of
industry and trade, for the removal of the feudal
burdens, for the securing of legal justice, and for the
welfare of humanity, of the Roumanian nation, and of
the common fatherland. They then proceeded to
ask for a separate national organization, for the use
of the Roumanian language in all national affairs, and
for representation in the Assembly in proportion to
their numbers. They further demanded a Roumanian
national guard to be commanded by Roumanian
officers. They claimed to be called by the name of
Roumanian, instead of the less dignified epithet of
Wallach. They also asked for an independent position for their Church ; for the foundation of a Roumanian University; for equality with the other races

---

[1] Out of the various efforts of the Roman Catholics to bring
back the Greeks to the Roman Church, there had arisen a community called the United Greeks, which acknowledged the power
of the Pope while maintaining the Greek ritual.

of Hungary in the endowment of their clergy and schools. These were the chief points of their petition; but along with these came the demands for the ordinary freedoms of the time, and for the redress of special local grievances. At the close of the petition, came the prayer which specially explained the urgency of their meeting at that time. They entreated that the Diet of Transylvania should not discuss the question of the proposed union with Hungary until the Roumanians were fully represented in the Diet. This petition Schaguna carried to Vienna on behalf of the meeting.

In the meantime the Saxons were preparing to express their opposition to the proposed union with Hungary in a separate protest of their own. The peculiar organization which the Saxons had enjoyed had become very dear to them; and they had hoped to retain their old institutions under the new Government. But when they appealed to the Hungarian Ministry, Deak told them that they had no right to make conditions; and it soon became evident that, in the larger matter of the union of Transylvania with Hungary, they would have as little chance of a fair hearing as in the smaller question of their own race organization. Count Teleki, the Governor of Transylvania, had announced, on May 2, that the union was practically settled already; and that only questions of detail had now to be arranged. This direct attack on the legal power of the Transylvanian Diet naturally alarmed the Saxons, and Count Salmen, the Comes der Sachsen or Chief Magistrate of the Saxon colony, organized the opposition to the proposed union. Hitherto the Saxons, with the exception of a few generous-minded men like Roth, had been as bitterly scornful of the Roumanians as any Magyar or Szekler could be; but now the sense of a common danger drew these races together; and the Saxons offered to allow the Roumanians to hold office in the Saxon towns and villages, and to be admitted to apprenticeships by the tradesmen of those towns.  The opposition of the Saxons to the Magyars was, no doubt, strengthened by the sympathy of the former with that German feeling which would lead to the strengthening of the influence of Vienna; and they declared that they would rather send representatives to a Viennese Assembly than to a Diet at Presburg.

And while, on the one hand, common danger to their liberties was drawing together the Saxons and the Roumanians, the sympathies of race and a common antipathy to aliens was drawing together the Magyar and the Szekler.  As early as May 10 Wesselenyi issued an appeal to the Szekler to arm themselves as guardians of the frontiers, and to be prepared to suppress any rising of the Roumanians; and on May 19 Batthyanyi appealed to them to march to Szegedin.  But it was not to the Szekler alone that the Magyars trusted to enforce their will on the Transylvanian Diet.  The fiery young students of Pesth hastened down, on May 30, to Klausenburg, where the deputies were gathering for the final meeting of the Diet.  A Roumanian deputation, coming to entreat the Parliament not to decide till the Roumanians were adequately represented in it, were contemptuously refused a hearing, and one of their leaders was roughly pushed back.  Banners were displayed bearing the words, "Union or Death!" and the young lawyers from Pesth filled the galleries

of the Assembly, and even crowded into the Hall.
The Saxon representatives, more used to quiet discussion, or to commercial transactions, than to the
fiery quarrels in which the Magyar and Szekler
delighted, tremblingly entered the Hall; and, unable
to gain courage for their duties, they gave way to
the storm, and voted for the union. Thus ended the
local independence of Transylvania, which was to
be revived twelve years later by the Germanizing
Liberalism of Schmerling, and then to be finally
swept away in the successful movement for Hungarian Independence.

The bitterness roused by the passing of the Act of
Union was not long in leading to actual bloodshed.
The immediate quarrel, however, arose out of a
matter connected, not with the race contest, but with
the new land laws of the country. The Hungarian
Diet had decided that the peasant should not only be
freed from his dependence on the landlord, but should
be also considered by his previous payment of dues
to have earned the land on which he had worked.
Naturally, disputes arose as to the extent of the land
so acquired; and in more than one case the peasants
were found to be claiming more than their own share.
It was to redress a blunder of this kind that, on
June 2, a party of National Guards, composed partly
of Szeklers and partly of Magyars, entered the Roumanian village of Mihalzi (Magyar, Mihacsfalva).
The exact circumstances of such a collision as that
which followed will always be told differently by the
most honest narrators; but it seems probable that
the Roumanians, in some confused way, connected
this visit with the recent struggle about the Union;
and it is certain that the race-hatred between the

Szekler and the Roumanians soon became inflamed.
The National Guard fired, and several of the Roumanians fell. The others fled; but their previous
resistance soon produced a rumour of a general
Roumanian insurrection. The Magyars were seized
with a panic; the Roumanian National Committee
was dissolved, and several of their clergy and other
leaders were imprisoned. Had the Roumanians been
now organized by Austrian officers it is possible that
less might have been heard of the savagery of the
new warfare. Had some of their own leaders, who
afterwards tried to control them, been ready at this
time to take the lead, many of the actual cruelties
might never have taken place. But just at this time
the Emperor answered the deputation of May 15 by
referring the Roumanians to the Magyar Ministry for
the redress of their grievances, and declaring that
equality could only be carried out by enforcing the
Act of Union. This rebuff was accompanied by a
letter from Schaguna written somewhat in the same
sense; and thus, finding that some of their leaders
had deserted them; that others were imprisoned;
that the Emperor was discouraging their complaints;
that the Magyars were denouncing them as rebels,
and the Szekler making raids on their territory, the
Roumanians began to defend themselves by a warfare which rapidly became exceptionally barbarous
and savage.

In the meantime the other subject races of Hungary were preparing in their own way for resistance
to the Magyars. The Croatian Assembly at Agram,
finding themselves discouraged by the Emperor, were
disposed to strengthen their union with the Serbs of
Slavonia; and, on June 6, Gaj and Jellaciç both sup-

ported proposals at Agram for uniting the Serbs and Croats under one rule. Rajaciç, who happened to be passing through Agram, heartily responded to these proposals; and it was resolved that the relations between the Ban of Croatia and the Voyvode of the Serbs should be left to be settled at a later period. But the Serbs, though heartily desiring sympathy with the Croats, were not disposed to trust to alliances, however welcome, or to Constitutional arrangements, however ingenious, for the settlement of their grievances against the Magyars; for they, too, had been forced to abandon peaceable discussions for actual warfare. Crnojeviç, not having been found sufficiently stern in the Magyar service, was being driven into more violent courses by the addition of a fiercer subordinate; and the cruelties inflicted on the Serbs of the Bacska had so roused their kinsmen in other parts of Hungary that an old officer of the military frontier had crossed the Danube at the head of his followers and seized the town of Titel.

At the same time the Serbs sent a deputation to Hrabowsky, the Governor of Peterwardein, to complain of the cruelties of the Magyar bands. Hitherto Hrabowsky had seemed to hesitate between the two parties; but he now grew angry in the conference with the Serb deputation, and disputed the right of of the Serbs to stay in Hungary. The Serbs, alarmed at these threats, began once more to gather at Carlowitz; and they now tried to draw recruits from friendly neighbours. Stratimiroviç had succeeded in persuading some of the regiments from the frontier to take up the Serb cause; but he perhaps relied still more on the help of those Serbs from the principality of Servia, who were now flocking in across the border

to defend their kinsmen against the Magyars. Of
the leaders of these new allies the most important
was General Knicsanin, who helped to organize the
forces in Carlowitz. The Serbs of Carlowitz had,
however, not yet entered upon actual hostilities,
when, on June 11, during one of the meetings of
their Assembly, Hrabowsky suddenly marched out of
Neusatz, dispersed a congregation who were coming
out of a chapel half way on the road between Neusatz
and Carlowitz, and reached the latter town before the
Serbs were aware of his intention. The Serbs, though
taken by surprise, rushed out to defend their town,
with a Montenegrin leader at their head. The contest
continued for several hours; but at last Hrabowsky
and his soldiers were driven back into Neusatz. Two
days later ten thousand men were in arms in Carlowitz to defend their town and their race.

But while the Slavs in Hungary were girding themselves for this fierce war, they had not forgotten the
more peaceable union proposed to them by the Bohemians; and on May 30 representatives from the
different Slavonic races of the Empire had been
welcomed in Prague by Peter Faster and other
Bohemian leaders. On June 1 the National Committee of Prague, while deliberating on the future
Constitution of Bohemia, were joined by several of
their Slavonic visitors; and out of this combination
the Congress was formed. It was speedily divided
into three sections : one representing Poles and Ruthenians, one the Southern Slavs (that is not only the
Serbs and Croats, but also the Slovenes of Krain and
the adjoining provinces), and the third the Bohemians, Moravians, Silesians, and the Slovaks of North
Hungary. Many of the members of the Congress

appeared in old Bohemian costumes, and from the
windows of the town waved the flags of all the different Slavonic races.    At 8 a.m. on June 2 the members
of the Congress went in solemn procession through
the great square called the Grosser Ring, so soon to
be be the scene of a bloody conflict, to the Teynkirche,
the church in which Huss preached, and where his
pulpit still stands.    In front of the procession went
the Students' Legion, singing patriotic songs; two
young men followed, one in the Polish dress, the other
bearing a white, blue, and red flag, which was supposed to symbolize the union of the Slavonic peoples.
A division of the Swornost corps followed these; then
came the Provisional Committee, and then the representatives of the three sections of the Congress.    The
Poles were led by Libelt, a leader in the recent rising
in Posen, and the Bohemians by the philologist Szaffarik.    At the altar, which was sacred to the bishops
Cyril and Methodius, the presiding priest offered
thanks to God for having put unity and brotherly love
into the hearts of the Slavs; and he prayed that the
Lord of Hosts would bless the work to the salvation
of the nation, as well as of the whole fatherland.  From
the church they proceeded to the hall in the Sophien-
Insel.    That hall had been decked with the arms of
the different Slavonic races.    At the upper end of it
was a table covered with red and white, the Bohemian
colours; and the choir began the proceedings with an
old national song.  The Vice-President, after formally
opening the Assembly, resigned his seat to Palacky,
who had been chosen President.

Palacky then rose and addressed the meeting.  He
spoke of the gathering as the realisation of the dreams
of their youth, which a month ago they could hardly

Y

have hoped for. "The Slavs had gathered from all sides to declare their eternal love and brotherhood to each other. Freedom," he continued, " which we now desire, is no gift of the foreigner, but of native growth, the inheritance of our fathers. The Slavs of old time were all equal before the law, and never aimed at the conquest of other nations. They understood freedom much better than some of our neighbours, who cannot comprehend the idea of aiming at freedom without also aiming at lordship. Let them learn from us the idea of equality between nations. The chief duty of our future is to carry out the principle of 'What thou wouldst not that men should do unto thee, that do not thou to another.' Our great nation would never have lost its freedom if it had not been broken up, and if each part had not gone its own separate way, and followed its own policy. The feeling of brotherly love and freedom could secure freedom to us. It is this feeling and Ferdinand that we thank for our freedom." For himself, Palacky continued, he could say, " Lord now lettest Thou thy servant depart in peace, for mine eyes have seen the salvation which Thou hast prepared for us before the face of the whole world. A light for the enlightenment of the peoples, and the glory of the Slavonic race." Then, addressing the Assembly, he concluded with these words: " Gentle-men, in virtue of the office entrusted to me by you, I announce and declare that this Slavonic Assembly is open; and I insist on its right and duty to deliberate about the welfare of the fatherland, and the nation, in the spirit of freedom, in the spirit of unity and peace; in the name of our old, renowned Prague, which pro-tects us in its bosom; in the name of the Czech nation, which follows our proceedings with hearty sympathy; in the name of the great Slavonic race, which expects from our deliberations its strengthening and eternal regeneration.  So help us God."  Other speeches followed from representatives of the different Slavonic races; and petitions to the Emperor were prepared in favour of the demands made by the Serbs at Carlowitz, and of the rights of the Poles and Ruthenians ; while plans were drawn up for the equalization of the rival languages in the schools.

But while these peaceable discussions were proceeding in the Slavonic Congress, more fiery elements were at work in other parts of the city.  During the months of April and May there had been signs of various kinds of discontent among different sections of the population.  Workmen's demonstrations about wages had attracted some attention; while one public gathering, approaching to a riot, had secured the release of an editor, supposed to have been unjustly arrested, and had hastened the resignation of Strobach, the Mayor of Prague.  But the most fiery agitations were those which had been stirred up among the students by a man named Sladkowsky, with the object of weakening as far as possible the German element in Prague.  So alarming did these demonstrations become that Count Deym resigned his seat on the National Committee ; and Count Leo Thun, the Governor of Prague, threatened to dissolve the Swornost in order to hinder further disorder; but the opposition to this proposal was so strong that he was obliged to abandon it.

The great cause of the students' alarm was the appointment of Windischgrätz to take the command of the forces in Bohemia.  His proceedings during the

March movement in Vienna were well known; and
the fear caused by his arrival was still further increased by the threatening position that he had taken
up; for he had mounted his cannon on two sides of
the city ; namely, on the commanding fortress of the
Wissehrad, on the South, from which he could have
swept a poor and crowded part of Prague; and in the
Joseph's barrack, on the North-East. The members
of the Town Council tried to check the demonstrations of the students, and to persuade them to appeal
to Windischgrätz in a more orderly manner. In order
to give dignity to the proceedings, the Burgomaster
consented to accompany the students on the proposed
deputation. Windischgrätz, however, answered that
he was responsible to the King, and not to the Council;
though, when Count Leo Thun appealed to him, he
consented to withdraw the cannon from the Joseph's
barrack, declaring that there was no need for its presence there; but that he had been determined not to
yield to the students.

While the students succeeded in further irritating
against them a man whose haughty and overbearing
spirit was naturally disposed to opposition, they were
still more rash and unfortunate in their relations with
some whom they had had greater hopes of conciliating.
The aristocratic leaders of the Bohemians, while
asserting the independence of Bohemia, and the need
for protecting Slavonic liberties, were most anxious
to make as many concessions to German feeling as
could be made consistently with these objects. One
of the noblemen, who had been fiercest in his denunciations of the rising of May 15th, even thought it
well to send to Vienna a long explanation and modification of his protest; while Palacky and other lead-

ing nationalists inaugurated a feast of reconciliation
in which many of the German Bohemians took part.
So successful had this policy appeared to be, that
the town of Saatz, which had been the first to express
alarm at the Bohemian attitude towards the Germans,
declared on May 20 its sympathy with the Prague
address to the Emperor, and its desire for union
between the German and Bohemian elements in
Bohemia. But the students seemed doomed to
weaken the effect produced by their more moderate
countrymen. They combined a strong Czech feeling
with a great desire for democratic government; and
while they thought they could enlist the sympathies
of the Vienna students by the latter part of their
creed, they seemed to be unaware that Germanism
was to the students of Vienna what Czechism was to
them. On June 5th, the very same day on which
the Slavonic Congress was deciding to send its petition to the Emperor, more than a hundred students
of Prague started on a deputation to their comrades
in Vienna. But on their way, they thought it necessary to attack and insult the German flag, wherever
it was displayed. They arrived in Vienna to find the
Viennese students suspicious even towards those who
had been their champions, and still smarting from the
recollection of a struggle between their Legion, and
the National Guard, who had attempted to suppress
them. It was while they were in this state of irritation, that the Czech students appeared in the Hall of
the University; and, unfortunately, at the same time,
there arrived from Prague the representatives of two
German Bohemian Clubs. Schuselka, Goldmark, and
other Viennese leaders, urged a reconciliation between
the two races; but the news of the insults to the

German flag so infuriated the Viennese students, that
they drove the Czechs from the Hall, and ordered
them to leave Vienna within twenty-four hours.

The unfortunate deputation returned to Prague to
find that the Slavonic Congress was approaching its
final acts, and was preparing two appeals, one to the
Emperor, and one to the Peoples of Europe. The
latter appeal was based on a general complaint of the
oppressions from which the Slavs suffered. It demanded the restoration of Poland, and called for a
European Congress to settle international questions;
" since free Peoples will understand each other better
than paid diplomatists." In the appeal to the Emperor,
the Congress went into greater detail, as to the special
demands of the different Slavonic races of Austria.
The Bohemians, indeed, mainly expressed their thanks
for the independence which now seemed legally
secured. The Moravians suggested an arrangement
which would combine the common action of Moravia
and Bohemia with a provision for Moravian local
independence. The Galicians pointed out how much
they had been left behind by the other Austrian provinces in the struggle for freedom, and proposed an
arrangement for securing equality between the Polish
and Ruthenian languages in Galicia, and for granting
to Galicia the same provincial freedom that had
already been secured to Bohemia. The Slovaks of
North Hungary demanded protection for their language against the Magyar attempt to crush it out;
equal representation in the Hungarian Assembly;
official equality between the Slovak, Ruthenian, and
Magyar languages; and freedom for those Slovaks
who had recently been arrested and imprisoned by
the Magyars, for defence of their national rights.

The Serbs, of course, demanded the acceptance of the programme put forward at Carlowitz; and the Croats the recognition of the legality of the acts of Jellaciç, and of the municipal independence of the Assembly of Croatia, Slavonia, and Dalmatia. Lastly, the Slovenes desired that the provinces of Steiermark, Krain, Carinthia, and some neighbouring districts, should be formed into a separate kingdom, in which the Slovenian language should be the official one. All the Slavs combined in the desire that Austria should be a federal State, and in the protest against that absorption in Germany, the fear of which had led to the calling of the Congress.

But sober and rational as was the tone of the Slavonic Congress, as a whole, there were turbulent spirits in Prague, who were determined that the matter should not end peaceably. The extremer representatives of Polish feeling desired the separation of Poland, and disliked any plan which would reconcile Galicia to remaining part of Austria. On the other hand, there had appeared in Prague at this period an adventurer named Turansky, who while professing to be a champion of the Slovaks of North Hungary, seems undoubtedly to have acted as an " agent provocateur." Such men as these were easily able to act upon the excited feelings of the students; and were further aided in stirring up violent feeling by a strike among the cotton workers which was just then going on.

Finally, the outburst came on June 12. The Slavonic Congress at Prague, already preparing to break up, met on that day to celebrate a last solemn mass. Once more they all gathered in front of the statue of S. Wenzel ; but now the numbers were so great that they spread down the whole length of the Wenzels Platz. In spite of the peaceable intentions of the majority, a number of the workmen had come bearing arms. The mass went off quietly enough; but several of those who had attended it, had had their national feelings excited to the utmost; and, as they left the Wenzels Platz, they marched back singing Bohemian songs, and howling against Windischgrätz. As they passed under the Pulverthurm into the narrow and busy Zeltnergasse, which leads to the Grosser Ring, some soldiers, as ill luck would have it, came out of the neighbouring barrack. The house of Windischgrätz was in the street, and the crowd were hooting against him. Under these circumstances a collision was unavoidable. The crowd were dispersed by the soldiers; some of the students attempted to rally them, and were arrested; the workmen then tried to rescue the students; the soldiers charged, and drove them back under the Pulverthurm, and round into the wider street of Am Graben, and right up to the National Museum, which was the head-quarters of the Swornost. After a fierce struggle the soldiers stormed the Museum, and captured many of the students; but the panic had now spread to other parts of the town. Sladkowsky, at the head of the workmen, broke into the depôt of the Town Watch, and seized arms; while others rushed into the country districts round Prague, and spread the rumour that the soldiers were trying to take away all that the Emperor had granted, and to restore the feudal dues.

In the meantime the leaders of the March movement were greatly startled at hearing of the outbreak. Some of them had already been alarmed at the growing tendency to disturbances in Prague; several of them hastened out to check the riots, and some of them even fought against the insurgents. Count Leo Thun, the Governor of Prague, hastened down to the Grosser Ring to try to still the disturbance; but the students seized him, and carried him off prisoner into the Jesuit College near the Carlsbrücke. They seem to have had very little intention of violence; but they thought to secure by this means his promise of help in a peaceful settlement of the contest. He refused, however, to promise anything while he was kept a prisoner. Some of the students went to the Countess to try to get her to persuade her husband to yield; but though she was so alarmed for his safety that her hair turned white from fear, she firmly refused to comply. Meanwhile, one of the more moderate men went to Windischgrätz to entreat him to give up the students who had been taken prisoners, on condition of the barricades being removed. But Windischgrätz demanded that Count Leo Thun should first be set free. While the discussion was going on, the fight was still raging in the Zeltner Gasse ; and Princess Windischgrätz coming to the windows was struck by a shot which mortally wounded her. Windischgrätz hastened to the room where his wife was dying, while the soldiers guarded the house against further attacks. With all his hardness, Windischgrätz was entirely free from the blood-thirstiness of Radetzky and Haynau; and under this terrible provocation he seems to have exercised a wonderful self-restraint. While the Burgomaster and some members of the Town Council were exerting themselves to restore order, Windischgrätz sent an offer to make peace, if Count Leo Thun were released, if guarantees were given for the peace of the town, and if Count Leo Thun and he were allowed to consult together about the restoration of order; and he even promised to await the deliberations of the Town Council on this subject.

But the fight was raging so hotly that the Town Council were unable, for some time, to deliberate. At last, however, temporary suspension of firing was secured, and the Burgomaster, with the assistance of Palacky, Szaffarik and others organized a new deputation to Windischgrätz. Windischgrätz insisted on his former terms; and at last Count Leo Thun was set free, giving a general promise to use his efforts for securing peace. The students, however, put forward the conditions, that Bohemia should be under a Bohemian commander who should be in most things independent of Vienna; that Bohemian soldiers, alone, should be used in the defence of Bohemia; that the officers and soldiers should take their oath to the Constitution, both of Bohemia and of Austria; that the gates of Prague should be defended by the citizens and students alone; and lastly that Windischgrätz should be declared the enemy of all the Peoples of Austria, and tried by a Bohemian tribunal. As Windischgrätz was, obviously, one of the people to whom these conditions would be referred, it was not very likely that the last of these requests would be complied with. He seems still, however, to have retained some desire for concession; and on June 15 he withdrew his soldiers from the other parts of the town to the North side of the river. But new acts of violence followed; and Windischgrätz began to cannonade the town. Again the Burgomaster appealed to him; and he consented to resign in favour of Count Mensdorff, on condition that the barricades should be instantly removed. On the 16th the town seemed to have become quiet; but the barricades were not yet removed ; the soldiers indignantly demanded that Windischgrätz should be restored to his command, as the conditions of his resignation had not been fulfilled; and the first act of Windischgrätz, on re-assuming power, was to threaten to bombard the town, if it did not surrender by six o'clock a.m. on the 17th.

The wiser students saw the uselessness of further resistance, and began to remove the barricades; but some stray shots from the soldiers, whether by accident or intention, hit the mill near one of the bridges; some women in the mill raised the cry that they were being fired on; the mill hands returned the fire, and Windischgrätz began at once to bombard the town. The barricades were quickly thrown up again; for four hours the bombardment continued; and, while the students were fiercely defending the Carlsbrücke against the soldiers of Windischgrätz, the fire, which had been lighted by the bomb-shells, was spreading from the mill to other parts of the town. Of such a contest there could be but one result. In the course of the 17th several thousand people fled from Prague; and on the 18th Windischgrätz entered the town in triumph, and proclaimed martial law.

The conspiracy had collapsed; but, except Peter Faster, who escaped from the town during the siege, none of the leaders of the March movement were at first suspected of any share in the Rising. Indeed, it was well known that many of them had exerted themselves to suppress it. But Turansky, the agitator above mentioned, suddenly gave himself up to the authorities, and offered to reveal a plot, in which he declared that Palacky, Rieger, and other Bohemian leaders were implicated. The evidence broke down; but it gave excuse for the continuance of the state of siege, for the arrest of many innocent men, and for the refusal to summon the Bohemian Assembly, which was to have met in that very month. This imaginary plot was used as the final pretext for the complete suppression of Bohemian liberty. Turansky was believed, rightly or wrongly, to have been sent by Kossuth to stir up the insurrection; that he had desired the failure of the movement which he stirred up was evident enough; and thus there arose an ineffaceable bitterness between the Bohemians and the Magyars. There also arose out of these events further cause for the bitterness between the Bohemians and the Germans. For, while Prague was still burning, and Windischgrätz was still enforcing martial law, a band of Vienna students arrived in Prague, to congratulate Windischgrätz on his victory over the liberties of Bohemia. The long-simmering hatred between the Germans and Bohemians seems to have found its climax in that congratulation; and from that time forth, whatever might be the political feeling of the leaders on either side, common action between Bohemians and Germans became less and less possible.

As for the effect of the fall of Prague on the position of the Slavonic races in Austria, they were deprived by that event of their last help of a free centre of national life round which their race could gather. For Prague had supplied such a centre in a

way in which none of the other Slavonic capitals ever
could supply it.  Its fame rested on a past, which
was connected with struggles for freedom against
German tyranny, and the leading facts of which
were clear and undisputed; while its geographical
position prevented it from coming into collision
with the other Slavonic races.  Agram and Carlowitz
might at times look upon each other as rivals; but
Prague had no interest in preferring one to the
other, or in destroying the independence of either,
while the connection in language between the Bohemians and the Slovaks of North Hungary ensured
the sympathy of the former for any attempts at
resistance to Magyar supremacy.  Lastly, wedged
in as Bohemia is between the Germans of the Archduchy of Austria, and that wider Germany with
which so many of the Austrians desired to unite, it
could never cherish those separatist aspirations which
would have prevented Lemberg, for instance, from
ever becoming the centre of an Austrian Slavonic
federation.  Thus the fall of Bohemian liberty prepared the way for a complete change in the character
of the Slavonic movement.  The idea of a federation
of the different Slavonic races of the Empire might
be still cherished by many of the Slavonic leaders;
and, for a short time, the struggle of the Slavonic
races against Magyar and German supremacy might
retain its original character of a struggle for freedom.
But it was unavoidable that this movement should
now gradually drift into an acceptance of the leadership of those courtiers and soldiers, who hated the
Germans and Magyars as the opponents, not of
Slavonic freedom, but of Imperial despotism.

# CHAPTER IX.

## THE REVOLUTION BREAKS INTO SEPARATE PARTS.
## APRIL TO OCTOBER, 1848.

Attitude of the other races to the Italian struggle.—Inconsistency of Kossuth.—Attitude of the Provisional Government of Lombardy.—Hesitation of Charles Albert.—His two declarations about the Lombard war.—The war adopted by Leopold of Tuscany.—By Ferdinand of Naples.—Confusions of the Pope.—General Durando.—Radetzky at Mantua.—The first battle of Goito.—Mazzini in Milan.—Casati, Charles Albert, and the Italian Volunteers.—The Southern Tyrol.—Venice.—Manin's error.—Durando and Manin.—Charles Albert's attitude towards Venetia. —The Pope's difficulty.—The Encyclical of April 29.—Its effect.—The Mamiani Ministry.—Effect of the Pope's attitude on Charles Albert's position.—The fall of Udine, and its consequences.—Charles Albert and Venetia.—Casati and Mazzini.—The question of the Fusion.—Its effect on opinion.—The Neapolitan Coup d'Etat of May 15.—The recall of the Neapolitan troops from Lombardy.—Pepe and Manin.—Battle of Curtatone. — "The handful of boys."—Second battle of Goito.—Capture of Peschiera. —The vote of fusion.—The émeute of May 29 and its effects.—The struggle and fall of Vicenza.—The Austrian conquest of Venetia.—The vote of fusion in Venice.—The attack on Trieste. German feeling in Frankfort.—The various difficulties of the Frankfort Parliament.—Effect of Archduke John's election.—Anti-Italian decisions.—The struggle in Italy grows fiercer.—Charles Albert's new blunders.—Mazzini's advice to the Lombard Government.—Charles Albert at Milan.—The final treason.—The Austrian reconquest of Lombardy. — The 8th of August in Bologna.—Repulse of Welden.—The struggle between Frankfort and Berlin.—The question of Posen.—The Schleswig-Holstein war.—The Assembly and the King.—The truce of Malmö.—The fatal vote.—The riots at Frankfort.—The "state of siege."—The

THE struggle of races described in the last chapter
had not been without its effect on the progress of
affairs in Italy.   Those Austrians, whose one desire
was for the unity of the Empire, spoke of Radetzky's
camp as the only place where Austria was truly
represented; while, on the other hand, the leaders of
the different race movements were divided in their
feelings about the Italian war.   The Germans, both
at Frankfort and Vienna, saw with chagrin that Lombardy and Venetia were slipping away from German
rule; but they felt, nevertheless, that they could not
entirely condemn a struggle for freedom and independence.   The Bohemians, especially in the first part of
the struggle, would gladly have let the Italian provinces go, if they could thereby have facilitated the
federal arrangement of the rest of the Austrian Empire.   Among the Croats there seems to have been
some division of feeling on the subject.   Gaj and the
purely national party had some sympathies with
Italian liberty; but Jellaciç, and that large body of
his followers who mingled military feelings with the
desire for Croatian independence, were eager to show
their loyalty to the House of Austria by supporting
the war in Italy; and they were, moreover, not un-
mindful of the rivalry between Slavs and Italians in
Dalmatia and Istria.   The Magyars, in the early days

of the March movement, had been more disposed than
any race in the Empire to show friendliness to Italy;
and Kossuth's Italian sympathies had been specially
well known.    But circumstances changed the attitude
of the Croats and Hungarians to Italy, as the struggle
went on; for, while the former desired to recall the
Croat forces from Italy to the defence of their home,
the latter became more and more desirous of conciliating the sympathies of the Emperor.    The wish to
preserve a strictly legal position led some of the
members of the Hungarian Ministry to dwell upon
the claims due to the Austrian Government under the
Pragmatic Sanction; and Kossuth, without sympath-
ising with this feeling, was easily induced to give way
to his colleagues, by his fear of the encouragement
which the recall of Croatian regiments would give to
the desire for Croatian independence; and therefore, in
spite of his belief in the justice of the Italian cause,
he strongly supported the use of Hungarian troops in
crushing out the freedom of Italy.

But, interesting as the Italian struggle was to all
the different races of the Austrian Empire, it was yet
working itself out in a way so distinct from either the
Austrian or the German movements, that we are compelled to ignore the exact chronological order of
European events in order to understand its full signi-
ficance; and we must therefore now go back to the
events which followed the March risings and the flight
of Radetzky and Palffy.    The centre of interest was
still in Milan, where Casati and the Town Council
had been changed by the force of circumstances into
the Provisional Government of Lombardy.    These
men had shown, during the siege, a continual uncertainty of purpose and readiness to compromise; and,

when Radetzky had been driven from Milan, they showed an equal unreadiness to follow up their advantages. In the people, however, there was no want of willingness to carry on the struggle; and at least one general rose to the occasion. Augusto Anfossi had died of his wounds during the siege; but Luciano Manara, the youth who had captured Porta Tosa, was following up the retreat of Radetzky, placing guards in the villages, and cutting roads. Manara found it very difficult to carry out his plans; partly owing to the distrust shown to him by the General whom the Provisional Government had placed over him, partly to the insubordination of Torres, one of the leaders of the Genoese Volunteers, who was nominally acting under him, and whose defiance of Manara seems to have been at least tolerated by the Provisional Government.

For Casati and his friends put their trust not so much in any Lombards as in the help derived from Charles Albert. That Prince, indeed, had hesitated as usual till the last moment. When the news of the Milanese rising had reached Genoa, the Genoese had risen and sent volunteers to assist the insurgents; but Charles Albert had not only forbidden their march, but had sent troops to drive them back from the frontier. So indignant were the students of Turin at this action that they rose against Charles Albert, and would not submit until they were allowed to volunteer. Several officers even threatened to leave the Army if war was not declared on Austria; Parma and Modena were rising at the same time against the Austrian forces, and demanding annexation to Piedmont; while Mazzini and his friends were issuing appeals from Paris to urge their followers to support

z

Charles Albert, if he would venture on war with
Austria.   At last Pareto, the most democratic of
Charles Albert's Ministers, assured him that, if he did
not act, a rebellion would break out in Piedmont; and
so, on March 23, having demanded of the Austrians
the evacuation of Parma and Modena, and having
been refused, Charles Albert ordered the Austrian
Ambassador to leave Turin, and straightway declared
war.   Yet even now he left doubtful the exact object
of the war; for, while he declared to the Provisional
Government that he came "to lend to the Peoples of
Lombardy and Venetia that assistance which brother
may expect from brother, and friend from friend," he
announced to the other Governments of Europe that
he had only intervened to prevent a Republican rising.
He then despatched General Passalacqua to Milan,
announcing that he himself would not arrive there
until he had won a victory over the Austrians.

But, however ungraciously Charles Albert had
done his part, he had succeeded in quickening the
enthusiasm of the Italians for a war against Austria.
Leopold of Tuscany had announced, two days before,
that the hour of the resurrection of Italy had struck,
and that his troops should march to the frontier of
Tuscany; and, on April 5, he frankly declared the
purpose of this march, and ordered his troops to help
their Lombard brothers.   Riots broke out both in
Naples and Rome, and the Austrian arms were torn
down.   Guglielmo Pepe hastened back to Naples,
after twenty seven years of exile, and demanded the
immediate departure of the troops for Lombardy.
Ferdinand yielded to the popular cry, and consented
to make Pepe general of the expedition.   Pius IX.
was less easy to move.   He had become thoroughly

scared at the progress of events; and though he had
consented to grant a Constitution, much like that of
other Princes, he could not reconcile in his mind the
contradictions between his position as Head of the
Catholic Church and as a Constitutional Italian
Prince.  The former position seemed' to require of
him a claim to absolute authority in home affairs,
and a perfectly impartial attitude towards the various
members of the Catholic Church, whatever might be
their differences of race or government.  The latter
position seemed, on the contrary, to demand that he
should adapt himself to the freer life which was
growing up in the different Italian States, and that
he should become the champion of Italian unity and
liberty against the Emperor of Austria.  His own
inclinations and sympathies would have led him to
sacrifice the new office to the old one.  He was,
as already explained, much more a priest than a
prince, much more a Conservative than a Reformer.
His priestly training combined with his weak health
to make new ideas distasteful to him; and his sense
of his duties as Head of the Catholic Church worked
in with that very kindliness of disposition which had
betrayed him into the position of a reformer, to make
him oppose a fierce and dangerous war.  Under these
circumstances, he looked with alarm on the new
impulse which Charles Albert had given to the anti-
Austrian feeling throughout Italy.

But he was, for the moment, in the hands of stronger
men, who were determined on driving him forward.
Massimo d'Azeglio was in Rome seconding the efforts
of Ciceruacchio for the war; and Giovanni Durando
(a brother of the Giacomo Durando who had written
on Italian Nationality) was appointed general of the

forces which were to march to Lombardy. Even
now the Pope refused to recognize the object of their
expedition; and as the troops filed past him, on
March 24, he blessed them, but only as the defenders
of the Roman territories against assailants; and when
a young man cried from the ranks, "Holy Father,
we are going to fight for Italy and for you," he
answered, "Not for me; I wish for peace, not war."
Durando, however, issued a proclamation to his
troops in which he declared that, since Pius IX.'s
approval of the war, "Radetzky must be considered
as fighting against the Cross of Christ." Pius IX.
angrily repudiated this speech in the Government
Gazette, declaring that he would soon utter his own
opinions, and that he did not require to express them
through the mouth of a subordinate. But nobody
took any notice of this protest, and the troops
marched to Lombardy.

In the meantime Charles Albert was beginning the
war in an unfortunate manner. Eager to distinguish
himself by an engagement with Radetzky, he was
resolved to march after him to Lodi instead of seizing
on the important fortress of Mantua. Mantua had
attempted to shake off the Austrian yoke at the time
when other cities of Lombardy were rising; but a
desire to act through the Municipal Council led the
citizens to hesitate in their movement. The want of
communication with other towns prevented them from
being aware of the position of the Austrian troops;
and, on the evening of March 22, Benedek, one of the
Austrian generals, was able to crush out the incipient
rising. But the news of the Piedmontese advance
once more stirred the Mantuans to action; on the
29th they rose again, threw up barricades, organized

a Civic Guard, and eagerly hoped that Charles Albert would come to support them. When Radetzky found that Charles Albert did not seize on this important fortress, he availed himself of the blunder to march at once to Mantua; and, on March 31, that city fell again into the hands of the Austrians. This victory at once alarmed the Piedmontese, who, under the command of General Bava, set out, on April 8, to Goito, a village a few miles from Mantua. The Austrians occupied the little bridge across the Mincio at the entrance to the village, and the Tyrolese sharpshooters sheltered themselves behind an inn which stands near the bridge on the Mantuan side. The Piedmontese, mistaking the stone ornaments on the inn for sentinels, fired at them; shots were returned by the Austrians, and a fierce encounter followed, during which several of the troops from the Italian Tyrol deserted the Austrian ranks and joined the Piedmontese. The Austrians, finding themselves beaten, attempted to blow up the bridge; but had only succeeded in destroying one arch before they were driven back. By this victory the Piedmontese obtained the command of the whole line of the Mincio from Mantua to Peschiera, and cut off all communication between the two wings of the Austrian army, one of which was in Mantua and one in Verona.

The battle of Goito roused the greatest enthusiasm for Charles Albert; and it unfortunately strengthened the Provisional Government of Milan in their determination to rely rather on him than on their own people. How much popular force they might at this time have gained was shown by an event which took place on the very day after the battle of Goito. On

that day, April 9, Mazzini arrived in Milan.  About
eight o'clock in the evening he appeared on the
balcony of the Albergo della Venezia, which stands
directly opposite the place occupied by the Provisional Government.  He addressed a few words to
the people, waving the tricolour banner.  He spoke
in terms of warm approval of the Provisional Government, and praised them for rejecting a truce which
Radetzky had proposed, and for endeavouring to
secure a complete representation of the Lombard
provinces in the Assembly which met at Milan; and
when Casati appeared he greeted him warmly.  But
Mazzini soon found that, neither in the camp of
Charles Albert, nor in Milan, were the leaders disposed to welcome the help of the Republican forces.
When Mazzini applied to the Provisional Government
to grant employment to those who had already had
experience in revolutionary wars, he was told that no
one knew where they were; and when he answered
this objection by producing the men, their services
were refused.  The Swiss, who flocked in from the
Canton Ticino, were in the same way repelled; and
even a more illustrious volunteer than any of these
found cold reception in Charles Albert's camp; for it
was at this period of the war that Garibaldi arrived
in Lombardy in the full splendour of the reputation
he had won as a champion of liberty in Monte Video.
But, when he offered his services to Charles Albert,
he was told that he might go to Turin, to see *if* and
*how* he could be employed.

One of the great points of difference between the
policy of the Republicans and that of Charles Albert
was that the former desired to press forward to the
Alps and excite an insurrection against Austria

amongst the population of the Southern Tyrol.
That population, in spite of its Italian blood and
language, had been loyal to Francis of Austria in
the time of Andrew Hofer; but the ungrateful policy
of the Austrian Emperor had gradually alienated the
sympathies of the Italian Tyrolese; and, while even
in Frankfort the representatives of the Southern
Tyrol were asking for local self-government in their
own country, the population were ready to rise on
behalf of Garibaldi and Manara. But the dislike of
many of the Piedmontese officers to the war, and the
hesitation of Charles Albert between war, diplomacy,
and complete abandonment of the cause, led the
official leaders of the Lombard movement to repel
any proposal for so extending the area of the war as
to drive the Austrians to extremities, and to make
them unwilling to accept a diplomatic settlement of
the contest.

Many of those who were repelled by Casati and
Charles Albert went to find a more generous welcome
at Venice. The extremely democratic character of
the Venetian insurrection had impressed all observers;
and it was specially noted that an artizan, named
Toffoli, had been admitted into the Provisional Govern-
vernment of Venice. But, hearty as Manin was in his
desire to enlist the sympathies of all classes, he could
not help being a Venetian, and not a Milanese. However narrow and aristocratic Casati and his friends
might be in their personal feelings, they were the
official representatives of a city whose glories were
connected with the memories of a time when it was
the head of a league of free cities;[1] while Venice, even

---

[1] To avoid needless controversy, I may add that I am perfectly
aware of the tyranny exercised by Milan over Lodi and other

in its long struggle against the Turks or in its resistance to the papacy in the seventeenth century, could never be taken as the champion of free civic government. Manin and Casati seem alike to have been influenced by these traditions; and while the future Council of Lombardy had been fully constituted by April 13th, it was not till the 14th of that month that the Provisional Government of Venice consented to allow the towns of Venetia to choose representatives, who should take a real share in the government of the province. The consequences of this hesitation were most unfortunate. Treviso, Padua, Rovigo, Vicenza, and Udine had formed Provisional Governments even before they knew that Venice was free; and they would then readily have joined the Venetian Republic; but observing some hesitation on the part of Venice to answer to their appeal, Vicenza offered herself to Charles Albert. This decision excited some indignation in Venice; for Manin had hoped that the old towns of Venetia would be willing, under whatever form of government, to act with the chief city; and whatever errors Manin may have committed in the delay, he was more zealous than either the Milanese or Piedmontese Governments for the protection of the Venetian towns from the Austrian forces.

Nor, indeed, was it wholly the result of the above-named hesitation that Manin was not able to secure that co-operation which he desired between Venice and the other Venetian cities. There seems to have been a tendency in the civic governments, and still more in those officers who came to help the Lombards

small towns; but the fact remains that the real force of the Lombard League, in its struggle against Barbarossa, lay in the *equal* union of the greater towns of Lombardy.

and Venetians, to look rather for orders to Casati and Charles Albert than to the rulers of Venice; and this tendency was still further increased by the anomalous position of the officers of the Papal troops. Durando, the chief of these officers, was vividly conscious that he had come to Lombardy in an independent manner, and in spite of the discouragement of the Pope; and, though he was willing to fight for Venice, he wished to do so in his own manner, and refused to listen to Manin's directions about the plan of operations. He felt no doubt that it was safer to take orders from an established sovereign, like Charles Albert, than from the head of an un-"recognised" revolutionary Government; and while he wished to march to the aid of Padua, he desired to do so as an officer of Charles Albert. But the same motives which led Charles Albert to abandon the Southern Tyrol were making him hesitate, at any rate, about extending his campaign to Venetia. So he forbad Durando to enter Venetia, and sent him instead to protect the Duchies of Modena and Parma.

While these conflicting interests were weakening the efforts of the defenders of Lombardy and Venetia, another apple of discord was thrown into the camp by an Encyclical from the Pope. As already mentioned, Pius had discouraged the march to Lombardy, and had promised to state his own opinions instead of accepting those of Durando. His Ministers, feeling the uncertainty of the position in which the Papal troops were placed, urged him to come to a more definite decision on this point. At no time was such strong pressure brought to bear from opposite sides on the feeble mind of Pius IX. On the one hand, disturbances were breaking out in the provinces; and the indignation at the Pope's hesitation was stirred to greater bitterness by the want both of food and of work which was being felt in Rome. On the other hand, two powerful influences were being exerted to induce Pius to abandon the Italian cause. In Germany great bitterness had arisen against the Italian war; and the German Catholics were threatening to break loose from the Papal authority. At the same time, Ferdinand of Naples, who had never heartily sympathised with the struggle for Italian freedom, was trying to inspire the Pope with jealousy of the designs of Charles Albert. To say the truth, Ferdinand was not without excuse in this matter; for, while he was being driven to declare war on Austria, the Sicilian Assembly were deposing him from the throne of Sicily, and discussing a proposal to offer their island to a son of Charles Albert. Therefore the Neapolitan Ambassador was directed to use his influence with Pius IX. for the promotion of a league between Rome, Naples, and Tuscany, which was to counteract the power of Piedmont. Thus, then, those rival instincts, of the Head of the Church and the Italian Prince, were both appealed to, to secure the opposition of the Pope to the war; and however much he may have been terrified by the disturbances in the provinces, those disturbances did not tend to increase his sympathy with the popular movement. Such was his state of feeling, when on April 28th, his Ministers, headed by Cardinal Antonelli, entreated him to give his open sanction to the war. The result of this petition was directly contrary to the desire expressed by the signers of it; for, on April 29th there appeared a Papal Encyclical absolutely repudiating the Italian war.

In this document, the Pope complained of the desire
of the agitators to draw away from him the sympathy
of the Catholics of Germany; and he proceeded to
justify and explain the course that he had hitherto
followed. He alluded to the demand for reform
which had been made in the time of Pius VII., and
to the encouragement which that demand had received
from the programme presented to Gregory XVI. by
the Great Powers. That programme had included
a Central Council, improvement in the Municipal
Councils, and above all the admission of the laity to
all offices, whether administrative or judicial. Gregory
had not been able to carry out these ideas completely;
and therefore Pius had been compelled to develope
them further. In this he had been guided, not by
the advice of others, but by charitable feeling towards
his subjects. But his concessions had not produced
the result which he had hoped; and he had been
compelled to warn the people against riots. These
warnings had been in vain; and he had been forced
to send troops to guard his frontier, and to " protect
the integrity and security of the Papal State." He
protested against the suspicion that he sympathised
with those " who wished the Roman Pontiff to preside
over some new kind of Republic to be constituted out
of all the Peoples of Italy." He exhorted the Italians
to abandon all such theories, and to obey the Princes
of whose benevolence they had had experience; and
he, for his part, did not desire any further extension
of his temporal power, but would use all his efforts
for the restoration of peace.

The greatest indignation was aroused by this
Encyclical; but it was still possible for the Pope to
find protection in that superstition which Ciceruacchio

had so industriously encouraged. The cry was again
raised that the Cardinals were misleading the Pope,
and special charges of treason were made against
Antonelli. Some of the more zealous patriots even
talked of carrying off the Pope to Milan, that he
might see for himself the real condition of the war.
At the same time appeals were made to the humanity
of Pius; it was pointed out to him that, if he disowned his soldiers, they would be liable to be treated
as brigands; and instances were quoted of the cruelty
of Austrian soldiers to those whom they had captured.
Partly moved by humanity, and partly by fear, the
Pope at last yielded; and on May 3 he summoned to
office Terenzio Mamiani, so lately under suspicion
as a half-amnestied rebel; and Mamiani speedily
avowed his zeal for the war, declaring it a holy cause.

But, in spite of this change of front, the Encyclical
produced a dangerous effect on the Lombard war;
and its first result was to strengthen the power of
Charles Albert, by compelling Durando to place himself more definitely than before under his orders, and
by leading the Italians in general to look to the King
of Sardinia as their only trustworthy leader. Fortunately, this accession of strength came to Charles
Albert at a moment when he was rousing himself
from that state of hesitation which had followed the
victory at Goito. That hesitation, however, had given
time for Radetzky to fortify Mantua more strongly;
while Nugent, at the head of another Austrian force,
had marched into Venetia. The Venetians, ill-sup-
ported, were little able to stand against the invader;
and the important town of Udine fell into the hands
of the Austrians. This startled both Charles Albert
and Casati; and, while the Provisional Government

of Lombardy turned to Mazzini for advice, Charles Albert at last consented to allow Durando to advance into Venetia. Durando sent his subordinate officer Ferrari before him; and on May 8, Ferrari encountered the Austrians at Cornuta, and drove them back. He then continued the struggle in hopes of new reinforcements from Durando; but, when Durando had not arrived at four o'clock in the afternoon, the soldiers were compelled to retreat. Then they were seized by a sudden panic, and they cried out that either Ferrari or Durando had betrayed them. The consciousness of the illegal position in which the Papal Encyclical had placed them, still further increased the panic of the soldiers; Ferrari was forced to retreat to Mestre, and Durando to Vicenza. In Vicenza, indeed, the latter defended himself gallantly enough; and the people seconded his efforts. Women, old men, and children, rushed to put out the lighted balls which the enemy threw into the city; and, after a struggle of about twelve hours, the Austrian forces were compelled to retreat.

But by this time Charles Albert had again repented of his invasion of Venetia; and, refusing to come to the help of Durando, he turned his attention to the fortress of Peschiera. The zeal of the Milanese Government had been even more short-lived than that of Charles Albert. Mazzini had proposed the formation of a Council of War, to be composed of three men, and to be accompanied by a levée en masse of what were called "the five classes." The Government consented to summon only the first three classes, alleging as their excuse, the distrust which they felt for many of the peasantry. Mazzini also proposed to issue an appeal for volunteers, and to place his own

name first on the list. The Government consented;
but, before the appeal had been prepared, they had
changed their mind and withdrawn their approval
from the proposal. The Council of War was changed
into a Committee of Defence for Venetia, then into a
Committee of aid for Venetia, and finally disappeared
altogether. Charles Albert's secretary announced
that the King did not choose to have an army of
enemies in his rear, and inscriptions on the walls of
Milan threatened Mazzini with death. The leaders
of the volunteers, who had been pressing forward to
the Alps, were discouraged; and General Allemandi,
their commander, was so ill supported that he resigned
his office.

The war seemed to be rapidly changing its character; and the desires of Charles Albert appeared to
be more exclusively concentrated on the aggrandise-
ment of his own Kingdom. When he had first
entered Lombardy, both he and the Milanese leaders
had announced that the form of Government would
be left undecided till the victory was won; but they
now changed their tone, and prepared for a union
between Piedmont and Lombardy. On May 12, the
Milanese Government issued a decree that the population of Lombardy should decide by a plebiscite the
question whether Lombardy should be immediately
incorporated with Piedmont under the rule of Charles
Albert. The Republicans, held in check to a great
extent by Mazzini, had hitherto refrained from giving
prominence to their political opinions. But Mazzini
now felt it necessary to protest against this proposal;
and all the more strongly because Charles Albert's
secretary had hoped, by the offer of the premiership
in the future Kingdom of North Italy, to induce him

to assist in promoting the fusion between Lombardy
and Piedmont.   He therefore now issued a protest
against the taking of any political vote of this kind
while  the  war  was  going  on;  both  because  it  was
absurd  and  unnatural  in  itself;  because  it  was  a
violation  of  the  promises  of  the  Government;  and
because it gave a pretext for foreign intervention, by
changing the war of liberation into one of conquest.
The champions of Charles Albert were infuriated at
this opposition; Mazzini's protest was publicly burnt
in Genoa; and  the  Provisional Government of Lombardy resolved  to  go  on  with  the  Plebiscite.   This
decision tended undoubtedly to bring great confusion
into  Lombardy.   It  weakened  the  sympathies  of
those Germans, Austrians, and Hungarians who had
been well disposed towards the Italian struggle for
independence; while it gave an excuse for the opposition of that larger body of politicians, who had
hesitated between  Liberal principles and  national
prejudice, and who were now eager  to declare that
the  war  had  ceased  to  be a  struggle  for  Italian
liberty, and was merely designed for the aggrandise-
ment of Charles Albert.

But,  however  much  Charles  Albert's  interests
might suffer from his changeable policy, he always
was helped out of his difficulties by the contrast
between his questionable acts, and the unquestion-
able badness of some other prince.   As the Papal
Encyclical had come at the right moment to redeem
the credit which he had lost by his slackness after the
Battle  of  Goito,  so  the  treachery  of  the  King  of
Naples served, at this crisis, to throw, by force of
contrast, a more favourable light on the ambitious
proposals for the fusion of Lombardy with Piedmont.

Ferdinand of Naples had reluctantly consented to join in the Italian war. The hearty dislike of Liberty, which he shared with the majority of the Bourbon family, combined with his special jealousy of Charles Albert to increase his desire to abandon this expedition. He feared that a Kingdom of North Italy would be the natural result of the war, even if the popular enthusiasm did not carry Charles Albert into schemes of greater aggrandizement; and he had a not unreasonable grievance against the King of Sardinia in the recent choice by the Sicilians of the Duke of Genoa as their King. The priests in Naples, unlike those in Lombardy and Venetia, were intriguing on behalf of Austria, and had circulated the rumour that St. Januarius was a friend to the Austrian Emperor. In spite of these intrigues, a Liberal majority had been returned to the Neapolitan Parliament; and the King, therefore, resolved to put still further limits on the power of that Parliament, by demanding of the members an oath which would have admitted Ferdinand's right to suppress the Sicilian movement, would have enforced the complete acceptance of the Roman Catholic faith, and would have prohibited any attempt to enlarge or reform the Constitution.

This oath the deputies refused; but in spite of the advice of his Ministers, the King resolved to insist upon it. Tumults arose in the city, and barricades were thrown up; but the deputies, while thanking the people for their zeal, urged them to remain quiet, and to pull down the barricades. Some of those who had taken part in the rising withdrew from the streets in consequence of this appeal; but others demanded that the royal troops, drawn up in the piazza of the palace, and near the church of San Francesco, should be withdrawn at the same time. The deputies went to wait upon the King; but whilst they were in conversation with him, they heard the first shots fired by the soldiers upon the crowd. Ferdinand then scornfully told the deputation to go home and consider themselves; "for the Day of Judgment is not far from you." He had one great advantage on his side. That degraded class, the Lazzaroni of Naples, had always been fanatical supporters of the King and St. Januarius; and it is even said, that, while the troops were firing on the people, Ferdinand was exclaiming to the Lazzaroni, " Go forward! " " Naples is yours! " While massacre and outrage were raging in the streets, the deputies sent a message to the French admiral, whose fleet was anchored in the Bay of Naples, to entreat him to intervene in the name of France. But he answered that he had been ordered not to interfere in the affairs of another people.

The deputies then passed a resolution, declaring that they would not suspend their sittings, unless compelled by brute force. An officer soon after came to disperse them; and, after a written protest, they yielded to this violence. Every liberty was shortly after crushed out; and, though, for about a month longer, a kind of spasmodic struggle went on, and though, after a time, the Sicilians consented to send some help to the insurgents, the movements were too ill-organized to have any permanent strength; and the Government were able to suppress them by repeated massacres.

Ferdinand's *coup d'état* had taken place on May 15. In the meantime, the Neapolitan forces under Pepe had been slowly advancing through the Papal territory collecting volunteers as they went. The slowness of their march had been due in part to the suspicious attitude of the Pope, who feared that the King of Naples might seize on those territories, which had always been a bone of contention between Naples and Rome. Pepe therefore had not yet left the Papal territory, when he received orders to abandon the war, and to return to Naples. At the same time he was told that, if he did not wish to return, he might resign his command to General Statella. Pepe was resolved to advance; but it seemed doubtful how far his authority would outweigh that of the King, and of the subordinate officers who were on the King's side. The Bolognese, who had risen in March to drive out those Austrian troops which had lingered in Ferrara, and to expel the Duke from Modena, now rose to insist that Pepe should lead on his forces to Lombardy. Statella was compelled to fly from the city; and those soldiers who returned to Naples were followed by the curses of the Romagnoli. Several of the officers were willing to act with Pepe; and he passed the Po with two battalions of volunteers, one company of the regular forces, and some Lombards and Bolognese. But many of these deserted him even after he had crossed the Po; and by the time he reached Venice, there remained with him only one battalion of riflemen, whose officer had served under him in 1815. But, however poorly attended, Pepe was heartily welcomed by Manin, and was soon after made Commander-in-Chief of all the land forces of Venice. These were composed not only of Venetians and Neapolitans, but also of Lombards, Romans, and even Swiss. The Neapolitan admiral, too, at first refused to obey the orders of the King, and continued for a time to defend Venice on his own authority.

In the meantime, while the resources of the Lombard towns were being drained to support the designs of Charles Albert, he was devoting his energies to the siege of Peschiera. Radetzky, seeing that the weakest part of the Italian army was stationed near Mantua, resolved to march from Verona, which was the headquarters of the Austrians, attack the right wing of the Italian army near Mantua, drive it across the Mincio, and so march to the relief of Peschiera. At a comparatively short distance from Mantua he reached the small collection of scattered houses which formed the village of Curtatone. A band of 6,000 Tuscans, chiefly composed of University students, and commanded by their professors, were marching along the road which lies between Curtatone and Montanara, on their way to join the Piedmontese army at Goito. There were, at that time, open fields on both sides of the road stretching along in an unbroken plain; and no defences had been made; for when Radetzky, at the head of 20,000 men, came upon the Tuscan band, the latter were far from expecting any attack. General de Laugier, who was in command of the Tuscans, resolved to resist; and for six hours this gallant little troop held its own against the overwhelming forces of the Austrians. But superiority in numbers and training at last prevailed; and, fighting inch by inch, the Tuscans were driven back to Montanara, and were either killed or captured. The same "fanaticism" which Radetzky had observed in Milan, seemed to show itself here also; and as his officers marched the young prisoners before him after the battle, he exclaimed in scorn, " Did you take six hours to beat a handful of boys?"

But the "handful of boys" had done their work; for, when Radetzky once more marched across the bridge at Goito, with his prisoners, he found Charles Albert at the head of his forces ready to receive him. The fight was fierce; the King and his eldest son, Victor Emmanuel, were both wounded; but at the close of the day, a new battalion dashed forward and compelled the Austrians to retreat. The day before this battle, while the Tuscans were still fighting between Curtatone and Montanara, the fortress of Peschiera had surrendered to Charles Albert; and while he was still exulting over his triumph, there had come to him the news that the Lombard plebiscite had been decided in favour of the fusion with Piedmont.

But it was not without much bitterness that it had been so decided. Mazzini's protest against the proposal of the fusion had been temperate and reasonable; but it had been sufficient to attract the attention of the enemies of Italy; and, while Gioberti had come to Milan to arouse sympathy with the movement for the fusion, a Jew named Urbino (who was unknown to the Republican leaders in Milan) was taking advantage of the differences of opinion to stir up riots against the Provisional Government. On May 28 (the day before the actual closing of the poll) an anonymous placard appeared, calling on the National Guard and the people to meet in the Piazza San Fedele, in front of the office of the Provisional Government. A deputation of the National Guard was about to demand the deposition of its captain; and the crowd which gathered in the Piazza San Fedele mixed itself up with the deputation. One of the agitators named Romani, demanded the convocation of a Constituent Assembly and denounced the proposed vote of fusion. Many even in the crowd opposed Romani; and the President, by promises of further security for personal freedom, was able to disperse them. The next day, however, they gathered again, with cries against the Piedmontese, and broke into the civic palace. The students heard of the disturbance, and rushed to the rescue of the Provisional Government. Casati had at first been panic struck; but he now gathered courage, and tried to address the people. Urbino attempted to drown his voice by shouting that the Government had resigned; and he exhibited a list of a new Government, composed of some of the leading Republicans in Milan. Casati snatched the list from his hand, and tore it in pieces. Many voices in the crowd denounced Urbino, and the rioters were speedily arrested or dispersed.

The unreality of this demonstration, as an exhibition of any popular feeling, was clear from every circumstance connected with it. The innocence of the Republican leaders might be gathered from a stern protest against the proceedings issued by Mazzini directly after; and the real source of the agitation might not unfairly be inferred from the cries of " Viva Radetzky," which broke out from some of the less cautious agitators. But the Provisional Government either was, or seemed to be, alarmed about the possible consequences of the riot of May 29; and Cernuschi, who had been the first to propose the deputation to O'Donnell which had preceded the struggle of the Five Days, and who had fought gallantly during that struggle, was arrested at midnight on the very night of the riot, and sent to prison. He was soon after set free, from want of any evidence against him; but the bitterness which his arrest had caused against the Provisional Government did not so soon come to an end.

This quarrel between the two sections of the national party in Milan tended to strengthen the power of Charles Albert. Casati had originally felt little sympathy for the Piedmontese aristocracy; but his growing distrust of Milanese feeling strengthened the effect produced by the victory at Goito, and the capture of Peschiera, and induced him to rest his hopes for the success of the struggle against Austria solely on Charles Albert, and the Sardinian army. And while the divisions in Milan strengthened Charles Albert's power in Lombardy, the weakness of the cities of Venetia, though due to a large extent to the previous vacillation of Charles Albert, was yet compelling them more and more to appeal to him as the recognised leader of the most important Italian force in the North of Italy. This tendency had been resisted by Daniel Manin, who was strongly opposed to the fusion of Venetia with Piedmont; and when he found that Charles Albert was unwilling to help the Venetians on any other terms, he had been disposed to turn for help rather to France than to Piedmont. But the prestige of Charles Albert's victories in Lombardy were attracting Vicenza and Padua to the scheme of fusion; and nothing but the proof that Venice could save Vicenza could counteract this tendency. Manin and Tommaseo felt so much the importance of this point, that they even left Venice for a few days to go to the help of Vicenza;

and the coldness of Charles Albert towards the defence might, if Vicenza had held out, have worked in favour of Manin's views.   But Radetzky also saw the importance of this siege, and resolved to lead the attack in person.   He appeared before the city on June 9, and on the following day succeeded, after a fierce struggle, in occupying the heights which surrounded it.   The defence speedily became hopeless; and, though Durando was afterwards blamed for the surrender, and even suspected of treason, there seems little reason to suppose that the town could have obtained better terms than those which were now granted it, if it had attempted a longer resistance. The garrison was allowed to go out with arms and baggage; the lives and property of the inhabitants were to be safe; and a full amnesty was to be granted for the past; the garrison only binding themselves not to bear arms for three months.   The fall of Vicenza seemed to mark the crisis of the struggle in Venetia.   Padua, Treviso, and Palmanuova rapidly fell into the hands of the Austrians; and the citizens of Venice now began to believe that, so far from being able to defend the freedom of their countrymen, they could only hope to secure their own freedom by surrendering themselves to Charles Albert.

It was while this feeling was at its height, that the Venetian Assembly met on the 3rd of July.   Manin recapitulated the circumstances of the war.   He had failed to obtain even recognition for his Government from the French Republic.   He admitted the growth of the feeling in favour of the fusion; and he advised his Republican friends to suppress for a time the assertion of their special political creed, and to accept the fusion as their only hope of safety.   Tommaseo, indeed, protested against the proposal; but Manin's influence, assisted by the growing sense of weakness, prevailed; and on July 4, the representatives of Venetia by 127 votes against six declared their province united to Piedmont. Manin, however, resigned his office, as being unable to act as Minister under a Monarchical Government.

But while Charles Albert seemed to be gaining partizans in Lombardy and Venetia by the growing necessities of those provinces, he was exciting against him the opposition of those who might at one time have been favourable to the Italian cause. On June 16, the Sardinian and Venetian fleets had attacked Trieste. As a military incident in the Italian war, this attack was probably of little importance; but its effect on the relations between the German and Italian movements for freedom and unity was of far greater importance than could be estimated by merely military results. For, in Germany more than in almost any other country of Europe, the movement for national freedom and unity was necessitating an amount of self-assertion on the part of the body which represented those ideas, which unavoidably brought it into collision with many whom it ought to have hailed as allies. Both the necessity and desire for this German self-assertion had been evident from the first opening of the Frankfort Constituent Assembly on the 18th of May. Even a small but picturesque incident which took place on the first day of its meeting indicated the strength of the exclusive and defiant German feeling. An old man of seventy-nine had attempted, during the first stormy sitting, to address the Parliament, but his voice had been drowned in the general hubbub. On

the following day, the member for Cologne called the
attention of the Parliament to the fact that the
deputy so unceremoniously treated was the poet
Arndt; and thereupon the whole Assembly rose, and
expressed to him their thanks for his song on the
German Fatherland.

This desire to assert its position as the representative
of German feeling had been quickened in the Parliament by two signs of resistance to its authority.   The
fiery Republicans of Baden had returned in indignation
to their State, when they found that the Preparatory
Parliament would neither establish a Republic, nor declare itself permanent; and, provoked by the arrest of
one of their members, they had rushed into open insurrection, which only the influence of Robert Blum
had prevented from spreading to the Rhine Province.
And, while they were preparing to suppress the
Republican opposition, the Frankfort Parliament were
startled to hear that an Assembly had met in Berlin,
which claimed, like them, to be a National Constituent Assembly; and this rivalry was made the
more alarming by the assistance which Prussian
soldiers were at that time giving to the Grand Duke
of Hesse-Darmstadt in suppressing a popular movement in Mainz.   The Frankfort Parliament indignantly resolved that, " This Assembly of the Empire
has alone the power, as the one legal organ of the will
of the German people, to settle the Constitution of
Germany, and to decide about the future position of
the Princes in the State." And they further resolved
that every Prince who would not submit to their
decisions " should be deprived, with his family, of the
princely rank, and should descend into the class of
citizens, and that his crown and family property

should become the property of the State." While
they thus boldly claimed to rule the internal affairs
of Germany, they were equally zealous in asserting
her rights against those who desired to infringe them.
They had resented the resistance of the Bohemians
to the proposed absorption of Bohemia in Germany;
and, while they were disposed to make some concessions to the Poles of Posen, they made them in a
somewhat grudging spirit, and were eager to retain
in Germany all of that province which they could
prove, to their own satisfaction, to be Germanized.

It was obvious that, while such was their state of
mind, the Frankfort Parliament would watch with
jealous eyes the movement for Italian liberty. They
could not, indeed, deny that the Italians had some
claim to freedom; or that the authority exercised by
Austria in Lombardy was, both in its origin and
character, exactly of the kind most opposed to the
ideas embodied in the Frankfort Parliament. But
the extreme desire to claim Austria as a part of united
Germany naturally led the Frankfort Parliament to
look at least with tolerance on the special prejudices
of the Viennese. While they were thus divided in
their minds between principle and prejudice, the news
of the attack on Trieste came like a God-send to those
who were looking for an excuse to sacrifice their
Liberal principles to the desire for German aggrandizement. The Parliament, therefore, resolved unanimously that any attack on the German haven of
Trieste was a declaration of war against Germany.
A resolution of this kind naturally prepared the way
for more decided hostility to the Italian cause; and
another decision at which they soon after arrived
gave new force to the anti-Italian feeling. Even if

some Viennese Democrats might desire, or at all events approve, the separation of Lombardy and Venetia from the Empire, there could be no doubt that this feeling was not shared by the members of the House of Hapsburg. When, therefore, on June 29, Archduke John was chosen Administrator of the German Empire, the Frankfort Parliament almost unavoidably identified itself with the domineering policy of the Austrian Germans. While, then, they claimed security for German freedom, the Parliament triumphed savagely over the fall of the liberties of Bohemia, refused even provincial independence to the Southern Tyrol, and demanded that Northern Italy should be retained in the Austrian Empire.

How far the support of the German Parliament gave any encouragement to Radetzky it may be difficult to say; but it is certain that, during the month of July, his efforts to recover his ground in Italy became more daring in character. No longer confining himself to Lombardy and Venetia, he now marched his troops into Modena, and attempted to restore the Austrian authority in that Duchy. Charles Albert was roused in his turn by this new invasion. His chief general, Bava, rallied his forces, and drove the Austrians first across the Po and then across the Mincio. Charles Albert's whole feeling seems to have been suddenly changed by these successes; abandoning the hesitating policy which he had pursued in the beginning of the war, he now became desperate even to rashness; and, rejecting the advice of General Bava, he tried to push forward to Mantua. Radetzky, during Charles Albert's delays and hesitations, had had time to reinforce his strength, to revive the discipline and vigour of the army, which had been utterly

broken during the retreat from Milan, and to choose
the best positions for defence and attack.  Therefore,
on July 24, he was more than ready for Charles
Albert's rash attack; and at the battle of Somma
Campagna he speedily routed the Piedmontese, and
drove them back across the Mincio.  But Charles
Albert's zeal for action was not yet exhausted, and
he marched against Valleggio, in the hope of cutting
off Radetzky from Verona.  In this march the King
seems again to have acted contrary to the advice of
his generals; and part of the march was conducted in
such tremendously hot weather, and with such bad
arrangements for the provision of food, that many of
the soldiers died on the road from heat and hunger.
A victory gained by General Bava, near Custozza,
strengthened the delusions of Charles Albert; but
Radetzky soon recovered his ground; the hasty march
and the want of food weakened the forces at Custozza,
and the Piedmontese were shortly after defeated on
the very ground on which they had just been victorious.  Charles Albert's assumption of military
authority and his defiance of his generals, led to
continual confusions and misunderstandings.  The
result of one of these confusions was that General
Sonnaz suddenly left an important fortified position,
under orders for which both Charles Albert and
General Bava denied their responsibility.  On discovering his mistake he hastened back to his position,
to find that it had been in the meantime occupied by
the Austrians; and when he then attempted to recover
it he received one of the most severe defeats of the
campaign.

In the meantime the Provisional Government of

Lombardy were exciting the greatest irritation by their want of vigour in the conduct of the war, and by the discouragement which they gave to the volunteers. As an extreme instance of this latter fault, may be mentioned their treatment of Francesco Anfossi. He was a brother of Augusto, the leader of the Five Days' Rising, and had served with distinction at Brescia; yet, on his arrival at Milan, he was suddenly arrested without any reason being given. When the news of Charles Albert's defeat arrived in Milan, the Provisional Government once more became alarmed, and again called Mazzini to their help. He had had much difficulty in preventing some of his more fiery followers from imitating the example of Urbino, and organizing an insurrection against the Provisional Government. Therefore Casati and his friends knew that they could depend upon his help whenever they should ask for it. His former proposal for a Council of War was now accepted, and he was asked to name the citizens of which it should be composed. Of the three whom he named, there was only one who had been a steady Republican; while one of them had laboured to promote that fusion of Venetia with Piedmont to which Mazzini had been opposed. The duties of this Committee were to fortify the town, and to provision the army. They proclaimed a *levée en masse*, and prepared to fortify the lines of the Adda. They also made special requisitions for corn and rice, and arranged for the bringing in of considerable provisions from the country; though some of these were lost by the refusal of the Piedmontese officers to provide guards for the protection of the convoy.

They then despatched Garibaldi to raise volunteers; and in three days he had under arms 3,000 men, and was marching to Brescia.

In the midst of these arrangements, the Committee suddenly heard that the Austrians had crossed the Adda, and that Charles Albert was retreating before them. They sent messengers to the Piedmontese camp to learn the intentions of the King; and were dismayed at receiving the answer that he intended to come himself to defend Milan. They then sent messengers to recall Zucchi and Garibaldi from the line of the Adda to the actual defence of Milan. But the management of the defence was now taken out of their hands; and on August 2 the Committee were obliged to resign their authority to the Piedmontese General Olivieri. Olivieri, while urging the Committee of Defence to remain in office, refused their proposal to summon the people to the barricades. But when Charles Albert was attacked by the Austrians under the walls of Milan, the barricades were thrown up in spite of Olivieri. It was, however, then too late to save the Piedmontese from defeat, and, on August 4, the King sent for the Municipal Council, to tell them that he had resolved to come to terms with Radetzky. Restelli, one of the Committee of Defence, denied the failure of food and money which Charles Albert had pleaded as one of his grounds of surrender; and when the Town Council assented to the proposal, Maestri, another of the Committee, denied their claim to speak on behalf of the citizens. The news that the King was intending to desert them, roused the Milanese to fury; and on August 5 Charles Albert promised in writing to stay to defend the city; and General Olivieri even

promised to go to Radetzky to obtain good terms.
But he did not go ; and Charles Albert, after a
secret agreement with Radetzky to put tho Porta
Romana into his hands, fled secretly from Milan on
August 6. Many of the Piedmontese officers were
so indignant at this desertion, that they offered to
remain in the city and share in its defence; and the
cry was raised of "Long live Piedmont!" and "Shame
to Charles Albert!" But resistance was in vain;
and on August 7 Radetzky entered Milan. Garibaldi,
who was already on his march to Milan, attempted,
with the help of General Medici, to carry on the
struggle on the banks of the Lago Maggiore; and
Mazzini joined this little band, encouraged them to
persevere in their defence, and attempted, though in
vain, to form a connection with the defenders of
Venice. But the struggle was hopeless. The Lombard cities rapidly fell into the hands of Radetzky;
and on August 11, Venice, left alone in her defence,
disowned her connection with Charles Albert, and
recalled Manin to power.

After this defeat thousands of Lombards left their
country; and the following extracts from a litany
composed at this period express, better than any
mere description, their feelings about this catastrophe :
—"All Italy is our country; and we are not exiles,
because we remain on Italian soil. Yet we are
pilgrims, because a vow binds us to go on a pilgrimage
to the Holy Land, that is to say to Lombardy when
it is freed. For the heart of our country is the
house of our fathers, the place where we were born,
where we have learned to pray, and where love was
revealed to us, where we have left our dead at rest,
our mothers, our sons, and our brothers in tears.

Kyrie Eleison," &c. . . . . . They then call on Christ, the Virgin, and the Saints to deliver Lombardy from the Austrians, and invoke them to their aid, by the memory of the special sufferers in the cause of Liberty, among whom they particularly specify the Brothers Bandiera, and the defenders of Milan and Pavia; and they end with a prayer that they may not die until they have saluted Italy "one, redeemed, free, and independent."

Radetzky, however, had another enemy to punish besides the Lombards and the Piedmontese. The action of the Pope, however uncertain, and one may even say unwilling, had given a force to the anti-Austrian movement which no other Prince could have given; and, as long as the Liberals ruled in the Papal States, Radetzky considered his work un-finished. About three weeks, therefore, before the surrender of Milan, a body of 6,500 Austrians had crossed the Po, and had once more entered Ferrara. The Bolognese, always the most politically energetic of any of the subjects of the Pope, desired at once to march to Ferrara; but the Pro-Legate, who ruled in Bologna, tried to check the popular movement; and refused to take any more energetic step than the issue of proclamations. He even appealed to the Bolognese to remember the fate of Vicenza as a warning against useless defences. But the people would not listen to him; and a declaration of the Pope that he would defend the frontiers of his State, increased their desire for action. Encouraged by the peaceable action of the Pro-Legate, and by no means alarmed at his proclamations, General Welden entered the Porta Maggiore of Bologna at the head of his forces on the 7th of August. Near that gate

a path leads up to a raised piece of ground called
the Montagnola, which is covered with grass and
trees.   To this the Austrian forces made their way;
but, in spite of the warnings of the Pro-Legate,
Welden's demand for hostages was flatly refused.
The people rang their bells, and rushed to the barricades; an old cannon was brought out and carried
up to the Montagnola, and by six o'clock in the
evening of the 8th of August, barricades had been
thrown up near every gate of the city.   The Austrians were driven out; and Monsignore Opizzoni,
who was in a country house outside the town, was
rescued by the citizens, and brought into Bologna.

The dreamy, old-world city at once became full of
new life; neighbours flocked in from the surrounding
districts; and soldiers who had left the city, in the
belief that it was indefensible, now returned to its
help.   The Pro-Legate issued an encouraging address
to the citizens; and Welden complained that the
rulers of Bologna were unable to control the excited
spirits of the city.   The Ambassadors of England,
France, Prussia, Denmark, Sweden, and even Naples,
who were resident at Florence, protested against the
renewal of the Austrian attack; the enthusiasm for
the Bolognese spread to Venice, where a large subscription was raised for the families of those who
had fallen on August 8; and finally on August 15
a meeting took place between Welden and the representatives of the Pope, which resulted in an order to
the Austrian forces to recross the Po.

In the meantime, whatever help the Austrian
generals might have received from the approval of
the Frankfort Parliament, that assistance must have
lost its value, as the position of the Parliament be-

came weaker and weaker. One great difficulty, as
already mentioned, was the growing rivalry of Berlin;
and this became the more dangerous to German
liberty, as the supporters of the original struggle
for freedom continued to lose their influence in the
Prussian Court. Camphausen, the new Prime Minister, repudiated the March Revolution as decidedly
as Schmaltz had repudiated the popular element in
the struggles of 1813. Prince William of Prussia,
the brother of the King, who was considered the
leader of the reactionary party, had returned to
Berlin; and, though he now professed to accept the
Constitution, he was believed to mean mischief.
The actual liberties, indeed, of the citizens of Berlin
had not yet been attacked; but a warning of their
future fate was given by the treatment inflicted
on Posen. Mieroslawski, the leader of the Polish
movement in Posen, had been received with enthusiasm in Berlin during the March rising; and the
King had then given permission to the different
provinces of Prussia to decide whether or not they
should be absorbed in the new Germany. The Posen
Assembly had decided by twenty-six votes to seventeen
against the proposed absorption; and as a means of
carrying out this decision, they had removed certain
Prussian officials from office in their province. The
King of Prussia had at first seemed to approve this
change, and had despatched General von Willisen to
secure the Poles in their national rights. But when
the German party in Posen offered resistance to this
policy, the King yielded to them, withdrew General von
Willisen, and sent in his stead General von Pfuel, who
placed Posen in a state of siege, and punished all who
had taken part in the Polish movement.

But, however alarming these signs might be to the
more Liberal members of the Frankfort Parliament,
the attitude of the majority of that Parliament towards the Poles had not been so generous as to
justify them in passing severe condemnation on
the Prussian Ministry. It was in another part of
Europe, and in a very different struggle, that the
power of the Frankfort Parliament over the King of
Prussia was to be finally tested. The March rising
in Denmark had, unfortunately, like the risings in
Pesth and Frankfort, been accompanied with a desire
to strengthen their own country at the expense of its
neighbours; and an Assembly in Copenhagen had,
on March 11, denounced the claims of Schleswig to a
separate Constitution as eagerly as the Liberals of
Pesth had demanded the suppression of the Transylvanian Diet, and the Liberals of Frankfort the
absorption of Bohemia in Germany. The Schleswig-
Holstein Estates, however, thought that the time had
come for a more definite demand for independence:
and, on March 18, they put forward five proposals
which they embodied in a petition to the King.
These were to the effect that the members of the
Estates of both Duchies should be united in one
Assembly for the purpose of discussing an Assembly
for Schleswig-Holstein; that measures should be taken
to enable Schleswig to enter the German Confederation; that in consideration of dangers both from
within and without, measures should be taken for a
general arming of the people; that liberty of the
Press and freedom of public meeting should be
granted; and that the Prime Minister of Denmark
should be dismissed. The arrival of the bearers of
this petition in Copenhagen caused great indignation

among the Danes; and, on March 20, a meeting was
held to pass five counter-resolutions in favour of the
claims of Denmark over Schleswig; and the temper
of the meeting was sufficiently shown by the fact
that, while the four resolutions which asserted the
power of Denmark were easily carried, a resolution
proposing a Provincial Assembly for Schleswig was
rejected by an enormous majority. War was declared
on the Duchies of Schleswig and Holstein; and, in
order to prevent those Duchies from having due
notice of the war, the members of the deputation
were detained in Copenhagen until the expedition
had actually sailed. On March 27 the Danish forces
appeared before Hadersleben; and thereupon the
Schleswig-Holstein Estates declared that the Duke
of Schleswig-Holstein was no longer free, and formed
a Provisional Government.

The meeting of the Preparatory Parliament at
Frankfort had naturally increased the hopes of the
people of Schleswig-Holstein; and they elected seven
representatives to take part in the deliberations of that
Parliament. But the Schleswig-Holstein question
seemed doomed to bring into prominence all the
difficulties which hindered the establishment of the
freedom and unity of Germany. The old Bundestag
had, even before the meeting of the Frankfort Parliament, declared its sympathy with the Estates of
Schleswig-Holstein; and, though it expressed its
approval of the election of the Schleswig-Holstein
representatives to the Frankfort Parliament, it
claimed, as against that body, the sole right of
directing the Federal forces of Germany. The King
of Prussia was, no doubt, glad enough to pit the
older body against the representatives of the newer

Germany; and it was avowedly under the authority of the Bundestag that, in the month of April, he marched his forces into Schleswig-Holstein. But it soon became clear that neither the representatives of the old League of Princes, nor the Assembly which embodied the aspirations for German freedom and unity, would be able to control the King of Prussia. Early in June he showed an inclination to come to an understanding with the King of Denmark and to evacuate North Schleswig. The leaders of the Frankfort Parliament felt that, in order to control this dangerous rival to their authority, they must create some central Power which should be able entirely to supersede the Bundestag; and it was, to a large extent, under the influence of this feeling, that the Archduke John was chosen Administrator of the Empire.

But, however much strength the Frankfort Parliament might gain in Germany by this election, it was hardly to be expected that the choice of an Austrian Prince would lead to more friendly relations between Frankfort and Berlin; and, in July, it began to be rumoured that a truce of a more permanent kind was about to be made between the King of Prussia and the King of Denmark, while the King of Hanover seemed disposed to second the former in his defiance of the Constituent Assembly at Frankfort. At last, in September, the crisis of the struggle came. It then became clearly known that a truce of seven months had been agreed to at Malmö between Prussia and Denmark. During that period both the Duchies were to be governed in the name of the King of Denmark as Duke of Schleswig-Holstein; and the man who was chosen to act in the King's name was

Count Moltke, who had been previously protested against by the people of Schleswig-Holstein on account of his tyrannical acts. He was to exercise all power except that of legislation, which, indeed, was to cease altogether during the truce; and he was to be assisted by four Notables, two of them to be nominated by the King of Denmark and two by the King of Prussia.

The Frankfort Parliament felt that this truce would sacrifice the whole object of the war; and, on the motion of Dahlmann, they resolved, on September 5, by 238 votes against 221, to stop the execution of the truce. The Ministry, who had been appointed by Archduke John, thereupon resigned, and Dahlmann was empowered by the Archduke to form a new Ministry. At the same time the Estates of Schleswig-Holstein met, and denied that any one had the power to dissolve them against their will, or to pass laws or lay on taxes without their consent. A public meeting of the Schleswig-Holstein citizens declared that they would not submit to the new Government; every one of the four Notables refused to act with Moltke; and, when he applied to the Provisional Government for protection, they sent him a passport to enable him to leave the country. But the Frankfort Parliament very soon began to shudder at its own audacity; and, when Robert Blum urged upon it the desirability of speedily putting in force its decree about Schleswig-Holstein, the Parliament decided that there was no urgency for this motion; and some of the more timid members began to plead the danger of a quarrel with Prussia. Arndt, who had voted for the condemnation of the truce, now changed sides, and urged that the Parliament should accept it, in order to convince the Danes "that they are a brother People;" while even those who still condemned the action of Prussia began to propose all sorts of compromises. At last, on September 16, the Assembly rescinded its former vote, declaring, by 257 against 236, that it was unadvisable to hinder the execution of the truce.

The leaders of the German Left had felt that concession to the King of Prussia in this dispute implied the sacrifice of the whole object of the Parliament's existence; and Robert Blum had declared, shortly before the final vote, that it must now be decided whether Prussia was to be absorbed in Germany or Germany to become Prussian. But the decision of the Frankfort Parliament so roused the fierce Democratic feeling in the city that the movement of resistance to Prussia passed out of the control of Robert Blum, and fell under the leadership of far fiercer and more intolerant spirits. Several thousand Democrats belonging to the Frankfort clubs held a meeting, on September 18, at which they called upon the members of the Left to leave the Frankfort Parliament and form a separate Assembly. Zitz, a representative of Mainz, and nineteen other members, accepted this proposal; and, in the meantime, the Frankfort mob, headed by a man who bore the ominous name of Metternich, threw up barricades in the streets, and prepared for a regular insurrection. The Ministry, in great alarm, sent for troops; and Bavarian, Prussian, and Austrian generals alike responded to the appeal. Robert Blum and Simon, the member for Breslau, in vain tried to make peace; entreating the Ministry to withdraw the troops, and the insurgents to pull down the barricades. But the

Ministry would not listen to any advice, and the insurgents threatened Blum and Simon with death. Auerswald and Lichnowsky, two members of the Right, were killed in the riot. Many fled from the city; and it is said that, when Archduke John wished, at last, to make a truce, no member of the Ministry could be found to countersign the order for the withdrawal of the troops. The struggle went on fiercely during the 19th; but there was no organization capable of offering permanent resistance to the soldiers; and, by ten o'clock at night, all the barricades had been swept away; and the Ministry soon after declared Frankfort in a state of siege.

These events gave a shock to the hopes for combining German freedom with German unity which they never after recovered; and the alternative which Blum had propounded, whether Prussia should be absorbed in Germany or Germany in Prussia, was, from that day, to be exchanged for the question whether Austria or Prussia should absorb Germany. There were some, however, who did not at once give up their hope for a solution more favourable to freedom than either of those alternatives. In several parts of Germany Republican feeling seemed to have been growing for some time past, and the fiercest and most daring of the Republican leaders were still to be found in Baden. The rising which had followed the dissolution of the Preparatory Parliament had, indeed, discredited Hecker and his friends with many of the more moderate Democrats; and this feeling, by alienating the party of Hecker from Robert Blum, had deprived that able and temperate statesman of the power which he might have gained as the head of a united Democratic party. That rising had also, unfortunately, brought about a collision between Baden and Bavaria, and, at least, a feeling of suspicion between Baden and Würtemberg. But, though the Democratic party, as a whole, had been weakened by the Baden rising, and though even the special South German movement, which had seemed, in March, to have gained so strong an influence, had been disunited, yet, on the other hand, a certain form of popular enthusiasm had undoubtedly been roused by Hecker, of a kind which the wiser Democrats had failed to excite; and the attempt of the members of the Right in the Frankfort Parliament to annul Hecker's election, on account of his insurrection, had marked him out as a martyr for liberty.

But when the Baden Republicans gathered for action after the Frankfort riots, it was, for some unknown reason, to Struve, rather than to Hecker, that they offered the leadership of the movement. Struve seems to have had fewer gifts for the work of a leader of insurrection than his colleague had possessed. He had been, as was proved by his programme in the Preparatory Parliament, interested rather in the redress of material grievances than in the assertion of Constitutional Liberties; and, though he now proclaimed the Republic from the Town Council House in Lörrach, he rested his appeal to the people mainly on the ground of the burdens still pressing on the cultivators of the land; and he did not allude to the Schleswig-Holstein question, nor did he allege any Constitutional reason for proclaiming the Republic. Blum had seen that Republicanism was not popular in Germany; and, though he looked forward to a Republic as the ultimate goal of his political aspirations, he felt, during the sitting of the Frankfort Parliament, as Mazzini had felt during the war in Lombardy, that any violent attempt to enforce Republican opinions would be dangerous to liberty. Indeed, it was clear that the only possibility for even a temporary success in an insurrection at that time would have lain in an appeal to the national feeling about the Schleswig-Holstein war. The movement, therefore, failed, and failed ignominiously. The Federal troops were sent against the insurgents; at the first collision the latter were easily defeated; and the insurrection was only remembered as the Struve-Putsch.

Since, then, the Frankfort Parliament no more embodied the hopes of the Liberals; since Republican risings seemed hopeless; and since it was hardly to be expected from human nature that those who had desired to establish German unity at Frankfort should consent at once to rally round that Prussian Parliament which had helped to defeat their efforts; the eyes of all who would not give up the cause for lost turned instinctively to Vienna. There, ever since July 10, a Parliament had been sitting, which seemed to enjoy securer freedom than could be found in other parts of Germany. This security was partly due to the influence of the same prince who had so much increased the dignity of the Frankfort Parliament; for the Archduke John was the one member of the Royal House who had a genuine respect for liberty. He had consented, not only to open the Viennese Assembly, but, a little later, to get Pillersdorf dismissed from office, on the ground of his having lost the confidence of the people; and, in August, Ferdinand himself was induced to return to Vienna, and

thus to give a still further sense of security to the
supporters of parliamentary government. Nor was
this Parliament without more solid results; for it
abolished in Austria that system of feudalism which
had already been swept away in Hungary.

But, in spite of this apparent success, the seeds of
division and bitterness were too deeply sown to allow
of lasting liberty in Vienna. The workmen's movements, so often leading to riot, had been one cause of
weakness ; but the most lasting and fatal cause was
that terrible race hatred, which, more than anything
else, ruined the Austrian movement for freedom in
1848. The opposition of the Bohemians to the May
rising in Vienna had intensified against them the
indignation which had already been roused by their
attitude towards the Frankfort Parliament ; and the
June insurrection in Prague had been exaggerated
by German panic-mongers into an anti-German " St.
Bartholomew." When Dr. Rieger, Palacky's son-in-
law, pleaded for delay in the election of the President
of the Assembly, on the ground that the Bohemian
members had not had time to arrive, he was hooted
in the streets, and only saved from actual violence by
the intervention of Dr. Goldmark ; and, when Rieger
protested against the illegal arrest and secret trial of
one of the Bohemian leaders in Prague, Bach, who had
now become the most popular of the Ministers with the
German party, evaded the appeal. Indeed the utterances of the German party in Vienna were marked by
a combination of a somewhat arrogant assertion of
popular authority, as represented by the Assembly,
with contempt for the aspirations of other countries.
This combination of feeling was perhaps best illustrated
by the meeting of July 29, when a majority of the

Assembly, in calling upon the Emperor to return to Vienna, indignantly rejected the word "bitten" (entreat) from the address, and substituted the word "fordern" (demand). On the day of this important assertion of popular rights, the news of Radetzky's victories in Italy was received with loud applause in the Chamber, and a solemn Te Deum was shortly afterwards decreed in honour of these victories.[1]

But, offensive as this contrast between the more vulgar side of democratic feeling, and the indifference to the liberties of Italy and Bohemia must seem to the student of this period, there was one direction in which the more generous instincts of the Viennese Democrats were shown; although, even in this matter, the generosity of principle was to be sadly clouded by the savagery of act. The political question which called out this better feeling was the relation of Vienna to Hungary. It will be remembered that the enthusiasm for Hungary, which had been awakened by Kossuth's speech of the 3rd of March, had been considerably damped by the attitude which the Magyar leaders had taken up towards the May rising in Vienna; and the more democratic tone of Jellacíç on that occasion had led the Viennese, for a time, to turn for sympathy to Agram rather than to Buda-Pesth. But no concessions to monarchical feeling which Kossuth might be disposed to make, could reconcile the most influential of Ferdinand's advisers to the independent position which the Magyar

---

[1] It must be admitted that a protest was made by some of the members against Radetzky's restoration of the Duke of Modena; but then the Duke of Modena was not subject to the Viennese Parliament, and Radetzky, in restoring him, had acted without their authority.

Ministers had obtained. The courtiers, indeed, who helped to form the Camarilla, might shrink at first from any sympathy with the daring and independent attitude of the Serbs and Croats. But the party in Vienna which was opposed to Hungarian liberty had been swelled, since March, by the accession of men who were not theoretic opponents of rebellion, but who simply desired that the new free Government should be as thoroughly centred in Vienna as the old system of Metternich had been.

The most important representative of this phase of opinion was the War Minister Latour. Ever since he had taken office, in the latter part of April, he had been trying to make use of the discontented races in Hungary to weaken the power of the Magyars and to strengthen the authority in Vienna. Although he could not at once bring round his colleagues in the Ministry to these intrigues, nor persuade the courtiers to sympathize with the national leaders at Agram and Carlowitz, yet there were points in the position of affairs of which Latour was able to make skilful use for the accomplishment of his ends. Of these circumstances one of the most striking was the character of the Emperor. Ferdinand had shown himself, ever since his accession, most desirous of doing justice between the rival races of his Empire. The great difficulty of balancing the claims of German and Bohemian, Magyar, Croat, and Serb, might well have perplexed a stronger brain and weakened a steadier will than that of Ferdinand the Good-natured (der Gütige) ; and when the painful disease, with which he was always afflicted, is taken into account, it will seem more wonderful that he ever maintained a steady political purpose for however short a period, than that he was constantly hesitating and changing his course, as new aspects of the question pressed themselves on his attention.

This confusion and its natural results are well illustrated by a story which, though obviously incapable of proof, yet, none the less, may be supposed to embody the popular feeling about this weak but well-meaning monarch. The story is, that during one of his conferences with a Serb deputation, Ferdinand had listened with tears to the descriptions of the cruelties inflicted by the Magyars ; but that, just when he seemed about to give them a favourable answer, he happened to glance at a note from Metternich which was lying beside him on the table, and, taking it up, he read these words : " Die Serben sind und bleiben Rebellen " (the Serbs are and remain rebels). This sentence checked Ferdinand's sympathy, and he at once dismissed the deputation with vague words.

Upon this desire to do justice to both sides, and this weakness under the pressure of a stronger will, Latour found it easy to act. A Conference at Vienna between representatives of the rival races was obviously an expedient, which it was easy to recommend to Ferdinand, while it gave admirable opportunities for secret intrigues. Moreover, whatever objections might be entertained by the courtiers to other leaders of the Slavonic races, there was one, at least, who stood on a somewhat different footing. Jellaciç was a personal favourite of the Archduchess Sophia, the wife of Archduke Francis Charles, the next heir to the throne. He had been a colonel in the Austrian army, and his appointment had been looked on at Buda-Pesth as quite as much an assertion of Imperial authority, as of Croatian independence. On the other hand, the fact that he had been entrusted by the Croatian Assembly, on June 29, with almost dictatorial powers, only ten days after he had been declared a traitor by the Emperor, made him a trustworthy representative of the independent nationalists of Croatia ; and while, therefore, Latour saw in him a fit tool for his purpose, Ferdinand naturally hoped that a meeting between Jellaciç and Batthyanyi in Vienna might lead to a satisfactory settlement of the quarrels between Hungary and Croatia.

In this hope the Emperor was encouraged by Archduke John, who offered himself as a mediator between the contending parties. But, unfortunately, the double responsibility which Archduke John had taken upon himself interfered with the execution of his good intentions; for while he was urging compromises on Magyars and Croats, the burden of his duties as Administrator of the German Empire compelled him to hasten away to Frankfort. And thus Batthyanyi and Jellaciç were left face to face in a city where there were few who desired to reconcile them, and where the most influential people desired to aggravate their divisions. It must be said, however, in justice to Jellaciç, that some of the points on which he insisted in the controversy have been somewhat misunderstood in respect of their spirit and intention. It has been urged, for instance, that in demanding the centralization at Vienna of financial and military administration, he was contending solely for the interests of the Court, and not at all for Croatian independence. This, however, is scarcely just; for Jellaciç had good reason to believe that Slavonic liberty needed protection from the Magyar Ministers of Finance and War, since, in July, Kossuth, as Minister of Finance, had refused supplies for the Croatian army; and even the Serbs, who were still in partially hostile relations with the Court, had discussed the question of placing themselves under the Ministry at Vienna, as a protection against the Magyars. There were, however, other proposals made by Jellaciç, which could scarcely be covered by this explanation, such as the demand that Hungary should take over a share of the Viennese debt, and that more troops should be sent to Italy; and it was natural, therefore, that Batthyanyi should construe the proposal about the War and Finance Ministry, rather as a blow at the liberties of the Magyars, than as an assertion of Croatian independence. It was obvious that for purposes of conciliation the Conference was a hopeless failure; and Batthyanyi, after in vain urging Jellaciç to abandon these proposals, rose in indignation exclaiming, " Then we meet on the Drave."[1] " No," said Jellaciç, " on the Danube." And so they parted with the consciousness that war was no longer avoidable.

But though the Conference had failed, so far as regarded its apparent purpose, it had served to complete the change in the policy of the Court, and in the position of Jellaciç. From this time forward he ceased to be the complete champion of Croatian liberty, and became the soldier of the Emperor; and from this time forward, therefore, the German Democrats of Vienna resumed their old faïth in Kossuth, and considered his enemies as their enemies. The policy of Latour had been accepted at Court, and Ferdinand was whirled away in the vortex of aristo-

---

[1] The boundary river between Croatia and Hungary.

cratic opinion, and official intrigue. On August 4 Ferdinand officially declared his confidence in Jellaciç; about September 1, the Viennese Ministry announced to the Hungarians that the March laws which had secured a responsible Ministry to Hungary were null and void, as having been passed without the sanction of Ministers at Vienna; and Ferdinand endorsed this opinion.

In the meantime, even the Serb movement which the Viennese courtiers had looked upon with special suspicion, was passing into hands more favourable to the authority of the Emperor. In the latter part of July, Stratimiroviç had gained great successes in the Banat; and his alliance with Knicsanin, the Servian General, had led him to hope that he might be able to throw off the authority both of Vienna and of Buda-Pesth. But the Patriarch Rajaciç, who had entered with such hesitation into the insurrection, saw his only possibility of safety in placing the movement under the authority of the Emperor. He therefore set himself against the influence of Stratimiroviç; and on his return from Agram to Carlowitz, he was able to use his authority as Patriarch, backed by the influence of Jellaciç, to recover the reins of government, and to limit the authority of Stratimiroviç to military affairs. At the time of the return of Rajacic, the war had begun to languish; but in the middle of August the Magyars renewed their attacks, and besieged the Serb town of Szent-Tomas. Stratimiroviç marched to the defence, and gained such successes that some of the Magyars raised the cry of treason against their Generals. General Kiss was therefore sent down to take the place of those who had forfeited the public confidence. At first the

c c

result of the war was doubtful; for victories were
alternately gained by the Serbs and the Magyars;
but at last Kiss, by a dexterous movement, succeeded
in preventing Stratimirovič from joining his forces
with those of Knicsanin, and thus turned the whole
tide of the war against the Serbs.  This change of
affairs naturally favoured the designs of Rajacič; Stratimirovič, finding that much of the popular feeling
was turning against him, resigned his authority, and
Colonel Mayerhoffer, an Austrian officer, was sent
down to take his place.  Some of the soldiers of
Stratimirovič were, indeed, indignant at this change;
and Rajacič was obliged to make some advances to
reconciliation; but Suplikač, the Voyvode, backed
Rajacič in his general plans; and by the help of their
joint influence, Latour was able to turn the Serb
cause into a new prop for the rule of the Emperor.

It is pathetic to see how, in spite of irresistible
evidence, Ferdinand still clung to the hope that he
might succeed in reconciling the leaders of the
different races in his Empire, and yet more strange to
see how he still believed that Latour would co-operate
with him for this object. He now chose as his mediator,
a Hungarian named Lamberg, to whom he gave a
commission to settle matters between the contending
parties, and to restore order in Hungary.  Lamberg
was known to Batthyanyi, and seems, to some extent,
to have enjoyed his confidence; for Batthyanyi declared that he would himself have counter-signed
Lamberg's commission, if Latour would only have
submitted it to him in time.  But Latour, whose
object was very different from that of his good-
natured master, despatched Lamberg to Buda-Pesth
without that sanction which could alone secure

him legal authority in the eyes of the Hungarian Ministers.

Some days before the arrival of Lamberg in Pesth, a striking proof had been given of the growing sympathy between the German Democrats of Vienna and the Magyars, and also of that fierce race-hatred between Germans and Bohemians which had been stirred up by the circumstances of the June rising in Prague. The Magyars had despatched a deputation to the Viennese Parliament, in the hopes of reviving the old alliance between Buda-Pesth and Vienna. The more generous side of the Democratic spirit had been reawakened in the Germans of Vienna by many of the recent events. Even those who had sympathized with the reconquest of Lombardy had been alarmed at the kind of government which the Austrian generals were trying to introduce into that province; and one of the members of the Assembly asked what should they think if the army which was now in Italy were to stand before tne gates of Vienna? This feeling of alarm at the growth of a military power independent of Parliament had naturally been increased by the suspicions of Latour's intrigues with the Serbs and the Croats. When, then, on September 19, the Magyar deputation, among whom were Eötvös and Wesselenyi, asked for an audience from the Assembly, that they might explain their position, the leading German Democrats urged their admission, but the Bohemian leaders protested against it, denouncing the Magyars both for separating from Austria and for oppressing the Slavs. Schuselka attempted to mediate between the two parties, maintaining that though the Magyars had done many indefensible things, yet, as a matter of justice, the

Parliament ought to hear their petition ; but the Ministerialists, combined with the Bohemians, were too strong for opposition ; and, by a majority of eighty, it was decided not to admit the deputation.

This refusal of the Viennese Parliament brought to an end the last hope of a peaceable settlement of the Hungarian difficulties.   On September 27, Lamberg entered Buda-Pesth, to which the Hungarian Diet had now been transferred.   It must be remembered that the Magyars had just been irritated at Ferdinand's denunciations of the March laws of Hungary, and alarmed at his expression of confidence in Jellaciç, who had just crossed the Drave and invaded Hungary. When, then, Lamberg arrived in Pesth, with a commission unsigned by any Hungarian Minister, his arrival was naturally looked upon as a further indication of an attempt of the Austrian Ministry to crush out the liberties of Hungary.   A slight thing was sufficient to cause these suspicions to swell into a panic ; and the news that Lamberg had at once crossed the Danube, to visit the fortress of Buda, seemed, to the excited Magyars, a sufficient proof of his dangerous intentions.   The cry was raised that the fortress was going to be seized and military law established.   The fiery students of Pesth hastened out into the streets ; and as Lamberg returned across the suspension bridge into Pesth, he was attacked and murdered.   Batthyanyi, terrified at this act, resigned his premiership and fled to Vienna ; and the Diet of Hungary passed a resolution condemning the murder.   Ferdinand was now more easily urged to violent action.   On October 3 he declared the Hungarian Diet dissolved, proclaimed Jellaciç Dictator of Hungary, and appointed Recsey

Prime Minister in place of Batthyanyi. Jellaciç, however, did not find it easy to assert the authority which was now given him. He had hoped that, in the confusion which followed the death of Lamberg, he would be able to carry Pesth by storm ; but he was driven back, and before the end of October the Croats had been expelled from Hungary.

In the meantime the suspicions of the Viennese had been increasing, and on the 29th of September Dr. Löhner, one of the original leaders of the March movement, publicly denounced Latour for his intrigues with Jellaciç. These intrigues had now been placed beyond a doubt by certain letters which had fallen into the hands of the Hungarian Ministry. Pulszky, who was at this time in Vienna, took the opportunity to publish these letters in the form of a placard, while he complained to Latour of the permission given to Jellaciç to raise recruits in Vienna, and threatened, if these proceedings continued, to excite a revolution in which the Viennese Ministers would be hung from lamp-posts. There were, indeed, revolutionary elements enough in Vienna at this time. The friendship between the workmen and the students had led to the formation of a special workman's Sub-Committee under the Committee of Safety. This body actually undertook to find employment for all who were out of work, and even to pay them wages while they were out of work. This offer naturally caused a rush of workmen to Vienna, from all parts of the Empire. The attempt to sift and regulate the claims for employment led to new bitterness ; and demands for impossibly high wages provoked rebuffs, which were answered by threats of violence. The Ministry tried to induce the workmen to leave the city, by urging them to join the army in Italy; but the students defeated this attempt by reminding the workmen that the war in Italy was a war against liberty. The suspicions of the Ministers were now excited, not only against the workmen, but against the students; and, after a riot in the latter part of August, the Committee of Safety had been dissolved, and the lecture-rooms of the University closed. But this repression, far from weakening the bitterness in Vienna, only drew closer the links between the poorer students and the workmen; for, while the richer students left the city, the poorer ones, finding it difficult to support themselves after the closing of the lecture-rooms, were subscribed for by the workmen. Thus then the suspicions roused by the intrigues of Latour were strengthened considerably by the general condition of Vienna at this period.

Latour, however, was resolved not to yield. The defeats which Jellacíç was experiencing in Hungary only made it the more necessary that those who sympathized with him should send him help; and on the 5th of October the news spread through Vienna that an Austrian regiment was about to march to Hungary to the assistance of Jellacíç. The students went to the head-quarters of one of the grenadier regiments, and urged them not to join in the march. An officer, who arrested one of the students, was attacked and wounded; and when one of the grenadiers, who had been wounded in a quarrel, was sent to his barrack, his comrades seemed to consider it as a kind of arrest, and demanded his surrender. The National Guard joined in this demand; and thus a state of confusion arose which made it easy for the students and the workmen to hinder the march of the regiments which were starting for Hungary. An Italian battalion refused to proceed further, and the march was hindered for that day. But General Auersperg, who commanded the forces in Vienna, was resolved to continue the attempt ; and so, on the following day, the soldiers were despatched to the station which lies beyond the Tabor bridge. But, when they arrived on the bridge, they found that the students and the National Guard were before them, and that the barriers had been closed against them. Auersperg was alarmed at this resistance, and recalled the troops ; but collisions had by this time taken place between the soldiers and the people in other parts of the town ; and a fierce fight was raging in the Stephansplatz, and even in the church itself.

Then suddenly there rose the cry " Latour is sending us the murderers of the 13th of March ;" and a rush was made towards the office of the Ministry of War. Fears had already been entertained by several members of the Assembly, that a personal attack would be made on Latour ; and Borrosch, one of the German Bohemian members, Smolka, the Vice-President of the Assembly, Dr. Goldmark, and others, hastened to protect Latour from the vengeance of the crowd. Borrosch, with the same humane ingenuity which Lafayette had shown on a similar occasion, promised that Latour should have a formal trial, if the crowd would spare him. The crowd cheered Borrosch and his friends; and many of them promised that they would protect Latour's life. Borrosch rode off, supposing Latour to be safe ; but Dr. Fischhof, feeling that matters were not yet secure, persuaded several members of the National Guard to act as special protectors to Latour; and as the best means of effecting

this object, some thirty or forty of them undertook
to arrest him.   But the excitement of the crowd had
been roused anew, and they burst into the War Office.
Smolka then entreated Latour to resign.   The Minister
consented ; but the passions of the crowd would not
be appeased.   The unfortunate man attempted to
hide from their pursuit : but they dragged him from
his hiding-place, and thrust aside his defenders.
Fischhof warded off the first blow that was aimed at
him.   A student, named Rauch, attempted also to
protect him; but all was in vain; and he was dragged
down the staircase and into the square in front of the
War Office.   With his white hair floating about him,
he was lifted on to the lamp-post which then stood
in the square.   He struggled against his enemies,
and compelled them to drop him once ; but again he
was lifted on to the post, and this time the hanging
was completed, the crowd tearing his clothes from
his body and dipping their handkerchiefs in his blood.
This outburst of savagery, instead of satisfying the
fury of the people, had quickened their thirst for
blood ;  and their desire for vengeance was now
turned against the Bohemian Deputies.   Strobach,
who had been chosen President of the Assembly,
had objected to hold a sitting at all on that
day, declaring that executive rather than legislative functions were needed just then.   For this
refusal some of the members wished to prosecute
him ; and armed men appeared in the gallery of the
Assembly threatening violence to the Bohemian deputies.   Those deputies, finding that they could no
longer deliberate freely, soon after fled from the city,
and issued from Prague a protest against the Reign
of Terror, which they declared to be dominating

Vienna. In the meantime Ferdinand, having consented, on the day of Latour's death, to the formation of a Democratic Ministry, fled, on the next day, from Vienna to Schönbrunn, and shortly afterwards to Innspruck ; and he soon notified his feelings to the Viennese by a proclamation in which he too denounced the reign of violence in Vienna.

Hardly had the Viennese recovered from the surprise caused by the flight of their Emperor, than they heard that Jellaciç, having abandoned his hope of conquering Hungary, was marching against Vienna. General Auersperg, who had withdrawn his troops to the Belvedere after the collision between the soldiers and the people, was still assumed by the Viennese to be in some degree favourable to their cause ; and they entreated him to repel the attack of Jellaciç, and to call for help from the Hungarians. Auersperg, however, rejected this proposal, withdrew his troops secretly from the city, and, on October 11, openly joined Jellaciç.

The Assembly were now anxious to appeal to the Frankfort Parliament for help, and entreated them to send representatives to Vienna. Robert Blum, who had grown weary of the state of affairs in Frankfort, and who believed that the only remaining hope for Germany was in Vienna, consented, in company with four others, to accept this embassy. The Parliament in Vienna still imagined that they could keep within legal forms ; but this desire irritated those fiery politicians who felt that the struggle was now on a revolutionary footing ; and they therefore desired to overthrow the Assembly, and to establish a more determined body in its place. But Blum, who had been accustomed to hold in check the violent members

of his own party in Frankfort, supposed that, in
Vienna also, he was boun. to resist revolutionary
methods; and, though he was ready to encourage
the Viennese in the defence of their city, he objected
to the proposal for the violent dissolution of the
Assembly, on the ground that such a proceeding
would give an excuse to the tyrants for a dissolution
of the Frankfort Parliament.

A man of much more importance in such a siege
than Robert Blum could be, arrived about the same
time in Vienna. This was Joseph Bem, a Galician
of about fifty-three years of age, who had served in
Napoleon's expedition to Russia, and had greatly
distinguished himself as colonel of the Polish artillery
at the battle of Ostrolenka. He had also commanded
the Polish artillery in the insurrection of 1830, and
had attempted to organize a Polish legion, for the
help of the Portuguese, during their struggle against
the Absolutist party. He had been wounded in one
of these wars, was obliged to use a staff in walking,
and was small and delicate in his appearance. He
had gained both friends and enemies in Poland, and
was known for his strong democratic sympathies.
Although he was not appointed to the official headship of the National Guard, he soon became the
centre and life of the defence. But he found that
the men with whom he had to act did not understand
the position in which they were placed; for, when
he attempted to urge the National Guard to march
out against the army of Jellaciç, they twice refused
to follow him, on the ground that they were only
intended for the defence of the city.

And, if the rulers of Vienna were feeble in their
attitude towards their enemies, they were not less

feeble in their treatment of the one people, from
whom they might have expected help in this emergency.  The advance of Jellaciç against Vienna had
naturally increased the sympathy of the Magyars for
the Viennese, and Pulszky urged the latter to summon
the Hungarian army to their rescue.  This formal
invitation was the more necessary because the Hungarian officers were in many cases confused in their
minds as to their strict legal duty in this war. Archduke
Stephen, the Count Palatine of Hungary, after pro-
fessedly assuming the command of the army, had
suddenly fled from the country, and thus weakened
the legal position, both of his subordinate officers,
and of the Hungarian Diet, of which he was the
nominal head.  Ferdinand had repeated his former
dissolution of the Diet in a proclamation of the
20th October ; Prince Windischgrätz, professing to
act in the name of the Emperor, issued a declaration
from Prague forbidding the Hungarian officers to
fight against Jellaciç ; and soon after, followed up
this proclamation by marching against Vienna.
General Moga, the Commander-in-Chief of the Hungarian forces, hesitated to resist the Imperial orders ;
but, whilst the generals were debating among themselves, Kossuth arrived in the Hungarian camp to
urge them to advance.  After some delay his influence
prevailed; and on October 28 began the march of the
Hungarian army for the relief of Vienna.

In the meantime, all those in Vienna, who really
cared to save it, were trying to rouse their fellow-
townsmen to action.  Robert Blum made an address
to the students in favour of making " no half-revolu-
tion, but a complete change of the system;" and on
the 25th October, three days before the Hungarians

had begun their march, Bem had succeeded in persuading the National Guard to make their sortie. But confusion followed this attempt; some of the Guard fled; others were mistaken in the darkness for enemies, and fired on by their comrades. Bem's horse was killed under him, and he was compelled to retreat. Windischgrätz, who had now been appointed to the complete command of the besieging force, demanded the surrender of " the Polish emissary Bem, who in a quite uncalled-for manner, had mixed himself up in the affairs of Vienna." This recognition of the independence of the Polish provinces of the Austrian Empire was not accepted by the Viennese; nor did they consent to surrender any of the other people who were demanded by Windischgrätz. Bem roused the soldiers again to the defence, and drove them to their work with abuse. The Students' Legion distinguished itself by its courage; and some of the workmen seconded them bravely. But Messenhauser, the official leader of the National Guard, declared that the struggle was hopeless, and urged the people to yield.

Many were now disposed to abandon the defence; when suddenly, on October 30, there arose a cry that the Hungarians were approaching. Messengers went up the high tower of St. Stephen's Church, and looked out towards the plain of Schwechat, where the Hungarians and Austrians had at last joined battle. The Viennese had been advised by their Hungarian friends to tear up the railway lines; but they neglected this precaution; and thus Windischgrätz had been able to send more troops to Schwechat. But the great weakness of the Hungarians was due to the hesitation of General Moga, and to the want of confidence felt in him by his subordinate officers. Troops were ordered to advance, and then suddenly to halt, without any apparent reason; several of the new recruits ran away; and at last a general panic seized the army, and they fled before the Austrians, continuing to retreat, even after the enemy had ceased to pursue them.

The rumours of Hungarian help had encouraged some of the Viennese to oppose the surrender of their city; and this opposition was continued even after the defeat of the Hungarians had been officially announced. This division of opinion between the leaders and a great part of the people, led to riots in various parts of the town. Under these circumstances, Windischgrätz refused to accept the peaceable surrender offered by the leaders, and, instead, bombarded the town, and then entered it, while it was still on fire. Bem managed to escape; and so did three of the representatives of the Frankfort Parliament; but Blum and Fröbel were arrested. The latter was discovered to have written a pamphlet, which implied a desire to maintain the unity of the Austrian Empire; and, on this ground, he was set free. But Blum was proved to have acted as a captain of one of the corps of the National Guard, during the defence; his speech to the students, about the complete change of system, was supposed to imply a desire for a Republican movement; and so on the 8th November he was condemned to death, and on the 9th he was shot.

Great indignation was excited in Germany by this execution; and the unpopularity which the Frankfort Parliament had incurred by their assent to the truce of Malmö, was increased by their having refused to interfere to protect Blum from arrest. Yet it seems

as if the remarks, made above in the case of Confalonieri, may be applied again to Blum.    That Blum
should die, and Windischgrätz triumph, was no doubt
sad; but Blum's execution was rather the result of a
system of Government, than a specially illegal or
tyrannical act.  Blum had staked his life on the issue
of the struggle, by coming to Vienna during the siege.
If there were any alternative to his death, it was the
one proposed by Socrates to his judges; and in the
case of Blum, as in that of Socrates, the actual result
was the best for his honour.

But, as for the capture of Vienna itself, it is difficult to over-estimate its importance in the history of
the Revolution.   As the fall of Milan had broken the
connection of the Italian struggle with the European
Revolution, so the fall of Vienna destroyed the link
which bound all the other parts of the Revolution
together.   Race hatred, and a narrow perception of
their own interests, might hinder the Viennese from
understanding their true position; but the March
rising in Vienna had given to the various Revolutions
a European importance, which they would scarcely
have attained without it; and the attention of each
of the struggling races in turn had been riveted on
the city which Metternich had made the centre of
the European system.  In a still more evident manner
was the link broken between Germany and the rest
of Europe, and apparently between the most vigorous
champions of liberty in the different parts of Germany.

This last aspect of the fall of Vienna has been embodied, by a poet named Schauffer, in verses, which
appeared a year after the event, and which contain
also a worthy tribute to those fiery youths whose
determination and enthusiasm were to so large an

extent the cause of all that was best in the Vienna insurrections; though their national prejudices, and their want of self-control, contributed largely to the ruin of the movement which they had inaugurated.[1]

## THE VIENNA LEGION.

Their hearts beat high and hopeful,
   In the bright October days;
Not March's glorious breezes
   Could bolder daring raise.
No more with idle drum beats,
   But with cannons' thundering tone,
Marched forth to guard the ramparts,
   Vienna's Legion.

Once more they come to guard it,—
   The freedom won by fight;
Once more 'tis force must conquer,
   When blood is shed for right.
A steely forest threatens,
   Ere yet the day be won;
But the Fatherland, they'll save it,
   Vienna's Legion.

And, as the Spartans hurled them
   On the Persian's mighty horde,
They burst on the barbarian,
   To smite with German sword.
Their lives into the balance
   In careless scorn they've thrown;
And victory crowns their daring,
   Vienna's Legion.

[1] It is also worth noting that the first production of the freed Press of Vienna in March, 1848, was a poem by L. A. von Frankl, in praise of the services of the students to the cause of liberty; but, though this poem gained some celebrity at the time, it does not as easily lend itself to translation as the one translated above.

Thus did they struggle boldly,
   For many a day and night ;
Thus were they crushed, o'er wearied
   By the tyrant's conquering might ;
Grey warriors wept in anguish
   O'er many a gallant son ;
E'en in defeat 'twas victor,
   Vienna's Legion.

Their deeds will well be honoured
   In the victor's glorious lay ;
Our youth lay dead in battle,
   But they would not yield the day.
Let others crouch and tremble !
   No pardon will they own ;
They dare not live in bondage,—
   Vienna's Legion.

In the days of bright October
   They shouted in their pride ;
Their blows fell thick and boldly,
   They struck their strokes—and died.
The gallant lads have fallen ;
   In blood the Legion lie ;
But in the grave that hides them
   Is buried—Germany.

# CHAPTER X.

## THE LAST EFFORTS OF CONSTITUTIONALISM.

### JUNE, 1848—MARCH, 1849.

Difference of the Prussian movement from the other March movements.—The Silesian question.—The Rhine Province.— The Berlin workmen.—The grievances of the other Prussian Liberals.—Hansemann and his concessions.—The proposal of a Workmen's Parliament.—The " German" movement in Prussia. —The fall of Hansemann.—The reaction in Berlin.—The deputation to Potsdam.—" Das Unglück der Könige."—" Brandenburg in the Chamber, or the Chamber in Brandenburg."—The struggle between the Parliament and the King.—The refusal to pay taxes.—The final dissolution.—Value of the resistance of the Prussian Liberals.—The offer of the Crown of Germany to Frederick William.—Consequences of his refusal.—Abdication of Ferdinand of Austria.—The Parliament at Kremsier.—Its character.—Its dissolution.—Difficulties of Pius IX. and of his Ministers.—Rossi as Prime Minister.—The contradictions in his position.—His opposition to Italian ideas.—His murder.—The rising in Rome.—The democratic Ministry.—The flight to Gaëta.—Mamiani's theories.—The Forli petition.—The summons to the Roman Assembly.—Leopold of Tuscany and Guerrazzi.— Flight of the Grand Duke.—Guerrazzi and Mazzini.—Difficulties of Gioberti.—His schemes for restoring the Pope and the Grand Duke.—Their failure.—Radetzky's breaches of faith in Lombardy.—The appeal of the Lombards.—The declaration of war by Charles Albert.—Attitude of the Roman Assembly.— Mazzini's appeal and its effect.—The blunders of Charles Albert and his officers.—Tito Speri at Brescia.—" Defeat more glorious

than victory."—The "Tiger of Brescia."—Novara.—Abdication
of Charles Albert.—End of the "Constitutional" efforts for
freedom.

WHILE the Frankfort Parliament had been discussing
personal liberties, Constitutional arrangements, and
the relation of the different races to each other; while
in Italy, Hungary, and Bohemia the questions of
national independence and race equality had thrown
every other into the background; while in Vienna
the republican aspirations of the students, the contest between German and Bohemian, and the discontent of the workmen, had all merged into one
common element of confusion, so as at last to make
government impossible; in Prussia the condition
of the workmen had assumed a position of such
paramount importance, during the period from
April to August, as to obscure even the most
pressing Constitutional questions. The workmen's
petition had been the first step in the March movement in Berlin; and the miseries of the Silesian
famine had quickened the desire for the improvement of the condition of the poor. This Silesian
question, indeed, may perhaps be reckoned as the
chief cause of the difference between the Prussian
movement, and those which were taking place in the
other countries of Europe. In that unfortunate
province, the aristocracy seem to have tried to combine the maintenance of their old feudal power with
such advantages as they could gain from modern
commercial ideas. Thus the millers, who carried on
the chief industry of Silesia, still paid enormous dues
to the landlords for the use of their mills, while, at
the same time, the landlords would start mills of
their own in competition with the millers, who were

paying dues to them; and, as the landlord was free
from those imposts, he was often able to ruin those
who were at once his rivals and dependents. Other
dues of a peculiar kind were paid for protection
supposed to be given by the landlord; others, again,
were exacted under the pretext of supplying education to the children; while at the same time excessive
preservation of game was hindering the natural
development of agriculture. At the same time on
the Western side of Prussia, in the Rhine Province,
the French influence was colouring the feelings of the
population; and the socialistic June risings in Paris
excited the sympathies of the citizens of Cologne.

All these causes, combined with those new hopes
for a change of condition which had been roused
by the Revolution, tended to excite the workmen
of Berlin to action of a more definitely socialistic
kind than was possible even in Vienna; and on May
21 the workmen's union of Berlin called upon all the
unions of workmen throughout the Kingdom to
send representatives to the capital. This naturally
tended to fix the attention of the Prussian politicians
on the questions specially affecting the working
classes; and Hansemann, a moderate Conservative,
promised to bring forward measures for curing the
distresses of the workmen. In Berlin, as elsewhere,
the suffering classes found that these things were
more easily promised than fulfilled; and the disappointment of their hopes produced a continual
tendency to riot and disorder.

But the discontent roused by these causes was
considerably strengthened by other grievances of
a different kind. The aristocratic character of
the Prussian Constitution which was proclaimed in

April, had excited indignation in members of the
Prussian Liberal party, who had little sympathy
with socialistic agitations.   The return of the Prince
of Prussia to Berlin was reckoned as a sign of still
further reactionary intentions on the part of the
Government; while a more justifiable ground of
complaint than either of these was found in the
cruelties with which General Pfuel was stamping
out in Posen a movement originally sanctioned by
the Prussian King and Parliament.   He had stirred
up riots and encouraged the Germans to insult the
Poles, some of whom were branded and had their
heads shaved; their priests had been murdered, and
images desecrated.   These cruelties and insults provoked not only anger, but fear; for some of the
Prussian Liberals believed that the troops then used
against the Poles might end in trampling out the
liberties of Berlin.   If we add to these causes of
discontent that tyrannical conduct of the Prussian
soldiers in Mainz, which had so provoked the Frankfort Liberals; the apparent defiance to the French
Republic, by the massing of troops in the Rhine
Province, combined with the neglect to guard the
North-eastern frontier of Prussia against the Russian
troops which were fast gathering there; and last, but
not least, the sluggishness and hesitation shown in
the Schleswig-Holstein war, we shall see how naturally the bitter disappointment of the workmen chimed
in with the feelings of suspicion felt by other classes
of Liberals. The Berlin students, indeed, endeavoured
to prevent the workmen from continually betaking
themselves to violence; but they were unable to
accomplish much in this direction.   The workmen
had despaired of peaceable remedies; and on June 8

they broke into the Assembly, attacked the Ministers, and were with difficulty restored to order.

This state of things naturally produced a general feeling of suspicion and bitterness among all classes; and while, on the one side, a movement began in Berlin, and some of the other Prussian towns, in favour of a more Conservative Ministry, and the extreme champions of reaction even talked of removing the Parliament to Potsdam, the miseries of Silesia and Posen so roused the feelings of the Prussian Democrats that every step in the Conservative direction, however apparently innocent, gave cause for new outbreaks. Thus when new gates were put up to bar the entrance to the royal castle at Berlin, they were seized and carried off by the crowd; and when a deputation of thirty starving workmen, bearing the German flag, with the red flag by its side, were repulsed by the Ministers, there arose a cry for the general arming of the people; and when this was refused, the workmen stormed the armoury and carried off about 3,000 weapons.

The Ministry now became alarmed for the peace of Berlin; and, in spite of a decision of the Assembly to the contrary, they sent for three new battalions of militia, and prosecuted the men who had taken part in the attack on the armoury. The time, however, had not yet come for a complete reaction; and it was therefore unavoidable that concessions should be made to so strong a popular movement. So on June 23 Camphausen fell; Hansemann, who had promised relief to the workmen, formed a Ministry; and on the same day a scheme was brought forward in the Prussian Parliament, for abolishing the feudal dues. Hansemann further promised to develope municipal government; and he repudiated the attacks which Camphausen had made on the March movement. Then proposals were brought forward, with the approval of the Minister of Trade, for a Commission of Enquiry into the condition of the Silesian workmen. But the workmen were determined, to a great extent, to keep matters in their own hands; and the proposal for a conference of their unions had now grown into a demand for a Workmen's Parliament which was to meet in August, and to carry out a great many points of the modern socialistic programme ; such as the guarantee of work for all ; the care by the State for those who were helpless or out of work ; the regulation of hours of labour; and the support by the State of workmen's associations. And if the programme of Hansemann did not prevent workmen from insisting on their extremer demands, neither did it suppress the riotous methods by which they asserted their claims. Many members of the Assembly were still alarmed by hearing of attacks on machinery in Breslau, and by seeing demonstrations of workmen in Berlin; and the provision of special work on the railways produced just as much, and just as little satisfaction, as such temporary expedients usually do.

In the meantime the growing collision between the power of Prussia and the power of the Assembly at Frankfort was exciting new divisions in Berlin. During the months of June and July the democratic feeling in Prussia had been strongly in favour of Frankfort as against Berlin; while, on the other hand, the military party desired more and more to assert the independence of the King of Prussia against any central Parliament, and more particularly against one which had given its highest post to an Austrian prince. The workmen's movement thus, by a natural process, began to be coloured by the desire of the more cultivated Liberals for a united Germany ; and the special demands of the workmen began to fall into the background as the larger questions of the freedom and unity of the whole country came more prominently to the front. The fears of the Ministry were naturally increased by this alliance ; and early in August several members of the Prussian Left were suddenly arrested ; and amongst them Rodbertus, one of the more moderate members who had helped to place Hansemann in power. The new quarrel threatened to be as bitter as the old one ; collisions took place in various parts of the kingdom between the Prussian soldiers and the champions of German unity ; and when the members of the Left began to demand the dismissal from the army of reactionary officers, and to make demonstrations against the Ministry, the Ministers met them by passing a law for the suppression of public meetings, while the fiercer reactionists circulated a petition in favour of making the Prince of Prussia the Commander-in-Chief of the forces.

The truce of Malmö brought the crisis to a head ; and the members of the Left resolved that if the Ministry would not remove the reactionary officers, the Liberal members would leave the Assembly. Thus the Schleswig-Holstein crisis consolidated completely the different elements of opposition ; and on September 16 a vote of want of confidence in the Hansemann Ministry was carried in the Assembly. The greatest enthusiasm was roused by this vote ; the members who voted for it were carried on the shoulders of the people, and it seemed, for a moment, as if a constitutional solution had been found for the difficulties of Prussia. But the riots at Frankfort, and the triumph which they secured to the reactionary party in Parliament, gave new courage to the King of Prussia in resisting the opposition ; and he entrusted the formation of a Ministry to General Brandenburg, a man of more fiercely despotic principles than any who had recently held office. New prosecutions were begun; and, for the first time since the March insurrection, a newspaper was seized and confiscated. The Liberals, however, were not disposed to yield ; and, as if to strengthen their alliance with the champions of provincial and class liberties, they carried by a small majority a motion in favour of securing special rights to the province of Posen, and adopted unanimously a report for finding work for the spinners and weavers in certain parts of the kingdom ; while demonstrations were made in favour of sending help to Vienna in its struggle against Windischgrätz.

The fall of Vienna, however, enabled the King of Prussia to take another step towards absolutism, and General Brandenburg was appointed Minister in spite of the opposition of the Liberals. The King himself had withdrawn to Potsdam : and the Assembly resolved almost unanimously to send a deputation to the King, to entreat him to dismiss this Ministry. The deputation had to wait for a long time in a dark gallery, the King refusing at first to receive them otherwise than through the Ministers ; but a Ministerial despatch arrived, calling attention to this deputation; and thus the King's scruple was removed, and he consented to hear them. When the address was completed he took it up, folded it, and prepared to withdraw ; but Johann Jacoby exclaimed, " We are not come here merely to present the address, but to explain to Your Majesty the true condition of the country. Will you not grant us a gracious hearing?" The King refused, upon which Jacoby uttered the memorable words : "It is the misfortune of Kings that they will not hear the truth." Then Frederick William withdrew in great anger, and refused to have any further communication with the deputies. On November 6 he announced that, if the Assembly did not accept the Ministry, they would be dissolved by force ; and two days later he declared unconditionally that he should remove the Assembly by force to the town of Brandenburg ; or, as he epigrammatically put it, the choice was between "Brandenburg in the Chamber, or the Chamber in Brandenburg."

Von Unruh, the President of the Chamber, read this announcement to his colleagues, but declared that he would not carry it out without the sanction of the Assembly ; and, when General Brandenburg tried to speak, in order to command the closing of the Assembly, the President informed him that he was out of order, and, if he desired to make an explanation, he must ask leave to speak. Brandenburg then declared that the further sitting of the Parliament was illegal ; and, accompanied by seventy members, he left the House. The Assembly then, by 250 votes against 30, decided to continue their sitting. They further resolved that "the Assembly finds at present no reason for changing their place of deliberation ; that it cannot grant to the Crown the right to remove, to adjourn, or to dissolve the Assembly against its will ; that the Assembly does not consider those officials who have advised the Crown to take this step capable of presiding over the Government of

this country ; and that those officials have become
guilty of grave violations of their duty to the Assembly,
the country, and the Crown." They further resolved
that, although they were obliged to adjourn, the
President and Secretaries should remain all night
at their post, as a sign of the permanence of the
Assembly. On November 9 General Brandenburg
answered this defiance by a letter, in which he
declared that these resolutions were illegal, and
that he held Von Unruh and others responsible
for the consequences. In the meantime Brandenburg
had appealed to the Civic Guard to prevent the Members from attending the meetings ; but the commandant of the Civic Guard denied the right of the
Ministers to send him this order, and further protested
against the proposal to remove the Assembly to the
town of Brandenburg. The Town Council tried to
reconcile the Parliament to the King; but Von Unruh,
while declaring his desire to avoid bloodshed, denied
that the Assembly could yield on any point, and
the Members issued an appeal to the country in
which they denounced the illegal conduct of the
King and his Ministers, but urged the people to maintain a strictly legal position in the defence of their
liberties. The address concluded with these words :
" The calm and determined attitude of a People that
is ripe for freedom will, with God's help, secure the
victory of freedom."

The situation had become terribly dangerous; for
General Wrangel, soon after his return from Schleswig-
Holstein, marched his troops into the market place,
in front of the building in which the Parliament was
sitting, and on November 11, Von Unruh and the
other Members, coming to hold their meetings, found

the doors locked, and the soldiers guarding the place. They then adjourned to the Hotel de Russie, where they declared Brandenburg guilty of High Treason, and called on the people to refuse to pay taxes. Deputations came in from Magdeburg, Breslau and Frankfort, declaring their sympathy with the Assembly; and the Civic Guard refused to give up their arms to Wrangel. Wrangel now declared all public meetings prohibited, announced that the Civic Guard was dissolved; and declared Berlin in a state of siege. But the addresses of sympathy came in more freely than ever; and it was rumoured that Silesia was actually in a state of insurrection. Even several citizens of Brandenburg itself sent an address to the Assembly, declaring that they would resist the transfer of the Parliament to their town. The opposition between the bourgeoisie and the workmen, which had been caused by the riots of June, July and August, had now entirely disappeared in a common zeal for Constitutional freedom; and the Town Council permitted the Assembly to meet in their Hall. But even there Wrangel would not leave them in peace, and soon after they were driven from this refuge also. Even the ex-Minister Hansemann became an object of denunciation to the Court party; and on November 15 the Assembly put into a formal vote the proposal which they had already hinted at, that no further taxes should be paid. This vote was carried just after they had been driven from the Town Council House to another meeting place. The next day soldiers were called out, who threatened the Civic Guard with violence, but finally marched off without firing; and some soldiers and officers were dismissed for not consenting to act against the people. Taxes

were beginning to be refused in various parts of
Prussia; several arrests were made in Cologne; and
Düsseldorf was declared in a state of siege. The
soldiers were forbidden to read the National Zeitung;
while on the other hand printers and publishers offered
to print the decrees of the Assembly without any compensation for loss of time. Attempts to enforce the
payment of taxes led to riots in Bonn and Breslau; and
in Coblenz the people attacked officers for speaking
evil of the National Assembly. The Government
tried, in some cases, to cut off the payment of deputies; but the people insisted on making the payment,
in spite of this prohibition; and even a Government
official in Düsseldorf declared his belief that if the
Brandenburg Ministry lasted three or four days more,
none of the official boards would consent to act. One
of the Roman Catholic bishops of Silesia appealed to
his flock not to refuse taxes, as otherwise they would
be damned for "refusing to give to Cæsar the things
that were Cæsar's." To this appeal several Roman
Catholics of Silesia retorted by an address in which
they expressed their fear for the spiritual condition
of the clergy, since they had never paid taxes at all.

On November 27, the Government resolved on a
new act of violence. While the deputies were met at
the Hotel Mylius, Major von Blumenthal entered
at the head of a band of soldiers, and ordered the
deputies to leave the Hall.[1] Jacoby asked him what
he wanted. The Major answered, "I come in the
name of the law." Jacoby: "Of what law?" Major:
"In the name of the highest law." Jacoby: "Of

[1] The following dialogue is taken from the "Neue Rheinische
Zeitung."

what law do you speak ? " Major: " I speak in the name of the Constitutional law." Jacoby: " There is no law that forbids us to meet in an hotel in the day-time." Elsner: " Even Wrangel's proclamations contain no prohibition of this kind; we are no club."[1] Major: " That does not concern me. I act under the authority of my board." Jacoby: " What is your name?" Major: " I am the Major Count Blumenthal." Jacoby: " Who has given you this authority? " Major: " The board set over me." Several voices: " Name the board." Major (after a pause): " Gentlemen, do not embarrass me." Jacoby: " Well, then, I declare to you that you are not acting in the name of law, but of force; and it is a sad thing that the soldiers are misemployed for such acts of violence." The Major then ordered them once more to leave the Hall, and seized on the parliamentary papers. Jacoby denounced this seizure as robbery, and attempted to make a copy of the documents. The Major snatched the papers from Jacoby's hands; upon which the latter exclaimed, " Go on with your robberies, and scorn all laws; some day you will be brought to account for this." Then the deputies, still refusing to leave the Hall, were driven out by the soldiers.

In the meantime, the members of the Right had been meeting at Brandenburg; and at last von Unruh and many of his friends joined them there; but demanded at the same time, that the Assembly should accept all the resolutions passed in Berlin between the 4th and the 15th of November. But, on December 5, the King finally dissolved the Parlia-

---

[1] This alludes to the dissolution of several clubs by Wrangel's orders.

ment, announcing that it should meet on February 26
in Berlin, and that he would then issue a new Constitution.  The Liberal members all flocked to Brandenburg to protest against this dissolution ; and the King
found it necessary to suppress meetings even in
Brandenburg, as dangerous to his authority.

It was impossible in the then state of Germany that
any organized insurrection could produce a satisfactory result.   On the one hand the Republican leaders
had weakened their cause by spasmodic and useless
appeals to insurrection, at times when Constitutional
action would have been perfectly possible; while in
Prussia itself, the differences between the workmen
and the bourgeoisie made the permanent coherence
of a Constitutional party almost impossible.   On the
other hand, the Parliament at Frankfort, abandoned
by many members of the Left, had been growing
ever more and more timid, and had not only passed
a resolution condemning the resistance of the Prussian
Parliament, but had even sent Bassermann, one of
the Frankfort Ministers, to Berlin, to persuade the
Parliament to yield.  Under these circumstances,
the passive resistance of Von Unruh and his friends
was, in all probability, the wisest and most dignified
course which was open to the champions of liberty;
and when the Assembly actually met again in
February, the leaders of the Left were received with
enthusiasm by the people, as men who had deserved
well of their country.  If the King of Prussia had
heartily accepted the new condition of affairs, he
might even now have done something to secure a
better future for Germany than any that it has since
achieved; for the Frankfort Parliament had come to
the conclusion that the only hope for the unity of

Germany lay in its acceptance of the King of Prussia
as its head. They had repudiated the connection of
Germany with Austria; Archduke John had resigned
his post as Administrator of the Empire; and on
March 28, 1849, they finally resolved to offer the
crown of Germany to the King of Prussia. But the
flavour of freedom and independence which still
lingered, even in these later months, about the
Frankfort Parliament, made this offer distasteful to
a King whose liberalism, always superficial, had now
quite evaporated. The Frankfort Parliament had
been the result of a popular movement; and it had
elaborated a free Constitution, which it desired to
treat as a necessary part of the proposed monarchy.
Under these circumstances, therefore, Frederick
William IV. refused to accept the crown of Germany, unless it were offered to him by the Princes
of Germany; and by this refusal he put an end to
the hope that the German question might be settled
in a peaceable and Constitutional manner.

In the meantime, experience was showing that
it was almost as difficult in Austria as in Prussia to
reduce parliamentary government to a mere tool of
despotism. The members of the Bohemian party in
the Viennese Parliament had withdrawn from its
sittings after the murder of Latour; and had
attempted to find a free place for deliberation in
Olmütz. About the same time Ferdinand, grown
weary of the struggles of parties and races, unsatisfied
as to the contending claims of Kossuth and Jellaciç,
and unable to reconcile himself to the proceedings
either of Windischgrätz, or of the Viennese Democrats, listened to the advice which the clique around
him were pressing upon him, and consented to resign

his throne, not to his brother and lawful heir, but to his nephew, Francis Joseph, who, being a mere boy at the time, would fall easily under the power of the Camarilla, who were governing Austria. The advisers of Francis Joseph, however, still thought that they could keep up an appearance of parliamentary government; and they, therefore, summoned a parliament to meet at Kremsier in Moravia early in December.

It soon became apparent, however, that the men who met in the Kremsier Parliament were by no means less zealous for freedom, hardly even less democratic than those who met at Vienna. Those Bohemian members, who had objected to the rule of terror in the Viennese Assembly, had appealed, even from Olmütz, to the Emperor not to deal too harshly with Vienna; and they now showed themselves as zealous for freedom as any German could be. Men, too, like Borrosch, Löhner, Schuselka and Fischhof, who had not acted with the Bohemians at Vienna, were ready to take part in the Kremsier Parliament. On the motion of Schuselka, that Parliament, early in January 1849, abolished all privileges of rank; the right of summary arrest was also taken away, and trial by jury secured; while the freest criticisms were passed on the action of the Austrian Government in Vienna, Hungary and Italy; and Rieger specially denounced the desire of the Ministry to crush out all feeling for the special nationalities. The Parliament began to attract the attention of many who were at first disposed to speak of it with scorn; and even those courtiers who had hoped to use it as a weapon against the Magyars, became alarmed at its evident democratic leanings. Acting under their advice, Francis Joseph, on March 7, announced that this Parliament, from which he had hoped so much, had driven off still further "the restoration of peace and law, and of public confidence," and had raised the hopes of "the not wholly conquered party of disorder." He therefore dissolved the Parliament, and announced, as the King of Prussia had done, that he would settle the Constitution without their help. The Bohemian leaders united with the Germans to protest against this final act of violence; and so ended for about ten years all hopes of Constitutional Government in Austria.

In the meantime affairs in Italy had been also hastening in the direction of a more violent solution of difficulties than had been wished for in the early days of the movement. In spite of his apparent abandonment of the policy embodied in the encyclical of April 9, in spite even of his acceptance of Mamiani as Minister, Pius was still hesitating between two different policies. He was disposed to rely continually on Cardinals who were out of sympathy with his Ministers; and he was particularly anxious to assert that, in introducing a Parliament, he had not surrendered his absolute authority as Pope. This conflict of feelings in Pius IX. led to a curious exhibition at the opening of the Roman Parliament of June 4, 1848. On this occasion the Pope entrusted Cardinal Altieri with a discourse which had not had the approval of Mamiani. Mamiani, on the other hand, as Prime Minister, read to the Chamber a discourse in which he declared that the Pope abandoned to the wisdom of the deputies the care of providing for temporal affairs, and spoke of entrusting the papal volunteers in Lombardy to the leadership of Charles Albert. In spite of the action of Altieri, Mamiani

E E

declared that his speech had been approved by the Pope; but the Papal Nuncio in Vienna repudiated the language of the Papal Prime Minister. This continual jar between the Pope and his Ministers naturally excited distrust in the Assembly; and when the Austrians crossed the Po and occupied Ferrara, the cry for war rose, not only in the Assembly, but also in popular meetings out of doors; and the feebleness of the papal protest against this second occupation of Ferrara, increased the distrust of the Pope which was now growing in Rome. At last, in August, Mamiani, finding his position impossible, resigned; and, for a time, an old man named Fabbri was accepted as Minister by the Pope, as a kind of stopgap. But he, too, speedily found the position impossible, and resigned his post.

It was under these circumstances that Pius IX. called to his counsels the man whom he had previously desired to employ, the former ambassador of Guizot, Pellegrino Rossi. Rossi was known for his previous services to the cause of liberty, in the early part of the century; for his careful study of Roman law, and for his attempt to devise a Constitution for Switzerland. He was a personal friend of Pius IX., and had desired even a wider Constitution than that which the Pope had granted. He was further known to have gained respect from some of the Italian exiles in Paris. On all these grounds he naturally seemed to Pius a fit person to be trusted with his confidence. But though a man of sterling honesty, he was the worst possible Papal Minister at this juncture. His friends expected him to be welcomed as a former sufferer in the cause of Italian liberty. He was, on the contrary, hated as a friend of Guizot, and as the former representative of Louis Philippe. Sterbini, one of the fiercest democrats in Rome, declared that, if Guizot's friend appeared in the Assembly, he would be stoned. And, while he was hated by the Jesuits for his desire for secular Government, and for his Protestant wife, an outcry was at once raised against his Ministry by the Liberals, when it was found that it contained two Cardinals. While, too, in his own way, he wished for the freedom and independence of Italy, his way was exactly opposite to that which was then desired by the people.

Professor Montanelli, who had been taken prisoner by the Austrians at Curtatone, but who had since been allowed to return to Tuscany, was propounding there his scheme for a Constituent Assembly, which was to embrace all Italy. And this proposal, welcomed eagerly in Tuscany, and accepted by the Grand Duke, was being advocated in Rome, especially by Charles Buonaparte, the Prince of Canino. On this plan Rossi threw cold water, desiring to substitute for it a League of Princes, to be begun by a Congress of Ambassadors at Rome. This idea, unwelcome and unpopular in itself, was made more unpopular still by Rossi's eager advances to Ferdinand of Naples, to whom he actually consented to surrender fugitives who had escaped from his tyranny. While, too, he made this alarming concession to the Prince, who was most deservedly hated throughout Italy, he allowed General Zucchi, whom he had sent to Bologna, to refuse Garibaldi entrance into that city on his return from Lombardy; and when Gavazzi, one of the most popular preachers of the Italian war, protested against this act, Rossi ordered him to be arrested. And as if the Clericals, the Republicans, and those who placed Italian unity above any special political creed, were not enemies enough for one man, Rossi proceeded, by special signs of suspicion towards Charles Albert, to irritate against him the powerful party of the Albertisti, who looked to the King of Sardinia as the necessary leader of a movement for Italian liberty.

All this was done in the most open and scornful manner. Rossi ridiculed the proposed Constituent Assembly as a Council of Drunkards, and scornfully told Sterbini that every one knows "that there are praises which injure and blame which honours." Rumours were spread of his intention to bombard Rome; and the students mobbed him in the streets. On one occasion when they were following him, he crossed a bridge; and as he passed he handed to the toll-man a much larger sum than was his due, saying, with a wave of his hand towards the students, " Take for them too." Rumours came to him of plots against his life, but he refused to pay any attention to them. At last, on November 15, as he was going down to Parliament, a priest came to him, and told him that he would die if he went. He answered, " The cause of the Pope is the cause of God. God will help me." As he passed through the square, the crowd hooted at him. He warded them off with his stick, and ascended the stair. Suddenly an umbrella struck him; he turned his head, so that his neck became exposed; and, in the same instant, a dagger pierced him, and he fell mortally wounded. So died Pellegrino Rossi, a man who undoubtedly deserved a better fate; but who was thrust upon a position and a time which required a man of genius and humanity; while he had nothing to give but cut-

and-dried maxims, enforced with a courage which was too nearly allied to insolence.

That the guilt of Rossi's death should be laid to the account of different parties by different people, with equal confidence, was natural enough, considering the variety of enemies which his policy and character had stirred up against him; but it is a strange fact that actual eye-witnesses dispute as to whether it was received with joy or indignation by the people of Rome. It is tolerably evident, however, that all feelings about the actual event were quickly merged in the panic about its consequences. A general demand was made for a popular Ministry; and Galletti, who had been Minister of Police under Fabbri, went to the Pope to ask leave to form a Ministry. The Pope refused, and the people who had followed Galletti soon came to blows with the Swiss Guard. The Guard were driven back, and the crowd succeeded in getting cannon into their hands; but Federico Torre thrust himself in front of the cannon, exclaiming, "Shame to point cannon at the men who gave us the amnesty." Pius had hoped that some of the inhabitants of the Trastevere would have risen on his behalf; but, finding no support from them, he yielded to the demand for a Liberal Ministry, and appointed as his Prime Minister Rosmini, a champion of Charles Albert, and suspected of heresy by the Cardinals. Mamiani, who was at the time absent from Rome, was made Minister of Foreign Affairs, and Sterbini Minister of Commerce and Public Works. On the refusal of Rosmini, the Premiership was given to Muzzarelli. But these appointments, like Ferdinand's acceptance of a Democratic Ministry under similar circumstances, did not

express the real feeling of the Pope. He was completely panic-struck by the events which had taken
place; and, urged by Cardinals and Ambassadors,
he fled secretly from Rome on the night of the 24th
of November disguised as a footman, and took refuge
at Gaeta, under the protection of the King of Naples.

Mamiani had reluctantly accepted the office of
Foreign Minister; but he still believed that it was
desirable to uphold the authority of the Pope, because, as he expressed it, "the only choice for Rome
lay between Pius IX. and Cola di Rienzi." Nor was
he shaken in his determination, even when a letter
came from the Pope at Gaeta, denouncing the acts of
the people, repudiating his Ministers, and appointing
as Commissioners of State men of the most violently
reactionary character.

But, in the meantime, a strong force of public
opinion was growing in the Roman provinces, in
favour of the election of a Constituent Assembly; and
at last Aurelio Saffi, who had been so prominent as a
champion of reform in the time of Gregory XVI.,
succeeded in gathering together, at Forli, representatives of different local Societies, and preparing an
Address to the Ministry, which set forth in a concise
form those feelings which were floating in the provinces at that time. This address expressed great
regret at the flight of the Pope, whose name the
petitioners declared they had been wont to reverence
as "the symbol of a magnanimous idea." They went
on to say, however, that, as Pius IX. had thrown
himself into the arms of the worst enemies of Italy, it
had become necessary to take steps to prevent civil
war and anarchy. As Constitutional Monarchy had
been cut short by the departure of the Pope, and as

it was impossible to accept Commissioners whom the Pope had appointed since his flight to Gaeta, it was necessary for the Council of Deputies to nominate a Provisional Government which should issue writs for the election of an Assembly by universal suffrage, and should settle definitely the political arrangements of the State, " saving only the rights of the nation united in an Italian Constituent Assembly, such as has been proclaimed by the Tuscan Parliament." This Address produced a great effect in Rome; and Armellini urged his colleagues to accept the proposals of the petitioners. Mamiani, seeing that the Constitutional compromise which he desired had become impossible, refused to remain a Minister of State. A Provisional Government of eight members was then formed, in which Sterbini, Galletti, and Armellini took part; and the new Government on December 29 issued an Address to the Roman people, calling upon them to elect an Assembly for the Roman State, which was to meet in Rome on February 5.

In the meantime, the flight of the Pope had startled the other Princes of Italy. Leopold of Tuscany had seemed more ready than most of his brother Princes to accept Constitutional Government, and even to look forward to arrangements for the unity of Italy. Guerrazzi, from what motives it may be difficult to guess, had discouraged Montanelli's plan of an Italian Constituent Assembly, and had warned the Grand Duke that his own position would be destroyed by such an institution. But, when the Pope fled from Rome, Guerrazzi had conceived the idea that Leopold might be chosen President of the new Assembly, and that the combination of Tuscany with the Roman

States might prove a check on the ambition of Charles Albert. Leopold, however, seems to have been actuated by very different motives from those to which Guerrazzi appealed. So far from being strongly moved by personal ambition, or by a sense of official dignity, he was particularly inclined to accept the lead of other Princes. He had imitated Ferdinand of Naples in proclaiming Constitutional Government; he had followed Charles Albert in proclaiming war on Austria; and he had accepted first the Italian League, and afterwards the plan of an Italian Constituent Assembly, without a sign, as far as is apparent, of any other motive than the desire to promote the unity of Italy. But this very willingness to act with other Princes made Leopold averse from the idea of standing alone in his policy. It was therefore that flight of the Pope which seemed to Guerrazzi to open a new chance for Tuscany, which awoke in Leopold scruples and hesitations; and when Pius issued from Gaeta his denunciation of the proposals of the Roman Council, Leopold lost heart, and secretly fled from Florence to Siena, leaving a written statement to the effect that the Pope's opposition to the Italian Constituent Assembly compelled him to revoke the decree by which he had just sanctioned that Assembly.

On February 8 the news of the Grand Duke's flight was received in Florence, and it was immediately followed by a rising, in which the insurgents demanded the appointment of a Provisional Government composed of Guerrazzi, Montanelli, and a man named Mazzoni. Just about the same time Mazzini arrived in Leghorn. Guerrazzi, who still wished to act in the name of the Grand Duke, tried to forbid Mazzini's entrance; but the Livornese went out to meet him

with banners bearing his motto, "Dio e il Popolo."
He exhorted them to preserve order, and then went
to Florence to urge the Tuscan Ministry to join their
country to the Roman State. But Guerrazzi succeeded in preventing the acceptance of this proposal,
and Mazzini went on to Rome.

Gioberti, on his part, had been much exercised in
his mind by the new aspect of affairs. His great
desire that the Pope should unite Italy seemed utterly
frustrated by the flight of Pius from Rome, and still
more by his placing himself under foreign protection.
For, though it was to the King of Naples that the
Pope first appealed, Gaeta soon became the gathering
place of the ambassadors of the extreme Roman
Catholic Powers; and, when Gioberti sent messengers
to Gaeta, they found the Pope surrounded by men
who had no sympathy with the ideas of the Primato.
When the Piedmontese envoys offered him a refuge
at Nice, and promised that their King would join
with other Italian Princes in restoring him to Rome,
the Pope answered that he had appealed to the
European Powers, and must await their decision ;
and he further reproached Charles Albert with the
sanction which he had given to the idea of an Italian
Constituent Assembly, accusing him of intriguing
with those who were opposed to the rights of the
Church. Though discouraged by this rebuff, Gioberti
hoped to find a new mission in the restoration of the
Grand Duke of Tuscany, who had now followed the
Pope to Gaeta. But in this plan he found himself
opposed at once by Guerrazzi, and by the Austrians ;
while his own colleagues were so indignant at the
proposal, that he was compelled to leave the Ministry
which he had only just joined.

In the meantime, the Austrian conquerors of
Lombardy had been supplying justifications for a new
Italian war.   The capitulation of Vicenza had been
violated almost as soon as it had been made, by the
infliction of new vexations on those to whom a free
pardon had been granted; and the more important
capitulation of Milan had been followed by similar
breaches of faith.   Special burdens had been laid on
those who had taken an active part in the struggle
against Austria; while some of the regulations of
General Welden in Pavia had been so cruel as to
excite a protest even from the Viennese Assembly.
He had ordered that anyone who went about with
arms was to be shot within twenty-four hours, and
that his patrols should fire on any group of men more
than three in number who were found in the streets
at night.   The Council of Lombardy had, therefore,
appealed to Charles Albert to secure them justice,
because Radetzky had acted " in defiance of his own
word, in defiance of the orders of his Sovereign, in
defiance of the military conventions, in defiance of
the mediation of England and France."   The stronger
Liberals of Piedmont soon began to cry out for war;
but, for a long time, Charles Albert and his Ministers
hoped to stave off action, and to secure a settlement
of these differences by diplomacy.   But the rebuffs
which Gioberti had received gradually convinced them
that no further help was to be found in appeals to
foreign Powers; and, urged on by a strong popular
feeling, Charles Albert for the last time declared war
upon Austria.

It might be reasonably doubted how far such a war
would excite the sympathies of the Romans.   The Piedmontese Ministry had recently attempted to suppress

the liberties of Rome; and although that Ministry
had fallen, Charles Albert was himself known to be
strongly Monarchical in his feelings about the government of Rome. The Roman Assembly, which met
on February 5, had, on the 9th, declared the Pope
deposed, and had proclaimed the Republic; a step
which they might naturally expect to widen the
breach between them and the Piedmontese. Some
were even disposed to think that Charles Albert
had given another sign of hostility in ignoring
the former league with Rome, and declaring
an Italian war without any consultation with, or
notice to the Roman Ministry. But any doubts or
hesitations as to the right attitude of Rome towards
Piedmont at this crisis were put an end to by Mazzini.
He had been chosen by Leghorn as their representative in the Roman Assembly, and had taken his seat
on March 6, the whole Assembly rising to greet him.
When, then, the news came that Charles Albert had
declared war once more on Austria, Mazzini appealed
to the Romans to join in the struggle. "There must,"
he said, "be only two kinds of Italians in Italy: the
friends and the enemies of Austria. Republican
Rome will make war by the side of Monarchical
Piedmont." Mazzini never considered that ready or
eloquent speech was a power that he possessed; and,
what is more to the point, some of those who loved
and admired him held the same opinion; but the
intensity of his conviction seemed to take the place
of readily-turned phrases or imagery; and, as he went
on to speak of the sacrifices that the war demanded
of all Romans, there fell upon the table beside him,
in showers, the jewels which the ladies in the gallery
had plucked off, as their offerings for the good of

their country. The Assembly voted war, almost unanimously, and twelve battalions of the National Guard were despatched to Lombardy.

The war was little worthy of their enthusiasm. The Piedmontese officers were so little trusted by Charles Albert that he chose a Pole named Chrzanowski as his Commander-in-Chief, while the second in command was that Ramorino who had betrayed Mazzini in the Expedition of 1833-4. The three or four days of the war were mere scenes of mutual distrust, mismanagement, and, possibly, treachery; and it is pleasant to turn for a moment from the Piedmontese battles to the one part of the struggle which redeemed this episode from utter contempt. On March 23, Brescia, from which a portion of the Austrian forces had, for a time, then withdrawn, sprang to arms, drove out the remaining troops, and raised the Italian flag. Tito Speri, a Mantuan, organized the poorer citizens, and led them against the forces of Nugent, which were advancing on the city. After a sharp struggle, the Brescians were driven back with some loss; but, two days later, Speri made another sortie, and, though attacked by the cavalry, succeeded in driving them back, and in occupying the hills which overlook Brescia. He now attempted to treat with the Austrians; but Nugent answered that he would enter Brescia, either by force or by love; to which Speri replied, "Perhaps by force, but never by love!" Rumours came of Charles Albert's defeat, but the Brescians refused to believe it; and Nugent was forced to retreat from Brescia, after having, apparently, concluded an armistice with the citizens. But, on March 30 or 31, Haynau appeared before the city; and, in answer to the appeal of the Brescians to the terms of the armistice, he declared that, if they did not yield in two hours, he would reduce the city to ashes. But the Brescians were resolved, as their own inscription tells us, to teach " that defeat may be more glorious and fruitful than victory;" and they, therefore, refused to yield. On April 1, Haynau bombarded the city; and, after a fierce struggle at Porta Torlunga, in which General Nugent was mortally wounded, Haynau forced his way into the city, and put men, women, and children to the sword—the cruelties of his proceedings gaining for him, among the Italians, the title of " the Tiger of Brescia."

But, before Brescia had fallen, Charles Albert, betrayed by his officers, distrusted by his soldiers, and out of heart, had been defeated at Novara; and, in response to a demand which he had made to Radetzky for a truce, he had been asked terms which he considered too dishonourable to accept. His officers, however, told him that his army was in too disorganised a state to be depended on, and he then answered in these words: " For eighteen years I have always used every possible power for the advantage of my people. It is painful to me to find my hopes deceived; not so much for my sake, as for my country's. I have not been able to find on the field of battle the death that I so ardently desired. Perhaps my person is the only obstacle to the obtaining of just terms from the enemy. The continuation of the war having become impossible, I abdicate the Crown in favour of my son, Victor Emmanuel, in the hope that a new King may be able to obtain more honourable terms, and to secure for the country an advantageous peace." So ended the chequered career of Charles Albert, a man of many attractive qualities and noble aspirations, but who, by a fatal weakness of will, made more evident by a painfully difficult situation, had been constantly dragged into acts of cruelty and treachery from which a man of stronger purpose would have been saved. With his fall ended the Constitutional struggles of this period; and, during the remaining months of the Revolution, the Peoples of Rome, Venice, Sicily, and Hungary had to depend, in their struggles for liberty, on the force of popular feeling, and on the guidance of those leaders whom they had themselves placed at the head of affairs.

# CHAPTER XI.

## THE DEATH-STRUGGLE OF FREEDOM.—
## OCTOBER 1848—AUGUST 1849.

Division of Feeling among the Magyar Leaders.—Arthur
Görgei.—Ground of his quarrels with Kossuth.—Bem.—The
Volunteers.—The Plan of Defence.—The Flight to Debreczin—
The Proclamation at Waitzen.—Effect of Hungarian Conscription Law in Transylvania. Puchner and the Roumanians.—
Puchner finally adopts their Cause.—Avraham Jancu.—The
Saxons and Roumanians.—Bem in Transylvania.—His Character
and Work.—The Appeal to General Lüders.—The Russians
in Transylvania.—The Capture of Hermannstadt.—Bem and
Csanyi.—The Reign of Terror.—The Death of Roth.—Görgei
and Dembinski.—Effect of Francis Joseph's coup d'état.—Why
it did not produce greater results.—The Race Feuds.—The Con-
stitutional Difficulty.—The Declaration of Independence.—
Kossuth's Power and its Causes.—The Struggle in Rome.—The
Triumvirate and their Difficulties.—Order and Liberty.—The
Danger from France.—A Pacific Candidate.—The Collapse of
the Tuscan Movement.—The Final Struggle and Fall of Sicily.
—The French Expedition.—The Landing at Civita Vecchia.—
Oudinot and Manara.—The Occupation of Civita Vecchia.—
The March to Rome.—Guerra! Guerra!—The Repulse of the
French.—The Debates in France.—The Defence of Bologna.—
Lesseps in Rome.—Lesseps and Oudinot.—French Treachery.—
Garibaldi and Roselli.—Further Treachery.—The Fight by the
Vascello.—Ledru Rollin's Insurrection.—The Final Struggle
for German Liberty and its Failure.—The Final Struggle in
Rome.—Mazzini's Proposals.—Decision of the Assembly.—

Garibaldi's last Effort.—"Cardinal" Oudinot in Rome.—The
Struggle in Venice.—Manin and Kossuth.—Kossuth's Blunder.
—Görgei's Policy.—The Russian Invasion of Transylvania.—The
Struggle at the Temos Pass.—Bem and Kossuth.—Kossuth's
Resignation.—The Surrender at Vilagos.—The Cholera in
Venice.—The Final Surrender.—Manin's Stone.—General Esti-
mate of the Struggle and its Results.

THE battle of Schwechat had brought into prominence the great difficulties with which the Hungarian
Government had now to contend. The flight of the
Count Palatine, and the resignation of Batthyanyi,
had thrown the government into the hands of the
Committee of Defence, over which Kossuth's power
was nearly supreme. But, however much this concen-
tration of authority in the hands of the most popular
leader may have given strength to the civil part of the
Executive, yet the revolutionary character which it
gave to the movement called out scruples in many
military men, who had hitherto been willing to work
with tolerable heartiness for the Hungarian cause.
The flight of Archduke Stephen deprived the Government of that Constitutional sanction which would
have been derived from the presence of an official
directly representing the Emperor; while at the same
time, Ferdinand's approval of Jellaciç, and the dissolution of the Hungarian Diet, placed the Emperor
and the Magyars in that condition of direct opposition
to each other, which most of the Magyar statesmen
had desired to avoid. This change of position considerably affected the feelings of the officers, especially
of those who had previously served in the Austrian
Army, and in whom the military preference for
Monarchical Government was strongly developed.
This feeling had shown itself even during the struggle

against Jellaciç's invasion; and it was this which had
led those Magyar officers, who were friendly to the
Viennese cause, to ask for a direct summons from the
Viennese Parliament before they would cross the
frontier.   Finally, it was this feeling which had led to
those orders and counter orders, and to that general
uncertainty of plan which had ruined the Hungarian
cause at the Battle of Schwechat.   Kossuth, and all
who wished to carry on the war vigorously, felt that a
change of generals was necessary, if the freedom of
Hungary was not to be destroyed by the internal
divisions of the country.   General Moga had therefore to be removed; and the question was, who was
to take his place?   It was under these circumstances
that Kossuth called to the front a man whose character
and actions have ever since been the favourite
debating ground of the students of the Hungarian
war.[1]

Arthur Görgei had been a lieutenant in the
Austrian Army, and, by his own account, had lived
away from Hungary until April, 1848, and was
" nearly ignorant of his country's customs, and above
all, wholly deficient in even a superficial and general
acquaintance with civil administration."   He had,
however, been made a captain in the newly raised
regiments of Honveds or Home troops of Hungary,
in the summer of 1848.   He very soon began to com-

[1] I must admit that my estimate of Görgei is, in many
respects, lower than that of men whose opportunities of observing
the facts, and whose general candour of judgment entitles their
opinion to great respect.   I can only plead that the severest
judgments which I have passed upon him are founded upon his
own memoirs ; that is, partly upon the facts narrated in them,
and partly upon the tone in which they are written.

plain of the men who had been placed over his head;
and specially at being superseded on one occasion by
Moritz Perczel.   To Perczel he soon began to show
the same insubordinate demeanour which remained
ever his characteristic attitude towards his superior
officers; and he was only saved by the intercession of
friends from being shot for disobeying orders.   He
had, however, gained credit with some of the fiercer
patriots among the Magyars, by his summary execution of Count Eugene Zichy, who had been suspected
of treason; and this act, though condemned by the
more temperate champions of the cause, was considered to have committed Görgei so strongly to an
anti-Austrian policy, that there could be no fear of
his lack of zeal in the coming struggle.   When then
General Moga had shown that, either from military
incapacity, or from want of sympathy with the cause,
he was not to be trusted with the command of the
army, Kossuth turned to Görgei, and offered him
the post of which Moga had been deprived.   Görgei
accepted it; and then there almost immediately began
that long series of differences and difficulties which
was to ruin the cause of Hungarian liberty.

The quarrel between Kossuth and Görgei will
always be judged differently by military and non-
military critics; for, setting aside those unfortunate
peculiarities of character which marked both these
leaders, the struggle was one between the ideas of a
statesman and the ideas of a soldier.   Kossuth had
already had experience of the difficulties which arose
from putting confidence in officers who are out of
sympathy with the cause for which they are fighting;
and he was therefore specially alive to any sign of
this want of sympathy in the successor of General

Moga.  Görgei, on the other hand, had that belief, so common in men of his profession, that all political questions were mainly to be judged from the military point of view; and that his admitted ignorance in matters of civil administration did not disqualify him from laying down the law on the most important affairs of Government.  Although he shared Kossuth's distrust for General Moga, he sympathised with Moga's preference for Monarchical Government; and although he had fought bravely against the forces of Windisch-grätz at the battle of Schwechat, he had previously declared that he did not see the solidarity between the cause of Hungary and that of Vienna; and he held that the oath which the officers had taken to the March Constitution implied their duty to preserve that Constitution in the exact form in which it had been originally granted.

But if Görgei went beyond his province in his interference with affairs of civil government, Kossuth no doubt, in turn, hampered Görgei in matters in which he was bound to trust him, so long as he retained him in his command.  But in periods of revolution there always arise a large number of questions which, in ordinary times, would be decided on purely military grounds, but which, in that abnormal state of affairs, become necessarily complicated with political considerations.  It is this peculiarity of circumstances, for which both statesmen and soldiers find it so hard to make allowance, and which makes it so difficult to judge justly in such a controversy as that which we are considering.

The first point of difference between Kossuth and Görgei related to exactly one of those matters in which military and political feeling seem most necessarily and reasonably to come into collision. This was the choice of Bem as a general in the Hungarian army. Bem had succeeded in escaping secretly from Vienna and coming to Hungary. He had, indeed, offered his services to the Hungarians at an earlier period, but Pulszky had persuaded him that he could best serve the cause of Hungary in Vienna ; and now that that city had fallen, he hastened back to Kossuth. Kossuth and Bem seem always to have recognized in each other that common faith in the people, and power of calling out popular enthusiasm, which, in different ways, was the great strength of both of them. Bem's conduct in the defence of Vienna had given sufficient pledge of his zeal against the power of Austria, a zeal which had produced such effect on the imagination of his enemies that it was said by the Vienna wits that Francis Joseph ordered the bells of Vienna to be muffled because they would ring out " Bem, Bem!" But Görgei disliked Bem for the very reason for which Kossuth approved of him. He considered him a knight errant who followed revolutionary methods of warfare which were quite unknown to correct military tacticians ; and he soon found that his own estimates of the different officers under him were quite opposed to those formed by Bem. Kossuth therefore wisely decided that Görgei and Bem could not work together, and he despatched Bem to take the command in Transylvania.

On the next question at issue the balance of opinion will probably be in favour of Görgei. The volunteers who had been raised by the national Government were naturally objects of special favour to them; but they had in some cases shown themselves disorderly; and this disorder was, no doubt, considerably in-

creased by the return to their country of Hungarian
soldiers who had been stationed in Galicia and other
parts of the Empire.  These soldiers had, in many
cases, thrown off the authority of their officers, and
asserted their national rights at the expense of military
discipline.  Görgei tried to make special arrangements for so redistributing these recruits as to utilize
their services while preventing the growth of any
such feelings of insubordination as might be likely to
spring from their previous mutiny.  In these methods
of re-organization the Committee of Defence saw a tendency to discourage patriotic feeling; and Görgei found
himself opposed in matters where he justly felt that he
should have been allowed some freedom of action.

But an even more important question of controversy was the general plan of the campaign.  Kossuth
and the Committee of Defence were extremely anxious
to defend the Western frontier of Hungary, partly in
order to weaken the fears produced by the battle of
Schwechat; partly, as Görgei believed, to make it
easier to draw the line between Hungary and Austria,
and so break off political connection between them.
Görgei, on the other hand, held that, since Hungary
was now threatened on north, south, and west, and,
since Windischgrätz's army was better disciplined
than the Hungarian soldiers, a defence of the frontier
was impossible, and that it would be better to retreat
to Raab and defend the principal passes across the
White Mountains, while removing the seat of Government beyond the Theiss.  In this plan he was at
first over-ruled.  But his ideas received apparent
justification in the defeats which he suffered from
Windischgrätz; and, on December 19 he was actually
compelled to retreat to Raab.

Then followed an episode which has brought much discredit on Kossuth. He issued a sensational address, declaring that the Committee of Defence would be buried under the ruins of Buda rather than desert the capital. Görgei ridiculed the idea of the defensibility of Buda Pesth; but the Committee of Defence insisted; and Görgei was preparing for battle, when, early in January, 1849, the news suddenly arrived in his camp that the Committee of Defence had left Pesth without waiting for the siege, and had retired to Debreczin. But, if Kossuth had been to blame in these earlier matters of controversy, Görgei now took a step which certainly seems to justify all Kossuth's subsequent suspicions. Görgei was, at this time, stationed at Waitzen, a little north of Pesth; and he there issued a declaration to the army condemning the policy of the Committee of Defence, and calling upon the officers to declare that the army was fighting for the maintenance of the Constitution of Hungary as sanctioned by King Ferdinand V.;[1] that it will oppose all those who may attempt to overthrow the Constitutional Monarchy by untimely Republican intrigues; and that it will only obey orders received from the responsible Minister of War, appointed by the King.

A few weeks later Görgei was again defeated by Windischgrätz, who, after the battle, offered him an amnesty, and free life out of Austria. In answer to this offer, Görgei sent a copy of the proclamation drawn up at Waitzen, declaring that this was the ultimatum, both of his army and of himself. By this act it is evident that he called the attention of the

[1] This was the title of the Emperor Ferdinand in his capacity of King of Hungary.

General against whom he was nominally fighting
to the internal party divisions of Hungary.  However brilliant Görgei's military abilities might be, and
however unfairly he had been interfered with by the
Committee of Defence, it cannot be wondered at that,
after this act of treachery, they looked upon him with
distrust.  In the following month Görgei was deprived
of his command and superseded by the Polish General
Dembinski.

In the meantime a struggle of far greater moral
importance, though possibly of less value to military
science, was being carried on in Transylvania.  The
Roumanian movement had been undergoing the same
change, which had already passed over the national
movements of the Serbs and Croats.  As early as
June, 1848, the Croatian Assembly had expressed
their sympathy with the struggle of the Roumanians;
and even from the Italians some utterances of sympathy had been heard, in favour of their kinsmen
in Transylvania.  The rejection of their petition by
the Emperor, and the consequent persecution by the
Magyars had led the Roumanians to rely upon themselves; and had induced some of their leaders to look
for help rather to the new State which was trying to
struggle into existence in Wallachia and Moldavia,
than to the Austrian Government.  In September,
however, a new element was introduced into the
struggle by the passing of a Conscription law by the
Hungarian Diet.  While the Roumanians resented
this, as an attempt to make them serve under the
military leadership of their persecutors, they also
saw that an attempt to enforce a law, passed without
the sanction of the Emperor, was a direct defiance
of his authority; and at a meeting in the town of

Orlat, they protested against this conscription, and declared their preference for the Austrian army, as against the Hungarian. They now openly announced their separation from Hungary, and demanded to be formed into an independent nation. The Hungarians met this demand by authorizing their Commissioner Berczenczei to summon the Szekler to a public meeting, nominally to plan the defence of their country, but really as a counterblast to the demands of the Roumanians.

But the Roumanians felt that it was necessary to strengthen themselves by an appeal to a recognized authority; and they saw that the desultory and barbarous warfare, which they had hitherto carried on, would never suffice to win them the rights which they had now resolved to claim; they therefore made advances to Field-Marshal Puchner, the General of the Austrian forces in Transylvania. Latour had for some time past been trying to stir up Puchner to action; but Puchner had hesitated to listen either to the Austrian Minister, or to the Roumanian leaders. He seems to have been a man of much higher type than most of the Austrian generals who were engaged in the struggles of this period ; and he shrank alike from the underhand intrigues of Latour, and from the dreadful cruelties of Roumanian warfare. The latter feeling would have had special force with him at this period; because the most urgent appeals for his help came from Urban, a former officer in the Austrian army, who had been the most notorious for his brutalities of all the leaders of the Roumanians. But, while Puchner was unwilling to commit himself definitely to the Roumanian cause, he opposed himself to the reckless persecution which

the Magyar Commissioner Vay had carried on against
all who had helped in organizing the petition of the
Roumanians; and Puchner had even gone to Karls-
burg, and sucessfully petitioned for the release of
some of the Roumanian prisoners. He had hoped,
however, to combine this merciful and moderate
policy with the recognition of Vay's authority, and
even with a kind of co-operation with him. But the
fiercely revolutionary character, which the Hungarian Diet began to assume after the death of
Latour, compelled Puchner into more decided opposition to their proceedings.

On the 8th of October, Kossuth issued an order to
the towns of Hungary, in which he told them that
anyone who did not hang out the Hungarian flag,
and express in writing his devotion to the Hungarian
cause, and his willingness to obey the committee
appointed by the Government, should be shot as a
traitor; and this savage proclamation was followed
the next day by a command from Commissioner
Vay, to the tax collectors of Transylvania, that they
should no longer send the taxes to the central office
at Hermannstadt, but to the office in Klausenburg,
which had hitherto been considered subordinate. As
Hermannstadt was at once the military head-quarters
of the Austrian army and the chief town of the Saxon
settlement in Transylvania, this was a direct attack
both on the Imperial power, and on the influence of
the Saxons. A few days later the Szekler, in the
meeting which had recently been summoned, denounced Puchner for his attempt to hinder that
meeting, and formally repudiated his authority.

Puchner now felt that the time had come for
action; and, on the 18th of October, he issued from

Hermannstadt an appeal to all the inhabitants of Transylvania, and especially to the official boards.   In
this he declared that, since the Count Palatine and
his Ministers had resigned their offices, there had
been no legal Government in Hungary.   The Government of Kossuth, which wrongfully claimed to act
for the Emperor, was substituting terror for equality,
and had falsely spread the rumour that the Government desired to use the Roumanians to oppress the
Magyar and Szekler.   In order, then, to put an end
to anarchy, and to protect the country from terrorism,
he, Puchner, had resolved to take advantage of the
Imperial Manifesto of October 3, which had placed
Hungary under military Government; and he called
upon all boards to act with him in restoring order,
and upon the volunteers and national guards to place
themselves under his command.

Nor were the Roumanians content with this official
appeal; for their own national committee issued about
the same time, on their own responsibility, an address
to the Szeklers and Magyars.   In this address they
declared that they, like the Szeklers and Magyars,
had sympathized with the March movement in Hungary; but that a faction had now usurped the Government of the country, and was aiming, at once, at
depriving the King of his crown, and the Hungarian
Peoples of their nationality.   They hoped that the
better part of the Magyars and Szeklers would unite
against this faction; but, if they would not, then the
Roumanians must declare war on them.   They
promised, however, to carry on the war in a humane
manner, and to spare women, old men, and prisoners.
At the same time, they issued an appeal to their
countrymen, urging them to abstain from cruelties

in warfare, as such practices were unworthy of a free people. The Saxons had, at first, been somewhat unwilling to act with the Roumanians; but the new movement seemed to give an opening for better co-operation. Joint committees of the two races were formed, and Puchner undertook to organize the soldiers of both races.

Of the Roumanian leaders who now came to the front, the most remarkable was Avraham Jancu.[1] He had been originally trained as a lawyer; but, after the meeting in September, he went off to organize the National Guard in his own mountains; and, when Puchner had issued his proclamation, Jancu received orders to give his assistance in disarming the Magyars. This process had been begun by the Roumanians, without waiting for orders; and it had, in consequence, been accompanied with many acts of cruelty. Jancu therefore sent down three tribunes with forces to protect the Magyar families from violence; and he also persuaded one or two of the towns to surrender to him, that he might then protect them from ill-treatment. Jancu also won several victories, and became so formidable to his opponents that he gained the name of the "Mountain King." But the humane exertions of Jancu and other tribunes, seconded with all his influence by Puchner, were not sufficient to keep in check the wildness of some of the Roumanian leaders. The cruelties which both the Magyars and Szeklers had committed in the struggle; the summary execution

---

[1] It will observed that the Roumanians used, wherever possible, the old Roman titles, in order to assert their connection with ancient Rome.

at Klausenburg of three leaders of the Roumanians,
before the actual rising had taken place, and the
reputed crucifixion of another at Maros Vasarhely,
roused the fury of the Roumanians to its highest
pitch.

The fiercest hatred of the Roumanians was directed
against the Szeklers who had been their most determined enemies; and General Gedeon marched against
Maros Vasarhely. Its specially isolated position,
and the bad roads in its neighbourhood made it an
easy prey for a General who had some skill in guerilla
warfare. The city fell into the hands of Gedeon, who
revenged the wrongs of the Roumanians by inflicting
every species of brutality on the Szekler inhabitants.
Horrified as Puchner was at these cruelties, he did not
wholly understand the character of the men with
whom he was working; for, in one of the orders
which he issued, he gave a distinct sanction to the
practice of burning villages. He seems, indeed, to
have intended this form of violence merely to be used
as an extreme measure in case of retreat; but the
Roumanians did not so understand it; and when, on
one occasion, Puchner was sternly rebuking some of
the Roumanian leaders for not better preventing the
cruelties of their followers, one of them retorted by
appealing to this order.

Besides the difficulties arising from these cruelties,
Puchner had to contend against the continual rivalry
between the Saxons and Roumanians. The former
were contemptuous towards their allies; and, according to the Roumanian theory, were disposed to take
unfair advantage of the Roumanians in the election
of the members of the Committee of Management.
Nevertheless, the help of the Saxons probably enabled

Puchner to secure a more orderly Government than he could have achieved without it; and, amongst others from whom he received this kind of help, was the Saxon clergyman, Stephan Ludwig Roth, who had already been known for his efforts to secure German emigrants to Transylvania. He was appointed by Puchner to govern the district of Mediasch, in the valley of Kokelburg, where he distinguished himself by his humanity to the Magyar families who came under his protection, and showed his large-hearted sympathy by adopting a Magyar child who had been deserted by its parents. Moreover, Bishop Schaguna, who, it will be remembered, had discouraged the first risings of the Roumanians, now joined in with Puchner's plans, and exerted himself to restrain the violence of his countrymen.

But while Puchner, aided by men like Schaguna, Jancu and Roth, was endeavouring to check the cruelties which his new followers were too ready to inflict, there was needed on the other hand an equally strong influence to restrain the savagery of the Magyar and Szekler. This was the more necessary, because, whatever injustice these races had committed towards the weaker races of Hungary, in the state in which things then stood, the Magyar cause had become identified with the cause of European freedom. Only in the success of the armies which Kossuth was trying to organize, did there seem even the least remaining chance for the overthrow of that Government which wes crushing out the life of Vienna, which had trampled on the freedom of Lombardy, and which threatened to be the complete inheritor of the old system of Metternich. But if the Magyar armies in North Hungary were to achieve either the

military or moral success which such a cause required,
it was necessary that, in Transylvania also, the same
race should deserve and obtain a similar success.
For that purpose, they would need a man who
would be the equal of Puchner both in generalship
and humanity.   For under Puchner's leadership, the
Saxons and Roumanians were gaining in military
prowess, even more than in self-restraint, and Klausenburg had fallen into the hands of the Imperial
forces.

Such was the state of things, when, on December 15,
it was announced that Bem had been appointed by
Kossuth Commander-in-Chief of the Transylvanian
Army.  He at once assembled the officers of the
Army which he was to command, and informed them
that he required from them unconditional obedience.
Those who did not obey, he said, would be shot.
Those who did obey he would know how to reward.
With these few stern words, he dismissed them. This
address was evidently one which might either be
delivered by a mere overweening tyrant, or by a man
of real genius and strong will, who understood the
work that was before him.   A few months served to
show in which class Bem was to be reckoned.
Ignoring the Commissioner, who had been sent down,
he armed and reclad his troops; punished disorder
with a stern hand, but showed such personal sympathy with his followers, that he became known as
" Father Bem; " while his enemies soon learned to
distinguish him from the other leaders by his generosity and humanity to the conquered.   He seems to
have been one of those born leaders of men, who
understand when to be stern, and when to be indul-
gent.   On one occasion an officer doubted if he could

hold a position. Bem told him that he must either
hold it, or be shot; and it was held. On another
occasion his troops, seized by the panic natural to
undisciplined levies, fled before the enemy, leaving
Bem in great danger. He announced afterwards that
he might have had to shoot or flog many of them;
but he would not do the first, because he thought
they might still serve their country; nor the second,
because he would not treat them as beasts; and,
therefore, he must forgive them. With regard to his
military capacity, although the conventional military
critics were disposed to discredit it, yet it could not
be denied that he taught an undisciplined mob to
stand fire before a regular army, to obey discipline,
and even to develope a courage and capacity which
won special applause and honours for the Szekler
nation; that he succeeded in about three months
in completely turning the fortunes of the war in
Transylvania; and at a later period in holding his
own for another two months against the powerful
armies of two nations. His personal daring was
more like that of a knight errant than of a modern
general. On one occasion, after a battle in which
he had been worsted, he saw some Austrians carrying
off one of his cannon. He darted forward alone, exclaiming, " That is my cannon "; and so cowed his
enemies, that they surrendered it at once. On another
occasion he sent an aide-de-camp to call up the rear-
guard of his Army, and found that they had all disappeared, and that he was continuing the struggle
with hardly any followers.

As if to mark the cause for which Bem was fighting
as more distinctly than ever the cause of liberty,
Puchner began, in January, 1849, those negotiations

with the Russians which were finally to stamp the Austrian invasion of Transylvania with the anti-national character which other circumstances of the struggle might have made doubtful. In this matter, as in his original adoption of the Roumanian cause, Puchner seems not so much to have taken the lead as to have keen driven into his position by unavoidable circumstances. Schaguna, whose prominence among the Roumanians had specially marked him out as an object of hostility to the Magyar Government, fled from Hermannstadt on the first news of Bem's arrival in Transylvania, and is believed to have made the first appeal for Russian help. The Roumanians, whose kinsmen of the Principalities (Wallachia and Moldavia) were in some alarm about the intentions of Russia, do not seem to have sympathized warmly with this action of their bishop; but the Saxons were less scrupulous; and the towns of Kronstadt and Hermannstadt sent a formal address to General Lüders, the Russian Commander in Bucharest, asking him to come to their assistance. Lüders answered that the Czar sympathized with the brave defenders of the Austrian throne, and wished to respond to their appeal; but that he was unable to do so without a direct request from the Austrian Commander-in-Chief. Under these circumstances, Puchner felt himself bound to yield to the wishes of the Saxons; some of the Roumanian leaders joined in the appeal; and so, on February 1, formal application was made for Russian help. The Russians do not seem to have come in great numbers, nor with that formal announcement of war which accompanied their later invasion, in June. Bem, at any rate, did not lose courage. Although he had recently been

repulsed by Puchner, he rallied his forces; and, on
March 11, he defeated the Russians before Hermannstadt, and followed up his victory by the capture of
the town.   This signal victory secured, for a time,
the reconquest of Transylvania by the Magyars; and,
if Bem had remained in that province, it is possible
that he would not only have retained the territory
under Magyar rule, but that he might have made
that rule acceptable to the Saxons, and, in time, even
to the Roumanians.

But behind Bem stood the dark figure of one who
had already brought disgrace and injury on the
Magyar cause, and who was still further to degrade
it on this occasion.   This was Ladislaus Csanyi, the
intriguer who had introduced into the election of
Zala County those elements of bribery and intimidation which had compelled Deak to refuse election.
Csanyi now desired to put Hermannstadt to the
sword; but Bem interfered, and the Saxons still
honour his memory as that of the man who saved
their countrymen from massacre and their chief city
from destruction.   Determined to counteract, so far
as he could, the brutal policy of Csanyi, Bem issued
a general amnesty to those who had opposed the
Magyar Government; but, unfortunately, that Government believed that they needed Bem's military talents
more than his civil wisdom; and they despatched
him into the Banat, to clear that province also of
the enemies of Magyar rule.   So, while Bem was
succeeding in battle in the Banat, Csanyi was
undoing his work in Transylvania.  With the approval, apparently, of Kossuth, Csanyi repudiated Bem's amnesty altogether, and established
tribunals in Transylvania for the summary exe-

cution of his enemies and the confiscation of their goods.

There was one victim of this reign of terror whose character and sufferings stand out in a manner which throws a halo over the Saxon cause. Stephan Ludwig Roth had, as above mentioned, distinguished himself by his humanity in the administration of the government of Mediasch under Puchner's rule; and the Magyar officials of the town of Elizabethstadt had sent him an address of thanks for his protection of their town from plunder. But he was hated by the strong partizans of Magyar rule, as the most illustrious embodiment of the feeling in favour of Saxon independence; and his attempts to promote the immigration of Germans into Transylvania had been remembered against him by those who wished to crush out, in Hungary, all national feeling except that of the Magyars. Bem had been so well aware of the hatred which Roth had excited, that he had thought it necessary to give him, in addition to the general amnesty, a special guarantee for his safety. In reliance on this security, Roth had retired to his parish of Meschen, and was living without any apparent fear, when he was suddenly arrested there by the soldiers of Csanyi, and brought, after some delay, to Klausenburg. There he was kept in prison, and, though at first leniently treated, he was, after a time, prevented from holding any communications with his friends. In the meantime, the tribunal which was to decide his fate was not allowed to come to a free decision. The Magyar mob of Klausenburg gathered round the court and demanded his death; and even those of the judges who were convinced of his innocence were terrified into voting for his condemnation. His friends appealed for mercy to Csanyi, but he indignantly rejected all petitions, declaring that Roth had deserved ten deaths.

After his condemnation Roth sent the following letter to his children:—

" Dear Children,—I have just been condemned to death, and in three hours more the sentence will be put into execution.  If anything gives me pain, it is the thought of you, who are without a mother, and who now are losing your father.  But there are good men who will advise and help you for your father's sake.  The Hungarian foundling whom I adopted, I entreat you to continue to take care of; only if its parents should wish for it, they have a nearer claim.  Except for this, I have nothing more in this world.  The children of my church at Meschen, and my Nimisch people I think of in love.  May God make these communities become rich in the fruits of godliness, like fruit-trees whose loaded boughs hang down to the ground!  In my writing-table are the prospectuses of the school and church newspaper which is to be published.  The body of the nation is broken to pieces.  I do not believe in any binding together of its limbs any more.  So much the more do I desire the keeping alive of the spirit which once lived in these forms.  For that purpose I entreat my brother clergy whom I leave behind to take care to carry on this newspaper, in order to keep alive the character, pure manners, and honesty of will of our people.  But, if it is decreed in the Counsels of History that it must perish, may it perish in a manner that shall not bring shame on its ancestors!  Time flies.  I know not if my sick body can honourably support my willing spirit.  All whom I have insulted I heartily entreat for pardon.  For my part, I leave the world

without hate, and pray God to forgive my enemies.
So let the end come in God's name!

"Klausenburg, 11th May, 1849.

"I must add that neither in life nor death have I
been an enemy of the Hungarian nation. May they
believe this, on the word of a dying man, in the
moment when all hypocrisy falls away!"

He was shortly after led out to execution.
When his sentence was read out to him, in which he
was accused of having taken the sword instead of the
Bible, and of having led on the Saxon and Wallack
hordes, he cried out indignantly, "It is not true. I
never carried a sword." He refused to have his
hands bound; and, with his face to the soldiers, he
fell, after the third shot. The captain in command of
the soldiers was so much impressed by the spectacle,
that he exclaimed, "Soldiers, learn from this man
how to die for one's people."

But long before Csanyi's reign of terror had
reached this climax, the aspect of affairs in other
parts of Hungary had gone through important
changes. The removal of Görgei and the appointment of Dembinski had caused great irritation among
the friends of the former. This irritation might be
somewhat excused by the fact that nearly a month
had elapsed between the time when Görgei had sent
his proclamation to Windischgrätz and his deposition
from command; and the deposition even received an
appearance of injustice and hardship from its announcement at the moment when Görgei had just
obtained a victory. But the opposition to this change
of command would have been almost as certain if the
removal had taken place earlier, and under different

circumstances.  It was looked upon as a blow struck
by the politicians of Buda Pesth at the politicians of
the army; and the appointment of a foreigner added
an element of national prejudice to the outburst of
professional irritation.  Moreover, Dembinski seems
to have been exactly the kind of officer whom Görgei
most disliked.  His reputation rested on certain brilliant feats of guerilla warfare in the Polish insurrection of 1830; and of course Görgei and his friends
may have been right in thinking that such a man was
ill fitted to carry on the more regular warfare which
was needed for the defeat of Windischgrätz.  But,
whatever excuse they may have had for opposition to the appointment, they clearly put themselves
in the wrong by their evident determination not to
allow Dembinski a fair chance.  Görgei, indeed, at
first affected to discourage the protests against Dembinski's appointment; but the language in which he
did so was so evidently defiant in intention as to
call forth a censure from his personal friend, the War
Minister Meszaros; nor was it long before Görgei
threw off even this slender mask, and openly defied
Dembinski's authority.

Görgei's faction among the officers was so strong,
and the dislike to Dembinski so general, that the
commanders of divisions at last agreed to demand
the deposition of their chief.  Kossuth came down to
the camp to inquire into the circumstances; and he
found the feeling against Dembinski so violent that he
consented to his removal.  Görgei seems to have
used this opportunity for once more discussing the
political situation with Kossuth; and, strange to say,
he made to him the very proposal which Batthyanyi
had rejected when it was put forward by Jellaciç;

namely, that the War and Finance Ministries should be removed to Vienna. If this proposal had been unsatisfactory when Vienna was free, and Ferdinand on the throne, it could have sounded little short of treason to the cause of Hungary, when Vienna was under the absolute rule of Windischgrätz; and it is not wonderful, therefore, that, though Kossuth was willing to remove Dembinski, he preferred appointing General Vetter as Commander-in-Chief to trusting Görgei with the leadership.

It was at this crisis that the event occurred which was mentioned in the last chapter, and which hastened on the final phase of the movement. Encouraged, as Görgei believed, by the victories of Windischgrätz, Francis Joseph and his advisers suddenly dismissed the Parliament at Kremsier, and proclaimed a Constitution "octroyè" for the occasion. Hungarians of all parties condemned this act as a violation of their old laws and customs, and an assertion of the arbitrary will of the sovereign. For, indeed, the discontent now aroused was far from being confined to the Magyars; and it would have been strange had it been otherwise. The dissolution of the Kremsier Parliament was, even irrespective of all that followed it, the most barefaced act of despotism that had been committed since the March risings of the previous year. Even Ferdinand of Naples could plead that barricades had been thrown up in the streets before his *coup d'état* of May 15. The unfortunate June insurrection at Prague had given a plausible excuse for preventing the meeting of the Bohemian Parliament; the murder of Lamberg had, no doubt, seemed to Ferdinand of Austria to supply at least a palliation for his dissolution of the

Hungarian Diet; the murder of Latour and the persecution of the Bohemian deputies supplied Windischgrätz with sufficient argument for depriving Vienna of its liberties; and even the violent dispersal of the deputies of Berlin could be defended by the King of Prussia by reference to the previous riots of August. But not a single excuse of this kind could, with the least show of plausibility, be urged in defence of the dissolution of the Kremsier Parliament. Indeed, Francis Joseph betrayed the weakness of his case by pleading in his defence the nature of the subjects that had been discussed in the Parliament; and he could not even pretend that it had either exceeded its powers or exercised them in a disorderly manner.

Nor was the Constitution, which was offered as a sequel to this dissolution, any more acceptable than the dissolution itself; and a general protest went up from nearly every race in the Empire. However much the Viennese might, under other circumstances, have liked a Constitution which was centralised at Vienna, they none of them would welcome it when it was combined with the rule of Windischgrätz. The Bohemian leaders felt themselves doubly offended; first by the dissolution of a Parliament to which they had specially trusted for justice; and secondly by the refusal of any real provincial independence to Bohemia. The Croats indignantly denounced the restoration of the military rule on the frontier, and the consequent separation from Croatia of the Slavs who inhabited the frontier district. The Serbs, ever since January, had been complaining of the advance of military rule in the Serb districts, and the gradual diminution of the power of the Voyvode; and they now felt that all their local institutions were

still further endangered by the centralisation of the
new Constitution.   Some of the bitterest protests
came from the Roumanians.   They had been treated
from the first with the greatest contempt by most
of the Imperialist officers; and directly after the
capture of Hermannstadt by Bem, they found themselves suddenly deserted by the Austrian forces,
which were withdrawn into Wallachia.   While they
were still smarting under this treachery, the news of
the new Constitution reached them; and they found
that they were as far off as ever from obtaining that
separate national organization for which they had so
long been pleading; while a part of the Banat, which
they considered specially Roumanian, was to be
placed, by the new arrangement, under the Serbs.

In this state of general discontent, it might have
seemed that Kossuth would have had a fair chance
of rallying round him all the races of the Empire, in
a common desire for local independence, and a common hostility to the rule of Francis Joseph.   But the
divisions and mutual suspicions between the various
races of the Empire had gone too deep to allow of
this change.   As for co-operation between the Bohemians and Germans, even if such a combination had
been possible after the various causes of bitterness
mentioned in the preceding chapters, little good could
be effected by it at this crisis, when both Prague and
Vienna were at the mercy of the conqueror.   The
important question, therefore, was the attitude to be
taken up towards the new Constitution, by the
various races in the Kingdom of Hungary; and here
it must be owned that it was not wholly the fault of
Kossuth, that he did not succeed in combining them
in this emergency.

Many both of the Croats and Serbs expressed plainly their discontent with the treatment which they had received from the House of Austria, but both Croats and Serbs were paralysed by the leaders whom they had accepted. The Banal Council[1] of Croatia protested against the publication of the new Constitution ; but Jellaciç declared that he was bound to see that it was published, and that the Council were only to carry out his orders. In a similar manner, many of the leading Serbs remonstrated with Rajaciç, on his acceptance of the vague promises, which were the substitute in the new Constitution, for those ancient liberties which the Serbs claimed as their due. But Rajaciç maintained his authority over his countrymen, and accepted a place of completer subordination to the Austrian General than that which he had hitherto held. On the other hand, Kossuth seems to have neglected the opportunity offered by the general feeling of discontent, which prevailed at this time among the Serbs and Croats; and it was not till months later, when driven to desperation, that he proposed to make those concessions, which had by that time lost all grace. Towards the Roumanians, indeed, Kossuth seemed disposed to make concessions, by which he hoped to draw them away from the Saxons; and he chose a negotiator, whom he thought well fitted for this purpose. But Jancu distrusted Kossuth's emissary, and perhaps also Kossuth himself; and so the negotiation broke down.

And if Kossuth failed to draw round him, at this crisis, the different races who were discontented with the new Constitution, it was a much stranger fact

[1] The Council which advised the Ban.

that he was unable to maintain the union between the different parties in the Magyar nation itself. This was all the stranger, because just at this time both the personal and political grounds for difference between Kossuth and Görgei seemed to be suddenly removed. Deep as had been Görgei's irritation at the appointment of Vetter, it had naturally been brought to a close by the sudden illness which removed Vetter from the command, and which was followed on March 31 by the appointment of Görgei as provisional Commander-in-Chief; while, as to political opinions, Görgei and Kossuth were both agreed in denouncing the circumstances under which Francis Joseph had been thrust on to the throne of Hungary, and the character and origin of the Constitution which he had just issued. Under these circumstances, it seemed as if there could be no further ground for division between the military party who followed Görgei, and the larger body of Magyars, who accepted Kossuth as their leader. But it soon appeared that this was not the case.

Kossuth and his friends naturally argued that as the only member of the House of Hapsburg who claimed the throne of Hungary was admittedly in an illegal position, the only logical course was to depose the House of Hapsburg from the throne of Hungary; and that as the only Constitution by which the rulers of Austria would consent to link themselves to Hungary was admittedly an illegal Constitution, the only logical course was to separate Hungary from Austria. Görgei and his friends, on the other hand, shrank with horror from the idea of fighting without the authority of a King. They had sworn to obey Ferdinand, and to accept the Constitution of March

1848; they therefore insisted on ignoring the abdication of Ferdinand, and the abolition of that Constitution, and continued to fight, in the name of a King
who did not wish to reign, and on behalf of a Constitution which had ceased to exist.   Kossuth and his
friends, however, were resolved to assert their principles; and on April 14 they issued the celebrated
" Declaration of Independence."

The strongly legal and historical character which
had marked the whole Hungarian movement since
the time of the meeting of the Diet in 1825, still
shows itself even in this semi-revolutionary document.  The Declaration goes back to the first connection of the House of Hapsburg with the throne of
Hungary, and declares that no House had ever had
so good a chance of governing successfully, and had
so misused it.  After mentioning some of the tyrannies
of the earlier Kings of this House, the Declaration
dwells on the fact that while Hungary had often had
to fight for its freedom, it had always been so moderate in its demands that it had laid down its arms as
soon as the King gave a new oath to preserve its
freedom; but these oaths had never been kept, and
for three hundred years this policy had never been
changed.  The people, after each promise, had forgotten the wounds of past years, in exaggerated
magnanimity ; but now the time had come to break
the union.  The House of Hapsburg had united itself
with the enemies of the people, and with robbers and
agitators, in order to oppress the people.  It had
attacked those of its subjects who would not combine
against the Constitution which it had sworn to protect,
or against the independent life of the nation.  It had
attacked with violence the integrity of the country,

though it had sworn to preserve it. It had used a
foreign Power to murder its own subjects and suppress
their lawful freedom. Any one of these crimes was
sufficient reason for depriving the Dynasty of its
throne. The Declaration then goes on to consider
the excuses which the Dynasty offered for its conduct.
As for the independence secured by Hungary in
March, 1848, that was only the confirmation of an
old tradition ; for the Pragmatic Sanction showed
that neither Hungary nor any of the provinces connected with it had ever been absorbed in Austria.
Joseph II. alone had ignored this fact, and his name,
therefore, never appeared in the list of the kings of
Hungary. As for the laws which the Diet had passed
in March, Ferdinand had sanctioned them ; but he
now wished to suppress them. Yet the Hungarians
had taken no advantage of the disturbances in different
parts of the Austrian Empire to secure greater independence for themselves, but had remained content
with what had been granted in March. They had
supported the monarchy; but Ferdinand had tried to
break his oath as soon as it was made. The Government at Vienna had at first tried to act through the
Count Palatine; but, as this combination had weakened
their power, they had gradually withdrawn more and
more power from him. They had tried to impose
customs duties which would have cut off Hungary
from the rest of the world ; and when this method
failed they tried to stir up the different nationalities
against the Hungarian Ministry. The proclamation
proceeds to say that dates and documents prove that
the Archduke Louis, the Archduke Francis Charles,
and the Archduchess Sophia had stirred up the movements in Croatia and Slavonia. They attribute Ferdi-

nand's first denunciation of Jellaciç as a traitor to
the difficulties caused by the war in Italy; but they
accuse him of having played a double part, both in
Croatia and Slavonia, and of having helped the Croats
and Serbs with money and ammunition at the very
time when he was denouncing them as rebels.   They
charge the Serbs with having committed great cruelties
in their rising.   They denounce, as illegal, the scatter-
ing of Hungarian troops in different provinces of the
Austrian Empire, and they declare that it was in consequence of this arrangement that they were unable
to save Fiume from Jellaciç.   They complain of the
order given to the soldiers and commanders of fortresses not to obey the Hungarian Ministry, and to
take orders only from Vienna.   They complain that
the Emperor had made a general of the Slavonic
priest who had headed the rising of the Slovaks in
North Hungary.   They complain of their desertion
by the Archduke Stephen, after his promises of support, and of the intrigues of Latour with Jellaciç
and with other generals against the liberties of Hungary.   Lastly, they complain of the abdication of
Ferdinand in favour of Francis Joseph.   Yet even
Francis Joseph they would have accepted had he
claimed his rights in a legal manner ; but he had
threatened to conquer Hungary by force, and had,
for the conquest of Transylvania, called in those
Russians who had crushed out the liberties of Rou-
mania.   They further stated that, although at first
the Hungarians had been driven back, they had now
recovered their ground in Transylvania, cleared North
Hungary of foes, suppressed the Serb rising, and
defeated the Austrians in five battles.   Under these
circumstances they now declared Hungary independent

of the House of Hapsburg, and appointed Kossuth as their President.

Kossuth's supremacy in Hungary had been an important fact for a considerable time past, and had been due, not only to his personal qualities, but to the gradual retirement from public life of most of the leading statesmen who had played a part in the earlier phases of the struggle against the ruling powers in Vienna. Batthyanyi had abandoned all direct initiative in Hungarian politics ever since his resignation of the Premiership, and had only attempted to mediate between the contending armies, a mediation which had been scornfully rejected by Windischgrätz. Deak had, from the first, announced that he was unfit for revolutionary propaganda; and, after devoting himself, in the early days of the March Ministry, to the compilation of a code of laws and the administrative work of his office, he had gradually assumed the same position of mediator which Batthyanyi had desired, and with equal want of success. Wesselenyi was now old and blind; and, though he had consented to go with Eötvös on that deputation to the Vienna Assembly which had been repulsed by the Bohemian Deputies, neither he nor Eötvös now took any regular part in public affairs. Szechenyi, horrified at the results which, as he considered, had flowed from his early encouragement of Magyar feeling, lost his reason, and was at this time under restraint. Thus, of the statesmen who had been prominent in Hungary during the struggle against Metternich, Kossuth was the only one who could still be said to be before the public.

Kossuth's unrivalled eloquence, and his keen sympathy, both with the intensity and the narrowness of

Magyar feeling, had given him a force which none of
the other leaders of the movement had ever possessed;
and his discovery of the military genius of Bem had
secured him an influence in Transylvania which considerably increased the strength of his position.  On
the other hand, his intolerant attitude towards the
subject races of Hungary had marked him out in a
special manner as the object of their hatred; while
his contempt for ordinary military arrangements, his
growing distrust of Görgei, and last, but perhaps not
least, the belief among many military men that he
was deficient in physical courage, tended to strengthen
against him a formidable party in the army which
was eventually to prove too strong for him.  But, if
the divided state of Hungarian feeling threw formidable difficulties in the way of Kossuth, he could find
compensations in the condition of the forces opposed
to him.  Windischgrätz does not seem to have been
reckoned, by military critics, a considerable general.
Stratimiroviç, whatever military qualities he may
have possessed, was continually held in check by the
cautious policy of Rajaciç.  Puchner, who had succeeded in giving such force to the Roumanian rising,
was becoming an object of suspicion to the more conventional Austrian generals, and was shortly to be
removed from Transylvania; while a cause of weakness, which was perhaps still more important, was to
be found in the withdrawal from the country of a
large body of Austrian and Croatian soldiers, who
were being despatched against the new Government
of the Roman States.

For in Italy, too, the champions of liberty were
preparing for their final struggle, though under
rather different auspices from those under which it

was being fought out in Hungary. On the very day when the Declaration of Independence was published in Hungary, Mazzini, Saffi, and Armellini, who had been elected Triumvirs of the Roman Republic, after the failure of Charles Albert's final war, appeared in the Assembly for the first time in their new capacity. They had no light task before them. Apart from the enemies who were threatening the Republic from outside, there were dangers arising from the feelings of the different parties within the Roman State. The deposition of the Pope had undoubtedly given a shock to the feelings of many strong Liberals, of a much keener, and if one may say so, more intelligible kind, than the deposition of the House of Hapsburg could possibly give to any Hungarian leader. Even Castellani, the Ambassador of the Venetian Republic, hesitated to identify the cause of his city with that of the opponents of the Pope; while the feeling among the priests of the Roman States had been shown by a formidable conspiracy in Imola and Ascoli. General Zucchi, who had taken part in this conspiracy, had even attempted to force his way into the Neapolitan territory, in order to put himself under the authority of the Pope. Garibaldi had defeated this attempt, and Zucchi had been sent as a prisoner to Rome; but the conspiracy was not forgotten; and, when the Triumvirs came into power, they found that these outbursts of priestly opposition were provoking savage reprisals on the part of the Republicans.

While Saffi had been only Minister of the Interior, and Mazzini only a private member of the Assembly, they had both warned the Government of the probability of this danger; and they now found that a Society had been formed at Ancona which threatened

death to the enemies of Liberalism.   The Triumvirs
first sent down two officers, who tried to organize the
local leaders into a committee for preserving public
order ; but, though their emissaries were satisfied
with their own action, the Triumvirs were less easily
contented.   Felice Orsini was sent down with full
powers to put down the insurrection; and, if necessary, to declare Ancona in a state of siege.   He at
once arrested twenty men, called out the National
Guard, put down opposition by force, and carried off
his prisoners to Rome, where they were shut up in
the Castle of St. Angelo.   From Ancona Orsini went
on to Ascoli, where he condemned three of the most
dangerous persons to be shot, and sequestrated the
goods of a cardinal, who had stirred up the clerical
insurrection.   But the Austrian forces were now
advancing into the Roman territory; and Orsini was
compelled to retire to Rome.

Even in the capital the Triumvirs had to use strong
measures to check the fierce feeling against the priests.
This feeling had just been roused to an unusual
height by special discoveries of priestly cruelty.   In
sweeping away the various irregular tribunals, which
had grown up under the papal tyranny, the Triumvirs
had to deal with the question of the Inquisition.
They appropriated the former offices of that celebrated institution, as dwellings for the poor; but, in
making the buildings available for this purpose, they
threw open the secret dungeons, and discovered prisoners who were slowly dying of their imprisonment.
One bishop, who had remained there since the time
of Leo XII., had absolutely lost the power of walking.
The horrible instruments of torture, which were found
in the same place, excited still further the indignation

of the people; and that feeling found yet a new cause for its expression, when a book was discovered in the library of the Inquisition, containing the secrets of the principal families of Italy, which had been obtained through the revelations of confessors. Several of the fiercer spirits in Rome at once made an attack on the pulpits and confessionals, and burnt some of them in the Piazza del Popolo. These tumults were sternly checked by the Triumvirs; and they succeeded in protecting from the popular vengeance the convent in which the chief Inquisitor lived. But while they protected the persons and private property of the priests, they appropriated the greater part of the ecclesiastical lands to the support of the poor, arranging that every family of three persons should have as much land as could be managed by a pair of oxen. At the same time the jurisdiction of the clergy over the universities and schools was taken away.

While the attention of the Government was thus devoted to the restoration of internal order, and the carrying out of necessary reforms, they did not neglect the vigorous measures which were needed for the resistance to foreign enemies. The forces which had been rather carelessly scattered in the outlying provinces of the Roman State, were concentrated by the Triumvirs near Bologna. That gallant little city had been in a state of alarm ever since the early part of February, when the Austrian forces had again attacked Ferrara; and the difficulties of communication between these two cities had increased the alarm of the Bolognese, though it had also strengthened their eagerness for resistance. But even before this Austrian invasion, the Roman Republicans had been alarmed at the threats issued by another Power.

Three days after the flight of the Pope, General
Cavaignac announced in the French Assembly that
he had sent three frigates to Civita Vecchia to secure
the safety of His Holiness.   This expedition had
excited much opposition in France; and, during the
subsequent contest for the Presidency, the following
letter was addressed by one of the candidates to the
editor of a French newspaper:—

" MR. EDITOR,
        " Knowing that my agreement to the vote for
the Expedition to Civita Vecchia has been remarked
upon, I think myself bound to declare that, whatever
may have been decided about the arrangements suitable for guaranteeing the liberty and authority of the
chief Pontiff, nevertheless I cannot approve by my
vote a military demonstration that appears dangerous
both to the sacred interests that they pretend to
protect, and that has a tendency to compromise
European peace.
                        " Yours respectfully,
                " LOUIS NAPOLEON BUONAPARTE.
" December 2, 1848."

As this pacific candidate had been shortly after
elected President of the French Republic, there seemed
little fear that an expedition " tending to compromise
European peace," would again be entered upon by
France ; and the Mountain of the French Assembly
had lately sent greetings to the Roman Republic.

Since then the immediate danger to Rome seemed
to come rather from the North than from the West,
the Triumvirs watched with much anxiety the hesitating attitude of Guerrazzi and the Tuscan Government.   So eager had the leaders of the Roman

Assembly been for a union between Tuscany and the Roman States that they had even offered to Montanelli and Guerrazzi places in the first Triumvirate, which had been formed before Mazzini and Saffi had been called to power. Guerrazzi, however, had refused to accept this offer; and, while declaring his desire for union with Rome, he professed his inability to find a means for effecting that union. Indeed, Guerrazzi held an almost impossible position. Though unable to make up his mind to accept a Republican Government, he was yet determined to resist any interference, either by Piedmontese or Austrians, in favour of the former Government of Tuscany. And while he still seemed to cherish Italian ideas, he felt that the defeat of Charles Albert had taken away the hopes for any satisfactory continuance of the War of Independence. Under these circumstances the champions of the restoration of the Grand Duke naturally gained ground in Tuscany. Guerrazzi, distrusted alike by Republicans and Royalists, was unable either to resist this movement, or to guide it according to his own theories; and on April 12 the Municipality of Florence took the matter out of the hands both of Guerrazzi and the Assembly, and decreed the recall of the Grand Duke.

This catastrophe, though a subject of regret, could scarcely have caused much surprise to the leaders of the Roman Republic. A feeling of far deeper pain must have been roused by the final failure of the earliest of all the struggles for liberty of this period. The *coup d'état* at Naples of May 15, 1848, though it had shattered the hopes of the Neapolitans, had only intensified the zeal of the Sicilians in their struggle against Ferdinand. As they had just de-

posed him from the throne, and proclaimed the Duke
of Genoa as their King, they thought themselves safe
against the restoration of Neapolitan rule; and the
Ambassadors of France and England tried to persuade
the King of Naples not to send an expedition to
Sicily. He refused, however, to listen to these
remonstrances; the expedition sailed; and, by his
bombardment of Palermo, Ferdinand won for himself
throughout Sicily the title of Il Re Bombardatore,
which was quickly shortened into Bomba. Ruggiero
Settimo, who had taken part in the struggles of 1812
and 1821, was placed at the head of the Sicilian
Government, and Garibaldi was invited to come to
defend the island. Garibaldi, however, did not arrive;
and the chief defence of the island was entrusted to
the Polish General Mieroslawski, who, having failed
to save Posen from the hands of the Prussians, had
become a kind of knight errant of liberty in other
parts of Europe. He brought, however, but little
good to the causes which he defended. He quarrelled
with the Italian General Antonini, and was so often
defeated, that the Sicilians began to fear treachery,
and at last compelled him to resign his command.
The struggle had, in fact, now become hopeless; and
on April 17, 1849, the Sicilian Parliament decided to
meet no longer. Then Ruggiero Settimo called his
friends together, and declared that he was ready to
undergo all his troubles again, if they decided to
continue the contest. But they believed that the case
was now desperate, and voted for peace. Then
Settimo consulted the National Guard, but also in
vain; and finding that any further efforts were useless, he resigned his Presidency, and left the island.
The separateness of the Sicilian movement lessened,

no doubt, in some degree the importance of this defeat; but the gallantry of their struggle had excited much sympathy in Rome; and their fall set free the Neapolitan forces for action against the Roman Republic.

This addition to the dangers which were harassing the Republic would not perhaps have been so formidable had not a new and more important enemy begun to show signs of hostility at the same period. The election of Louis Napoleon as President of the French Republic had been hailed with some satisfaction both in Venice and Rome; and, after the Roman Republic had been established, two envoys were sent to Paris, who reminded the President of the share he had taken in one of the insurrections against Gregory XVI. Louis Napoleon replied that the time of Gregory XVI. had gone by in Rome, and that his youth was also gone by. Both remarks were undoubtedly true, nor were they in themselves very alarming; but Ledru Rollin, one of the few Frenchmen who really sympathized with Italy, warned Mazzini that danger was coming; and the nature of the danger soon became apparent. On April 16 Odillon Barrot moved in the French Assembly a proposal for a vote of twelve hundred thousand francs for an expedition to Italy; an expedition, he said, which was not to restore the Pope; but to protect liberty and humanity. On April 20 General Oudinot took the command of the expedition, and told his followers that his object was to maintain the old legitimate French influence, and to protect the destinies of Italy from the predominance of the stranger, and of a party who were really in a minority. So kindly was the tone of the French Ministry towards the Romans,

that Colonel Frapolli, one of the envoys of the Roman
Republic, obtained the leave of the French President
to organize a French Legion, which was to fight for
the defence of Rome, and to be commanded by Pierre
Buonaparte. But Pierre Buonaparte suddenly resigned his command; the prefect was ordered to
hinder the embarkation of the Legion; and a large
supply of muskets, which had been bought by the
Roman Republic, were confiscated by the French
Government. In the meantime Oudinot had set sail,
and on April 24 he appeared before Civita Vecchia.

About the time when the French troops were land-
ing, there arrived at the same place a very different
force. The leader of this force was Luciano Manara,
who had fought so gallantly in the " Five Days " of
Milan, and who had afterwards been so hampered by
Casati and Charles Albert in his attempt to rescue the
Southern Tyrol from Austrian rule. He, like others,
had been disappointed by the failure of Charles
Albert's final war; but he had refused to join in the
Genoese insurrection, which followed the defeat at
Novara, and had preferred to set out with 8,000 men
to help the Roman Republic. The difficulties thrown
in the way of their march were, however, so great that
only 600 remained with Manara by the time that he
reached Civita Vecchia. Oudinot, with extraordinary
impudence, disputed the right of the Lombards to
interfere on behalf of Rome; and he even tried to
persuade them that the cause of Rome was so distinct
from that of Lombardy, that the Lombards could
consistently join their forces with the French against
Rome. Manara indignantly repelled the suggestion;
and then Oudinot in vain attempted to exact a promise that the Lombard forces should not act against

him until the 4th of May. Manara, having refused this further demand, Oudinot was forced to allow the Lombards to pass; and Manara marched to Rome to tell the Romans how the French Republic was preparing to defend the cause of " liberty and humanity."

In spite of this plain evidence of his intentions, Oudinot still attempted to play his double part; and, since his utterance about the government of a party in a minority had alarmed the inhabitants of Civita Vecchia, he authorised the Secretary of the Legation to declare the sympathy of the French for the Romans, and to assure the citizens of Civita Vecchia that the French Army had only come to defend them against the Austrians. Mannucci, the Governor of Civita Vecchia, had wished to oppose the first landing of the French; but he was overborne by the Chamber of Commerce and the Municipal Council, who were convinced that the French could not really intend to destroy the freedom which they so much professed to cherish. No sooner, however, had Oudinot effected a landing, than he announced that he would not protect the Anarchical Government of Rome, which had never been officially recognised. The Municipality became alarmed; and Oudinot again altered his tone, and declared that the French would respect the vote of the majority of the population, and did not desire to impose any special form of Government upon them. In spite of the warnings given by Oudinot's previous proclamation, the Municipal Council consented to admit him into the town; and, no sooner was he there, than he disarmed the battalion which was to have defended the town; and still further showed his zeal for the interests of " Liberty and humanity," by suppressing a printing office in Civita Vecchia, because it had recently printed an address in which the Papacy was condemned.

In the meantime the news had spread to Rome; and the Assembly were debating how they should receive Oudinot. So deep was the conviction of the reality of the French zeal for freedom, that Armellini actually suggested that Oudinot should be received as a friend. But, while the Assembly were debating, Mazzini entered the hall, and announced that Colonel le Blanc had confessed that the expedition was sent to restore the Papacy. Thereupon the Assembly voted that the Triumvirs should have power to resist force with force. But another difficulty arose; the officers of the National Guard declared that they did not believe their soldiers would fight. Thereupon Mazzini ordered that the battalions of the Guards should defile next morning in front of the Quirinal, where the Assembly were meeting; and, as the Guards passed, he put to them the question whether they were for peace or war. A loud shout of " Guerra, guerra!" answered his appeal; and the defence was at once resolved on.

In every district the heads of the people and the representatives of the Assembly were to organize the defence of every inch of the country. Barricades were thrown up; arms were to be given to all the people; while the municipality undertook to provide them with corn, meat, and other eatables. At the same time all foreigners, and particularly all Frenchmen living in Rome, were to be placed under the protection of the nation. Anyone who injured them was to be punished as having violated the honour of Rome. With regard to the actual soldiers to be used in the first defence of the city, they were arranged as follows:—the 1st brigade, commanded by Garibaldi, guarded the line outside the walls, which extends from the Porta Portese to the Porta San Pancrazio. The 2nd brigade, commanded by Colonel Masi, was drawn up before the Porta Cavalleggieri, the Vatican, and the Porta Angelica. The 3rd, under Colonel Savini, stood in reserve in the Piazza Navona. Colonel Galletti commanded the 4th, which was stationed in the Piazza Cesarini; while a reserve force under General Galletti, in which Manara and his Lombard volunteers were included, was held back for the present, to come up when needed. The whole of the forces were supervised by General Avezzana, who had organized the insurrection in Genoa after the defeat at Novara, and who now acted apparently both as Minister of War and Commander-in-Chief.

On April 29 Avezzana took his staff up to Monte Mario, from which point he could see the French army advancing from Civita Vecchia. As they marched along the road, the French saw everywhere a singular inscription painted upon the walls and posts. It ran as follows:—"Article 5 of the preamble of the French Constitution. The French Republic respects foreign nationalities as it intends to make its own respected. It does not undertake any war of conquest. It will never use its own forces against the liberty of any people." Whether as a kind of answer to this challenge, or in contempt of it, Oudinot announced to his troops that they came to liberate Rome from the factious party which had expelled the Pope, and which had answered his words of conciliation with ill-considered provocations.

It was at 11.30 a.m. on April 30 that the French and Roman armies first came into collision. Gari-

baldi advanced from Porta San Pancrazio to meet
the French, who were entering the grounds of the
Villa Pamfili, and who, hearing the bells of the city
ring for the attack, supposed that an insurrection
had broken out in favour of the Pope, and that they
would have an easy victory. Garibaldi, however,
repelled them, after a sharp fight, and made 300 prisoners. But the main attack of the French was in the
meantime directed against the Porta Angelica. There
one of the French captains had hoped to lead a column
into Rome by a secret way near the Vatican. But a
fire was poured on the advancing column from the
Papal gardens, while the troops from Monte Mario
attacked them in the rear. The battle lasted for four
hours. The French captain Picarde managed at first
to drive back the University battalion; but as he
advanced, Colonel Arcioni at the head of a regiment
of the Lombard exiles attacked him on one flank,
and Galletti at the head of the National Guard on
the other; finally Garibaldi, having disposed of his
original opponents at the Villa Pamfili, charged the
French force, and compelled them to lay down their
arms.

Several acts of special valour marked this battle.
One officer, named Montaldi, having been surrounded
by the French, was beaten to his knees, and fought
on with only a piece of his sword left. He had
fought under Garibaldi at Monte Video, and was a
Genoese by birth. Ugo Bassi[1] distinguished himself
by riding about the field urging the Romans to
battle. His horse was killed under him, and, as he

---

[1] A Bolognese priest, who followed Garibaldi partly in the
character of a chaplain and partly as aide-de-camp. See "The
Disciples," by Mrs. E. H. King.

was embracing it with tears, the French came up and took him prisoner. Garibaldi himself was wounded; but would not allow it to be known until the battle was over, when he sent privately for the doctor.

On the following day the battle was renewed; the people flocking to the defence of the walls, and the French sharp-shooters being finally driven out from the Pamfili gardens. Garibaldi would now have been able to cut off the French retreat and destroy their army; but the Triumvirs, though they had no faith in Oudinot's promises, believed that, if the French were generously treated, the Republican feeling would awake again in France and overthrow the Government, or defeat their plans; but that, if they were driven to extremities, the French vanity would hinder even the most consistent Republicans from opposing the war. On these grounds, they allowed the French to retreat, granted them a short truce, and set free the prisoners who had been captured.

But the hope of any change of feeling in the French was soon found to be utterly vain. A debate, indeed, had been begun in the French Assembly soon after the sailing of the expedition, and a Committee had been appointed to enquire into the object of the expedition; but Jules Favre, the chairman of that Committee, reported that the Government had no intention of making France a party to the overthrow of the Roman Republic; and that it only interfered in order that, under the French flag, humanity might be respected; and that a limit might be placed on the pretensions of Austria. In spite, therefore, of the opposition of Ledru Rollin, the money for the expedition had been voted by 325 against 283. But even Jules Favre could not be entirely blinded by

such phrases as these, when considered in the light
of Oudinot's actions; and on May 8 the National
Assembly invited the Government to take, without
delay, the necessary measures for preventing the
expedition to Italy from being diverted from the
scope assigned to it; and they therefore decided
to send Ferdinand Lesseps to negotiate with the
Triumvirs for terms of peace.

In the meantime, the Roman Republic realized that
it had to guard itself against two other enemies. On
May 2, a Neapolitan army was found to be on its way
to Rome. On the 4th, Garibaldi marched to Pales-
trina, and, with the help of Manara and his Lombard
battalion, utterly defeated the Neapolitan forces.
Just at the same time, the Bolognese became aware
that the threatened attack of the Austrians was about
to become a reality. Ferrara was occupied on May 7;
but, even with the Austrian troops present in the city,
the Municipal Council of Ferrara voted, by thirty-
seven to three, in favour of the Roman Republic.
Such a protest was undoubtedly of use in proving
the earnestness of the Roman provinces on behalf of
the new Government. But something more was
expected from a city so heroic in its traditions as
Bologna. On May 6 it had been announced by the
President of the Municipality that medals were about
to be distributed in memory of August 8, 1848. On
May 8 it was announced that the Austrians were
advancing upon Bologna. In that city, as in Rome,
the internal defence was organized in special districts
under special leaders, while the National Guard and
the University battalion were to fight side by side
with the regular troops. By nine o'clock in the
morning of the 8th the Austrians were at the gates

of Bologna, and before eleven o'clock fierce struggles
had taken place at the Porta Galliera, the Porta San
Felice, and the Porta Saragozza.   The people indignantly refused every proposal for capitulation, and
at about four o'clock the Austrians began to bombard
the city.   Before the end of the day, the President
had resigned his office, believing that resistance was
useless; but the Municipality having in vain endeavoured to obtain the terms which they had hoped
for, the assault was renewed, and the Austrians dis-
charged rockets into the city from the bell-tower of
the Franciscan convent.   A special Commission was
appointed to carry on the struggle, and the band of
one of the regiments, standing under the tree of
Liberty in the Piazza San Petronio, encouraged the
combatants with music and songs.   The struggle,
however, was a desperate one, and, on May 10, it was
again necessary to send a deputation to ask for a
truce.   But the combat was soon renewed, and the
Bolognese troops were so eager in the attack that the
general had to warn them against firing off their
pieces needlessly.   The pastrycooks were ordered to
suspend the making of mere confectionary, in order
that there might be more bread for the defenders of
the city, and reinforcements were expected from the
country districts of the Romagna.   General Wimpffen,
who was leading the Austrian troops, denounced the
defence as "the stupid work of a blind faction;" but
the Provisional Government answered that the proclamation signed by Marshal Wimpffen, and for-
warded by him to the magistrates, having come
without any accompanying evidence, could not be
received by them.   Weary of acting merely on the
defensive, the Bolognese made a sortie from the Porta

Maggiore, repelled an attack of the Austrians, and succeeded in joining a body of the Romagnoli, who were coming to the relief of the city. But the chances of uniting with the outside world became less and less; for the Austrian troops drew ever more closely round the city, and, on the 15th, the bombardment was renewed. Then a number of the citizens requested leave to go to Rome, to find out how things were going on there, in order that they might know what was still required of them at headquarters. But this proposal seems to have been a mere utterance of despair; for, on the 16th, it became necessary to abandon the defence and arrange for terms of surrender.

While the Bolognese were engaged in this desperate struggle, Ferdinand Lesseps had arrived in Rome, and was rapidly becoming converted to the belief that the Republican Government was the free choice of the people, and that it was better able to maintain order than the Papacy had been; while a conversation with Mamiani had shown him that even the so-called Moderate Liberals were unwilling to act against the Republic. But, though Lesseps was honest enough to confess these facts, his vanity, both personal and national, prevented him from making the natural inference that neither he nor Oudinot were needed in Rome. He, therefore, proposed that the Roman States should request the paternal protection of the French Republic; that the Roman populations should pronounce freely on their form of government; that Rome should receive the French as their friends; and that Roman and French troops should act together in defence of the city. The Assembly rejected these proposals, on the ground that Rome had no need of

protection, and that the name of the Roman Republic
was not mentioned in the negotiation; and they
further complained that, on May 19, while the truce
was still in force, the French soldiers had crossed the
Tiber.   Then the Triumvirs proposed, in their turn,
that the Roman Republic should acknowledge the
help offered by the French nation against foreign
intervention; that the Constitution which had been
adopted by the General Assembly should be sanctioned by a popular vote; that Rome should welcome
the French soldiers as brothers; but that they should
stay outside the city till the Roman Republic called
for them.   These proposals were accepted, with some
modifications, by Lesseps, within the time of the
truce; and he left Rome, well satisfied with Mazzini,
still better with himself.

Great, however, was the indignation of this unfortunate diplomatist, when, on reaching the camp of
Oudinot, he found that the general, without waiting
for the expiration of the truce, had suddenly occupied Monte Mario!   Lesseps was divided between his
feelings as a man of honour and his unwillingness to
oppose his countrymen.   He threatened at first that
if the order for assault were not withdrawn, he would
himself go back to Rome and give the alarm; but
when, on his return to the city, the Triumvirs questioned him about the breach of the truce, he assured
them that Monte Mario had only been occupied in
order to prevent its falling into the hands of the
French reinforcements, which were on their way to
Rome.   The fact was that, from first to last, Lesseps
had been the dupe of the unscrupulous men who
were ruling France.   While he had been entrusted
with apparently peaceful negotiations, secret instruc-

tions had been sent to Oudinot to the following
effect:—"Tell the Romans that we do not wish to
join with the Neapolitans against them.  Continue
your negotiations in the sense of your declaration.
We are sending you reinforcements.  Wait for them.
Manage to enter Rome by agreement with the inhabitants; and if you should be compelled to assault it,
do it in the manner that shall be most likely to secure
success."  Oudinot fully understood his instructions.
On May 31 he scornfully rejected the convention
which had been accepted by Lesseps; and on the
same day Lesseps received his recall to Paris, and
Oudinot received orders to take Rome by force.

In the meantime an unfortunate occurrence had
called attention to another danger which was threatening the Roman Republic.  General Roselli had
now been appointed Commander-in-Chief of the
Roman army; but he found it very difficult to control Garibaldi.  After the defeat of the Neapolitan
forces, Garibaldi had desired to push on to Velletri.
Roselli forbad him to do so; but Garibaldi disobeyed
the orders of his chief, and marched forward.  Part
of the troops who followed him had not learned to
stand fire, and fled at the first attack.  Garibaldi was
in such danger that he was obliged to send to Roselli
for fresh troops.  With the help of these reinforcements, Garibaldi drove back the Neapolitans; but he
then disobeyed Roselli's orders for the second time,
marched forward to Velletri, and entered it on
May 20.  Fierce recriminations followed between the
friends of Garibaldi and those of Roselli; Garibaldi
and his friends maintaining that, but for Roselli's
delay, the victory would have been more complete;
the supporters of Roselli declaring that, if it had not

been for Garibaldi's rashness, Ferdinand himself, and
a great part of his army, would have fallen into the
hands of the Romans. Roselli further demanded
that Garibaldi should be summoned before a Court-
Martial for his disobedience to orders. But the
Triumvirs felt that there would be a certain incon-
gruity in such a trial, which could only lead to
mischief, and they persuaded Roselli to abandon his
proposal. Garibaldi's influence, indeed, was strong,
not only among his soldiers, but also among the
members of the Assembly; and Sterbini, who seems
generally to have suspected all existing Governments,
demanded that Garibaldi should be made Dictator,
and that Roselli's command should be taken from
him. This proposal, however, the Assembly rejected,
and, on June 3, declared itself in permanence.

On that very day Oudinot gave another proof of
his peculiar ideas of French honour. The day
before, he had promised to defer the attack until
June 4. The grounds of the Villa Pamfili lie at a
short distance from the Porta San Pancrazio, and were
then more thickly wooded than they are now. On
the night of June 2 they were occupied by three
companies of Bolognese. These soldiers, trusting
to the honour of Oudinot, were sleeping peace-
fully, when suddenly two French divisions entered
the wood. They surrounded and captured 200 of
the soldiers; but the remaining 200 retreated fighting,
before a body of 8,000 French. Garibaldi hastened
up with reinforcements, and the fight lasted from
2 A.M. till 6 P.M. on June 3. Four times were
the houses in the grounds of the Villa Pamfili
lost and won. The walls shook with the thunder of
the French and Roman artillery; and the houses

were filled with the dead and wounded of both armies. But the treachery of Oudinot had been successful in securing him so good a position, that the houses at last remained in the hands of the French, although they were so ruined that they afforded them very little protection.

This struggle seemed only to rouse the energies of the Romans to new efforts. Between the Villa Pamfili and the Porta San Pancrazio, stood an old house which, from its shape, was known as the Vascello or little ship; and it was by the walls of this house that, for nearly a month from this time, General Medici and Garibaldi held their own against the numbers, the training, and the treachery of the French. Nothing could exceed the enthusiasm of the Romans in the defence of their city. The walls were crowded with people during the fight; youths, not able yet to bear arms, rushed into the crash of battle. And girls went, while the cannon was still firing, to search for the dead, to encourage the combatants, and to heal the wounded. But treachery steadily gained ground upon valour. Enrico Dandolo, a young captain in Manara's regiment, was about to attack a company of Frenchmen, when the French captain cried out, "We are friends!" Dandolo ordered the attack to be suspended, and advanced to the Frenchman, holding out his hand. The French at once fired, and Dandolo and more than a third of his company fell dead. Oudinot, however, over-estimated the credulity of the Romans; for on June 12 he demanded to be admitted into Rome, on the ground that his intentions had been misunderstood, and that he wished to secure Roman liberty. When, however, he was reminded of his violation of Lesseps's agree-

ment, he showed his zeal for Roman liberty by proceeding to bombard the city.

But there were still some Frenchmen who held
different views from Oudinot's on the subject of their
country's honour.  On the very day when the bombardment of Rome began, Ledru Rollin and his
friends, having in vain tried to secure a condemnation
of the Roman expedition from the French Assembly,
took up arms for a final effort to vindicate the honour
of France against its faithless rulers.  But the revo-
tionary force of France had been wasted in the
Socialist insurrection of the previous year; and, after
a gallant struggle, the champions of French honour
and liberty were suppressed by General Changarnier.
The failure of this effort must, no doubt, have been
terribly disappointing to those Romans who had
hoped to the last that France would vindicate herself
against those who were dishonouring her.  And, as
if to bring home to the Romans how isolated their
position was becoming as defenders of liberty, there
came to them, shortly after, the news of the final
downfall of German liberty.

Ever since April 24, when the King of Prussia
refused the crown of Germany, he had been following
a steady course of opposition to the Liberal movements in favour of German unity; and on May 24
he had recalled the Prussian Deputies from the
Frankfort Assembly.  This had encouraged the
other Princes of Germany to dissolve their local
parliaments and recall their subjects from the Frankfort Parliament ; while the strengthening of the
troops near Frankfort seemed to limit the freedom
of debate among the few deputies who remained.
At last, on June 6, the few remaining representa-

tives of German unity decided to transfer their place
of meeting from Frankfort to Stuttgart.  The Baden
Republicans had in the meantime taken the stronger
course of appealing for the last time to insurrection;
but both the constitutional and the revolutionary
attempt to save the liberties of Germany proved
hopeless.  On June 18 the remnant of the German
Parliament was dispersed by the Würtemberg soldiers; the Baden rising failed, to a great extent from
the quarrels between the Polish general Mieroslawski
and the Baden general Sigel; and the Prussian soldiers
trampled out the last remains of German liberty.

In the meantime the Austrians were capturing
city after city in the Roman provinces; and the
French were pressing nearer to the city.  But the
enthusiasm of the Romans did not slacken.  As
Garibaldi went through the hospitals to visit the
wounded, several of the sufferers sprang from their
beds to embrace his knees, with cries of " Papa,
papa"; and the women exerted themselves gallantly
to relieve the sufferings of the wounded.  The French
did not even now seem absolutely certain of victory;
for when a sortie, planned by Garibaldi on June
22, had ended in a fiasco, a certain M. Corcelles
attempted to reopen diplomatic negotiations.  But
Mazzini, warned by his experience of Lesseps, sternly
repelled all proposals for negotiation; and the struggle
was renewed.  The state of the Roman Republic was,
however, really desperate.  On June 24 came the news
that, after twenty-five days' struggle, Ancona had
fallen into the hands of the Austrians, who had
almost immediately violated the understanding on
which it had been surrendered.

In the meantime the French slowly advanced in

the struggle by the Vascello, Medici continually driving them back. Many of the houses were battered down, but the inhabitants were provided by the Triumvirs with fresh lodgings in the deserted houses of the Cardinals. When the French knocked down part of the walls, the citizens picked up the stones to repair them. At last, however, on June 29, Oudinot resolved to make a final effort, and directed his forces against Garibaldi's house, which was known as the Villa Spada. Twice the invaders attacked this house, and twice they were repelled. Then they succeeded in capturing a barricade which had been raised in front of the house; but again the Romans recaptured it. Garibaldi fought in the midst of his followers, singing a war-song; and more than a hundred of his soldiers fell round him. Seven times the barricade was taken and retaken; the gallant Manara was killed; and at last, after twelve hours' fighting, it was discovered that the Porta San Pancrazio was no longer tenable.

On June 30 the Roman Assembly met, and Mazzini propounded to them three alternatives. Either they should continue the defence, which now seemed impossible; or they should yield altogether; or, thirdly, they should cut their way out into the provinces, and continue the struggle there. Mazzini strongly urged the third course. While the debate was still proceeding, Garibaldi in his red shirt, covered with mud, sprang into the Assembly. He declared that further defence was impossible, unless they were prepared to abandon the Trastevere, and break down the bridges. Under these circumstances, he supported Mazzini's recommendation, that they should cut their way out into the provinces, and

carry on the struggle there.  Cernuschi, however, proposed the following resolution:—" The Roman Constituent Assembly abandons a defence which has
become impossible, and remains at its post."  This
motion was carried; the Triumvirs resigned their
post to the Municipality, and a new Triumvirate was
elected to carry out the terms of peace.

Then Garibaldi called round him his followers in
the Piazza San Pietro, and addressed them as follows:
—" I have nothing to give you but hunger, sufferings,
and battles; the bare earth for your bed, and the
burning sun for your refreshment.  Yet let him who
does not yet disbelieve in the fortune of Italy follow
me."  He then marched out from the Porta San
Giovanni, followed by 4,000 men.  They made their
way to the northern part of the Roman States; but
after much suffering and privation, they were forced
to abandon the struggle.  Ugo Bassi and others fell
into the hands of the Austrians, and were shot.
Garibaldi and a small remnant of his followers succeeded in escaping from the country.

In the meantime the Roman Municipal Council
attempted to make terms with Oudinot; but finding
it impossible to secure honourable conditions, they
declared that they yielded only to force.  On July 3
the French troops entered Rome; and while they
marched through the city they found all the shops
closed, and heard from every side the cries of " Death
to Cardinal Oudinot!  Death to the soldiers of the
Pope!  Death to the Croats of France!"  On the
same day the Roman Assembly proclaimed from the
Capitol the Constitution of the Republic.  On the
next day a regiment of French infantry dissolved
the Assembly by force; and soon after a Commis-

sion of three Cardinals was appointed to govern Rome.

The hopes of Italy now centred in Venice, where, ever since the abandonment of Milan by Charles Albert in the previous August, the Republican Government had struggled alone against Austria. So fierce had been the feeling caused by Charles Albert's treatment of Venice, that it had required all Manin's influence to hinder a violent attack on the Sardinian Commissioner. The Sardinian Admiral, indeed, attempted at first to disregard the orders of Charles Albert, and to continue the defence of Venice, but he was compelled after a time to withdraw. Manin, however, was anxious to secure foreign allies for Venice; and, shortly after his abandonment by Charles Albert, he appealed to France for help. The French Government answered by those vague and cheap promises which meant nothing; while the English Consul at Venice tried to form an Austrian party in the city; and Lord Palmerston worried Manin with all sorts of useless proposals for diplomatic compromises. But if Manin found little help from foreign Governments, he received much encouragement from those Italians who had not yet despaired of their country. In September, 1848, 1,200 soldiers who had served under Durando arrived in Venice; and on October 3 a vessel brought 6,000 guns from Genoa. The Austrian blockade, indeed, pressed ever closer, and on October 10 it had become so close that food could not be brought into the town. But so little did Manin lose heart that on October 11 he declared to the Assembly that Venice was in a better state for defence than when the Dictatorship had been established in August; and the Assembly in turn voted that Manin and the two colleagues who had been appointed to assist him should be entrusted with all political negotiations, saving the ratification by the Assembly of the final treaty. So great was the mutual confidence between Manin and the poorer classes of Venice, that in January, 1849, two Gondoliers were chosen to assist him in the Government.

The proclamation of the Republic in Rome had excited both the sympathies and the fears of Manin; for while he saw in it a step towards an Italian Republic, in which Venice might take a part, he also saw that it might hasten an Austrian intervention in the Roman States. The failure of Charles Albert's final effort in April, 1849, so alarmed the Venetians that Manin began to speculate on the desirability of accepting an Austrian Prince as Constitutional Sovereign of Lombardo-Venetia. But the Hungarian Declaration of Independence once more revived his hopes, and from that time his one aim in foreign policy was to secure and strengthen an alliance between Venice and Hungary. Yet the month of May, in which this alliance was concluded, seemed one of the most desperate periods in the fortunes of Venice. The fortress of Malghera, which lies on an island in the lagunes, about two hours' gondola journey west of Venice, was the scene of one of the fiercest struggles between the Austrians and Venetians. General Haynau had effected a landing on this island, and attempted to seize the fortress; but the Venetians on their side let loose the waters to swamp the Austrian trenches, sent boats under the fire of the Austrians to bring food to the defenders, and made expeditions to carry off oxen, even from

the country already occupied by the Austrians. So
desperate was the resistance that Radetzky treated
Haynau's attempt as a failure, and sent General
Thurn to take his place. But, partly by breaking a
truce, partly by force of superior numbers, the
Austrians succeeded in carrying the day; and on
May 26, when the fortress had been reduced to
ruins, the Venetians were compelled to abandon
Malghera, and to retreat to some islands nearer the
city. In the following month Manin again tried to
enter into negotiations with Radetzky; but a letter
from Kossuth encouraged him to stand firm; and he
made such demands for independence that the
Austrians scornfully rejected them.

In spite, however, of the encouragement which he
had sent to Manin, Kossuth's own position was one of
increasing danger. The Declaration of Independence
of April 14 had been followed by the resignation of
several Hungarian officers; and Görgei, though
unwillingly retaining his command, became more and
more antagonistic in his attitude towards Kossuth.
This mutual distrust was one of the main causes of
a step not very creditable to either party, and which
is reckoned by military critics one of the most
unfortunate in the war. On April 26, Görgei
and General Klapka had, by a desperate march,
rescued the fortress of Komorn from the Austrians;
and Klapka and others believed that, if Görgei had
followed up this success by marching to Raab, he
might have been able to reopen communications with
Vienna. Kossuth, however, was anxious that Buda-
Pesth should not be allowed to remain in the hands
of the Austrians, and he therefore desired Görgei to
turn his forces to the deliverance of the capital.

Görgei, in common with all the military leaders, believed this proposal to be a mistake; but he has frankly recorded his reasons for readily obeying Kossuth's orders. If he had followed up his advantages and marched into Austria, a Republic, he believed, would have been proclaimed in Hungary; and a compromise with the Austrian Government would have become impossible; whereas, by occupying Buda-Pesth, he thought that he should gain a vantage ground which would enable him to persuade both parties to accept the modified Constitution for Hungary which he desired. Hence it came to pass that the greater part of May was taken up by the siege of the fortress of Buda, while Görgei was intriguing with Kossuth's opponents in the Diet, and the Austrians were gaining ground in Hungary. And while he was with difficulty holding his own against Görgei's intrigues, Kossuth was alarmed by the news that a more formidable enemy had once more appeared on the scene.

On May 1 the Emperor of Austria had formally appealed to the Russians to assist him against his Hungarian subjects; and in June the Russian forces began to gather near the passes of the Carpathians. On the 17, Colonel Szabò encountered the Russians near the Temos Pass. When he first advanced to meet them, he believed that he had only to do with some skirmishing troops, such as those with whom he had previously dealt. But more and more soldiers pressed in to the attack, and Szabò was compelled to retreat. Two days later Colonel Kiss, at the head of a band of Szeklers, came up to resist the invaders; and, while those who were on the hills above hurled down stones and wood on the Russians, the soldiers below, though only 400 in number, resisted so gallantly that the Russians at first fled before them. At last, kowever, Kiss was laid senseless by a shot, and his soldiers were seized with a panic and fled in disorder.

Bem, who had returned to Transylvania about the end of May, now attempted to rally the Szekler by inspiriting appeals to the memories of their former struggles. On June 25 he recaptured the Saxon town of Bistritz, and then encountered in the open field a combined corps of Russians and Austrians. For seven hours he held out against them ; but new reinforcements came up, and he was compelled to retreat. The enormous numbers of the Russians seem to have impressed Bem's followers, and to have increased their original panic. The country was overrun by the enemy; Hermannstadt was captured and recaptured, and when, on August 5, it at last fell into the hands of the Russians, Bem narrowly escaped with his life. Even then he wished to continue the struggle; but on August 7 he was summoned to North Hungary by Kossuth, to advise him in his difficulties with Görgei.

After an attempt to supersede Görgei by Meszàros, Kossuth had been compelled to allow the former to resume the command; but he had by no means recovered confidence in him, and he felt ready to clutch at any proposal which would extricate himself and his country from their difficulties. Amongst other suggestions he proposed to offer to Jancu and the Roumanian leaders independent commands in the Hungarian Army, and to concede to them most of the points about which they had been fighting. He had even opened negotiations with Jancu for this purpose;

but Bem steadily opposed the scheme, and the negotiations came to nothing.    But Kossuth's great hope
was to supersede Görgei by Bem.    This proposal,
however, was opposed, not only by Görgei himself, but
also by Csanyi, who seems throughout to have
sympathised with Görgei, as against Kossuth.    Bem,
therefore, returned to the war.    Kossuth, left unsup-
ported, became more and more alarmed.    Csanyi and
Görgei pressed for his resignation; and, while he was
doubting, he received the news that Bem had been
dangerously wounded in battle.    The report, indeed,
was exaggerated; and Bem wrote a letter to assure
Kossuth of the slightness of his wound, and to
encourage him to stand firm.    But this letter never
arrived, and the next news which Bem received was
that Kossuth had abdicated, and Görgei been declared
Dictator of Hungary.    Bem wrote a letter of remonstrance to Kossuth, and, at the same time, marched
towards Lugos, in the Banat, to meet the Russians.
Dembinski, who was now in Bem's army, disobeyed
his orders, and Bem was defeated.    On that very day,
August 13, Görgei surrendered at Vilagos with all
his forces to the Russian general.

This surrender is now believed to have been
necessary on military grounds.    The advances made
by the Austrians during the siege of Buda, and the
Russian conquest of Transylvania had placed Hungary at the mercy of the conqueror.    Nevertheless,
it cannot be doubted that the quarrel between Görgei
and Kossuth, and the factions which the former had
stirred up in the army, had tended considerably to
bring about this result; while, with regard to the
terms of surrender, General Görgei has never
been able to explain how it was that, while the

amnesty was so scrupulously observed towards himself both by the Austrians and Russians, the generals, whose only fault was that they had served under him, were ruthlessly put to death by Haynau. Anyhow, whatever may have been the excuses for the act, the surrender of Vilagos produced a startling close to the Hungarian War. Bem, indeed, hastened back to Transylvania, and attempted to rouse his former followers; and General Klapka held out for a month longer at Komorn. But Bem's efforts were of no avail; Klapka's defence only served to secure rather better terms; and both these generals, as well as Kossuth, were forced to take refuge in Turkey.

The news of the surrender of Vilagos did not reach Venice till August 20. There Manin had had much difficulty in still retaining the control which had been necessary for the guidance of affairs; and on August 6 a minority of 28 in the Assembly had protested against his reappointment as Dictator. The cholera had now been added to the other horrors of the siege; provisions were growing scarce; and thus the news of Görgei's surrender came as the last straw to break down the hopes of the defenders of Venice. On the 22nd, therefore, the Government agreed to yield. Manin succeeded in preventing the riots which seemed likely to break out on the news of the capitulation; and on August 30 the final surrender of Venice to the Austrians brought to a close the long struggle for liberty which had begun with the Sicilian rising of 1848.

On December 20, 1849, there appeared the following statement in a Swiss paper: "In front of Manin's door was a stone on which his name was engraved. The Austrians broke it to pieces; but the

smallest fragments of it have been collected by the
Venetians as sacred relics."

So ended the revolutionary period of 1848 and
1849. [Those Revolutions had displayed, in a way
unknown before, the strength and the weakness of
the national principle.   The enthusiasm for liberty,
and the power of generous self-sacrifice, which was
kindled by the feeling for a common language and
common traditions, had been shown in each of the
Revolutions; and they had struck a blow at the
merely diplomatic and military settlements of States
which produced a lasting effect.   But, on the other
hand, with the love for men of the same race and
language there awoke in all these nations, with
terrible force, the hatred and scorn for men of other
races and languages; and thus, while the leaders of
the movement taught tyrants their danger, they
supplied them at the same time with a defence
against that danger,—with another justification of
the old maxim of tyrants, " Divide et impera."   And
so the work of the Revolutionists did not fail; but
yet it could not achieve all the noble ends for which
it was intended.

The time which followed the defeat of the Revolutionists was to show both their failure and their
success.   The dreary period of reaction from 1849
to 1859 could not have been expected by any sane
man to be of long duration.   But the time of reawak-
ening was not like the time of the first dawn of hope.
The work which had been ennobled by the thought
of Mazzini, by the sword of Garibaldi, by the states-
manship of Manin, and the eloquent enthusiam of
Ciceruacchio, was to be carried to completion by the
intrigues of Cavour, and the interested speculation

of Louis Napoleon. In the place of the wisdom of Robert Blum, and the wild popular energy of Hecker, was to arise the stern hard policy of "blood and iron"; and, as Germany had failed to absorb Prussia, Prussia was finally to absorb Germany. The blunders and prejudices of the leaders of the Vienna Revolution were to be reproduced by Schmerling, without their self-sacrifice or generosity. But at the same time Francis Deak, the wise statesman, who had stood aside in dislike of the fiercer and more unscrupulous policy of other Magyar leaders, was to re-establish gradually for his country the freedom which she had lost for a time during the Revolutionary struggle. The race struggles of the Austro-Hungarian Empire were to be renewed in a milder form, and the solution of their difficulties postponed to a distant future; while the yet more dangerous problems of Socialism, which had forced themselves in so untimely a manner on the citizens of Vienna and Berlin, were gradually to assume ever greater prominence in the affairs of Europe. Thus it will be seen that the Revolutions of 1848 to '49 were but the climax of movements of which we have not yet seen the end; but, for good and for evil, they left a mark on Europe, which is never likely to be entirely effaced.

THE END.

# INDEX.

## A.

Aargau, 152, 155, 160.

Agram, Bishop of in Gaj's time, 99; Assembly at, 144-5; May Meeting at, 318-19; contrasted with Prague, 333.

Albrecht (Professor), 92. *See* also Arch Dukes.

Alessandria, occupation of, 3; in 1821, 39-40, 43; threatened by Radetzky, 182.

Alexander I. of Russia, character of, 3-4; relations with Mme. de Krudener, 7; plan of Holy Alliance, 8; supports Sardinia, 27; attitude in 1820, 32; treatment of Greece, 46-7; death, 49.

Alfieri, Vittorio, influence of, 23; Manzoni's feeling to, 25, 54; influence in Piedmont, 35.

Allemandi, 350.

Alliance, Holy. *See* Holy Alliance.

Altieri, Cardinal, 417.

Ancona, in 1831, 61, 118; treatment of by French, 159; by Triumvirs, 464-5; fall of, 485.

Andrian, 208.

Anfossi, Augusto, conspiracy against Charles Felix, 61; early career, 263; in Milan, 263, 265, 267, 269; death, 337.

—— Francesco, 365.

Antologia, of Florence, 54-5.

Antonelli, Cardinal, supports Italian war, 346; suspected of treachery, 348.

Antonini, General, 469.

Apponyi, Chancellor of Hungary, 201.

Arch Duchess Sophia, opposed to

Metternich, 207; favours Jellaciç, 288; denounced by Hungarians, 460.

Arch Duke Albert, in March insurrection, 239, 241.

—— Francis Charles, in Imperial Council, 207; appealed to by merchants, 231; attitude to Metternich, 241; denounced by Hungarians, 460.

—— John, promises to Italy, 21; his toast at Cologne, 209-10; his liberalism, 241; pressure on Metternich, 243; made administrator, 363, 373; forms new ministry, 374; opens Viennese Parliament, 378; intervenes in Croatian question, 383.

—— Louis, helps to govern Vienna, 206; opposes removal of Hye, 207; warns Metternich, 232; his proposal about Windischgrätz, 240; denounced by Hungarians, 460.

—— Maximilian, in March rising, 242-3.

—— Sigismund, 268.

—— Stephen, deserts Hungary, 395, 432; denounced by Hungarians, 461.

Arcioni, at defence of Rome, 475.

Armellini, in provisional government, 423; Triumvir, 464; feelings to French, 473.

Arndt, relations with Stein, 10; professor, 12; in 1816, 12; restored by Frederick William IV., 94; thanked at Frankfort, 361; vote on truce of Malmö, 374-5.

Arthaber, 245.

Ascoli, Duke of, 34-5.

—— conspiracy in, 464-5.

K K

504　　　　　　　　　　INDEX.

plans for Leopold, 423-4 ; in provisional government, 423-4 ; opposes Mazzini, 424-5 ; opposes Gioberti, 425 ; failure of his government, 467-8.
Guizot, relations with Metternich,
159 ; policy in Switzerland, 162.

H.

Hanover, constitution granted, 90 ;
abolished, 91 ; protest of professors
in, 91-2.
—— King of, resists March move-
ment, 226 ; opposes Frankfort As-
sembly, 373.
Hansemann, 403, 405, 407, 411.
Hapsburg. See Austria, house of.
Haulik, Bishop, 105.
Haynau, 428-9, 489-90.
Hecker, causes of popularity, 219-20 ;
attitude of at Heidelberg, 233 ;
effect of insurrection, 376-7.
Heidelberg, March meeting at, 232.
Herbst, Dr., note to 134.
Hermannstadt, importance in Tran-
sylvania, 441 ; treatment by Bem,
449 ; fall of, 492.
Hesse Cassel, March rising in, 222.
—— Darmstadt, March rising in,
222 ; position of Gagern in, 233.
—— Duke of, his action in Mainz,
361.
Hofer, Andrew, 10.
Holy Alliance, end of, 50. See also
Alexander, Krudener (Mᵉ. de),
Frederick William III., Metternich.
Honveds, 433.
Hormayr, 204.
Horn, Uffo, 258.
Hoyos, 307.
Hrabowsky, 312, 320.
Hungary, difference from other coun-
tries, 73-5 ; division of races in, 96,
276, 288 ; relations of with Croatia,
97, 276-7, 287-8 ; growth of national
feeling, 106-7 ; "nobles" 102-3 ;
compared with Lombardy, 191 ;
feelings of, for county government,
201-3 ; relations of, with Vienna,

209, 226-30 ; Gagern's admiration
of, 233 ; responsible ministry in,
246-7 ; relations of with Bohemia,
250, 253 ; treatment of by Ferdinand, 384-7 ; invasion of by Jellaciç, 388-9 ; position of after
Schwechat, 432-3 ; division of parties in, 433-9 ; later struggles in,
433-63 ; relations of with Venice,
489-90 ; final effort of, 490-2 ; fall
of, 493-4.
Hungary, Diet of, in 1825, 75-6 ; in
1832, 81 ; in 1840, 100 ; in 1843, 102 ;
in 1849, 439, 441.
Hye, share in debating Society, 207 ;
denounces annexation of Cracow,
212 ; hesitations in March, 234-5 ;
appealed to by Windischgrätz, 245 ;
attitude about press law, 303-4.
—— House of Magnates of, their
concession to Croats, 105.

I.

Illyrian Movement, 99, 283.
Imola, conspiracy in, 464. See also
Pius IX.
Innspruck, 308, 310, 393.
Inquisition, 465-6.
Istria, influence of Venice in, 97.
Italy, conquerors' promises to, 20-1 ;
condition of, in 1820-30, 52-3 ; question of unity of, 56-8, 170, 190, 419,
423 ; contrasted with Hungary,
117-18 ; position of Charles Albert
in, 62-4 ; relations of with Switzerland, 157, 159 ; feelings of other
races to, 335-6 ; separateness of
struggle in, 336 ; feeling of Frankfort parliament to, 362-3 ; of
Viennese to, 387, 389-90 ; feelings
in towards Roumanians, 439 ; final
struggles in, 463-88.
—— Young. See Mazzini.

J.

Jacoby defies King of Prussia, 409 ;
interview with Blumenthal, 412-13.
Jahn, 14-15, 16, 94.

after Pope's fall, 423; interview with Lesseps, 479.

Manara, in rising in Milan, 269; difficulties in Lombard war, 337; march to Civita Vecchia, 471; controversy with Oudinot, 471-2; at defence of Rome, 474-7; death, 486.

Manin, promotes railway with Piedmont, 137; his petitions, 193-5; imprisonment, 196; its effect, 270; his release, 271; in March rising, 271-4; influenced by Venetian traditions, 343-4; relations with Durando, 345; welcomes Pepe, 354-5; resists fusion, 358; tries to help Vicenza, 358-9; resignation, 359-60; recall, 367; final struggle, 488-90; surrender, 494; his stone, 494-5.

Mannheim, 221.

Mantua, in March rising, 340; captured by Radetzky, 341; fortification of,· 348; movements of Radetzky about, 355.

Manzoni, career and aims, 24-5; growth of influence, 54.

Margherita, Solaro della, opposed to Gioberti, 123; politics, 137; sympathy with Sonderbund, 157.

Maria Theresa, agrarian reforms of, 81; treatment of Transylvania, 110, 115; of Bohemia, 253; of Serbs, 282-3.

Marinovich, 272.

Maros Vasarhely, 108, 444.

Maximilian. See Arch Duke.

Mayerhoffer, 386.

Mazzini, 51; early career, 55-6; attitude to Carbonari, 56-7; political creed, 57-9; first banishment, 59; first insurrection, 60; letter to Charles Albert, 63-4; personal influence, 66-7; contrasted with other revolutionists, 67-8; founds Young Italy, 68-9; invasion of Savoy, 69-71; impression on Metternich, 71; relation with Brothers Bandiera, 118-20; sympathy with Poland, 129; effect of on working classes,

191; relations with Tommaseo, 194; appeal for Charles Albert, 337-8; visit to Milan, 342; appealed to by Lombard Government, 349; advice rejected, 349-50; protest against fusion, 350-1; opposes May insurrection, 356-7; plan for defence of Milan, 365-6; last struggle in Lombardy, 367; in Leghorn, 424-5; attitude to Charles Albert, 427; work as Triumvir, 464; warned by Ledru Rollin, 470; urges resistance to French, 473; feeling of Lesseps to, 480; repels Corcelles, 485; his final advice to Assembly, 486.

Mazzoni, 424.

Medici, last effort in Lombardy, 367; defends Vascello, 483-6.

Menotti, Ciro, 50.

Mensdorff, 331.

Menz, 71-3, 157.

Messenhauser, 396.

Messina, in 1820, 34; Ferdinand's visit to, 169; September rising in, 171.

Meszaros, in Batthyanyi's Ministry, 279; rebukes Görgei, 453; supersedes Görgei, 492.

Metternich, Prince, rise to power, 1; system of government, 2; feeling to Alexander, 3-4; to religion, 5-7; opposition to Stein, 8-10; to S. German States, 13; a "moral power," 15; triumph in 1819, 16-18; surprise at movement of 1820, 32; treatment of Lombardy in 1821, 44; of Confalonieri, 44-6; attitude to Greece, 46-7; opinion of Canning, 48; change towards England, 48-9; triumph in 1832, 50-1; policy towards Tuscany, 53; opinion of Mazzini, 71; feelings to Hungary, 73; quarrel with Szechenyi, 78; defeat in 1839, 86-7; attitude to Gaj, 99; denounces Grand Duke of Tuscany, 128; treatment of Cracow, 134; feeling to Charles Albert, 135-6; treatment of Canton Ticino,

despotism, 27-8; attitude in 1820, 35-6; abdication, 41.

Victor Emmanuel, Duke of Savoy, afterwards King of Italy, wounded at Goito, 356; accession to throne of Piedmont, 429.

Vienna, effect of on Lombardy, 189-90; Metternich's government of, 204-8; effect on of Ferdinand's accession, 206-8; double position of, 209; movements in, 210-14, 225-6; March rising in, 229-47; its effect in Bohemia, 259; in Milan, 262; in Venice, 271; relations of with Prague, 325-6; July Parliament in, 378-80; relations of with Hungary, 380, 384, 387; with Bohemia, 379, 392; with Italy, 379-80, 387; October rising in, 390-7; fall of, 397-9; effect of fall on Prussia, 408.

—— Concluding Act of, 17-18.

—— Decrees of 1834, 90, 221.

—— Treaty of, 3, 8, 17, 130, 146, 149, 151, 155, 160, 164. See also Congress.

Vilagos, 493-4.

Villamarina, 135.

## W.

Waizen, declaration of, 438-9.

Wallachia, rising in in 1821, 46-7.

Wallacks. See Roumanians.

Warsaw, trade with Cracow, 130; insurrection in, 131.

Wartburg, Feast of, 14-15.

Weimar, Duke of, his policy, 13-16.

Welden, General, besieges Bologna, 368-9; cruelty of in Pavia, 426.

Wellington, his opinion of Navarino, 49; small effect of his rule, 50.

Wesselenyi, position and influence, 79; speech at Presburg, 83; imprisonment and its results, 85-6; appeal to Szeklers, 316; joins de-

putation to Vienna, 387; retirement from politics, 462.

Willisen, General von, 370.

Wimpffen, General, 478.

Windischgrätz, made commandant of Vienna, 240; proposed Dictatorship of, 240-1, 244-5; protest against deposition of Metternich, 243; announcement on March 22nd, 247; irritation of Bohemians with, 323-4, 328; attitude in June rising in Prague, 329-32; besieges Vienna, 395-7; defeats Görgei, 437-8; his offer to Görgei, 438; rejects mediation in Hungary, 462; military opinion of his generalship, 463.

Workmen's movements, in Vienna, 239-40, 305, 389-90; in Berlin, 247, 402, 403, 405-6, 408; in Prague, 323, 328; in Silesia, 402, 405, 406.

Wrangel, 410-11.

Würtemberg, first two Kings of, 13; protest of against Concluding Act, 18; Roth's relations with, 115; resistance of to Metternich, 218; March rising in, 221-2; quarrel with Baden, 377. See also Stuttgart.

## Y.

Ypsilanti, 46.

## Z.

Zay, his circular, 101-2.

Zichy, Governor of Venice, 272, 273.

—— Hungarian Count, his execution, 434.

Zitz, action of in Frankfort riots, 375.

Zollverein, 93, 210.

Zucchi, recalled to Milan, 366; treatment of Garibaldi, 419; defeated by Garibaldi, 464.

Zug, Canton, 162.

Zurich, 152, 154, 156. See also University.